MW01055023

The Travelers' Charleston

The Travelers' Charleston

Accounts of Charleston and Lowcountry, South Carolina, 1666–1861

EDITED BY

Jennie Holton Fant

The University of South Carolina Press

© 2016 University of South Carolina

Published by the University of South Carolina Press
Columbia, South Carolina 29208

www.sc.edu/uscpress

Manufactured in the United States of America

25 24 23 22 21 20 19 18 17 16
10 9 8 7 6 5 4 3 2 1

Library of Congress Cataloging-in-Publication Data
can be found at http://catalog.loc.gov/.

ISBN 978-1-61117-584-4 (cloth)
ISBN 978-1-61117-585-1 (ebook)

This book was printed on recycled paper with 30 percent postconsumer waste content.

Contents

List of Illustrations

Acknowledgments

I have incurred many debts of gratitude in the research and preparation of this manuscript with its combination of letters, documents, and illustrations. I owe special thanks to my editor, Alexander Moore at the University of South Carolina Press, who accompanied me on this long journey to publication, and to whom I am infinitely grateful for his support, his expertise, and his belief in this book. The research for this volume would not have been possible without the faculty library privileges I was granted as an employee of Duke University Libraries, with its wonderful resources. I am infinitely grateful to the staff of Interlibrary Loan at Duke Libraries, who, over a number of years, granted my fathoms of requests for materials in and beyond the university, some relatively obscure. I am further indebted to Interlibrary Loan at Durham County Library, Shannon Road, for granting my many requests as well.

I owe appreciation to the William L. Clements Library at the University of Michigan for permission to publish the Joseph Woory 1666 account. My gratitude to the Massachusetts Historical Society for permission to reproduce a portion of the original journal of Josiah Quincy Jr. from the Quincy Family Papers. During the research for this book, the Library of Congress digitized the handwritten correspondence of Samuel F. B. Morse. My appreciation to them for permission to publish a number of letters written to and from Morse while he was in Charleston between 1818 and 1821. My sincere gratitude to Michael Mallon, literary executor of the Sir John Pope-Hennessy estate, for permission to publish from the original letters of Margaret Hunter Hall. Additional thanks to Mallon's literary agent and agency, Darryl Samaraweera and Artellus Ltd. in London for help locating Mr. Mallon in Paris. Further, I am indebted to Catherine Wilson, great-great-granddaughter of William Makepeace Thackeray, for her kind guidance through the various rights of the Thackeray estates in my quest to obtain permission to reprint a number of the Thackeray letters first published by Gordon N. Ray some years ago.

My deep appreciation goes to staff members of innumerable libraries, archives, and museums: Michelle Gait at the Special Collections Centre, the Sir Duncan Rice Library, Aberdeen University; Jamie Cutts at Aberdeenshire Council, Aberdeenshire Museums Service; Ondine LeBlanc, Elaine Heavey and Anna

Clutterbuck-Cook at the Massachusetts Historical Society, Boston; Jennifer Johns at Ruthmere Museum, Elkhart, Indiana; Dale Sauter at Manuscripts and Rare Books, Joyner Library, East Carolina University; Jeffery Flannery and Lewis Wyman at the Manuscripts Division, Library of Congress; Márta Fodor at the Museum of Fine Arts, Boston; Alice Hickcox at the Beck Center, Emory University Libraries; Diana Sykes at the William L. Clements Library, University of Michigan. My added thanks to the National Portrait Gallery, London; Victoria and Albert Museum; National Library of Scotland; New-York Historical Society; Library of Congress Prints and Photographs; Thomas Cooper Library, University of South Carolina; United States Office of Medical History; and the National Library of Medicine.

Finally, my love and gratitude to friends and family who supported me over the long gestation of this project, especially Rhet Wilson-Deehan and John Deehan, Eleanor Hawkins and Mary Cecil Hawkins Parker. I salute your long-suffering belief that one day this tome would, indeed, make it to the reader. My regard to the many friends (you know who you are) who tolerated my long sequester; nevertheless, at every stage in the preparation for this book showed such interest. I further owe a debt of gratitude to my friend and excellent on-call IT resource, James Wood, a genius with technology.

INTRODUCTION

These charming gardens, in connection with the piazzas resting on ornamental pillars, make the whole town graceful. One sits, in the morning, in these open chambers, inhaling the refreshing air from the sea, its perfume mingled with that of the flowers below; and, at midday, closing the Venetian shutters to exclude the sun, he rests in grateful shade. Here, too, throughout the longer portion of the year, may be spread, at evening, the tea table; while the heavens still glow with the purple-and amber of the sunset. And here lingers the family until the bells from the tower of St. Michael's, sweetly ringing their silver chimes through the calm, starry air, announce, at last, the hour of repose.

John Milton Mackie, *From Cape Cod to*
Dixie and the Tropics, 1864

Soon after he was restored to the English throne in 1660, King Charles II rewarded eight men who had supported him in exile with a large section of the American continent. These men, constituted "lords proprietors," were granted the province of Carolina by a charter dated 1663, which gave them permission to develop "all that territory, or tract of ground called Carolina scituate, lying, and being within our dominions of America." Carolina extended over a vast and unexplored terrain from Virginia to Florida.

Five months later, a group of Barbados businessmen sponsored an expedition to explore the coastal regions of the grant. Commanded by Captain William Hilton, the expedition left Barbados in August of 1663 and arrived in the province of Carolina. They sailed in the proximity of the Combahee and Edisto rivers, Port Royal, and St. Helena Sound. In a report, Hilton described the region as "one of the greatest and fairest havens in the world."

Influenced by Captain Hilton's favorable description, at the end of 1663 a second English group set out from Barbados to settle an area on the Charles River (later named the Clarendon River, now the Cape Fear River), which they named Charles Town. When that colony proved unsuccessful, the lords proprietors encouraged the Barbadians to explore the territory further south for settlement, "that region described by Hilton." An expedition ensued in two small vessels, the *Speedwell* and the *Rebecca,* commanded by Lieutenant-Colonel Robert Sandford.

It is here that this book begins—with an account written four years before Charles Town was founded in what is now South Carolina. The Sandford expedition set out on June 16, 1666, and explored down to Beaufort (Port Royal). Lieutenant Joseph Woory, a crewman aboard, wrote an account of the discovery of these coastal regions. As a result of this sighting by Sandford and his crew, Port Royal became the original destination for ships carrying the first settlers of Charles Town in 1670. They arrived near Beaufort only to be convinced by Kiawah Indians that the territory around what is now Charleston was a better choice for farming, and realized it was (thankfully) even further away from the Spanish settlement of St. Augustine.

From its beginnings, the lowcountry region was considered distinctive. A unique geography formed by an intricate system of sea-islands, sounds, rivers, inlets, and creeks, it was a watery "paradise" rich in untamed nature and graced with a subtropical climate. Isolated in a lush coastal wilderness, a tiny struggling colony hewed out an existence. By 1670, John Locke wrote a memorandum that described Carolina: "*Country:* "Healthy, delightful. Bears anything." From little more than an outpost, boundaries expanded as the colony was relocated to the peninsula, and a society was formed. Land was reclaimed from the sea; creeks and marshes were filled in. Streets were laid, city walls were built, houses and churches constructed. In the outlying region, planters cleared and diked inland swamps for the cultivation of crops. Author Dubose Heyward wrote, "Where others failed, the English succeeded, and perhaps the reason lies in the fact that they came armed not with pikes and arquebuses, but with plows and sickles."* Fast fortunes were made in the cultivation of indigo, rice, and eventually cotton. As slaves toiled in the fields, wealth and leisure were created for planters who, due to the threat of "country fevers" in the swamplands, escaped to town with their families from May to November. There the "social season" was contrived, like so much of Charleston tradition and custom, an adaptation to climate. Cousins married, which resulted in families as intertwined as lowcountry waterways. An oligarchy ensued, families interrelated by marriage and business. It was a convivial populous, one that enjoyed a "certain high gloss of living"—hunts, rides, balls, concerts, dances, feasts, horse races, and duels. "All decent travellers" were welcomed, civilized travelers with "no other Recommendation, but their being Human Creatures" could "depend upon being received with Hospitality." A number of travelers and visitors documented exactly what they saw and perceived. As the

*Heyward, "Charleston: Where Mellow Past and Present Meet," 273–74.

region evolved through an increase in population due to the draw of economic prosperity and social and cultural development, their written records leave a map of history through the centuries to the Civil War.

Over time, a complicated civilization shaped and reshaped this province, and Charleston has forever held a fascination for its visitors. Today there remains the nacreous patina that overlays the city, a pentimento suggesting artifacts beneath the surface, and gradations of history. It suggested to me an excavation of centuries-old layers through records left by travelers and visitors to the region. Their firsthand accounts provide a means of travel by proxy, as close as we can venture back in history to "being there." Travel narratives, travelogues, journals, diaries, correspondence, and a memoir present a breadth of documentation in synthesis over time, allowing the reader to visualize and examine the region anew. These particular accounts were chosen to contribute to the larger narrative, a composite picture and chronology of Charleston and the surrounding region—a range from Lieutenant Woory's recording of the 1666 exploration, to 1861, when a Yankee schoolteacher in Charleston witnessed the start of the Civil War. My further objective was to look behind the myth of the tea-table—indicative of the southern code of manners, polite conversation, culture and refinement that Charleston espouses—into a more realistic past.

"Travel writing" may be too loose a definition. There are a number of more traditional narratives, but I have included herein the private correspondence of Samuel F. B. Morse, a portrait artist in Charleston over four social seasons. The Morse correspondence includes letters written from Charleston to members of his family, as well as letters written to him in Charleston by John Ashe Alston, his art patron in Georgetown, and letters exchanged between Morse and Caroline Ball, a difficult Charleston client who commissioned the artist to paint her portrait. Further included are the private letters of William Makepeace Thackeray, who traveled to Charleston on two lecture tours; and an account by educator Anna Brackett, written as an article for *Harper's Weekly*, which bears witness to the last days of antebellum Charleston. The focus is less on "travel," "travel writing," or travelers per se, but rather on these travelers and what they have to tell us about Charleston, what they add to the story from varying perspectives or different eras of history, or by having witnessed key events. Most of these texts were subtracted from larger works, the visit to Charleston or the lowcountry being but a brief period in a larger narrative.

These travelers came for a range of reasons and from a variety of backgrounds, none from the South. They were from England, Germany, Scotland, Sweden, and the American North. First to arrive were the English explorers and surveyors, represented here by Joseph Woory and John Lawson. Bostonian Josiah Quincy came for his health. Some came to the South to investigate a specific topic, such as democracy or slavery. Johann Schoepf, a German doctor, came to investigate the effects of the American Revolution. After Charleston became a popular travel destination, Europeans arrived in the course of an extended "Grand Tour" of American cities, Charleston being fashionable on that itinerary. None traveled so grandly as Scottish aristocrat Margaret Hunter Hall. Other travelers, not so well off, ventured to town for a variety of purposes. Some worked in the region for a short time; among accounts are those of a Englishman John Davis, a tutor; Morse as itinerant artist; Thackeray as famous lecturer; Scot William Ferguson, a businessman from London; and Bostonian Anna Brackett, a schoolteacher. John Lambert came intending to publish his travels after a failed attempt in Canada to foster the cultivation of hemp for England. James Stuart traveled from Scotland to escape publicity after he killed his cousin in a duel. Englishman John Benwell was largely making a surveillance of slavery. John Milton Mackie came from Massachusetts on a pleasure trip. Some travelers were famous in their day, such as Englishwoman Harriet Martineau and Fredrika Bremer from Sweden. A number were professional writers, who hoped their accounts would be published; others wrote narratives never meant to be published. They arrived with their own interests, their own biases and prejudices, and those of the times. Like most travelers, they reveal a preference for their own countries or states, which serve as points of comparison in most accounts. They traveled the beaten track of Charleston tourism in their day and describe many of the same sights, scenes, or people; however, their experiences contribute to the validity of another visitor's observation or offer an alternative view, or additional information. They were attentive to a vast variety of subjects, and describe and assess historic events and historic figures of the city and state. From Charleston, they ramble into the outlying regions, from Georgetown to Beaufort, with detours and digressions.

After 1830, slavery was an increasingly prevalent topic. Travelers witnessed slave sales in Charleston at slave markets or in the streets, whether by accident or design, and chronicled them. Some writers reveal themselves as racist even as they denounce slavery. Others grow confused by their own moral reactions. Many are subject to myths concocted by Charlestonians concerning slavery, and they were persuasive. Together, these writers describe a complicated, multidimensional landscape.

In the interest of the reader, spelling and typography have been modernized in a number of the earlier accounts. Further, all facts stated by these travelers—dates, people encountered, situations or events chronicled—have been scrutinized to validate fact and probability. What can be verified has been, and corrections or clarification, as well as further information, have been included in the footnotes.

After a great deal of research into the many resources available, it was apparent that the accounts of these particular travelers afford the reader a credible body of information over time. Most of the actual detail proves dependable. The mention of a person, plantation visited, or an event was too compelling not to pursue an identity or further information, therefore extensive annotation is provided. Something as small as identifying the authors and books they read or the actors they saw on the stage adds texture to past eras. Granted, my curiosity got the best of me, and I went much further to track down the full facts behind any comment written. Yet it was such a fascinating journey, and my footnotes contain some great Charleston-region stories.

It is impossible to extract an absolute, just as an archeological reconstruction is only an approximation. However, these accounts create a reasonable and cumulative history as told by travelers. Their impressions enable the reader to discover the captivating essence, the sense of history and heartbreak, of one of the nation's most distinctive regions.

And nowhere is that trick of history—the art of transcending time—more in evidence than through these witnesses' words. Centuries disappear and pages obscure and fade away as a landscape becomes visible and people step into sight like ghosts passing over water. There is a resonance in the imagery evoked from these fragments of a vanished past: At a stagecoach stop at Pocotaligo, a company of colonial Charleston actors and comedians dismount a stagecoach and enter a tavern to dine and bed in the desolate countryside between Charleston and Savannah. In the woods of Ashepoo, a traveler encounters an elephant and his trainer between appearances in Charleston and Savannah, the first elephant to set foot on American soil. In the middle of a forest, there appears a fast-moving coach drawn by four horses, the carriage of a fine lady "attired in the dress of the ladies of Queen Dido's court" with a train of servants following, clad in a "magnificent livery." Downtown there strides a newly-fashioned "Carolinian buck," resembling an "ancient Roman." An ever-hospitable Charlestonian, Dr. Tidyman welcomes all (well-heeled) visitors to town. In a remote field out of town, bedlam ensues during a militia muster of an ill-disciplined corps under a "Captain Clod-pol." In the Charleston mansion of a lady Nullifier hangs a portrait of Andrew Jackson; once loved by southerners but now reviled, his face is shrouded in black cloth. The funeral cortege of Senator John C. Calhoun queues through Charleston streets in reverent cavalcade, "solemn and magnificent," before he was laid to rest in St. Philip's graveyard. On a round of Charleston parties, visiting author William Makepeace Thackeray exchanges insults with the controversial Charlestonian, Susan Petigru King. Standing over a laden dining-room table, a small black child waves a giant fan of peacocks'-tail feathers to fan flies off the table for the seated white folk. At the Charleston races, the ladies are "in full feather" in "ermine and point lace, brocades and cashmeres of India," and two dowagers sport "diamonds and jewels more appropriate for the ballroom." While in the slave market, people are examined like cattle, families separated, and horrors abound in heartbreaking imagery. A runaway slave, caught and shackled and being led to the city jail, has "STR" branded in his forehead, a personal brand to identify ownership between planters, and which means: "Stop The Rascal." Then as war becomes inevitable, there is described a "last hour of repose," where yet "may be spread, at evening, the tea table; while the heavens still glow with the purple-and-amber of the sunset."

"Charles II, King of England, ca. 1660–65." Portrait by John Michael Wright or his studio. Copyright National Portrait Gallery, London.

Joseph Woory (1666)

"Discovery"

Lt. Joseph Woory (d. 1692) was a crew member of Captain Robert Sandford's 1666 expedition to explore Carolina. Sandford wrote: "I was accompanied by Capt. George Cary, Lt. Samuel Harvy, Lt Joseph Woory, Ens. Henry Brayne, Ens. Richard Abrahall and Mr. Tho. Giles, and several other inhabitants of the county of Clarendon to the number of 17 besides myself (and the ships company, which alas were but two men and a boy)."

Woory was the nephew of Englishman Sir John Yeamans (1605–1676), chief among the Barbadian planters and businessmen who had hoped to found a Carolina colony. Yeamans had been instrumental in the founding of the Cape Fear settlement; his nephew Woory had participated in that venture as well.

Sandford and his crew sailed along the coast and explored the area from Cape Romano (Cape Fear) down to Port Royal (Beaufort) in twenty-six days, during which they landed at St. Helena, Kiawah, and Edisto Island, anchored off Hilton Head, and visited Indian villages. On June 23, Sandford took formal possession of Carolina for England and the lords proprietors. Sandford documented his experience on the venture, as did Joseph Woory.

Sometime after the 1666 expedition, Woory emigrated from Barbados to Isle of Wight County, Virginia, where he was a merchant and represented John Yeamans's interests in Virginia trade. Woory was sheriff and justice of the peace for Isle of Wight. A Quaker, he married Elizabeth Godwin, daughter of Colonel Thomas and Elizabeth Godwin, a well-established Quaker family in Nansemond County, Virginia. At his death in Isle of Wight County in 1692, he owned a sizable estate and eight slaves.

The Joseph Woory account is believed to have originated from the papers of Sir Edmund Andros (1637–1714). It was owned by various collectors before being acquired in 1994 by the William L. Clements Library at the University of Michigan.

"Discovery" from "A Discovery of the Coasts Rivers Sounds and Creeks of that Part of the Province between Cape Romano and Port Royal vizt, by Joseph Woory." Woory Manuscript, William L. Clements Library, University of Michigan Manuscripts Division.

SOURCES

Brayton, John Anderson, ed. *Colonial Families of Surry and Isle of Wight Counties, Virginia.* Vol. 8. Memphis: J. A. Brayton, 1999.

———, ed. Isle of Wight County, Virginia Will and Deed Book 2, 1666–1719. Memphis: J. A. Brayton, 2004.

"Historical and Genealogical Notes and Queries." *Virginia Magazine of History and Biography* 15, no. 3 (1908): 321.

King, Helen Haverty. *Historical Notes on Isle of Wight County.* Isle of Wight, VA: Isle of Wight County Board of Supervisors, 1993.

Worrall, Jay. *The Friendly Virginians: America's First Quakers.* Athens, GA: Iberian Publishing Co., 1994.

"Discovery"

Saturday June 1666—We set sail on the ship *Rebecca* and with the shallop *Speedwell* from the mouth of the Charles River and Sunday the 17th in the afternoon we [discovered] a large opening against which we came to an anchor and sent the shallop* in to sound the channel, but she could not get in by reason of creeks and shoals yt lay out. That evening, the wind blowing fresh from sea, we weighed and stood of. On Tuesday the 19th we lost the shallop by foul weather.[†] Thursday the 21st after noon we [discovered] a very fair opening and stood of that night 'til Friday the 22nd at which time we stood in &c. Sounding as we went in [but] had not in the narrowest place then 2-fathom and then 3, 4, 5, 7, 8-fathom water. We ran up with our ship about five miles from the river's mouth. On both sides the river is a great store of oyster banks and good creeks that run to the main and about an hour after we came to an anchor two Indians came aboard us who told us we were in the River Grandee[‡] and that that country was called Edisto. Presently after there came several other Indians with venison, corn bread, fish amongst whom was two of those Indians that were at Barbados.[§]

*A shallop, a small open boat used in shallow water, had two masts and a lugsail yet could be rowed with oars.

[†]Sandford had placed Ensign Henry Brayne in charge of the shallop. The night was cloudy and dark, and Brayne in the shallop "parted company" with Sandford's vessel.

[‡]North Edisto River.

[§]From an earlier (1663) Carolina expedition, Capt. William Hilton took two Indians, "Shadow and Alush," back to Barbados. Shadow was a Kiawah chief, and Alush was "a chief of Edisto." They were later returned to the region.

Saturday the 23rd* some of us went on shore to get fresh water but could find none near the river side, but the Indians taking our casks carried them about half a mile into the woods to a large pond where was water enough. The land is generally very choice, and good. The mold is mellow and black and about a foot deep under a red marly sand. It bears large oaks, walnut and few pines unless spruce pines. The woods afford very good pasture for cattle being richly laden with English grass; for fowl and fish it affords like that of Charles River, there is turtle in abundance. The same afternoon we went a mile eastward from our ship and landed on a dry marsh where we found an Indian path which we kept, and it led us through many fields of corn ready to gather, also other corn, peas and beans which had been later planted there and was not so forward as the rest. They keep their ground very clean. We also found many peach trees with fruit thereon near ripe. After that we crossed a large creek and marched three miles into the country upon an island and did not see an inch of bad land but all choice and good timber trees growing thereon, as oak, walnut, chestnut, maple, ash, elder and many other good trees.

Sunday the 24th we went up with our boat about 4 miles from our ship, and then the river divides itself into branches, one of which we went up 8 or 9 miles and then landed upon very good land and saw abundance of very good and large timber trees. The worst land we saw that day was spruce pine swamps and that better then the oak land at Cape Fear for it is plantable and black mold free from sand & dry. Monday the 25th there came aboard one of the Indians that was at Barbados[†] and was very desirous that some of us might go to see their town so Lieutenant Colonel Sandford commanded four of us to go with them which we did. It lies about 5 miles from the river.[‡] All the way as we traveled we saw very good oak land and large pleasant meadows as good as England can afford. When we came to their town, they kindly entertained us and were very desirous to have us stay with them that night which we did, and on Tuesday the 26th some of them returned with us to our ship. There is turtle in such abundance that small vessels might make good profit by going thither.

---

*While Woory was ashore on Saturday June 23, Sandford ventured into Bohicket Creek and wrote: "Being gone about a mile up I landed and, according to my instructions, in presence of my company took a formal possession by turf and twig of that whole country from the Lat. of 36 deg. north to 29 d. South and west to the South Seas by the name of the Province of Carolina" (Sandford, "A Relation of a Voyage," 88).

[†]Sandford describes this Indian as a "Capt. of the Nation named Shadoo" ("A Relation of a Voyage," 93).

[‡]Edisto Island.

Wednesday the 27th some Indians told us that we might go with our vessel to the River Jordan* through land. One of them promised to go with us. The same day we weighed and sailed according to the directions of the Indian up a branch of the river and by reason of contrary winds we [shoaled] in some parts of the passage. It was Sunday July 1st before we got into the other river, which we thought had been Jordan. We stayed not there but went through to sea and about 3 hours after the wind shifted and having a lee shore under us, thought it best to get in again to the river which we did and anchored within the river's mouth. After which we went on shore upon a point that runs out into the sea where we saw one of the Indians that was at Barbados who told us that the river we were in, and which we called Jordan, was not so named, and that Hilton had never been there, so that we supposed that the passage we came through from the River Grandee to this river's mouth makes Edisto an island. Monday July the 2nd in the morning we weighed with the tide of ebb intending to see Port Royal. But it being calm the tide set us almost upon a point of creeks that lies to the eastward of the river's mouth. We lay in so that we were forced to come to an anchor and had but 5-foot water. We [struck] 7 or 8 times, and was in great danger of being lost but carrying anchors out we saved our vessel without harm. We rode 'til the ebb was done and then weighed and stood into a large opening—which we supposed to be Port Royal at which time we [discovered] the shallop as we thought coming to us, but contrary winds would neither permit her to come to us nor we to stand any longer in, therefore were forced to lie by 'til Wednesday July the 3rd in the morning when we [discovered] land again, and found out [to] be to the northward of Port Royal and no wind stirring. We came to an anchor about a league from the shore an hour or two after we weighed and stood to the southward with a fresh gale and [discovered] a large opening unto which we made and found a good large channel in the shallowest part not less than 3 fathom and the 5, 6, 7, 8 & more. It was midnight before we got into the river's mouth and then came to anchor about 3 leagues from the river's mouth in 8-fathom water.[†]

Wednesday July the 4th we went with our ship higher up, and the same depth of water from side to side. We went on shore up a small creek to the Indian town, where the Indians received us very gladly in that place. We saw many fields of corn, peas & beans, peach trees with fruit thereon; grapes, figs but not ripe, water melons, musk melons, squashes, pumpkins & other fruit. The Indians seemed

*Combahee River.

[†]They ran upon the shoals and nearly lost the vessel in St. Helena Sound. They sailed around St. Helena Island and anchored off Hilton Head, which Sandford named Woory Island in honor of his crewman. They then steered between Hilton Head and Port Royal and came to anchor in the Port Royal River.

very willing to have us settle amongst them. The land is generally such as Edisto and no whit worse. Whilst we were ashore the shallop arrived in Port Royal River who informed us that she had been in the River Jordan where they saw very good land and large timber. The same day we took the shallop and ran up the river about 30 miles and then the river divides itself into several branches and small creeks into one of the branches we went up about 3 miles and traveled into the country, and found the land very good, and many good timber trees growing thereon. In that march we found a pleasant running spring. We lay in that place all night and Thursday July the 5th early in the ebb we returned downward, and went on shore in several places of the river, where we found the land as in other places. The river is of so good a depth, and the channel so large that ships of 500 tons may go up to the division. About 1 o'clock we returned to our ship and found that Indians had been there with great store of fish. The Indians call the whole country St. Helena. We suppose the Spaniards usually come amongst them, because where they live is a large wooden cross erected, which they say the Spaniards had put there;* the same day we ran the shallop to the west side of the river where goes in a large creek which we ran up about 7 miles, and then came to a sound which hath a passage into the sea.† We went on shore that evening upon an island and found the land very good and laden with large trees, walnut, white oak & live oak, palm trees. That night we lay in the sound. Friday July the 6th we fell about a league lower with the shallop and went on shore of the other side the sound upon a large pleasant island which runs 4 or five miles before it comes to the sea. It was well stored with deer. The land thereon we found to be a black color with a small mixture of sand & that is where the pines grow but in another part of the island the land is far better than the former and laden with large timber trees. In that sound are many creeks which run up to the main land. That night we returned to our vessel and Mr. Brayne informing us that he had been with his shallop in the River Jordan, and came to Port Royal through land. We fell down with our ship to the mouth of the passage intending to go that way, but fearing we might meet with the like inconveniences, as we did from the River Grandee, and the shallop having been there already and given us good satisfaction as to the goodness of the land in Jordan thought it more convenient to take in wood and water at St. Helena, and so to see Kiawah on our way home.

---

*Both Hilton and Sandford noted that in front of a large council house at "St. Ellens" they saw a large wooden cross, a sign of prior Spanish presence in the region. The town was burned by Indians in 1667. Spaniards landed at Port Royal as early as 1520 and named the cape Santa Elena. In the mid-1600s another village was established nearby. The vicinity is Parris Island (Kovacik and Rowland, "Images of Port Royal," 331–33).

†Calibogue Sound.

Saturday July the 7th we took in wood and water, and the same evening one of the principal Indians of Port Royal came on board and made signs that he would go with us, upon which Lieut. Colonel Sandford thought it fit to leave one of our men in his room to learn the Indian tongue. Sunday the 8th of July we carried one of our company by name Henry Woodward on shore to the Indian town, and informed their king that we would leave the said Woodward with him and take the Indian in his place, at which he seemed very joyful and promised to use him very friendly showing his great desire of having the English to settle there.* We left the said Woodward with him at St. Helena taking the Indian in his place with another that came with us from Edisto, with as great a desire to go with us.

The same evening we set sail from Port Royal river and Wednesday the 10th we [discovered] an opening which we supposed to be Kiawah but an Indian of that place which we took in at Edisto told us that it was not the river but that it lay farther eastward, and about two hours after the Indian having been asleep and looking about him told us that the river we had seen before was Kiawah but the wind then would not permit us to go thither. A little after we saw another small opening at the mouth of which we saw great fires. The Kiawah Indian desired to be put on shore there, then making signs for the shallop to come up with us ordered her to put him on shore. And having been absent about two hours, she returned saying she could not come near the land nor opening for shoals and breakers, so that we took the advantage of the wind to sail homeward. Wednesday the 11th we stood in & made Charles River into which we stood, and about 5 o'clock that evening arrived before Charles towne with the shallop with all our men well and lusty only 4 of which had been sick of the fever & ague, at their first going to sea. What I have here written is no more than I have seen and I am sure the truth. I have not in the least been guided with falsehood but have rather writ the worst than the best, and those that travel into any of these parts, will I am confident say that they find things rather better than worse for 'twas my great care to observe the ground, timber trees, rivers &c and I am sure it may be settled at less charge than Cape Fear was; and a far greater benefit may accrue to those that settles it. And indeed it is a great pity, that such brave places should lie unpeopled and [an] abundance of our nation want land.

*Henry Woodward (d. 1686), the twenty-year-old ship's surgeon, remained to learn the Indian language and culture, and the Indian's young nephew was taken in exchange. Sandford gave Woodward formal possession of the country to hold for the lords proprietors. Woodward was later an agent for Lord Shaftesbury in setting up an Indian trade for the lords proprietors.

"Portrait of a man reputed to be John Lawson holding a book entitled
John Lawson." Courtesy of Joyner Library Special Collections,
East Carolina University, Greenville, NC.

John Lawson (Early 1700s)

"Charles Towne" and "Travel Among the Indians"

John Lawson (1674–1711), explorer, surveyor, naturalist, and author of *A New Voyage to Carolina*, was a native of Yorkshire, England, the son of Dr. John Lawson and his wife, Isabella Love. The family owned estates in the vicinity of Kingston-on-Hull, Yorkshire, where it is likely young Lawson first attended Anglican schools, followed by lectures at Gresham College near the family's London residence. At Gresham an endowment supported the teaching of astronomy, geometry, physics, law, divinity, and other subjects, while the natural sciences, mathematics, inventions, travel, and discoveries were subjects of special interest. It was also the usual meeting place of the Royal Society, and Lawson apparently yearned to accomplish something so notable that he would be chosen for membership.

He wrote in his preface to *A New Voyage to Carolina:* "In the Year 1700, when People flock'd from all Parts of the Christian world, to see the Solemnity of the Grand Jubilee at *Rome,* my Intention at that Times, being to travel, I accidentally met with a Gentleman, who had been Abroad and was very well acquainted with the Ways of Living in both *Indies;* of whom, having made Enquiry concerning them, he assur'd me, that *Carolina* was the best Country I could go to; and, that there then lay a Ship in *Thames,* in which I might have my passage." Although he did not name his informant, there is evidence that it was either Christopher Gale, a native of Yorkshire and an official in the northern part of Carolina, or James Moore from Charles Town, then in London seeking the governorship. Moore, already a friend of Lawson, owned the ship on which he sailed from England. When, three months later, they arrived in "Britain's colony in the New World," Moore, as Lawson's host, introduced him to the area.

Lawson was commissioned by colonial authorities to lead a small expedition from Charles Town into the interior. He arrived in the colony on August 15, 1700,

Taken from *A New Voyage to Carolina; Containing the Exact Description and Natural History of That Country: Together with the Present State thereof. And A Journal Of a Thousand Miles, Travel'd thro' several Nations of Indians. Giving a particular Account of their Customs, Manners, &c.* (London, 1709).

and remained until December 28, 1700. Then, traveling first in a cypress dugout canoe and then on foot, he ventured into the unchartered Carolina wilderness, accompanied by his spaniel, five unnamed Englishmen, and four Indians. They headed north to the mouth of the Santee River, where they encountered the last of the Indian tribes living in the interior. Lawson took vigilant note of the region's vegetation, wildlife, and the Indian tribes. He later wrote: "We took his earthly paradise and butchered it." He visited the early French Huguenot settlements on a section of the French Santee. From there, Lawson and company headed off toward the Congarees and to the High Hills of Santee, traveling into rivers, swamps, and over Indian paths. He ended his six hundred-mile journey near the Pamlico River in what was later designated North Carolina.

In February of 1701, Lawson settled on the Pamlico River and made his living as a land surveyor. There he met a companion, Hannah Smith, who bore him children. Near the fork of the Trent and Neuse rivers, he built a cabin on a creek. In 1705, he bought a plantation in Pamlico and laid out the settlement of Bath, the first town of North Carolina. He built a house for Hannah and their offspring, and from there he took long forays into the wilderness to collect natural specimens to send back to England. In 1705 he was appointed deputy surveyor of Carolina by the lords proprietors. In 1708 he became surveyor-general of the colony.

In October of 1709, Lawson returned to England to find a publisher for the journal of his journey. It was initially published in serial form, but the first issue proved so popular that the publisher combined installments under one title, *A New Voyage to Carolina*, with Lawson's added sections. It was widely read in Europe and various editions and translations (also retitled *The History of Carolina*) appeared between 1709 and 1722.

Early in April of 1710, Lawson returned to North Carolina, with several hundred Palatines, and laid out the town of New Bern. In September 1711, he was tortured and slain by Tuscarora Indians on the Neuse River.

SOURCES

Holloman, Charles R. "John Lawson, 1674–1711." In *Dictionary of North Carolina Biography* ed. William S. Powell. Chapel Hill: University of North Carolina Press, 1979–96.
Savage, Henry, Jr. *Lost Heritage.* New York: William Morrow & Co., 1970.

"CHARLES TOWNE"

After a fortnight's stay here, we put out from Sandyhook, and in 4 days after, arriv'd at Charles-Town, the metropolis of South Carolina, which is situate in

32, 45 north latitude, and admits of large ships to come over their bar up to the town, where is a very commodious harbor, about five miles distant from the inlet, and stands on a point very convenient for trade, being seated between two pleasant and navigable rivers. The town has very regular and fair streets, in which are good buildings of brick and wood, and since my coming thence, has had great additions of beautiful, large brick-buildings, besides a strong fort, and regular fortifications made to defend the town. The inhabitants, by their wise management and industry, have much improv'd the country, which is in as thriving circumstances at this time, as any colony on the continent of English America, and is of more advantage to the Crown of Great Britain, than any of the other more northerly plantations, (Virginia and Maryland excepted). This colony was at first planted by a genteel sort of people, that were well acquainted with trade, and had either money or parts, to make good use of the advantages that offer'd, as most of them have done, by raising themselves to great estates, and considerable places of trust, and posts of honor, in this thriving settlement. Since the first planters, abundance of French and others have gone over, and rais'd themselves to considerable fortunes. They are very neat and exact in packing and shipping of their commodities; which method has got them so great a character abroad, that they generally come to a good market with their commodities; when oftentimes the product of other plantations, are forc'd to be sold at lower prizes. They have a considerable trade both to Europe, and the West Indies, whereby they become rich, and are supply'd with all things necessary for trade, and genteel living, which several other places fall short of. Their cohabiting in a town, has drawn to them ingenious people of most sciences, whereby they have tutors amongst them that educate their youth a-la-mode.

Their roads, with great industry, are made very good and pleasant. Near the town is built a fair parsonage-house, with necessary offices, and the minister has a very considerable allowance from his parish. There is likewise a French Church in town,* of the reform'd religion, and several meeting-houses for dissenting congregations, who all enjoy at this day an entire liberty of their worship; the constitution of this government, allowing all parties of well-meaning Christians to enjoy a free toleration, and possess the same privileges, so long as they appear to behave themselves peaceably and well: It being the Lords Proprietors intent, that the inhabitants of Carolina should be as free from oppression, as any in the universe; which doubtless they will, if their own differences amongst themselves do not occasion the contrary.

They have a well-disciplin'd militia; their horses are most gentlemen[ly], and well mounted, and the best in America, and may equalize any in other parts:

*The French Huguenot Church, first built in 1687 on Church Street in Charleston.

Their officers, both Infantry and Cavalry, generally appear in scarlet mountings, and as rich as in most regiments belonging to the Crown, which shows the richness and grandeur of this colony. They are a frontier, and prove such troublesome neighbors to the Spaniards, that they have once laid their town of St. Augustine in ashes, and drove away their cattle; besides many encounters and engagements, in which they have defeated them, too tedious to relate here. What the French got by their attempt against South Carolina, will hardly ever be rank'd amongst their victories; their Admiral Mouville being glad to leave the enterprise, and run away, after he had suffer'd all the loss and disgrace he was capable of receiving.* They are absolute masters over the Indians, and carry so strict a hand over such as are within the circle of their trade, that none does the least injury to any of the English but he is presently sent for, and punish'd with death, or otherwise, according to the nature of the fault. They have an entire friendship with the neighboring Indians of several nations, which are a very warlike people, ever faithful to the English, and have prov'd themselves brave and true on all occasions; and are a great help and strength to this colony. The chief of the savage nations have heretofore groan'd under the Spanish yoke, and having experienc'd their cruelty, are become such mortal enemies to that people, that they never give a Spaniard quarter; but generally, when they take any prisoners, (if the English be not near to prevent it) scalp them, that is, to take their hair and skin of their heads, which they often flea away, whilst the wretch is alive. Notwithstanding the English have used all their endeavors, yet they could never bring them to leave this barbarity to the Spaniards; who, as they allege, use to murder them and their relations, and make slaves of them to build their forts and towns.

This place is more plentiful in money, than most, or indeed any of the plantations on the continent; besides, they build a considerable number of vessels of cedar, and other wood, with which they trade to [Curaçao] and the West Indies; from one they bring money, and from the other the produce of their islands, which yields a necessary supply of both to the colony. Their stocks of cattle are incredible, being from one to two thousand head in one man's possession: These feed in the savannas, and other grounds, and need no fodder in the winter. Their mutton and veal is good, and their pork is not inferior to any in America. As for pitch and tar, none of the plantations are comparable for affording the vast quantities of naval stores, as this place does. There have been heretofore some discoveries of rich mines in the mountainous part of this country; but being remote from the present settlement, and the inhabitants not well versed in ordering minerals,

*Lawson mistakes "Admiral Mouville" for Gaspard de Coligny, admiral of France and Protestant chief.

they have been laid aside 'till a more fit opportunity happens. There are several noble rivers, and spacious tracts of rich land in their Lordships dominions, lying to the southward, which are yet uninhabited, besides Port Royal, a rare harbor and inlet, having many inhabitants thereon, which their Lordships have now made a port for trade. This will be a most advantageous settlement, lying so commodiously for ships coming from the Gulf, and the richness of the land, which is reported to be there. These more southerly parts will afford oranges, lemons, limes, and many other fruits, which the northerly plantations yield not.

The merchants of Carolina are fair, frank traders. The gentlemen seated in the country, are very courteous, live very nobly in their houses, and give very genteel entertainment to all strangers and others that come to visit them. And since the produce of South and North Carolina is the same, unless silk, which this place produces great quantities of, and very good,* North Carolina having never made any trial thereof as yet, therefore I shall refer the natural produce of this country to that part which treats of North Carolina, whose productions are much the same. The Christian inhabitants of both colonies pretty equal, but the slaves of South Carolina are far more in number than those in the North. I shall now proceed to relate my journey thro' the country, from this settlement to the other, and then treat them of the natural history of Carolina, with other remarkable circumstances which I have met with, during my eight years abode in that country.

"Travel Among the Indians"

[Saturday.]

On December the 28th, 1700, I began my voyage from Charles-Town, being six Englishmen in company, with three Indian-men, and one woman, wife to our Indian-guide, having five miles from the town to the Breach we went down in a large canoe, that we had provided for our voyage thither, having the tide of ebb along with us; which was so far spent by that time we got down, that we had not water enough for our craft to go over, although we drew but two foot, or thereabouts. This breach is a passage through a marsh lying to the northward of Sullivan's Island, the pilot's having a look out thereon, lying very commodious for mariners, (on that coast) making a good land-mark in so level a country, this bar being difficult to hit, where an observation hath been wanting for a day or two;

---

*French Huguenots were encouraged by the lords proprietors to cultivate silk, wine, and olive oil. Experiments resulted in some progress, but these commodities ultimately proved unsuccessful as products of trade.

north east winds bringing great fogs, mists, and rains; which, towards the cool months of October, November, and until the latter end of March, often appear in these parts. There are three pilots to attend, and conduct ships over the bar.

The harbor where the vessels generally ride, is against the town on Cooper's River, lying within a point which parts that and Ashley-River, they being land locked almost on all sides.

At 4 in the afternoon, (at half flood) we passed with our canoe over the breach, leaving Sullivan's Island on our starboard. The first place we designed for was Santee River, on which there is a colony of French Protestants, allowed and encouraged by the Lords Proprietors.* At night we got to Bell's-Island, a poor spot of land, being about ten miles round, where lived (at that time) a Bermudian, being employed here with a boy, to look after a stock of cattle and hogs, by the owner of this island. One side of the roof of his house was thatched with palmetto-leaves, the other open to the heavens, thousands of musketoes, and other troublesome insects, tormenting both man and beast inhabiting these islands.

[Palmetto-trees.]

The palmetto-trees, whose leaves growing only on the top of the tree, in the shape of a fan, and in a cluster, like a cabbage; this tree in Carolina, when at its utmost growth, is about forty or fifty foot in height, and two foot through: It's worth mentioning, that the growth of the tree is not perceivable in the age of any man, the experiment having been often tried in Bermudas, and elsewhere, which shows the slow growth of this vegetable, the wood of it being porous and stringy, like some canes; the leaves thereof the Bermudians make women's hats, bokeets, baskets, and pretty dressing-boxes, a great deal being transported to Pennsylvania, and other northern parts of America, (where they do not grow) for the same manufacture. The people of Carolina make of the fans of this tree, brooms very serviceable, to sweep their houses withal.

We took up our lodging this night with the Bermudian; our entertainment was very indifferent, there being no fresh water to be had on the island. The next

*In 1679, Rene Petit, the King's agent in Rouen, and Jacob Guerard from Normandy petitioned the lords proprietors for "money, land and transportation" to transport eighty families of French Huguenot refugees to Carolina. In return, the Huguenots would apply their experience and skills to the production of silk, olives, and wine. The petition was approved by King Charles II. In December of 1679, His Majesty's Ship, the HMS *Richmond*, sailed from England for the Carolinas with the first contingent of the Petit-Guérard Colony, forty-five French Protestants. They landed in Charles Town in April of 1680 and were assigned three thousand acres on the south Santee River (Bates and Leland, *Proprietary Records of South Carolina*, 61n, 69).

morning we set away thro' the marshes; about noon we reached another island, called Dix's Island, much like to the former, tho' larger; there lived an honest Scot, who gave us the best reception his dwelling afforded, being well provided of oat-meal, and several other effects he had found on that coast; which goods belonged to that unfortunate vessel, the *Rising Sun,* a Scotch Man of War, lately arrived from the Isthmus of Darien, and cast away near the bar of Ashley River, the September before, Capt. Gibson of Glass then commanding her, who, with above an hundred men then on board her [on September 5, 1700], were every soul drowned in that terrible gust which then happened; most of the corps being taken up, were carefully interred by Mr. Graham, their Lieutenant, who happily was on shore during the tempest.*

After dinner, we left our Scotch landlord, and went that night to the north east point of the island: It being dark ere we got there, our canoe struck on a sand near the breakers, and were in great danger of our lives, but (by God's blessing) got off safe to the shore, where we lay all night.

[Monday.]

In the morning we set forwards on our intended voyage. About two a clock we got to Bulls Island, which is about thirty miles long, and hath a great number of both cattle and hogs upon it; the cattle being very wild, and the hogs very lean. These two last islands belong to one Colonel Cary, an inhabitant of South Carolina.†

---

*As the *Rising Sun* attempted to return home from the abandoned Scottish Presbyterian colony of Stuart's Town near Beaufort, it was damaged in a storm. Traveling north, the ship anchored off Charleston bar for rest and provisions. The crew was in the act of removing the ship's guns and preparing to cross the bar when a hurricane arose. The ship sank, and three hundred aboard were lost, "their bodies strewn on the beach at James Island." Capt. James Gibson of Glasgow, commander, went down with the ship. Presbyterian Rev. Archibald Stobo (1670–1737), a passenger earlier induced to preach in a Charleston church, had disembarked with his wife and twelve other passengers, including Graham (McCrady, *South Carolina under the Proprietary Government,* 310–11).

†Bulls Island is the largest of four barrier islands in what is now Cape Romain National Wildlife Refuge. The island was inhabited by Sewee Indians before the arrival of the first European settlers. According to *Names in South Carolina,* it was originally known by its Indian name of Oni:see:cau (also spelled "Oneiscau," meaning island people). In 1696 one Small Hartly was granted all that "Island commonly called Anisecau or Bullings Island." Thomas Cary owned innumerable islands nearby, but this author could find no record of his having owned Bulls. By 1708–9 the island was owned by Capt. John Collins. His son, Jonah Collins, sold it prior to 1743 to John Atchison, who sold it to Daniel McGregor and William Bohannan. In the latter deed, it is referred to as Bulls Island. In 1925, the island was purchased by

Although it were winter, yet we found such swarms of musketoes, and other troublesome insects, that we got but little rest that night.

[Tuesday.]

The next day we intended for a small island on the other side of Sewee-Bay, which joining to these islands, shipping might come to victual or careen; but there being such a burden of those flies, that few or none cares to settle there; so the stock thereon are run wild. We were gotten about half way to Raccoon-Island, when there sprung up a tart gale at N.W. which put us in some danger of being cast away, the bay being rough, and there running great seas between the two islands, which are better than four leagues asunder, a strong current of a tide setting in and out, which made us turn tail to it, and got our canoe right before the wind, and came safe into a creek that is joining to the north end of Bulls Island. We sent our Indians to hunt, who brought us two deers, which were very poor, and their maws full of large grubs.

[Wednesday.]

On the morrow we went and visited the easternmost side of this island, it joining to the ocean, having very fair sandy beeches, paved with innumerable sorts of curious pretty shells, very pleasant to the eye. Amongst the rest, we found the Spanish oyster-shell, whence come the pearls. They are very large, and of a different form from other oysters; their color much resembles the tortoise-shell, when it is dressed. There was left by the tide several strange species of a mucilaginous slimy substance, though living, and very aptly moved at their first appearance; yet, being left on the dry sand, (by the beams of the sun) soon exhale and vanish.

At our return to our quarters, the Indians had killed two more deer, two wild hogs, and three raccoons, all very lean, except the raccoons. We had great store of oysters, conks, and clams, a large sort of cockles. These parts being very well furnished with shell-fish, turtle of several sorts, but few or none of the green, with other sorts of salt-water fish, and in the season, good plenty of fowl, as curleus, gulls, gannets, and pelicans, besides duck and mallard, geese, swans, teal, pigeon, & c.

[Thursday.]

On Thursday morning we left Bulls Island, and went thro' the creeks, which lie between the bay and the main land. At noon we went on shore, and got our

---

New York Senator Gayer Dominick, who built an estate on the island as a winter residence and hunting preserve. In the 1930s, he turned it over to the U.S. Fish and Wildlife Service (Neuffer, *Names in South Carolina*, Volumes 1–30: see vols. 12 [Winter 1965] and 16 [Winter 1969]).

dinner near a plantation, on a creek having the full prospect of Sewee-Bay: We sent up to the house, but found none at home, but a negro, of whom our messenger purchased some small quantity of tobacco and rice. We came to a deserted Indian residence, called Avendaugh-bough,* where we rested that night.

[Friday.]

The next day we entered Santee-River's mouth, where is fresh water, occasioned by the extraordinary current that comes down continually. With hard rowing, we got two leagues up the river, lying all night in a swampy piece of ground, the Weather being so cold all that time, we were almost frozen ere morning, leaving the impressions of our bodies on the wet ground. We set forward very early in the morning, to seek some better quarters.

[Saturday.]

As we rowed up the river, we found the land towards the mouth, and for about sixteen miles up it, scarce any thing but swamp and percoarson, [a sort of low land] affording vast cypress-trees, of which the French make canoes, that will carry fifty or sixty barrels. After the tree is molded and dug, they saw them in two pieces, and so put a plank between, and a small keel, to preserve them from the oyster-banks, which are innumerable in the creeks and bays betwixt the French settlement and Charles-Town. They carry two masts, and Bermudas sails, which makes them very handy and fit for their purpose; for although their river fetches its first rise from the mountains, and continues a current some hundreds of miles ere it disgorges it self, having no sound bay or sand-banks betwixt the mouth thereof, and the ocean. Notwithstanding all this, with the vast stream it affords at all seasons, and the repeated freshes it so often alarms the inhabitants with, by laying under water a great part of their country; yet the mouth is barred, affording not above four or five foot water at the entrance. As we went up the river, we heard a great noise, as if two parties were engaged against each other, seeming exactly like small shot.

[Sewee Indians.]

When we approached nearer the place, we found it to be some Sewee Indians firing the canes swamps, which drives out the game, then taking their particular stands, kill great quantities of both bear, deer, turkeys, and what wild creatures the parts afford.

---

*Awendaw, incorporated as a town in 1992, was originally named by the Seewee Indian tribe, who built a large mound in the region.

These Sewees have been formerly a large nation, though now very much de-creased, since the English hath seated their land, and all other nations of Indians are observed to partake of the same fate, where the Europeans come, the Indians being a people very apt to catch any distemper they are afflicted withal; the small-pox has destroyed many thousands of these natives, who no sooner than they are attacked with the violent fevers, and the burning which attends that distemper, fling themselves over head in the water, in the very extremity of the disease; which shutting up the pores, hinders a kindly evacuation of the pestilential matter, and drives it back; by which means death most commonly ensues; not but in other distempers which are epidemical, you may find among 'em practitioners that have extraordinary skill and success in removing those morbifick qualities which afflict 'em, not often going above 100 yards from their abode for their remedies, some of their chiefest physicians commonly carrying their compliment of drugs continually about them, which are roots, barks, berries, nuts, &c. that are strung upon a thread. So like a pomander, the physician wears them about his neck. An Indian hath been often found to heal an Englishman of a malady, for the value of a match-coat; which the ablest of our English pretenders in America, after re-peated applications, have deserted the patient as incurable; God having furnished every country with specific remedies for their peculiar diseases.

[Rum.]

Rum, a liquor now so much in use with them, that they will part with the dearest thing they have, to purchase it; and when they have got a little in their heads, are the impatientest creatures living, 'till they have enough to make 'em quite drunk; and the most miserable spectacles when they are so, some falling into the fires, burn their legs or arms, contracting the sinews, and become cripples all their life-time; others from precipices break their bones and joints, with abun-dance of instances, yet none are so great to deter them from that accursed practice of drunkenness, though sensible how many of them (are by it) hurried into the other world before their time, as themselves oftentimes will confess. The Indians, I was now speaking of, were not content with the common enemies that lessen and destroy their country-men, but invented an infallible stratagem to purge their tribe, and reduce their multitude into far less numbers. Their contrivance was thus, as a trader amongst them informed me.

They seeing several ships coming in, to bring the English supplies from Old England, one chief part of their cargo being for a trade with the Indians, some of the craftiest of them had observed, that the ships came always in at one place, which made them very confident that way was the exact road to England; and seeing so many ships come thence, they believed it could not be far thither, esteeming the English that were among them, no better than cheats, and thought, if they could carry the skins and furs they got, themselves to England, which were inhabited with a better sort of people than those sent amongst them, that then they should purchase twenty times the value for every pelt they sold abroad, in consideration of what rates they sold for at home. The intended barter was exceeding well approved of, and after a general consultation of the ablest heads amongst them, it was, "Nemine Contradicente," agreed upon, immediately to make an addition of their fleet, by building more canoes, and those to be of the best sort, and biggest size, as fit for their intended discovery. Some Indians were employed about making the canoes, others to hunting, every one to the post he was most fit for, all endeavors tending towards an able fleet and cargo for Europe. The affair was carried on with a great deal of secrecy and expedition, so as in a small time they had gotten a Navy, loading provisions, and hands ready to set sail, leaving only the old, impotent, and minors at home, 'till their successful return. (They never hearing more of their fleet.) The wind presenting, they set up their mat-sails, and were scarce out of sight, when there rose a tempest, which it's supposed carried one part of these Indian merchants, by way of the other world, whilst the others were taken up at sea by an English ship, and sold for slaves to the islands. The remainder are better satisfied with their imbecilities in such an undertaking, nothing affronting them more, than to rehearse their voyage to England.*

There being a strong current in Santee-River, caused us to make small way with our oars. With hard rowing, we got that night to Mons. Eugee's[†] house, which stands about fifteen miles up the river, being the first Christian dwelling we met withal in that settlement, and were very courteously received by him and his wife.

Many of the French follow a trade with the Indians, living very conveniently for that Interest. There is about seventy families seated on this river, who live as decently and happily, as any planters in these Southward parts of America. The French being a temperate industrious people, some of them bringing very little of effects, yet by their endeavors and mutual assistance amongst themselves, (which is highly to be commended) have out-stripped our English, who brought with 'em larger fortunes, though (as it seems) less endeavor to manage their talent to the best advantage. 'Tis admirable to see what time and industry will (with God's

*This event occurred around 1696 (www.fws.gov/caperomain [accessed December 1, 2012]).
[†]Daniel Huger (1651–1711) first left France for England before he came to Carolina in 1686 with his wife, Margaret, and daughter, Margarite. Huger, a French merchant trader and tax collector, was able to preserve his wealth. He purchased three lots in Charleston and several hundred acres of land, and settled at Wambaw Creek at a farm they named Waterhorn. Two more children, Daniel and Madeline, were born in Carolina after 1696 (Leiding, *Historic Houses of South Carolina*, 93; Salley, ed., *Warrants for Land in South Carolina*, 34, 58, 175).

blessing) effect. Carolina affording many strange revolutions in the age of a man, daily instances presenting themselves to our view, of so many, from despicable beginnings, which in a short time arrive to very splendid conditions. Here propriety hath a large scope, there being no strict laws to bind our privileges. A quest after game, being as freely and peremptorily enjoyed by the meanest planter, as he that is the highest in dignity, or wealthiest in the province. Deer, and other game that are naturally wild, being not immured, or preserved within boundaries, to satisfy the appetite of the rich alone. A poor laborer, that is master of his gun, &c. hath as good a claim to have continued courses of delicacies crowded upon his table, as he that is master of a greater purse.

We lay all that night at Mons. Eugee's, and the next morning set out farther, to go the remainder of our voyage by land: At ten a clock we passed over a narrow, deep swamp, having left the three Indian men and one woman, that had piloted the canoe from Ashley-River, having hired a Sewee-Indian, a tall, lusty fellow, who carried a pack of our cloths, of great weight; notwithstanding his burden, we had much a-do to keep pace with him. At noon we came up with several French plantations, meeting with several creeks by the way, the French were very officious in assisting with their small dories to pass over these waters, (whom we met coming from their church) being all of them very clean and decent in their apparel; their houses and plantations suitable in neatness and contrivance. They are all of the same opinion with the church of Geneva,* there being no difference amongst them concerning the punctilio's of their Christian faith; which union hath propagated a happy and delightful concord in all other matters throughout the whole neighborhood; living amongst themselves as one tribal, or kindred, every one making it his business to be assistant to the wants of his country-man, preserving his estate and reputation with the same exactness and concern as he does his own; all seeming to share in the misfortunes, and rejoice at the advance, and rise, of their brethren.

Towards the afternoon, we came to Mons. L'Jandro,† where we got our dinner; there coming some French ladies whilst we were there, who were lately come from England, and Mons. L'Grand,‡ a worthy Norman, who hath been a great

---

*Four French congregations established in the colony—Santee, Orange Quarter, Charleston, and St. John's Berkeley—professed the doctrines and forms of the Church of Geneva.

†"L'Jandro" was Capt. Philip Gendron, who arrived on an English ship in 1686. He invested in land and local commercial ventures, was a moneylender in the region, and a commissioner for the settlement. He lived a short distance from Daniel Huger. His daughter, Elizabeth, eventually married Daniel Huger's son, also named Daniel (Harrell, *Kith and Kin*, 62–66).

‡Isaac Le Grand, a native of Caen "of minor nobility," who fled Normandy with his wife, Elizabeth, and their son, Isaac. Actually he moved significant funds out of France. In

sufferer in his estate, by the persecution in France, against those of the Protestant religion: This gentleman very kindly invited us to make our stay with him all night, but we being intended farther that day, took our leaves, returning acknowledgments of their favors.

About 4 in the afternoon, we passed over a large cyprus run in a small canoe; the French doctor* sent his negro to guide us over the head of a large swamp; so we got that night to Mons. Galliar's the elder,† who lives in a very curious contrived house, built of brick and stone, which is gotten near that place. Near here comes in the road from Charles-Town, and the rest of the English settlement, it being a very good way by land, and not above 36 miles, altho' more than 100 by water; and I think the most difficult way I ever saw, occasioned by reason of the multitude of creeks lying along the main, keeping their course thro' the marshes, turning and winding like a labyrinth, having the tide of ebb and flood twenty times in less than three leagues going.

[Monday.]

The next morning very early, we ferry'd over a creek that runs near the house; and, after an hour's travel in the woods, we came to the river-side, where we stayed for the Indian, who was our guide, and was gone round by water in a small canoe, to meet us at that place we rested at. He came after a small time, and ferry'd us in that little vessel over Santee River 4 miles, and 84 miles in the woods, which the over-flowing of the freshes, which then came down, had made a perfect sea of, there running an incredible current in the river, which had cast our small craft, and us, away, had we not had this Sewee Indian with us; who are excellent artists in managing these small canoes.

London in 1686, he purchased one hundred acres of Carolina land. A daughter, Elizabeth, was born in Carolina (Van Ruymbeke, *From New Babylon to Eden*, 60; Bridges and Williams, *St. James Santee*, 17).

*Rev. Pierre Robert (1656–1715), born in Switzerland, emigrated from France with his wife, Jeanne Bayer, and their son Pierre in 1686. Their ship was joined in route by the ship with Philip Gendron aboard. In Carolina, Robert was an itinerant pastor, then rector of St. James Santee, the parish church. He served with Gendron as commissioner of Jamestown. Both of their home sites were located across from the church. Robert later founded the village of Robertsville (Harrell, *Kith and Kin*, 61–66; Lawton, *Saga of the South*, 32–33).

†Joachim Gaillard, a wealthy merchant from France, purchased 600 acres of Carolina land in London in 1687. He arrived the same year with his wife, Ester, and two sons, Barthelemy (Bartholomew) Jr. and Jean (John). In 1705, a grant of 360 acres from the plantation of Philip Gendron was made to Gaillard, Rene Ravenel, and Henry Bruneau for the town of Jamestown (Orvin, *Historic Berkeley County*, 15, 16, 136).

"Josiah Quincy Jr.," painted posthumously by Gilbert Stuart ca. 1825.
Courtesy of Museum of Fine Arts, Boston.

Josiah Quincy Jr. (1773)

"Society of Charleston"

Josiah Quincy (1744–1775), the first American attorney to compile and publish law reports, was considered a legal prodigy in New England. He was born into an old Massachusetts family that had first arrived in Boston in 1633. His father was Colonel Josiah Quincy (1710–1784), a militia officer who owned ships and a glass factory. His son, Josiah Quincy III (1772–1864), would become a member of Congress, mayor of Boston, and president of Harvard.

Quincy Jr. grew up at his ancestral homestead at Braintree Plantation township (now Quincy, Massachusetts), south of Boston. He graduated from Harvard in 1763 and received his master's degree there in 1766, at which time he delivered a passionate address "on liberty," or "the meaning of being a patriot." The gifted orator's speech caught the attention of Boston's patriot leadership. By 1767, he contributed regularly to the *Boston Gazette,* initially under the name "Hyperion." At the age of twenty-six and against his father's advice, he assisted his cousin John Adams in the legal defense of the British officers and soldiers accused in the Boston Massacre, one of the most celebrated criminal trials in colonial history, which famously won acquittals or reduced sentences for the accused.

In failing health in 1773, Quincy was advised to seek a southern climate. In February, he took passage to the provinces and traveled through the Carolinas to Charleston. By spring, relations between the colonies and England would become critical, followed by the overthrow of the royal government in 1775. Despite the approaching war, he arrived during the social season and found Charleston society endeavored in horse races, dancing assemblies, and "the most brilliant season in the history of the colonial American theatre."

It was said that Quincy's journey brought southern patriots into closer relations with the popular leaders in Massachusetts. In September of 1774, he secretly left America for England to argue the American cause to British politicians. While

Taken from Josiah Quincy Jr.'s journal, February 28—March 21, 1773, Quincy Family Papers, Massachusetts Historical Society.

sailing back to this country in April of 1775, he died aboard ship of tuberculosis within sight of the Massachusetts shore. He was only thirty-two years old.

Quincy's journal was first printed by his son in 1825 in *Memoir of the Life of Josiah Quincy, Jun. of Massachusetts,* a heavily edited version of the original. In 1874, it was reprinted by his granddaughter, Eliza Susan Quincy, who once again edited the original, excluding any personal or critical remarks. In 1916, the Massachusetts Historical Society compared the original manuscript to the edited family versions and found the comparison intriguing. They published an edition closer to the original in an issue of the society's magazine that year. However, the following account was transcribed directly from Quincy's handwritten manuscript to follow verbatim his wording and punctuation. The original journal is located in the Quincy family papers at the Massachusetts Historical Society.

SOURCES

Harris, J. William. *The Hanging of Thomas Jeremiah: A Free Black Man's Encounter with Liberty.* New Haven, CT: Yale University Press, 2009.

Howe, Mark De Wolfe, ed. "Journal of Josiah Quincy, Jr., 1773." *Proceedings of the Massachusetts Historical Society* 49 (1915–16): 426–81.

McCullough, David. *John Adams.* New York: Simon and Schuster, 2001.

Quincy, Josiah. *Memoir of the Life of Josiah Quincy, Jr. of Massachusetts.* 2nd ed. Boston: John Wilson and Son, 1874.

Quincy, Josiah, III. Papers. Harvard University Archives, Boston.

—————

"SOCIETY OF CHARLESTON"

Feb. 28. We now were off Charlestown-Bar, and the wind being right in our teeth we were the whole day beating up. Just before sunset we passed the fort. Charlestown appeared situated between two large spacious rivers, (the one on the right called Cooper River and the other on the left, Ashley-River) which here empty themselves into the sea. The number of shipping far surpassed all I had ever seen in Boston. I was told there were then not so many as common at this season, tho' about 350 sail lay off the town. The town struck me very agreeably; but the New Exchange which fronted the place of my landing made a most noble appearance.* On landing, Sunday Evening just before dark, the numbers of Inhabitants and appearance of the buildings far exceeded my expectation. I proceeded to

---

*The Exchange or Custom House (ca. 1767 to 1771), at Broad and East Bay streets, initially faced the harbor to impress visitors arriving on ships. It was built on the site of the guard post of the early colonists.

the Coffee-house, where was a great resort of company as busy and noisy as was decent.

I here met with Mr. Lavinus Clarkson* to whom I had letters, who much befriended me in getting lodgings, which we were put to very great difficulty to obtain. By ten o'clock however we procured one near the State-house, and this night I had the most sound and refreshing slumber I have ever enjoyed.

March 1. In the morning the same gentleman politely attended me to introduce me to those to whom I had letters of recommendation.

This and the next day I spent in traversing the town from one end to the other, viewing the public buildings and the most elegant mansion houses.

March 2. This day I was waited upon by several gentlemen to whom yesterday I had delivered letters—those who came in my absence left cards with their names. Received a ticket from David Deis, Esq.,[†] for the St. Cecilia Concert, and now quit my journal to go.

March 3. The concert-house is a large, inelegant building[‡] situated down a yard at the entrance of which I was met by *a Constable with his staff.* I offered him my ticket, which was *subscribed by the name of the person giving it,* and directing admission of me *by name,* the officer told me to proceed, I did, and was next met by a white waiter, who directs one to a 3rd to whom I delivered my ticket and was conducted in. The Hall is (preposterously) and out of all proportion large, no orchestra for the musical performers, though a kind of loft for fiddlers at the Assembly. The performers were all at one end of the hall and the company in front and on each side. The musick was good. The two bass-viols and French horns were grand. One Abercrombie,[§] a Frenchman just arrived played the first fiddle and solo incomparably, better than any one I ever had heard. Abercombie can't speak a word of English and has a salary of 500 guineas a year from the St. Cecilia Society.—Hartley[¶] was here, and played as I thought badly on the harpsichord. The capital defect of this concert was want of an organ.

*Levinus Clarkson (1740–1798) was a commission merchant and slave trader involved in the rice trade from 1772 until he returned to the North a few years later. He was a member of the merchant families of Van Horne and Clarkson of New York.

[†]David Deas (1720–1775) emigrated from Scotland in 1738. At the time of Quincy's visit, he was treasurer of the Charleston Chamber of Commerce.

[‡]The concert hall was Thomas Pike's New Assembly Room or "Long Room," located on the west side of Church between Elliott and Tradd streets.

[§]John Abercrombie (elsewhere described as a "Scotchman") achieved fame as a first violinist and was among the select few professional musicians offered positions by the St. Cecilia Society.

[¶]Oscar Sonneck identifies the harpsichordist as Thomas Hartley, who had arrived in Charleston from Boston in February. His major instrument was the violin. It could as easily have been musician George H. Hartley (*Early Concert Life in America,* 27).

Here was upwards of two hundred and fifty ladies, and it was called no great show. I took a view of them, but there was no E———.* However, I saw "*Beauty* in a Brow of Egypt": To be sure not a Helen's.

In loftiness of head-dress these ladies stoop to the daughters of the North: in richness of dress surpass them: in health and floridity of countenance veil to them: in taciturnity during the performances greatly before our ladies: in noise and flirtations after the musick is over pretty much on a par. If Our Women have any advantage it is in white and red, vivacity and fire.

The gentlemen many of them dressed with richness and elegance was common with us—many with swords on. We had two Macaronis present—just arrived from London. This character I found real, and not fictitious. "See the Macaroni," was a common phrase in the hall. One may well be styled the Bag, and the other the Cue-Macaroni.[†]

Mr. Deis was very polite:—he introduced me to most of the first character. Among the rest to Lord Charles G[reville] Montague, the Governor[‡] (who was to sail next day for London) and to the Chief Justice,[§] two of the Assistant Judges, and several of the Council.

Nothing that I now saw raised my conceptions of the mental abilities of this people: but my wrath enkindled, when I considered a King's Governor.

March 3. Spent in viewing horses, riding over the town and into the vicinity, and receiving formal compliments.

March 4, Thursday. Dined (with four other Gentlemen) with David Deis, Esq. (Table decent and not inelegant: provisions indifferent, but well-dressed: no apology: good wines and festivity. Salt fish brought in small bits in a dish made a corner.) The first toast the king: the second, a lady: the third, our friends at Boston and your (meaning my) fire-side. The master of the feast then called to the *Gentleman* on his right hand *for a Lady:*—this was done to every one, except to the Ladies at table (Mr. D's daughters about sixteen and ten) who were called upon *for a Gentleman* and gave one with ease. The ladies withdrew after the first round—the father seemed displeased at it. Glasses were changed every time different wine was filled. A sentiment was given by each gentleman and then we

---

*"Eugenia" was a name Quincy gave his wife, Abigail.

[†]"Macaroni," an elite, flamboyant young British man, otherwise called a fop or dandy, who came into fashion in the early 1770s.

[‡]Lord Charles Greville Montague (1741–1783), royal governor from 1765, was making his last public appearance at the St. Cecilia concert. On March 8, he sailed on the *Eagle* for England.

[§]Thomas Knox Gordon (1728–1796), the last chief justice elected by the king.

were called to coffee and tea. No compulsion in drinking, except that a bumper was called for at the third toast. Politicks an uninteresting topick.

March 5, Friday. Dined at a very elegantly disposed and plentiful table at the house of John Mathews, Esq. (son-in-law of Colonel Scott)* in company with the Chief Justice of St. Augustine,[†] and several other gentlemen. Puddings and pies brought in hot after meats taken away. The flour of the place in general is indifferent. First toast The King and his friends. The master of the feast calls upon *his lady* for *a gentleman* as a second toast: given with ease. Ladies go round as toasts. The females withdraw, and sentiments succeed. No compulsion in drinking: no interesting conversation. Good wines.

March 6. This day was to have been spent with Thomas Loughton Smith, Esq.[‡] at his country seat. Bad weather prevents, and I take what is called a family dinner with him. A prodigious fine pudding made of what they call rice flour. Nick-nacks brought on table after removal of meats. Ladies ask the gentlemen to drink a glass of wine with them: Upon a gentleman's asking a lady to do the like, she replies, "G— bless you, I thought you would never ask. I have been waiting for you this half hour."

First toasts Our Boston friends and your good health. Sir:—the unmarried lady (of nineteen) at my right, "Your good health and best affections, Sir!"—Miss ——— your toast, madam. "Love and friendship and they who *feel them*!"

Toasts called for from the guests. Until coffee and etc. Mr. Smith's house furniture, pictures, plate etc. very elegant—wines very fine.

Mrs. Smith showed me a most beautiful white satin and very richly embroidered lady's work-bag, designed as a present for a lady in London. Miss Catherine Ingliss, her sister, a still more finely embroidered festoon (as they called it) of flowers. Both their own work; and far surpassing anything of the kind I ever saw.

Before dinner a short account of the late disputes with the Governor, Lord Charles G. Montague, and the state of matters at present.

No Politicks after dinner.

---

*John Mathews (1744–1802) was educated at the Inns of Court, London, before he began to practice law in Charleston in 1764. He married Sally Scott, the daughter of Col. John Scott, a wealthy merchant from Boston.

[†]William Drayton (1732–1790) was chief justice of East-Florida, ceded to England by Spain.

[‡]Thomas Loughton Smith (1741–1773) was killed in a fall from his horse shortly after Quincy's visit. He was said to have lived "according to the new fashion" and "quite ostentatiously." He was married to Elizabeth Inglis, daughter of George Inglis, a Charleston merchant (Rogers, *Evolution of a Federalist*, 60).

In walking with ———— occurred a singular event, of which Balch* could make a humorous strory.

March 7, Sabbath. Went to St. Philip's Church: Very few (comparatively speaking) present, tho' this former part of the day is the most full: A young scarcely-bearded boy read prayers, with the most gay, indifferent and gallant air imaginable: very few men and no women stand in singing-time: a very elegant piece of modern declamatory composition was decently delivered by another clergyman, by way of sermon from these words in Job: "Acquaint now thyself with God, that good will or may come of it."[†] Having heard a young church-parson very coxcomically advance a few days before, that no sermon ought to exceed twenty-five minutes, I had the curiosity to see by my watch whether our clerical instructor was of the same sentiments, and found that he shortened the space above seven and one-half minutes. It was very common in prayer as well as sermon-time to see gentlemen conversing together. In short, taking a view of all things, I could not help remarking in the time of it, that here was not, certainly, "*solemn* mockery."

This church is the most decorated within, tho' not the most splendid without, of any in the place.

I find that in the several places of public worship, which I have visited, that a much greater taste for marble monuments prevail here, than with us in the northward.

I had noticed before, and could not help renewing a remark, that a majority of both sexes at public assemblies appear in mourning.

I have seen and have been told, that mourning apparel at funerals is greatly in fashion.

Dined with considerable company at Miles Brewton's, Esq,[‡] a gentleman of very large fortune: a most superb house, said to have cost him £8000 sterling. The grandest hall I ever beheld. Azure Blue Satten—window Curtains, rich blue paper with gilt, Mashee Borders, most elegant pictures, excessive grand and costly looking glasses etc. Politicks started before dinner: a hot sensible flaming tory, one Mr. Thomas Shirley (a native of Britain) present: he had advanced that Great Britain had better be without any of the Colonies; that she committed a most

---

*Nathaniel Balch (1735–1808), a Boston hatter known for "his extraordinary talent at humorous pleasantry," and who "treasured up an inexhaustible fund of Anecdotes and witty Sayings of all Kinds" (John Adams to James Warren, Boston, Dec. 17, 1773. Taylor, *The Adams Papers*, Papers of John Adams 2, 1-2.)

[†]The exact quote (Job 22:21) is "Acquaint now thyself with him, and be at peace: Thereby good shall come unto thee."

[‡]Miles Brewton (1732–1775) made a fortune as a merchant. His Georgian mansion at 27 King Street was completed in 1769.

capital political blunder in not ceding Canada to France; that all the Northern Colonies to the Colony of New York, and even New York, were now working the bane of Great Britain: that Great Britain would do wisely to renounce the Colonies to the North and leave them as prey to their continental neighbors or foreign powers: that none of the political writings or conducts of the Colonies would bear any examination but Virginia, and none could lay any claim to encomium but that province, etc.

[Shirley] strongly urged that Massachusetts [was] aiming at sovereignty; that they now took the lead, were assuming, dictatorial, etc. "You may depend upon it (added he) that if Great Britain should renounce the Sovereignty of this Continent or if the Colonies shake themselves clear of her authority, that you all (meaning the Carolinas and the other provinces) will have governors sent you from Boston; Boston aims at nothing less than the sovereignty of this whole continent; I know it."

It was easy to see the drift of this discourse. I remarked that all this was new to me; that if it was true, it was a great and good ground of distrust and disunion between the colonies; that I could not say what the other provinces had in view or thought but I was sure that the Inhabitants of Massachusetts paid a very great respect to all their sister provinces; that she revered, almost, the leaders in Virginia and much respected those of Carolina. Mr. Shirley replied, when it comes to the test Boston will give the other provinces the shell and the shadow and keep the substance. Take away the power and superintendency of Britain, and the Colonies must submit to the next power. Boston would soon have that—power rules all things—they might allow the other a paltry representation, but that would be all.

The company seemed attentive—and incredulous—were taking sides—when the call of dinner turned the subject of attention.

Shirley seemed well bred and learned in the course of the afternoon, but very warm and irascible. From his singular looks and behavior I suspect he knew my political path.

A most elegant table—three courses. Nick nacks, jellies, preserves, sweetmeats, etc.

After dinner, two sorts of nuts, almonds, raisins, three sorts of olives, apples, oranges, etc.

By odds the richest wine I ever tasted: Exceeds Mr. Hancock's, Vassall's, Phillip's* and others much in flavor, softness and strength.

I toast all your friends, Sir. Each gentleman gave his toast round in succession.

---

*John Hancock (1737–1793) and Maj. Henry Vassall (1721–1769) owned summer estates near the Quincys at Braintree, Massachusetts. William Phillips Sr. (1722–1804) was Quincy's father-in-law, a Boston merchant.

A young lawyer Mr. Pinckney,* a gentleman educated at the Temple and of eminence dined with us. From him and the rest of the company I was assured, by the provincial laws of the place any two justices and three freeholders might and very often did *instanter* upon view or complaint try a negro for any crime, and might and did often award execution of death—issue their warrant and it was done forthwith. Two gentlemen present said they had issued such warrants several times. This law too was for *free* as well as *slave* negroes and mulattoes. They further informed me, that neither negroes or mulattoes could have a Jury;—that for killing a negro, ever so wantonly, as without any provocation, there could be nothing but *a fine;* they gave a late instance of this; that (further) to *steal* a negro was death, but to *kill him* was only fineable. Curious laws and policy! I exclaimed. Very true cried the company, but this is the case.

At Mr. Brewton's side-board was very magnificent plate: a very large exquisitely wrought Goblet, most excellent workmanship and singularly beautiful.

A very fine bird kept familiarly playing over the room, under our chairs and the table, picking up the crumbs, etc., and perching on the window, sideboard and chairs: vastly pretty!

March 8th. Received complimentary visits, from Charles Cotesworth Pinckney, Esq., Messrs. Bee, Parsons, Simpson and Scott,[†] all gentlemen of the Bar, and others.

Was much entertained with Mr. Pinckney's conversation, who appeared a man of bright natural powers, and improved by a British education at the Temple.

This gentleman presented me with the only digest of the laws of the Province, made some years since by Mr. Simpson, late Attorney-General in the absence of Sir Egerton Leigh.[‡] This present was the more acceptable, as there is no collection of the Laws of this Province in a book to be had.—No wonder their lawyers make from £2000 to £3000 sterling a year!—The rule of action altogether unknown to the people!

March 9. Spent all the morning in viewing the Public library, State-house, public offices, etc. being waited upon Messrs. Pinckney and Rutledge,[§] two

*Charles Cotesworth Pinckney (1746–1825).

[†]These were attorneys Thomas Bee (1739–1812), James Parsons (1724–1779), and John Scott. James Simpson was serving as royal attorney general.

[‡]James Simpson had replaced Sir Edgerton Leigh (1733–1781) as attorney general after Leigh was removed from office in disgrace, accused of seducing his wife's young sister, and both nieces of his influential friend, Henry Laurens (1724–1792) (Bellot, "Presidential Address," 161, 187).

[§]Thomas Pinckney (1750–1828), younger brother of Charles Cotesworth Pinckney, and Edward Rutledge (1749–1800).

young gentlemen lately from the Temple, where they took the degree of barrister at law. The public library is a handsome, square, spacious room, containing a large collection of very valuable books, cuts, globes, etc.

I received much entertainment and information from the above gentlemen; and Mr. Charles Cotesworth Pinckney informed me of an anecdote to which he was personally knowing, which I desired him several times to repeat that I might be the better able to relate it.

He said that two gentlemen being at a tavern, one of them gave *the Pretender's health,* the other refused to drink it, upon which he who gave the toast threw his glass of wine in the refuser's face. For this an action of trespass was brought, and Sir Fletcher Norton* closed the case on behalf of the plaintiff, before *Lord Mansfield,*† which is nisi prius.

His Lordship in summing up the case told the jury it was a most trifling affair, that the action ought never to have been brought, and they ought to find the offender *Not Guilty.* Sir Fletcher after his Lordship had sat down rose immediately in some heat and asked his Lordship if he did not intend to say anything more to the jury?

Lord M: No, Sir Fletcher, I did not!

Sir F: I pray to be heard, then; and I do here publicly aver it to be law, that if one man throws wine out of a glass at another in anger, this is an assault and battery; this I declare for law, and I do here pawn my reputation as a lawyer upon it.

Lord M: Poo, poo, poo! Sir F., it is a most trifling affair.

Sir F.: Poo, poo, poo! My Lord, I don't intend to be poo, poo, poo'd out of it neither!—I renew my declaration, and affirm it to be law—and *if the jury don't hear law from the Court, they shall from the Bar.* I affirm again that it is an assault and battery.

Here Sir Fletcher sat down, and spoke so loud as that the whole Court, bar, and jury heard him,—"He had as good's retract his opinion now, as do it another time." Meaning on a motion for a new trial for misdirection of the Judge on a point of law.

Lord Mansfield did not think fit to take any notice of all this.

Compare this with some maneuvers of the *little* Gods at the North.

Mr. C. C. Pinckney who was a member of the General Assembly told me, that the members of the House, like those of the Commons of England, always sat with their hats on.

---

*Sir Fletcher Norton, First Baron Grantley (1716–1789), speaker of the British House of Commons.

†William Murray, First Earl of Mansfield (1705–1793), British judge who held high office in the House of Lords.

March 9. Same day. Dined with Thomas Smith;* several gentlemen and ladies: decent and plenteous table of meats: the upper cloth removed a compleat course, table of puddings, pies, tarts, custards, sweetmeats, oranges, macaroons, etc., etc.—profuse. Excellent wines—no politicks.

March 10. Evening. Spent the evening at the Assembly. Bad musick, good dancing, elegantly disposed supper, bad provisions, worse dressed.

March 11. Dined with Roger Smith,† son to Mr. Thomas Smith: good deal of company, elegant table, and the best provisions I have seen in this town, One cloth removed, a handsome desert and most kinds of nicknacks. Good wines and much festivity. Two ladies were being called on for toasts, the one gave—"Delicate pleasures to susceptible minds." The other, "When passions rise may reason be the guide."

In company were two of the late appointed Assistant Justices from Great Britain. Their behavior by no means abated my zeal against British appointments: one of them appeared, in aspect, phiz, conversation etc. very near an ———.

In company dined one Mr. Thomas Bee, a planter of considerable opulence. A gentleman of sense, improvement, and politeness; and one of the members of the house—just upon the point of marrying Mrs. McKenzie, a young widow of about twenty with eight or nine thousand guineas independent fortune in specie, and daughter to Mr. Thomas Smith.‡

From Mr. Bee, I received assurance of the truth of what I had before heard: that a few years ago, the Assistant Judges of the Supreme Court of the province, being natives, men of abilities, fortune and good fame, an act of assembly passed to settle £300 Sterling a year upon them, when the King should grant them Commissions *quamdiu se bene gesserint.* The act being sent home for concurrence was disallowed, and the reason assigned was the above clause. I am promised by Mr. Bee a transcript of the reasons of disallowance, with the Attorney and Solicitor-General's opinion relative to the act.

Upon this, the Assembly passed an act to establish the like salary, *payable but of any monies that shall be in the treasury,* not restricting it to any alteration in the tenure of their commission.—

Mark the sequel. No *Assistant* Judge, had ever before been nominated in England. Immediately upon the King's approving this last act, Lord Hillsborough§

*Thomas Smith (1720–1790), Charleston merchant.

†Roger Moore Smith (1745–1805).

‡Thomas Bee's first wife, Susannah Holmes, died in 1771. On March 16, he married widow Sarah Smith McKenzie, Roger Moore Smith's sister.

§The Earl of Hillsborough or Wills Hill, First Marquess of Downshire (1718–1793), Irish peer first appointed British secretary of state for the Colonies. He was president of the Board

in his zeal for American good forthwith sends over, one Chief Justice, and two Assistant Justices, Irishmen, the other two, was the one a Scotchman, and the other a Welshman.*

How long will the simple love their simplicity? And ye, who assume the guileful name, the venerable pretext of *friends to Government,* how long will ye deceive and *be deceived?* Surely in a political sense, the Americans—"are lighted the way—to study wisdom."

I have conversed with upwards of one half the members of the General Assembly and many other ranks of men on this matter. They see their error, and confess it: they own it a rash, imprudent, hasty step, and bitterly repent it. A Committee of the house has ranked it in their list of grievances. The only *solamen* is—"it is done; we will take care, never to do the like again." The only apology is, that the Assistant Judges of the province, were unwilling to have Circuit Court without a fixed salary: the remote parts of the province complained of being obliged to attend all causes, at Charlestown: they had great reason of complaint: the Regulators of this province were up as well as those of North Carolina:† Such was the influence of some, that upon the disallowance of the first act, no act for creating Circuit Courts could be got through till salaries were fixed.—May Heaven forgive, but *the people* never forget them! Think you, that they who eyed the fleece, have got it? No. As in like cases,—American fools—thirsting for honor and riches—beat the bush:—British harpies seize—*the poor bird.*—Righteous is the measure of God.

Spent an agreeable evening with Mr. Roger Smith and was entertained with a much genteel supper.

I have also learned from several gentlemen, that it was common in this province for an executor of a will to make several hundred guineas by his office;— and that with reputation. Mr. R[oger] S[mith] told he made the last year, by

----

of Trade from 1768 to 1772, a significant period leading up to the Revolution, from which he opposed concessions to the colonists.

*This was Chief Justice Thomas Knox Gordon and the three assistants, Edward Savage, John Murray, and John Fewtrell (Ramsay, *History of South Carolina,* 154).

†The Regulators were a "law and order league" or vigilante group formed to keep order in the backcountry of North and South Carolina, where there were no courts—a fact that pitched seacoast slaveholding regions, where there were common courts, against small farms of the interior. The Circuit Court Act was passed in 1769 to correct this problem, but there were still disputes over native judges who wanted larger salaries for increased duty in the backcountry. Quincy blames the South Carolina Assembly and refers to placemen judges, whose appointment he detested. He blamed the assembly for not upholding the principle that salaries should be given for good behavior (Brown, *South Carolina Regulators,* 107–9).

three executorships upwards of seven hundred guineas; and Mr. Bee told me, that Thomas L. Smith's father made 10,000 Sterling and more the same way,

Who would not be *his own* Executor?

March 12. Dined with Thomas Lynch, Esq.,* a plain, sensible, honest man, upon a solid, plentiful, good table; with very good wines.

Spent the evening with the Friday-night Club, consisting of the more elder substantial gentlemen: About twenty or thirty in company. Conversation on negroes, rice, and the necessity of British Regular troops to be quartered in Charlestown: there were not wanting men of fortune, sense and attachment to their country; who were zealous for the establishing such troops here.

I took some share in the conversation; and can't but hope I spoke conviction to many sensible minds. At the close of the evening; plans were agitated for the making a certain part of the militia of the province (to take in rotation) answer instead of foreign aid.

I here learned in a side conversation with Mr. Brewton, that two of the late Assistant Judges (gentleman now in high and popular repute) of the Supreme Court: (men too of great opulence!) who were in the General Assembly at the time of the Act, mentioned two pages back, were the very means of getting it passed: *Quid non mortalia pectora cogis, Auri sacra fames?* That they hoping to enjoy the emoluments of government were hot, zealous, and perpetually persevering till they got it through: He informed me also of the specious arguments they used, and the advantages that they took of the popular commotions. Good heavens, how much more noble a part might they have taken: They are now knawing their tongues in rage.

March 13. Spent all the morning transcribing Mr. Edward Rutledge's MS. Law Reports.† At eleven set off *in state* for the Retreat of T. L. Smith, Esqr.‡ Dined there and spent the remainder of the day.

This day spent most agreeably of any since my arrival in Charlestown.

A delightful place indeed!

March 14. Bad weather: spent the day at my lodgings. Visited by Mr. Lynch, Deis, and others.

---

*Thomas Lynch (1720–1776).

†A manuscript among Quincy's papers contains forty-eight pages of these reports in Quincy's handwriting. Fifty pages of the public records of the Province of South Carolina were copied under his direction by a clerk (Quincy and Quincy, *Memoir of the Life of Josiah Quincy, Jr.*, 84:1n).

‡The Retreat was Thomas Loughton Smith's plantation at his country seat at Goose Creek.

Mr. Lynch gave me a long account of the conduct of the Regulators; with the cause of their ill-success; the ease with which Tyron might have been defeated.* He said he had the best information of the facts he related, and good grounds for his opinions on the matter.

March 15. Dined with company at Mr. Lynch's on turtle.—

Spent the morning and afternoon in transcribing Law reports of Edward Rutledge, Esq. late student of the Temple.

Spent the evening with the Monday-night Club; introduced by Mr. Brewton. Cards, feasting, and indifferent wines.

N.B. This is at a tavern, and was the first time of my meeting with ordinary wines since my being at Charlestown.

March 16. Spent this morning ever since five o'clock in perusing Public Records of the Province: which I was favored with by worthy Mr. Bee;—have marked many to be copied for me:—Am now going to the famous races.

The races were well performed; but Flimnap[†] beat Little David (who had won the sixteen last races) out and out. The last heat the former distanced the latter. The first four mile heat was performed in eight minutes and seven seconds, being four miles.—Two thousand pounds sterling was won and lost at the race, and Flimnap sold at Public Vendue the same day for £300 sterling.

Took a family dinner with Mr. Brewton—had a fine dish of politicks—had further light from one of the company (a prerogative-man) into the arts used to disunite the Colonies. Sounded Mr. Brewton and Mr. Erving, when alone, with regard to a general and permanent Continental literary correspondence: the matter takes mightily.

At the races I saw a prodigious fine collection of excellent, though very high-priced horses—and was let a little into the singular art and mystery of the Turf.

March 17. Spent all the morning in the copying Mr. Rutledge's reports. Feasted with the Sons of St. Patrick.[‡] While at dinner six violins, two hautboys and bassoon with a hand-tabor beat excellently well. After dinner six French horns in concert—most surpassing musick!—Two solos on the French horn by one who is

---

*On May 16, 1771, William Tryon (1725–1728), governor of North Carolina, with a militia had defeated some two thousand Regulators in Alamance County, hoping to decisively crush the Regulator rebellion.

†Flimnap, bred in England and imported into South Carolina in 1772, was one of the most celebrated horses of the Carolina turf. Descended from France and England's legendary stallion the Godolphin Arabian, he sired many fine racehorses and broodmares in the region (Irving, *A Day on the Cooper River*, 182).

‡The Friendly Sons of St. Patrick, founded in 1774, later merged with the Hibernian Society.

said to blow the finest horn in the world: he has fifty guineas for the season from the St. Cecilia Society.*

March 18. Spent in reading farther reports of Mr. Rutledge—paying complementary visits of departure, and in preparation for my journey—Northward.

N.B. this day advanced to Miles Brewton Esqr. thirty-one pounds sterling for one pipe of Best London Particular Madeira Wine to be sent for to the house of Pantalium, Fernandez and Co. in Madeira—and took Mr. Brewton's receipt of this date.

March 19. By reason of order of the house of Assembly enjoining attendance of all members, Mr. Lynch cannot set out.—I am therefore to be detained this day.

Spent all the morning in hearing the debates of the House, had an opportunity of hearing the best speakers in the province.

The *first* thing done at the meeting of the House is to bring the mace (a very superb and elegant one which cost ninety guineas) and lay it on the table before the speaker. This I am told is the way in the Commons of Great Britain.

The next thing is for the Clerk to read over in a very audible voice, the doings of the preceding day.

The Speaker is robed in black and has a very large wig of State, when he goes to attend the Chair (with the Mace borne before him) on delivery of speeches, etc.

T. Lynch, Esqr. spoke like a man of sense and a patriot—with dignity, fire, and laconism. Gadsden Esqr.[†] was plain, blunt, hot and incorrect—though very sensible. In the course of the debate, he used these very singular expressions for a member of Parliament: "And, Mr. Speaker, if the Governor and Council don't see fit to fall in with us, I say, let the General duty law and all *go to the Devil,* Sir. And we go about our business." Parsons, J. Rutledge,[‡] and old Charles Pinckney[§] (the three first-lawyers in the Province) spoke on the occasion:—the two last very good speakers indeed.

The members of the House all sit with their hats on, and uncover when they rise to speak: they are not confined (at least they do not confine themselves) to any one place to speak in.

The members conversed, lolled, and chatted much like a friendly jovial society, when nothing of importance was before the House:—nay once or twice while the

---

*The French horn player was likely Thomas Pike, noted for playing concertos of both French horn and bassoon (Cobau, "The Precarious Life of Thomas Pike," 230–31; Sonneck, *Early Concert Life in America,* 18).

[†]Christopher Gadsden (1724–1805).

[‡]John Rutledge (1739–1800), elder brother of Edward Rutledge.

[§]Col. Charles Pinckney (1731–1782), cousin of the aforementioned Pinckney brothers.

speaker and clerk were busy in writing the members spoke quite loud across the room to one another.—A very unparlimentary appearance. The speaker put the question sitting, and conversed with the House sitting: the members gave their votes by rising from their seats—the dissentients did not rise.

March 20. Set out with Mr. Lynch for his plantation on Santee River on my way to the Northward. In crossing Hobcaw ferry we were rowed by six negroes, four of whom had *nothing on* but their kind of breeches, scare sufficient for covering.

Had a most agreeable ride, and received much information from Mr. Lynch of the maneuvers at the Congress in 1765.

N.B. from what I learned from Mr. Lynch it is worth trying the experiment of planting rice in our low, marshy lands, for the purpose of feeding cows and making the most excellent flavored and yellow butter.—he said he did not doubt it would answer well.

March 21. Mr. Lynch's plantation is very pleasantly situated and is very valuable.

Had a three hours tedious passage up Santee river: Crossed Georgetown river or Sampit River just at dusk. Lodged in the town and now held in duress by a very high equinoxial gale from crossing Winyah Bay, formed by the union of Waccamaw, Peedee and Black rivers. 'Tis prodigious fine travelling weather and requires no small share of philosophy to be contented with my situation.

"Dr. Johann David Schoepf." Courtesy of U.S. Army Medical Department, Office of Medical History.

Johann David Schoepf (1784)

"After the Revolution"

Johann David Schoepf (1752–1800), German physician and naturalist, was the son of a wealthy merchant in Bayreuth. He graduated in 1773 from the University of Erlangen, where he studied medicine and natural sciences. After a year of travel through Germany, he returned to Erlangen and in 1776 received his MD. He established a medical practice in Ansbach. When, as a business enterprise, Karl Alexander, Margrave of Brandenburg-Ansbach, decided to pay down the principality's debts by sending hired troops to help the English crown in the American Revolution, Schoepf voluntarily accompanied a regiment of Hessian troops as chief surgeon and doctor. Between 1777 and 1783, he was stationed at New York, Long Island, Rhode Island, and Philadelphia. After peace was declared, he traveled for two years throughout the eastern and the southeastern United States, which brought him to Charleston. As a result, Schoepf wrote a rare assessment of the country, including Charleston, in the aftereffects of the Revolution. Possessed of a broad scientific acumen in biology, botany, geology, ethnology, and meteorology, he noted everything relative to Charleston in 1784. The reader may recognize his oft-repeated Charleston quote: "Carolina is in the spring a paradise, in the summer a hell, and in the autumn a hospital."

After his experiences in America, Schoepf returned to Europe by way of the Bahamas. He opened a medical practice in Bayreuth but continued his natural history observations. In 1787, he published the first study of the medicinal plants of North America. In 1788, a two-volume account of his American travels was published in Erlangen, entitled *Reise Durch Einige Der Mittlern und Südlichen Vereinigten Nordamerikanischen Staaten Nach Ost-florida und Den Bahama-inseln: Unternommen in den Jahren 1783 und 1784.* In Europe this proved to be a significant work on American geology. In America, an English translation was not published for many years because to Americans, the German language remained that of the detested Hessians of the Revolution.

Taken from *Travels in the Confederation,* ed. and trans. Alfred J. Morrison (New York: Burt Franklin), 1911.

Schoepf remained in Germany and from 1792 onward published works of natural history. He was president of the United Medical Colleges of Ansbach and Bayreuth at the time of his death in 1800. His travels did not appear in English translation until 1911, when Alfred Morrison edited and translated an edition published as *Travels in the Confederation*, from which this extract on Charleston is taken.

SOURCES

Elliott, Clark A. *Biographical Dictionary.* Westport, CT.: Greenwood Press, 1979.
Lloyd, J. J. "Johann David Schoepf, Hessian Traveller." *Earth Science History* 11, no. 2 (1992): 88–89.
Merrill, George P. Review of *Travels in the Confederation (1783–1784)* by Johann David Schoepf, ed. and trans. Alfred Morrison, *Science* 3 (November 3, 1911): 610–11.
Morrison, A. J. "Dr. Johann David Schöpf." *German American Annals* 8 (1910): 255–64.
New York (State). Legislature. Assembly. *Documents of the Assembly of the State of New York.* Vol. 18. Albany: J. B. Lyon, 1900.

"After the Revolution"

Charleston is one of the finest of American cities; Philadelphia excepted, it is inferior to none, and I know not whether, from its vastly more cheerful and pleasing plan, it may not deserve first place, even if it is not the equal of Philadelphia in size and population. The city contains a number of tasteful and elegant buildings, which however are mostly of timber. This circumstance is explained by the natural scarceness of stone in this region; but there seems no reason why bricks might not be used here for building quite as well as at Philadelphia and New York, since nowhere are better materials to be had, or in greater plenty. The number of the houses is estimated to be about 1500. In the plan of the houses especial regard is had to airy and cool rooms. Most of the houses have spacious yards and gardens, and the kitchen is always placed in a separate building, the custom throughout the southern provinces, to avoid the heat and the danger of fire.

Both the rivers named are navigable, but for trading-vessels only the Cooper, as much as 20 miles above the city. Merchantmen find commodious and safe anchorage between the city and a little island in the Cooper river. This part of the river is called the Bay, and along this side of the city the shore is furnished with excellent wharves of cabbage-trees. The entrance to the harbor is made more difficult by a bar which ships of more than 200 tons cannot pass without lightening cargo. The advantageous site of the city has not been neglected in its fortification;

towards the land side as well as at the south-western point there have long been regular works of masonry, which during the war were considerably increased and improved both by the Americans and the English, but are now again fallen to decay. On the landside the city has but one approach, protected by a gate with several walled defenses of oyster-shells and lime. Among the public buildings of the city the handsome State-house, the Main-guard opposite, the Bourse, and the two churches, St. Philip and St. Michael, are conspicuous, all designed after good plans. Two lines of framed barracks, for the one-time English garrisons are not at present made use of. The tower of St. Michael's church is 190 feet high, and has long served as landmark for incoming ships. It was formerly painted white; the American Commodore Whipple* hit upon the idea of painting it black on the side towards the sea whence it can be seen very far, so as to be made invisible to British ships, whose visits were dreaded. But the result so far from being that desired was directly the opposite, for in clear weather the black side is far more distinct, and on gloomy, cloudy days it is seen quite as far and appears, if anything, larger than before.

There is a German Lutheran congregation here,[†] with its own church and minister, but it is not very numerous.

The name of the city, since the last peace, has been changed from Charlestown to Charleston and at the same time its rank, that of a Town until then, made that of a City. By the English rule those towns only are called cities which have a Bishop and are Incorporated, or those which exercise their own granted privileges under the presidency of a Mayor and other officers and use a special city-seal. A bishop Charleston has not, but the dignity of a Mayor, called Superintendent, has been given it under this elevation of rank conferred by the Provincial Assembly.

The number of the inhabitants was formerly reckoned at 10–12000, of which half or probably two thirds were blacks, but at present it is not possible to say exactly what the number is, since no precise baptismal or death lists are kept. The population, besides, has considerably diminished both by voluntary emigration and by the banishment of many of the most estimable citizens of the royalist party. But certainly the number of the white inhabitants is greatly less than that of the blacks, browns, and yellows to be seen here of all shades. In winter the city is less active than in summer. About Christmas most of the families retire to their country-seats and spend there the greater part of what remains of the winter. One reason for this is that at that festival season the negroes are allowed somewhat more liberty, and fearing they might use it in a bad way the proprietors deem

*Continental Naval Commodore Abraham Whipple (1733–1819).
[†]St. John's Lutheran Church.

it well to be present themselves and at the same time look after the progress of their plantation affairs. With the coming of the sweltery summer days all that can hasten back to town. The nearness of the sea and the cooler winds blowing thence make summer in the city pleasanter and wholesomer than farther inland among woods and swamps.

The manners of the inhabitants of Charleston are as different from those of the other North American cities as are the products of their soil. The profitable rice and indigo plantations are abundant sources of wealth for many considerable families who therefore live their lives to the enjoyment of every pleasure and convenience to which their warmer climate and better circumstances invite them. Throughout, there prevails here a finer manner of life, and on the whole there are more evidences of courtesy than in the northern cities. I had already been told this at Philadelphia, and I found it to be the case; just as in general on the way hither, the farther I travelled from Pennsylvania towards the southern country, there were to be observed somewhat more pleasing manners among the people, at least there was absent the unbearable curiosity of the common sort, which in the more northern regions extends to shamelessness and exhausts all patience. There is courtesy here, without punctiliousness, stiffness or formality. It has long been nothing extraordinary for the richer inhabitants to send their children of both sexes to Europe for their education. The effect of this on manners must be all the greater and more general since there were neither domestic circumstances to stand in the way nor particular religious principles, as among the Presbyterians of New England or the Quakers of Pennsylvania, to check the enjoyment of good-living. So luxury in Carolina has made the greatest advance, and their manner of life, dress, equipages, furniture, everything denotes a higher degree of taste and love of show, and less frugality than in the northern provinces. They had their own play-house, in which itinerant companies from time to time entertained the public, but it was burned some time ago.* A like misfortune overtook an elegant dancing-hall. A French dancing master was the promoter of this building; the necessary amount was advanced him by the first minister of the town who not only had no hesitation in a matter of furthering the pleasure of his parishioners, but afterwards when the property fell to him, the Frenchman being unable to return the loan, made no scruple of receiving the rent; whereas in the New England states the bare thought of such a thing would have disgraced any minister.† Pleasures of every kind are known, loved, and enjoyed here. There are

---

*The "New Theatre in Dock Street."

†Thomas Pike's New Assembly Room, the concert hall mentioned in the Quincy account. Pike, a French dancing master, was advanced the money to build it by Reverend Robert

public concerts, at this time mainly under the direction of German and English musicians left behind by the army, for as yet few of the natives care greatly for music or understand it. A liking for exclusive private societies, Clubs so-called, prevails here very generally. There are as many as 20 different Clubs, and most of the residents are members of more than one. These social unions give themselves strange names at times, as: Mount Sion Society, Hell-fire Club, Marine Anti-Britannic Society, Smoking Society, and the like. All the games usual in England are in vogue here. As regards dress, the English taste is closely followed; also the clergy and civil officers wear the garb customary in England. The ladies bestow much attention upon their dress, and spare no cost to obtain the newest modes from Europe. Milliners and hair-dressers do well here and grow rich.

Charleston, at sundry times and by opposite elements, has been threatened with complete destruction. A great part of the town has several times gone up in fire, and with loss of considerable stores of merchants' wares. Again, violent and lasting hurricanes have seemed as if certain to destroy the place. The low situation of the town exposes it, if northeast storms hold somewhat long, to the danger of furious overflow, these winds checking the northwestern course of the gulf-stream flowing along the coast from the Mexican gulf, and driving it and other water of the ocean against the flat coast of Carolina. From the same causes also the two rivers flowing by the town are checked, and in a very brief space the water often rises to an incredible height.

In the item of weather Carolina is subject to the same changes as the rest of the eastern coast of North America; warmth and cold, fair and rainy days are the effects or consequences of the winds. The Northwest spreads cold over this southern region as over all the coast besides. In January and February 1784, the time of my stay at Charleston, the weather was almost regularly cyclical. Towards the end of January and February we had this year mostly very cold weather. The thermometer often fell to 24, 26, 28, and almost every morning it was at least 32 by Fahrenheit. But this was an extraordinarily cold winter, of no common severity also in the higher middle province. Here at Charleston there was ice to be seen every morning on shallow water and ponds, and in the houses. The poor negroes, who can bear cold by no means well, crept about stiff and sluggish, whereas in the hottest weather, when the European is relaxed without strength, they are brisk and industrious. But of snow there was none; however in the year 1776 it fell a

---

Smith (1732–1801), first rector of St. St. Philip's. Pike subsequently fell into debt and borrowed further from cabinetmaker Thomas Elfe (1719–1775). By August 1773, his "estates and effects" were placed on auction for the benefit of his creditors (Cobau, "The Precarious Life of Thomas Pike," 229–62).

foot deep, and lay nearly a week. Chalmers, from 10 years' observations,* gives the lowest station of the quicksilver at 18 Fahrenheit and the highest at 101 in the shade; but he mentions that the quicksilver had once been known to fall as low as 10 Fahrenheit; certainly extraordinary for so southern a place. Such cold and frosty days are rarer in customary winters, and never hold long without a change to warm days; at any rate, only the evenings and mornings are so cold, the midday sun soon giving the atmosphere pleasant warmth. During these cold days of January and February, in the neighborhood of Charleston not an indigenous plant was to be seen in bloom; for in this climate spring does not really come before the middle of March or the beginning of April. But in sundry gardens the following European plants might be found greening and blooming: *Alsine media—Lamium amplexicaule,—Leontodon Taraxacum,—Rumex crispus & Acetosa,—Poa annua,—Vitica dioica and Sonchus arvensis.*† Of garden-flowers there were blooming at this time narcissuses and jonquils. Also the orange-trees, which are everywhere in the houses and in the open in gardens, standing the severe weather pretty well; they were full of fruit and burgeons. But often they are frozen, and this is seldom the case even to the south, at Pensacola in Florida. A palm-tree, 7–8 feet high, standing out in a garden, suffered from this weather and its leaves hung slack. Several other trees from warmer regions, such as *Croton sebiferum, Sapindus Saponaria*‡ &c, which hitherto had withstood the cold well in the open, it was feared would this time hardly escape damage. These and other tender plants which Carolina has in common with the West Indies, either naturally or from transplantation, thrive only on the sea-coast where in comparison with the inland country milder and more temperate weather prevails generally. Some 60–80 miles inland from Charleston snow was seen to fall during this time more than once. The variable winter-weather often gives rise to inflammatory diseases which at other times are less frequent in this region, and require bleedings neither powerful nor often repeated. Carolina is in the spring a paradise, in the summer a hell, and in the autumn a hospital. The more oppressive months are June, July, and August, during which the Fahrenh. Thermometer commonly stands anywhere from 70 to 90° and not seldom rises to 96 or more. The summer heat, in itself, is more

*Dr. Lionel Chalmers (1715–1777), Scottish-born physician, studied meteorology and recorded observations on the weather of South Carolina for ten successive years beginning in 1750. The results were published as "A Treatise on the Weather and Diseases of South Carolina" (London, 1776) (Waring, "Lionel Chalmers and Williams Cullen's Treatment of Fevers," 445–47).

†Chickweed, henbit, dandelion, curly dock, garden sorrel, meadow grass, chamomile, and thistle.

‡Chinese tallow and soapberry.

overpowering on account of the calms usual at that season and the little circulation of air. To be sure, few summer-days pass without a violent thunderstorm to set the air in motion and for a short time cooling it, but the pleasant effect is soon gone and the oppressive, swelty heat again has the upper hand. At Augustine and along the whole of the east coast of Florida there is vastly less cause to complain of this still, heavy heat, although that region lies nearer the sun. But the nature of that country, which is low and extends in the form of a tongue of earth into the West Indian waters, brings about a freer and more refreshing passage of air from sea to sea, which is not the case in the situation of Carolina. Besides, there must be taken into the account the immeasurable forests which cover the interior of the country, the upward rise of the land from the coast inwards, and the absence of large streams penetrating into the interior, all which circumstances are unfavorable to movements of the atmosphere.

Pleasant regions or diverting changes of prospect are not to be found about Charleston; the whole landscape is flat and sandy; tracts next the sea and the rivers are swampy. The greatest part of the fore-country is taken up in pine-forest. In Carolina there are to be found almost all the varieties of oak which appear elsewhere in North America. Besides the pines and oaks the woods and open fields about Charleston are pranked with many fine evergreen plants, which with temperate winter-weather keep up in some measure the charm of a perennial spring. Orange-trees, planted in the gardens and in the houses, are not originally indigenous, but they hold their leaves in the winter, as in the case with the lemon-tree even here. Orange-trees left to themselves and gone half wild, arm themselves with long thorns, and are used here and there as hedges.

With so fine a store of lasting plants, it would be very easy to have the pleasure of a continual green in the gardens, and to make famous winter-gardens. Many of the European annual plants keep green and in bloom throughout the winter, but in the heat of summer die away, at which time the indigenous annuals begin to shoot, and last through the hot season into September. But gardening is not very much in vogue and is generally left to ignorant negroes. Nor is it very long since all cabbages, pot-herbs, colly-flowers, and other garden vegetables, were brought from the Bermuda islands to the Charleston market. A skillful English gardener, Mr. Squibb,* had first to show the inhabitants that they could abundantly supply themselves if they would only make the necessary change on the culture of vegetables, which the nature of the climate demanded. For these do not thrive so well throughout the summer as in the spring and the fall, and are to be kept in the

---

*For more on Squibb, see Robert Squibb, *The Gardener's Calendar For South-Carolina, Georgia, And North-Carolina* (1787) (Athens: University of Georgia Press, 1980).

open the winter through, green and growing. Root-plants, as radishes and yellow and white turnips hold their own and grow even during the summer, but far less well than in the spring and the fall.

Of fruit trees they have pears, apples, peaches, plums and cherries. Apples and peaches, which are not particularly good, are ripe in June. These and other transplanted fruits mature so rapidly that they have not, it may be for that reason, so good a taste as in the northern country. Most of these fruits bloom twice a year; but seldom ripen the second time. The fig-tree bears 3 and 4 times, in May and June, September and October. There are a few European olive-trees, which do well and yield heavily, but they have not yet learned how to conserve the fruit properly.

Next to indigo, already touched upon, rice is the chief staple of South Carolina. Only this province and Georgia have hitherto cultivated rice on the large scale; for although North Carolina and Virginia are in places well-suited for this grain, its culture has always been too much neglected there. The greatest part of rice grown in North America is exported to the northern states of Europe. In the years 1768, 1769, and 1770 the total export of rice from the southern colonies of North America amounted annually to 140,000 casks which at an average price of 45 shillings sterl. the cask brought in the sum of 316, 0000 Pd. Sterl. Of that figure South Carolina alone supplied about 110,000 casks.

The yearly profits from an acre (166 perches) of rice-land may be counted at 8–12, even 14 Pd. Sterling, according as the price is high or low. Hence the taking in of suitable new lands is zealously prosecuted. Rice is raised so as to buy more negroes, and negroes are bought so as to get more rice.

Rice, indigo, and in the back parts, tobacco, have so far chiefly engaged the attention of the inhabitants of Carolina; but from the nature of the climate and the situation of the country, it is to be expected that, population and industry advancing, very many other valuable products may be raised here at a great profit. The olive-tree, the carob-tree, the mastich, the almond, saffron, liquorice, honey, silk, fine wool, and the like, might, with indefatigable effort, be had of an especial goodness and yielding a great profit.

In a country which of itself brings forth such a quantity of wild vines as is the case almost throughout North America, it might be naturally expected that vine-culture would be carried on easily and profitably; and yet this is not so, at least was not so. From the first much wine has been drank in America, and much money has gone out for it to foreign states. Whether wine in general is a necessary article is not the question here. Enough, that people in America find pleasure in it, and greatly desire to partake of it. The produce of North America would not be sufficient to pay for its wine, if it became a universal drink. But then there are many fruitful orchards which yield an abundance of good apple and pear-wine; barley and hops are raised, to brew beer; they distill whiskey, and get cheap rum from the sugar-islands, or prepare it from molasses fetched thence.

The sorts of wine, which were formerly best known and liked in America, came from Spain and Portugal, on account of the trade-relations of those countries with England; that is to say, red, and less often white, Oporto or port-wine, and then Sherry, Lisbon, Teneriffa, Fayal, and Madeira. Of the last named there was a distinction made between the so-called "New-york and London quality," according as the taste was more suited to the one or the other of those cities. Madeira-wine was more prized if it had passed the ocean once or several times, especially if it came by way of the West Indies for it betters by a voyage in warm regions. Formerly French wines came rarely to America, but because of that, so much the oftener now. The considerable sums which were drawn from America for wine, induced the English government repeatedly to set premiums on the raising of domestic wines. Following these encouragements, attempts at wine-culture were made in several provinces, and a little wine produced for test here and there; the purposes of the government were not fulfilled; beyond these few trials, nothing was done, because the work was not found profitable, seemed not to promise greatly, and, as it appears, was not in any way to the taste of the Americans.

In South Carolina, almost 40 year ago, there was offered by Provincial Act a reward of 60 Pd. to any one exhibiting a pipe of good, drinkable wine made in the country. A Frenchman settled near Orangeburg, encouraged by this, made a few tuns of very good wine, and for several years together received his premium. But so soon as the premiums were discontinued, he gave up vine-culture, saying that he could find a better use for his land. Another resident of South Carolina, by the name of Thorpe, planted a vineyard 30 miles from Charleston, under the oversight of a Portuguese, whom he had brought in for the purpose. He also received premiums on 3 pipes of wine; but after his death his heirs gave over any further attempts, using the land in some other way. Later, there were other attempts made, in a region called Long Canes, 200 miles from Charleston, and good samples of wine were produced. But the reason why vineyards have not been set and vine-culture taken up by the farmer is the great labor which the tending of the vines requires, and the time that must go by before there is a profit . . . a vineyard from its first establishment hardly yields a fair profit in 6–7 years. A number of insufficient reasons have been brought forward to show that America is absolutely ill-suited for vine-culture, but similar statements might be made of vine-countries elsewhere.—

The Charleston market can by no means be called equal to that of Philadelphia, either as regards the plenty or the quality of provisions. Butcher's meat here is neither fat, nor of a good taste, because they are at no pains to fatten the cattle, which is slaughtered direct from the thin pasture found in the woods and swamps. In general the black cattle of the southern colonies are not of the good and large sort to be seen in the northern; they give themselves less trouble in keeping up and feeding a good breed, because they have a plenty of cattle. But of the fowl-meat there is no lack, and very good, because fed on rice and corn. And there is plenty of venison; a doe, weighing 60–70 pounds, commonly brings 7–8 Span[ish] Dollars. Wild ducks and other water-fowl are often brought in; they are not all to be recommended for their taste; among these are many sorts which America has in common with Europe.

Garden-vegetables are gradually beginning to be raised in more abundance, but a head of cabbage or cole-wort still bring 6d. Sterl. Potatoes are brought in from the northern colonies and from Europe; they are little raised here, but battatas and "tan-yards" in quantities, and gourds, cashaws, squashes, melons, pease, and beans of many sorts. And the nearness of the West Indies brings to this town the manifold enjoyment of the fruits of those regions. Finally, the rivers and the ocean according to the season, yield a great abundance of fish.

Between Charleston and the ocean lie several islands which help form the bay and the harbor. Those that became the best known during the last war are: Long,* Sullivan's, and James Islands. On James Island, which is of considerable extent, there is placed Fort Johnson, for the protection of the harbor; the irregular works, of no particular strength or compass, are run up of oyster-shells and lime. They were in part blasted by the Americans themselves when they abandoned this fort in 1780, and storm and wave have done for the rest.† There were there at the time only 3 cannon, and a guard of a dozen invalids, to hail in-going and out-going ships, examine their passes, and make signals to the town, whenever a vessel is sighted coming in; for the fort standing on a high bank, there is an open prospect to the city, 3 miles away, and also out to sea. From the fort there extends along the shore a long bank or wall of oyster and other shells, cast up by the water. Next the fort it is at least 4–5 ft. high and almost as wide; father off, it diminished by degrees.

In the middle of February, one small plant excepted, not a bloom was to be found on this island, although in other winters (mild as this was severe) one plant or another is at this season in bloom. I looked about, to no purpose also,

*Isle of Palms.

†Fort Johnson (ca. 1708), the first fortification built for the defense of the Charles Towne harbor, had many uses before it was seized by local patriots at the start of the Revolutionary War. Upon the nearby landing and advance of British troops under Sir Henry Clinton, patriots abandoned the fort.

for the "Cabbage-tree," which was once plentiful there, but now is as good as exterminated, because everywhere cut down during the war for fortifications and bulwarks. But there are a few still left on Morris and other neighboring islands, whither I had no occasion to go. The trunks of this palm-tree are excellent for breast-works; their fibre and whole structure so soft they do not split. They last but a few years exposed to the air, and hence are for temporary use only. The works on Sullivan's Island, which the English men-of-war grew weary of firing upon at the first attack upon Charleston in 1776, are built largely of these; as also most of the works in the city on the Bay side. There are many other uses for which this palm serves, ropes, for instance, and nets made from the soft threads of the leaves, and it is well-known that its top-most point, green and conical, may be eaten, composed as it is of soft undeveloped leaves; hence the name cabbage-tree. Raw this substance tastes a little bitter, something like an almond; boiled it is said to be like a cabbage; but it is mostly put up in vinegar or used as a salade.

The middle of February there opened at Charleston the winter-session of the Assembly of South Carolina. Any discreet man may be present at the sittings, and no one can come away without instruction, and seldom any without fear of man, without reserve, and with manifest zeal for the best good of their father-land and their fellow-citizens. The form of government of the state of South Carolina, a few small particulars excepted, is like that of the other states. The executive administration of the laws is in the hands of a Governor, assisted by a Lieutenant-Governor and a Privy Council, all these being chosen every other year by the Assembly. The law-making power consists of a Senate and House of Representatives, elected every two years by the people. The Governor, Lieutenant-Governor, and members of the Privy Council must have lived in the state, the first two ten years and the others five years. Each of these must be possessed of estates of at least 10,000 Pd. A Senator must be 30 years old, have been a citizen of the state five years, and own property worth 2000 Pd. in minimum. A representative in the Lower House must have lived 3 years in the country and own besides property in a certain amount. Eligibility for naming these members of the government is vested in every free white man, who has lived a year in the state, and pays taxes equal in amount to the land-tax on 50 acres. The various parishes and counties of South Carolina return some 170 members to the Assembly, but the City of Charleston alone sends 30. The latter figure is, to be sure, vastly out of proportion, considering the number of people in the city and the country; this was very well known, but the larger number was chosen at the beginning of the war so as to give more certainty of a majority of votes for the war, the inhabitants of the city, for reasons well known, being more inclined to the war and its prosecution than were the country-people. The members from the city are for the most part attorneys, considerable merchants, and others, intelligent and well-informed; hence they are fluent, enterprising, and easily get the upper hand of the representatives from the country, when it is a matter of address and a little intrigue. The full number of representatives is never together; the remoter and poorer districts dread the expense of sending all their representatives to Charleston. But those who do not appear, if they have not courage or eloquence enough to oppose matters which might seem to them undesirable or burdensome at home, at least they know their interests enough to refuse their assent to a vote. Thus it is often a matter of astonishment, that proposals fall through, the possible use or necessity of which has been urged by members from the city or the hither districts with all the charms of eloquence, and no representative from the hinterland has said anything publicly in opposition. However, they are often a little obstinate or even a little suspicious and many a time, in a good cause, it is necessary to influence them by innocent subterfuge. But at times they have good grounds for opposition; this was the case during this Assembly. It was proposed to increase the land-tax, and to raise it equally over the entire state. Now the rice and indigo-plantations of the fore-country produced vastly greater returns than the wheat and corn-fields of the interior—hence the owners of the former would have felt the increase not at all or very little but to the latter it would have been an insupportable burden. So they demanded, and with all justice, that the increase in the tax should be reckoned not according to the land's extent, but by its quality and yield.

The revenues of the state of South Carolina for the year 1783 were from the following sources:

2 1/2 per cent. tax on the proceeds of all merchants' goods sold at public auction, and on other merchandize thus sold, negroes, horses &c. The amount of tax was estimated at 10–12000 Pd. Sterling.

2 1/2 per cent. entrance-duty on all merchants' goods brought into the country, not otherwise specially listed or taxed. Last year the value of all merchandize imported into Carolina is said to have been 7–800,000 Pd.; and so this duty might be reckoned at 15–16000 Pd.

Extra entrance-duty on sundry specifically fixed European and West Indian articles of trade.

1 dollar, or 4 shill. 6d. Sterling, on every 100 acres of land.

1 dollar head-tax on every negro, without distinction of age. Shortly before the war the number of negroes was counted at 93,000 head. This number was diminished by the war; however, a considerable sum is thus raised.

A tax on capitals, as were, a fixed per cent. Of the value of stocks in trade; and a species of trades-tax for professional men.

The revenues from these taxes, which are considerable, were applied to the payment of debts and interest, and to other needs of the state. The 2 1/2 per cent. entrance-duty was to be devoted to the Congress, and although this was really collected in Carolina there was at the time a hesitation whether to deliver the proceeds to the Congress, none of the other states having so done, and several of them having flatly refused, not even collecting the duty.

For the current year 1784 the Assembly has devised "ways and means" to raise in taxes the sum of 104000 Pd. Sterling if it should be necessary; but provisionally the assessment has been fixed at only 79400 Pd. The tax on negroes was raised from one to two dollars, and it was a question whether 3 dollars would not be more advantageous; especially as the proportional increase of the land-tax from 1 to 2 dollars the 100 acres was strongly opposed by the inhabitants of the back country. These would have less to say against an increased tax on negroes, because in that interior region few or no negroes are used. The civil disbursements of the state amount to about 40000 Pd. Sterling. The Governor alone receives 1000 Pd. Salary, and the other servants of the state are paid in proportion.

Beside these taxes coming into the State's treasury, there were still other imposts for the maintenance of the police, city-watchmen, lamps &c. For these purposes especially the revenues were applied which rose from such negroes as worked in the city. That is to say, a license-badge showing the negro's occupation must be paid for by every master for his slaves or by every free negro for himself. But this concerned only those negroes who hired themselves out or were hired out by their masters. For a butcher 40 shillings a year was paid. For a carpenter, mason, farrier, goldsmith, cartwright, house-painter, fisherman &c., 20 shillings a year. For a tailor, tanner, harness-maker, tin-man &c. 15 shillings. For a sea-man, cooper, shoemaker, hatter, rope-maker &c. 10 shillings. For every other hired negro, not specifically described,—5 shillings. In explanation of this tax levied on hired negroes, one must know that in Virginia, Carolina, Georgia, as well as in the West Indies, this class of men are to their owners an interest-bearing capital, and if the owners have no use for them themselves, they hire them out and live on their wages as is elsewhere the case with horses let. The meanest negro, if he has no regular trade and can carry on no fixed occupation, must earn his keep in some heavy work or as a day laborer, and must give in to his owner a certain part of his wages. He may have earned little or much, but he turns in at the least a shilling sterling a day, and besides he must feed and clothe himself. There are various conditions, according to the good nature of the owner and the skill of the negro; but in the average it may be accepted that a hired negro is worth a yearly interest of 15–20 per centum. Thus many idlers place their capital in negroes and, in the strict sense, are by them supported, living careless on the bitter sweat of the hired.

Notwithstanding the material injury suffered by South Carolina during the war, recovery is more rapid there than in any of the other states; commerce is almost as flourishing and as extended as before the disquiets, and there is every reason to expect further incr.

It is generally admitted, and is a matter of surprise to every incoming European, that at Charleston finer manners and a more tasteful mode of life are unmistakably prevalent, and if there was need, the fact might easily be proved by numerous observations. And it is quite as certain that this refinement of manners and taste has a positive influence on the opinions, those whose characteristic this is showing on many occasions nobility and magnanimity of thought and conduct. The Assembly had appointed a committee to examine the list of banished citizens and their confiscated property, in order to determine the degree of their offences against the state, and so bring them back again or continue their banishment. Even this investigation was held behind open doors. The opinions of the worthiest and most esteemed citizens and gentlemen of Charleston were to the effect that all, except those guilty of very serious offences against the state, should be dealt with as gently as possible, they being permitted to return on payment of 10–15–20 per centum of their property, and the sin of their adherence to Great Britain forgiven them. Mr. Burke,* Mr. Hutson,† Mr. Vanhorsh‡ and many other high-minded and estimable men used all their influence to recommend indulgence, forgiveness, and gentle measures; they desired that only those who in their zeal for the cause of the King had been plainly guilty of murder, or of serious wrong committed in respect to members of the American party, such as fire, devastation, and the like, that only such offenders as these should be deprived of all hope of returning to their homes—and of more than a hundred and fifty on the black list not more than 15 could have been so described. However, the magnanimous views of these many worthy men were opposed by others, of the lower and rougher class, with a veritably raging obstinacy; they breathed nothing but the bitterness of vengeance, and would hear of no forgiveness, although their grounds were neither sufficient nor seemly. I was witness at another time to a noble answer given in court by one of the Judges to the plaintiff who hoped greatly to weaken the argument of defendant by bringing out that he had belonged to the King's party and deserved, like many others, to be banished

---

*Irishman Aedanus Burke (1743–1802), state circuit judge and legislator.
†Richard Hutson (1747–1795) had become the city's first intendant (mayor) in 1783.
‡Arnoldus Vanderhorst (1748–1815) served in the South Carolina Senate 1780 to 1786.

from the country. "Here before the court," answered the Judge, "is no question of Whig and Tory. Your adversary has not been banished; he has thus permission to live here; and in consequence must have the same claims before the court as you to an impartial examination and an unprejudiced decision." Such opinions as these are all the more commendable, held and openly expressed by upright men repeatedly, at a time when the blind zeal of the people was still everywhere crying for vengeance, holding it for a crime unpardonable to think in any way different from the crowd.*

The laws of South Carolina are no more favorable than those of the other states to distinctions of rank. But even if there are no class distinctions as such, it is observable that many circumstances and conditions have almost that effect, certain members of society being more nearly and closely associated, and to them is tacitly ascribed more or less superiority. America knows no nobility, rather hates the thought of such a thing, and refuses any respect demanded by those whose only claim is that of descent and birth. There is however a class of citizens who by natural gifts, useful acquirements, or wealth, are plainly enough superior to the rest, know how to make themselves influential and regarded in many situations and to maintain their hold, and in many respects think and act precisely as do the nobility in other countries.

At this time discontented officers were to be found here in great numbers. The grounds of their dissatisfaction were valid enough. Many of them had for years devoted health and property to the service of their country, and now saw themselves abandoned to their fate. A Major of South Carolina troops assured me that during the whole of the war he had received no more than 70 Pd. pay in cash money, and that in order to live conformably to his position he had been obliged to sell many negroes, and even land, and as circumstances were, at prices far below the real values. For 2 and 3 years' service many officers had been paid not a bare shilling, and the settlement of their claims by the state is as far off as ever. Therefore it should not be a matter of surprise if one hears these men let fall words and judgments not to be expected of those who had, one might have

*In 1783 and 1784, the Loyalists named by the Confiscation Act buried the legislature in work appraising Loyalist claims through petitions and hearings, dominating this branch of state government. In the General Assembly, Aedanus Burke "consistently used a series of carrots and sticks to get Loyalists to recommit to the state and to South Carolina society." The Proclamation of 1781 allowed Loyalists to reclaim their citizenship and standing in return for six months of military service. Burke favored clemency. He felt anti-Tory legislation was destructive to the legal and moral framework of society, and would embitter people who would otherwise be loyal to the state. In 1784, the General Assembly passed a general clemency act that removed a majority of proscribed Loyalists from confiscation.

supposed, been fighting out of pure patriotism. Was it patriotism alone that put arms in their hands, they would have ample cause to be content and to regard themselves as richly repaid in the self-satisfaction arising from the happy outcome of their war. But besides the honor of being called liberators of their country they desire pay, and loudly grumble at being so put off. How superior then are they to those whom they thought to dishonor with the injurious name of hirelings? In their expressions of ill-will, elicited by the withholding of their pay, they swear that neither they nor any one else would ever be so foolish again as to dedicate themselves to the service of the state, fighting for empty promises, and that if another war should break out after 10 or more years it would be impossible to assemble another army, since the small attention and gratitude given the first would not so soon be forgotten. Moreover it is believed and affirmed pretty generally that the Americans do not show a natural disposition for war and pleasure in military service such as are to be remarked in other nations. Love of softness and desire of riches incline them more to the peaceful and monotonous pursuits of agriculture and commerce. Nothing but a positively hostile attack would in the future move them to take up arms again. These opinions are doubtless mistaken. America, as well as other nations, has men enough who from natural disposition take pleasure in war as war; this may be inferred in part solely from the general impulse to fist-fights. However repulsive certain disadvantages and difficulties inseparable from war may be, there is on the other hand so much that is tempting and dazzling that men will never cease to be attracted to the fame-promising enterprises of war. Without being tedious in this matter, I may mention a trifling circumstance, how remarkable it was that those very officers who complained with such bitterness of the losses their military service had brought upon them, showed the greatest pleasure in their military uniform, their cockades, and their swords. Many who had gone into trade, still retained the outward appearance of officers and the title. Even older and serious persons showed this preference. An esteemed lawyer here always appeared in public in black velvet, but with a white cockade to his hat, and a ribbon-knot on his sword, for he had been a General, but was now again managing cases at law.

THE

ELEPHANT,

ACCORDING to the account of the celebrated BUFFON, is the moſt reſpectable Animal in the world. In ſize he ſurpaſſes all other terreſtrial creatures; and by his intelligence, makes as near an approach to man, as matter can approach ſpirit. A ſufficient proof that there is not too much ſaid of the knowledge of this animal is, that the Proprietor having been abſent for ten weeks, the moment he arrived at the door of his apartment, and ſpoke to the keeper, the animal's knowledge was beyond any doubt confirmed by the cries he uttered forth, till his Friend came within reach of his trunk, with which he careſſed him, to the aſtoniſhment of all thoſe who ſaw him. This moſt curious and ſurpriſing animal is juſt arrived in this town, from Philadelphia, where he will ſtay but a few days.————He is only four years old, and weighs about 3000 weight, but will not have come to his full growth till he ſhall be between 30 and 40 years old. He meaſures from the end of his trunk to the tip of his tail 15 feet 8 inches, round the body 10 feet 6 inches, round his head 7 feet 2 inches, round his leg above the knee 3 feet 3 inches, round his ankle 2 feet 2 inches. He eats 130 weight a day, and drinks all kinds of ſpirituous liquors; ſome days he has drank 30 bottles of porter, drawing the corks with his trunk. He is ſo tame that he travels looſe, and has never attempted to hurt any one. He appeared on the ſtage, at the New Theatre in Philadelphia, to the great ſatisfaction of a reſpectable audience.

A reſpectable and convenient place is fitted up adjoining the Store of Mr. Bartlet, Market-Street, for the reception of thoſe ladies and gentlemen who may be pleaſed to view the greateſt natural curioſity ever preſented to the curious, which is to be ſeen from ſunriſe till ſundown, every day in the week.

☞ The Elephant having deſtroyed many papers of conſequence, it is recommended to viſitors not to come near him with ſuch papers.

Admittance ONE QUARTER OF A DOLLAR——Children ONE EIGHTH OF A DOLLAR.

NEWBURYPORT, Sept. 19, 1797.

"The Elephant" (Newburyport, MA: William Barrett, 1797). Broadside SY1797 no. 26. Collection of the New-York Historical Society, New York.

JOHN DAVIS (1798–99)

"*The Woods of South Carolina*"

John Davis (1775–1854) was born in Salisbury, Wiltshire, England, the son of a wool draper. He wrote that he was "reared in the lap of opulence," but facts suggest the family fortunes declined before 1790. He was educated at home with access to a "well-selected but outdated" family library. At the age of fourteen, he entered naval service with the East India Company as ship's boy on a vessel that sailed for the West Indies and China. In 1793, he served in the British Navy on the "fastest sailing ship" in a flying squadron. By his release in 1797, he had sailed for eleven years. He had lived in the East Indies, navigated to the chief countries of the Orient, four times skirted the coasts of Africa, and sailed near parts of Spain, France, and Germany. An autodidact, over the course of these voyages he made an exhaustive study of literature, the classics in French and Greek, and Latin.

A love of adventure brought Davis to America at the age of twenty-two. He sailed from Bristol to New York, carrying three hundred volumes from his family library. In New York, he lodged with Dr. DeBow, a young physician. He befriended proprietors of bookstores and writers and was recommended to translate Bonaparte's *Campaign in Italy*, from which he gained a reputation as a translator. This attracted the attention of Vice-President Aaron Burr, who gave Davis access to his library at Richmond Hill (Burr's home in New York) in which to work on his *Travels*. Davis soon set out to record further impressions and made acquaintances from literary figures of the day to Thomas Jefferson. He traveled mostly on foot, financing his travels by writing low-quality, quick-paying "potboilers" for New York and Philadelphia booksellers and newspapers.

When Davis left New York for Charleston, he was accompanied by Dr. DeBow, who planned to set up a medical practice there. They sent their luggage ahead and walked to Trenton, New Jersey, then traveled by boat from Philadelphia to Charleston. They arrived in the autumn of 1798. Davis served six weeks

Taken from *Travels of Four Years and a Half in the United States of America; during 1798, 1799, 1800, 1801, and 1802*. London, 1803, vol. 1.

as assistant professor at the College of Charleston before establishing himself as tutor to one of Charleston's oldest families, the Draytons, at Ocean Plantation.

Davis wrote his *Travels* to cater to the desire for travel literature in his day. He was an impressionist who wrote whatever he saw but romanticized it, and a poet who wrote what can only be called travel odes. He claimed to have been influenced by Oliver Goldsmith's *Citizen of the World*. He was further inspired by Alexander Pope (1688–1744), a top seller in America between 1794 and 1796, and Jean-Jacques Rousseau (1712–1788), whose work was also popular at the time. When *Travels* was published in 1803, English reviewers criticized Davis as a "mediocre writer, monotonous and verbose," and his travels as "marred by a conceit." On the other hand, Thomas Jefferson was flattered when this "enlightened foreigner" dedicated the book to him. History has been kinder to Davis's *Travels*.

While he was in the region, his odes were published in Charleston newspapers. Included in *Travels,* they were also published separately in Charleston as *Poems Written at Coosawhatchie in South Carolina* (1799). Davis published a number of books in America. His first novel, *The Original Letters of Ferdinand and Elizabeth* (1798) was followed by novels he wrote after leaving Charleston that concern his walking trip through fifteen American states, including *The Farmer of New Jersey* (1800) and its sequel, *The Wanderings of William* (1801), and *Walter Kennedy: An Interesting American Tale* (1805). He wrote *Walter Kennedy* and *The Post Captain; or, The Wooden Walls Well Manned* (1805), which is now said to have initiated the nautical literary genre. While engaged as a tutor in Virginia, he published *Captain Smith and Princess Pocahontas* (1805) and *The First Settlers of Virginia: An Historical Novel* (1806). The latter is now recognized as the first historical novel, the second being Sir Walter Scott's "true modern version of the genre," *Waverley* (1814). Davis is today acknowledged as the first author to resurrect the American legend of John Smith and Pocahontas, which inspired novelists, dramatists, and poets to draw on the legend for generations. In 1981, scholar Jan Bakker established *First Settlers of Virginia* as the first direct statement of a major national theme in American fiction: the loss of a second Eden in the New World.

However, other than for his *Travels*, Davis attained little success in his own day. He returned to England and published his last book, *The American Mariner; or, The Atlantic Voyage* (1822). He worked as a stationer and bookseller in Winchester, England, and spent the last ten years of his life destitute.

SOURCES

Bakker, Jan. "Parallel Water Journeys into the American Eden in John Davis's *First Settlers of Virginia* and F. Scott Fitzgerald's *The Great Gatsby.*" *Early American Literature* 16, no. 1 (Spring 1981): 50–53.

Byrd, Max. "The Brief History of a Historical Novel." *Wilson Quarterly* (Autumn 2007): 25–31.

Ellis, Scott. "Reviewers Reviewed: John Davis and the Early American Literary Field." *Early American Literature* 42, no. 1 (Winter 2007): 157–87.

Jenkins, William Warren. "The Princess Pocahontas and Three Englishmen Named John." In *No Fairer Land: Studies in Southern Literature before 1900*, ed. J. Lasley Dameron and James W. Matthews. Troy, NY: Whitston Publishing, 1986.

Kellogg, Thelma Louise. *The Life and Works of John Davis, 1774–1853*. Orono: Maine University Press, 1924.

Kribbs, Jayne K. "'Reserved for My Pen': John Davis's Place in American Literature." In *Early American Literature and Culture*, ed. Kathryn Zabelle Derounian-Stodola. Newark: University of Delaware Press, 1992.

Law, Robert. "The Bard of Coosawhatchie." *The Texas Review* 7 (October 1921–July 1922): 133–56.

Morrison, A. J. *Travels in Virginia in Revolutionary Times*. Lynchburg, VA: J. P. Bell Co., 1922.

"THE WOODS OF SOUTH CAROLINA"

Projects at Charleston.—Solemnity the Mask of Ignorance.—Interview with a Planter and his Lady.—The Erudition of a Professor.—A new and desirable Acquaintance.—College Toils.—A Journey on foot from Charleston to Coosawhatchie.

I landed at Charleston with Doctor De Bow,* who had clad himself in his black suit, and though a young man, wore a monstrous pair of spectacles on his nose. Adieu jollity! adieu laughter! the Doctor was without an acquaintance on a strange shore, and he had no other friend but his Solemnity to recommend him. It was to no purpose that I endeavored to provoke him to laughter by my remarks; the Physician would not even relax his risible muscles into a smile.

The Doctor was right. In a few days he contrived to hire part of a house in Union-street;† obtained credit for a considerable quantity of drugs; and only wanted a chariot to equal the best Physician in Charleston.

---

*According to a December 1797 notice in the *New York Diary*, William DeBow was insolvent, which may explain his relocation to Charleston. He is listed as a Charleston druggist at 104 East Bay in 1816; an "oil and color man" at 102 E. Bay in 1819; and owner of a distillery at 53 State Street in 1829 (*New York Diary*, December 25, 1797, 3; Hagy, *Charleston, S.C. City Directories for the Years 1816, 1819, 1822, 1825, and 1829*, 7, 38, 142).
†Now State Street.

The Doctor was in possession of a voluble tongue; and I furnished him with a few Latin phrases, which he dealt out to his hearers with an air of profound learning. He generally concluded his speeches with *Nullius addictus jurare in verba magistri.*[†]

Wishing for some daily pursuit, I advertised in one of the papers for the place of Tutor in a respectable family; not omitting to observe that the advertiser was the translator of Bonaparte's *Campaign in Italy.* The editor of the *Gazette*[‡] assured me of an hundred applications; and that early the next morning I should not be without some. His predictions were verified; for the following day, on calling at the office, I found a note left from a Planter who lived a mile from the town, desiring me to visit him that afternoon at his house. I went thither accordingly. Every thing indicated opulence and ease. Mr. H—— received me with the insolence of prosperity. You are, said he, the person who advertised for the place of Tutor in a respectable family? I answered with a bow.

Planter. What, Sir, are your qualifications?

Tutor. I am competently skilled, Sir, in the Latin and French languages, not unacquainted with Greek, conversant with Geography, and accustomed to composition in my vernacular idiom.

Planter. But if you possess all *that there* learning, how comes it you could not get into some College, or School.

Tutor. Why, Sir, it is found even in Colleges that dunces triumph, and men of letters are disregarded by a general combination in favor of dullness.

Planter. Can you *drive* well, Sir?—*

[**Davis's note:* The term *drive,* requires some little note explanatory to the English reader. No man forgets his original trade. An Overseer of a Plantation, who preserves subordination among the negroes, is said to *drive* well; and Mr. H—— *having once been an Overseer himself,* the phrase very naturally predominated in his mind.]

Tutor. Drive, Sir, did you say? I really do not comprehend you.

[†]Part of a quote from Homer which reads: "Accustomed to swear in the words of no master."

[‡]Peter Freneau (1757–1814), younger brother of Philip Freneau, the "Poet of the Revolution," arrived in Charleston in 1782. Tall, handsome and dashing, he was known as "the Apollo of Charles Town." He served as deputy secretary of South Carolina in 1784 and secretary of state in 1787, for which he was reappointed in 1791. Freneau had business interests, including land speculation, ship-owning, and the Madeira trade. In 1795, he and a partner purchased the *Charleston City Gazette and Daily Advertiser.* In 1798, they founded the *Carolina Gazette,* which was soon influential in the state. Freneau published John Davis's odes in his newspaper (Davis and Seigler, "Peter Freneau," 395–405; Mills, *Historic Houses of New Jersey,* 170).

Planter. I mean, Sir, can you keep your scholars in order?

Tutor. Yes, Sir, if they are left entirely to my direction.

Planter. Ah! that would not be. Mrs. H——, who is a woman of extensive learning, (she lost a fine opportunity once of learning *French*, and only a few years ago could write the best hand of any lady in Charleston,) Mrs. H—— would superintend your management of the school.

Tutor. Mrs. H——, Sir, would do me honor.

Planter. Mrs. H——, Sir, is, in the real sense of the word, a woman of literature; and her eldest daughter is a prodigy for her age. She could tell at nine years old whether a pudding was boiled enough; and now, though only eleven, can repeat Pope's "Ode on Solitude" by heart. Ah! *Pope* was a *pretty* poet; my wife is very fond of Pope. You have read him, I make no doubt, Sir. What is your opinion of his works?

Tutor. In his "Rape of the Lock," Sir, he exhibits most of the *vis imaginandi* that constitutes the poet; his "Essay on Criticism" is scarcely inferior to Horace's Epistle to the Pisos; his Satires——.

Planter. But I am surprised, Sir, you bestow no praise on his "Ode on Solitude." Mrs. H——, who is quite a critic in those matters, allows the "Ode on Solitude" to be his best, his noblest, his sublimest production.

Tutor. Persuaded, Sir, of the critical acuteness of Mrs. H——, it is not safe to depart from her in opinion;—and if Mrs. H—— affirms the "Ode on Solitude" to be the sublimest of Mr. Pope's productions, it would be rather painful than pleasant to undeceive her in opinion.

Planter. That is right, Sir, I like to see young men modest. What spelling-book do you use?

Tutor. What spelling-book, Sir? Indeed—really—upon my word, Sir,—any—oh! Noah Webster's, Sir.

Planter. Ah! I perceive you are a New England man, by giving the preference to Noah Webster.*

Tutor. Sir, I beg your pardon; I am from Old England.

Planter. Well, no matter for that,—but Mrs. H——, who is an excellent speller, never makes use of any other but Matthew Carey's spelling-book.† It is a valuable work, the copyright is secured. But here comes Mrs. H—— herself.

*Noah Webster (1758–1843) produced the first American spelling book as *The First Part of the Grammatical Institute of the English Language* in 1783. The title was changed in 1786 to *The American Spelling Book.*

†Mathew Carey (1760–1839), a Philadelphia bookseller and printer, asked for the copyright of Webster's *American Spelling Book*, but they disagreed on price. Instead Carey compiled one similar to Webster's, which was not a success.

Mrs. H—— now entered, followed by a negro girl, who held a peacock's feather in her hand. Mrs. H—— received my bow with a mutilated curtsey, and throwing herself on a sofa, called peremptorily to Prudence to brush the flies from her face. There was a striking contrast between the dress of the lady and her maid; the one was tricked out in all the finery of fashion; while the black skin of the other peeped through her garments.

Well, my dear, said Mr. H——, this young man is the person who advertised for the place of tutor in a respectable family. A little conversation with him will enable you to judge, whether he is qualified to instruct our children in the branches of a liberal education.

Mrs. H. Why independent of his literary attainments, it will be necessary for him to produce certificates of his conduct. I am not easily satisfied in my choice of a tutor; a body should be very cautious in admitting a stranger to her family. This gentleman is young, and young men are very frequently addicted to bad habits. Some are prone to late hours; some to hard drinking; and some to Negur girls: the last propensity I could never forgive.

Mr. H. Yes, my dear, you discharged Mr. Spondee, our last tutor, for his intimacy with the Negur girls:—Prudence had a little one by him.—Prudence looked reproachfully at her master; the child was in reality the offspring of Mr. H——, who fearing the inquiries of the world on the subject, fathered it upon his last tutor. But they must have been blind who could not discover that the child was sprung from Mr. H——; for it had the same vulgar forehead, the same vacant eye, and the same idiot laugh.

Mr. H. Do, my dear, examine the young man a little on literary matters. He seems to have read Pope.

Mrs. H. What, Sir, is your opinion of Mr. Pope's "Ode on Solitude?"

Tutor. It is a tolerable production, madam, for a child.

Mrs. H. A tolerable production for a child! Mercy on us! It is the *most sublimest* of his productions. But tastes sometimes differ. Have you read the words of Dr. Johnson? Which do you approve the most?

Tutor. Why, Madam, if you allude to his poems, I should, in conformity with your judgment, give a decided preference to his "Epitaph on a Duck," written, if I mistake not, when he was four years old. It need scarcely fear competition with Pope's "Ode on Solitude."

At this moment the eldest daughter of this learned lady, of this unsexed female, tripped into the room on light, fantastic toe.—Come, my daughter, said the lady, let this gentleman hear you repeat the "Ode on Solitude."

Excuse me, Madam, cried I, taking up my hat and bowing.

Do hear the child, bawled Mr. H——.

I pray you Sir to excuse me, rejoined I.

Mrs. H. It will not take the child ten minutes.

Tutor. Ten minutes, madam, are the sixth part of an hour that will never return!

Mr. H. Politeness dictates it.

Tutor. Excuse me, I entreat you, Sir.

Mr. H. I cannot excuse you, I shall hire you as tutor, and I have a right to expect from you submission. I may perhaps give you the sum of fifty pounds a year.

Don't mention it, Sir, said I. There again you will have the goodness to excuse me. Madam, your most obedient. Miss, your very obsequious. Sir, your humble servant.—*

[*Davis's note:* It has been my, object in this scene to soften the condition of private tutors in America, by putting up Mr. H——— *in signum terroris et memoriæ,*† to other purse-proud planters. I write not from personal pique, but a desire to benefit society. Happy shall I think myself should this page hold the mirror up to the inflation of pride, and insolence of prosperity.]

My walk back to Charleston was along the shore of the Atlantic, whose waves naturally associated the idea of a home I despaired ever again to behold. Sorrow always begets in me a disposition for poetry; and the reflections that obtruded themselves in my lonely walk produced a little ode.

Ode On Home

DEAR native soil! where once my feet
Were wont thy flow'ry paths to roam,
And where my heart, would joyful beat,
From India's climes restor'd to home;
Ah! shall I e'er behold you more,
And cheer again a parent's eye?
A wand'rer from thy blissful shore,
Thro' endless troubles doom'd to sigh?
Or shall I, pensive and forlorn,
Of penury be yet the prey,
Long from thy grateful bosom torn,
Without a friend to guide my way?
Hard is the hapless wand'rer's fate
Tho' blest with magic power of song;
Successive woes his steps await,
Unheeded by the worldly throng.

†From Virgil's *Aeneid*: "I am *Aeneas*, the good, who carry with me in my fleet my household gods, snatched from the foe; my fame is known in the heavens above" (1.378).

It was not long before my advertisement brought me other applications. The principal of Charleston-College honored me with a letter, whom, pursuant to his desire, I waited on at his house.

I found Mr. Drone* in his study, consulting with great solemnity the ponderous lexicon of Schrevelius.[†] I could not but feel a secret veneration from the scene before me. I was admitted to the presence of a man who was not less voluminous than learned; for no book under a folio ever stood on his shelf. How stupendous, thought I, must be the erudition of this professor, who holds in sovereign contempt a volume of ordinary dimensions! Every animal has an aliment peculiarly suited to its constitution. The ox finds nourishment only from the earth; and a professor cannot derive knowledge from any volume but a folio.

Mr. Drone received me with all the little decorums of dullness. He, however, talked learnedly. He lamented the degeneracy of literature in England and America; discovered that taste was on the decline; and despaired of ever beholding the spirit of that age revived when writers sought not for new combinations of imagery, but were content to compile lexicons, and restore the true punctuation to an ancient poet.

Mr. Drone asked me whether I was conversant with Latin; and on my replying in the affirmative, he produced a Horace in folio, and desired I would construe the Ode of *Quem tu, Melpomene.*

Horace had never before assumed so formidable an aspect. In the ordinary editions he had always looked at me *placido lumine;*[‡] but he now appeared crabbed and sour, and I found his text completely buried amidst the rubbish of annotations.

By making *Isthmius labor* the agent to *clarabit,* the difficulty of the inversion vanished; but when I came to analyze the construction of the ode, not having some rule for verbs construed at memory, I think it was the important one of *mo*

---

*In the fall of 1798, "Drone" appointed Davis teaching assistant in Latin and Greek. In 1935, J. H. Easterby identified Mr. Drone as Thomas Bee Jr., second principle of the college, who replaced Robert Smith in 1798. Bee was described as a "cloistered scholar and an ineffective administrator." Easterby writes that, in 1821, Bee founded a journal known as the *Omnium Gatherum*, which revealed him to be an "eccentric, if not pedantic, scholar." William Gilmore Simms described Bee as "better known for his memory and his fund of anecdotes than his wisdom" (Easterby, *History of the College of Charleston*, 40–43).

†Cornelius Schrevelius (1615–1664), headmaster of the German Gymnasium in Leiden, published variorum editions of the major classical Greek and Latin authors from Homer to Claudian. Schrevelius's major independent work was the Greek-Latin *Lexicon Manuale Graeco-Latinum et Latino-Graecum*, first published in 1661.

‡"With smiling eye."

fit ui, as vomo vomui the Professor, with a shake of his head, which doubtless put all his sagacity into motion, told me very gravely I had yet something to learn.

I ought to apologize to my reader for detaining him so long in the company of Professor Drone; but it is a link in the chain of my history, however rusty. To be brief, he engaged me as an Assistant to his sublime College for three months; and had the vanity to assert, that in consequence of it I should become *fama super æthera notus.*

I was about to take leave of Mr. Drone, when his principal Tutor entered the room, to whom he introduced me. Mr. George taught the Greek and Latin classics at the College, and was not less distinguished by his genius than his erudition.*

On surveying my new acquaintance, I could not but think that he deserved a better office than that of a Gerund-grinder. Nature seemed to have set her seal on him to give the world assurance of a man.

Mr. George laughed obstreperously at the pedantry of the Professor. Peace, said he, to all such! Old Duffey, my first school-master in Roscommon, concealed more learning under the coarseness of his brogue, than Drone will ever display with all his rhetoric of declamation. It is true he can talk of Luitprandus, Bertholdus, and Lamberlus; but an acquaintance with these writers, however it may display reading, discovers little judgment.

Two young men, of similar pursuits, soon become acquainted. The day of my introduction to Mr. George, we exchanged thoughts without restraint; and during three months that I continued at Charleston, we were inseparable companions.

I know not whether I was qualified to fill the vacant chair of instruction at the College; but I remember, that zealous to acquit myself with dignity in my new office, I assumed the aspect of a pedagogue, and when an idle boy stared at me, I checked him with a frown. I, however, was not ambitious of this honor more than six weeks; a space of time, which, however it cannot be long, may surely be tedious. The Professor complained that I was always the last in the College; and I replied by desiring my discharge.

I was now dismissed from the College; but I was under no solicitude for my future life. A Planter of the name of Brisbane,† had politely invited me to his

---

*Lucas George, Davis's immediate superior, was principal tutor for the college. By the following summer, he was teaching at the Winyah Indigo Society in Georgetown. He remained a figure in Davis's literary career until the two engaged in a heated editorial exchange in a Philadelphia newspaper, which ended badly (Death Notice, *New York Evening Post*, November 11, 1808, no. 2087, 3; Kellogg, "The Life and Works of John Davis," 28–29; Easterby, *History of the College of Charleston*, 45).

†This was probably planter John Stanyarne Brisbane (1773–1850), who married Maria Hall (1769–1831) in 1795. He owned Otranto Plantation from 1801 to 1804 and later resided at Malona (Acabee) Plantation on the Ashley River.

plantation, to partake with him and his neighbors, the diversion of hunting, during the winter; and another of the name of Drayton, the owner of immense forests,
had applied to me to live in his family, and undertake the tuition of his children.
Of these proposals, the first flattered my love of ease, and the other insured me
an augmentation of wealth. I was not long held in suspense which of the two to
choose; but I preferred the summons of industry to the blandishments of pleasure.

The winters of Carolina, however piercing to a native, who during the summer months may be said to bask rather than breathe, are mild to an Englishman
accustomed to the frosts of his island. In the month of November my engage-
ment led me to [Coosawhatchie], an insignificant village about seventy-eight
miles from Charleston;* for the plantation of Mr. Drayton was in the neighboring woods. The serenity of the weather invited the traveller to walk, and, at
an early hour of the morning, I departed on foot from Charleston, having the
preceding evening taken leave of Mr. George.

The foot-traveller need not be ashamed of his mode of journeying. To travel
on foot, is to travel like Plato and Pythagoras; and to these examples may be
added the not less illustrious ones of Goldsmith and Rousseau. The rambles of
the ancient sages are at this distance of time uncertain; but it is well known, that
Goldsmith made the tour of Europe on foot, and that Rousseau walked, from
choice, through a great part of Italy.

An agreeable walk of ten miles, brought me to the bank of Ashley River, where
I breakfasted in a decent public-house, with the landlord and his family. That
man travels to no purpose who sits down alone to his meals; for my part I love
to mingle with the sons and daughters of industry; to mark the economy of their
household, and compare their mode of living with that of the same class of people
in my own country. The opulent of every nation are nearly the same; refinement
has polished away the original stamp of character: the true estimate of manners is
to be made among those in a middle rank of life.

Having crossed the ferry, I resumed my journey through a country which
might be assimilated to one continued forest. Tall trees of pine, planted by the
hand of nature in regular rows, bordered the road I travelled; and I saw no other
animals, but now and then a flock of deer, which ceasing awhile to browse, looked
up at me with symptoms of wonder rather than fear.

At three in the afternoon I reached Jackson-borough,[†] the only town on the
road from Charleston to Coosawhatchie. Though a foot-traveller, I was received

---

*Coosawhatchie remains an unincorporated community located in Jasper County, south
of Charleston.

[†]At the time of Davis's visit, Jacksonboro was the county seat of Colleton County, with a
courthouse, jail, racetrack, and over 113 lots.

at the tavern with every demonstration of respect; the landlord ushered me into a room which afforded the largest fire I had ever seen in my travels: yet the landlord, rubbing his hands, complained it was cold, and exclaimed against his negroes for keeping so bad a fire. Here, Syphax, said he, be quick and bring more wood: you have made, you rascal, a Charleston fire: fetch a stout back-log, or I'll make a backlog of you.

The exclamations of the landlord brought his wife into the room. She curtsied, and made many eloquent apologies for the badness of the fire; but added, that her waiting man Will had run away, and having whipped Syphax till his back was raw, she was willing to try what gentle means would do.

A dinner of venison, and a pint of Madeira, made me forget I had walked thirty miles; and it being little more than four o'clock, I proceeded forward on my journey. The vapors of a Spanish segar promoted cogitation, and I was lamenting the inequality of conditions in the world, when night overtook me.

I now redoubled my pace, not without the apprehension that I should have to seek my lodgings in some tree, to avoid the beasts that prowled nightly in the woods; but the moon, which rose to direct me in my path, alleviated my perturbation, and in another hour I descried the blaze of a friendly fire through the casements of a log-house. Imaginary are worse than real calamities; and the apprehension of sleeping in the woods was by far more painful than the actual experience of it would have been. The same Being who sends trials, can also inspire fortitude.

The place I had reached was Ashepoo,* a hamlet consisting of three or more log-houses; and the inhabitants of every sex and age had collected round a huge elephant, which was journeying with his master to Savannah.

Fortune had therefore brought me into unexpected company, and I could not but admire the docility of the elephant, who in solemn majesty received the girls of the children with his trunk. But not so the monkey. This man of Lord Monboddo† was inflamed with rage at the boys and girls; nor could the rebukes of his master calm the transports of his fury.

I entered the log-house which accommodated travellers. An old negro-man had squatted himself before the fire. Well, old man, said I, why don't you go out to look at the elephant? Hie! Massa, he calf! In fact the elephant came from Asia, and the negro from Africa, where he had seen the same species of animal, but of much greater magnitude.

*Ashepoo, named for a Cusabo Indian tribe, remains a town in Colleton County.

†James Burnett, Lord Monboddo (1714–1799), Scottish judge, evolutionist, and founder of comparative historical linguistics, published *Origin and Process of Language* in six volumes from 1774 to 1792, in which he suggested man was descended from apes, the "tail bone being a vestige of simian ancestry."

Travelling, says Shakespeare, acquaints a man with strange bed-fellows; and there being only one bed in the log-house, I slept that night with the elephant-driver. Mr. Owen was a native of Wales, but he had been a great traveller, and carried a map of his travels in his pocket.—Nothing shortens a journey more than good company on the road; so I departed after breakfast from Ashepoo, with Mr. Owen, his elephant, and his monkey.*

Mr. Owen related to me the wonders of his elephant, which at some future day, I may perhaps publish in a separate treatise; but they would be irrelevant to my present journey, which towards noon I was left to prosecute alone. The elephant, however docile, would not travel without his dinner; and Mr. Owen halted under a pine-tree to feed the mute companion of his toils.

---

*In 1795, the first elephant to set foot on American soil was brought from Bengal by Jacob Crowninshield, a ship captain from Salem, Massachusetts. He purchased the elephant as a two-year-old for $450 and boarded it on the ship *America* for a four-month trip to New York City, a voyage by author Nathaniel Hawthorne's father, a member of the ship's crew who kept a log. In April 1796, *The Argus* or *Greenleaf's New York Advertiser* reports the elephant journeying on the *America*. According to an advertisement in *The Argus* a few days later, it was exhibited on Beaver and Broadway streets at the Bull's Head Tavern, which was frequented by ship's captains, drovers, and businessmen. Newspaper accounts report the elephant was sold for $10,000 to a "Mr. Owen," to exhibit "up and down the United States." Hachaliah Bailey (1774–1845), later known as "the father of the American circus," was a regular guest at the Bull's Head Tavern. A farmer and cattle merchant from Somers, New York, he frequently brought his cattle to a nearby abattoir. Bailey purchased and toured the second elephant in America. Mr. Owen has been conjectured to be John Owen, who married Hachaliah Bailey's sister, Anna, in 1815. However, Owen was born in 1784, which would have made him fourteen years old at the time he encountered John Davis at Ashepoo. The elephant walker was no doubt a member of the Owen family, possibly John's father Joseph Owen, also from the Somers, New York, area. The *Aurora* of July 28, 1796, states, "There just arrived from New York, in this city, on his way to Charleston, an elephant." The paper mentions the elephant traveling from New York to Philadelphia before it shows up in the Baltimore papers. By spring of 1797, the elephant was in Philadelphia, where it appeared on stage in an epoch-making performance of *Alexander the Great*, or *The Rival Queens*, a benefit with tragedian Thomas Cooper, which reportedly gained "Mr. Owen" $60. In the next few years, it was exhibited in New York, Providence, Boston, Salem, Marblehead, and other New England towns before northern advertisements announced the elephant was headed back to Charleston, "presumably its winter home." In the winter of 1798, Lailson's Circus performed in Charleston, advertising "Exhibits of an Elephant—a Stupendous Beast." On February 18, 1799, the South Carolina *State Gazette* ran the advertisement: "(Last Day but One.) The Elephant. The inhabitants of Charleston and people coming from the country are informed, that this surprising animal will positively leave the city next Tuesday, February 19; and may perhaps never return, during these three days the doors will be open til nine o'clock in the evenings. To be seen in King Street, near the Tobacco Inspection."

For my own part, I dined at a solitary log-house in the woods, upon exquisite venison. My host was a small Planter, who cultivated a little rice, and maintained a wife and four children with his rifled-barrel-gun. He had been Overseer to a Colonel Fishborne,* and owned half a dozen negroes; but he observed to me his property was running about at large, for four of them had absconded.

As I purposed to make Pocotaligo† the end of my day's journey, I walked forward at a moderate pace; but towards evening I was roused from the reveries into which my walking had plunged me, by a conflagration in the woods. On either side of the road the trees were in flames, which extending to their branches, assumed an appearance both terrific and grotesque. Through these woods, belching flames and rolling smoke, I had to travel nearly a mile, when the sound of the negro's axe chopping of wood, announced that I was near Pocotaligo.

At Pocotaligo I learned that the conflagration in the woods arose from the carelessness of some back-wood-men, who having neglected to extinguish their fires, the flames had extended in succession to the herbage and the trees.

I was somewhat surprised on entering the tavern‡ at Pocotaligo, to behold sixteen or more chairs placed round a table which was covered with the choicest dishes; but my surprise ceased when the Savannah and Charleston stage-coaches stopped at the door, and the passengers flocked to the fire before which I was sitting. In the Charleston coach came a party of comedians. Of these itinerant heroes the greater part were my countrymen; and, as I was not travelling to see Englishmen, but Americans, I was not sorry when they retired to bed.§

I was in a worse condition at Pocotaligo than Ashepoo; for at Pocotaligo the beds were so small that they would hold only respectively one person. But I pity the Traveller who takes umbrage against America because its houses of entertainment

---

*Gen. William H. Fishburne (1760–1819) owned Marcello Plantation nearby.

†Pocotaligo remains an unincorporated community located in Jasper County, close to the border of Beaufort County.

‡The tavern of Jacob Van Bibber, postmaster, was located at the Pocotaligo Bridge. Van Bibber was said to keep "an excellent house." He died in 1785, although the tavern continued operation. According to Grace Perry, "a tavern known as Van Bibber's, built of logs and tapia (tabby), existed on the stagecoach road in the village and was famous for its entertainment." The inn was a party spot, and served cognac, Jamaica rum, and Madeira wine. In his diary, George Washington mentions that he stopped overnight and was entertained at Van Bibber's on his 1792 southern tour. The tavern was also known as Faunce (Perry, *Moving Finger* of *Jasper*, 5; Zubly, *Journal of the Reverend*, 61).

§These were likely members of the Charleston Comedians, who played a short season in Savannah through March of that year and returned to Charleston in April. Charleston Theater was at a standstill over the 1798–99 season, due to a major quarrel among stage players in

cannot always accommodate him to his wishes. If he images no other happiness to himself in travelling, but what is to be obtained from repasts that minister to luxury, and beds distinguished by their softness, let him confine his excursions to the cities of polished Europe. The Western Continent can supply the Traveller an employment more noble than a minute attention to the casualties of the road, which are afterwards to be enlarged upon with studied declamation.

The world is called upon to sympathize with the sufferer; he who at home had been accustomed to the luxury of a bed, groaned the night out in America on the rack of a mattress; and for this the country is to be execrated, and the beautiful scenes of nature beheld with a jaundiced eye.

Finding there was no bed to be procured, I seated myself in a nook of the chimney, called for wine and segars, and either attended to the conversation of the negro-girls who had spread their blankets on the floor, or entertained myself with the half-formed notions of the landlord and coachman, who had brought their chairs to the fire, and were disputing on politics. Both Americans and English are subject to loquacious imbecility. Their subjects only differ. The American talks of his government, the Englishman of himself.

Early in the morning, I resumed my journey in the coach that was proceeding to Savannah; I had but a short distance more to go; for Coosawhatchie is only ten miles from Pocotaligo. In journeying through America, the Indian names of places have always awakened in my breast a train of reflection; a single word will speak volumes to a speculative mind; and the names of Pocotaligo, and Coosawhatchie, and Occoquan, have pictured to my fancy the havoc of time, the decay and succession of generations, together with the final extirpation of savage nations, who, unconscious of the existence of another people, dreamt not of invasions from foreign enemies, or inroads from colonists, but believed their power invincible, and their race eternal.

I was put down at the post office of Coosawhatchie. The post-master was risen, expecting the mail. He invited me to partake of a fire he had just kindled, before which a negro-boy was administering pap to a sickly infant, whom the man always addressed by the Homeric title of "My Son."

Charleston, and on November 27, 1798, the *Columbian Museum and Savannah Advertiser* advertised: "Messrs Williamson and Jones, managers of the Theater in Charleston (South Carolina) announce . . . their intention of performing for a few nights with the Charleston company—to commence in the course of the present week, with a view to establish a regular plan of theatrical Exhibitions in conjunction with their Theaters in Charleston and Savannah." The company opened in Savannah on December 1, 1798, and continued for many nights (Patrick, *Savannah's Pioneer Theater*, 25–32; Curtis, "John Joseph Stephen Leger Sollee," 285).

I sat with the post-master an hour, when I sought out the village tavern, where with some trouble I knocked up a miserable Negress, who, on my entrance, resumed her slumbers on an old rug spread before the embers of the kitchen fire, and snored in oblivion of all care. After all, I know not whether those whose condition wears the appearance of wretchedness, are not greater favorites of nature than the opulent. Nothing comes amiss to the slave; he will find repose on the flint, when sleep flies the eye-lids of his master on a bed of down. I seated myself in a nook of the chimney till daylight, when the landlord came down; and, not long after, a servant was announced with horses, to conduct me to the house of Mr. Drayton.*

An hour's ride through a forest of stately pines, brought me to the plantation, where I was received with much affability, by Mr. Drayton and his lady, and where I was doomed to pass the winter in the woods of Carolina.

Ocean Plantation.—Poetry delightful in Solitude.—Walks in the Woods.—Family of Mr. Drayton.—Midnight Lucubrations.—Sketches of Natural History.—Deer-Hunting.—Remarks on Slaves and Slavery.—Militia of Coosawhatchie District.—A School Groupe.—Journey into Georgia.

In the Woods of South Carolina

Deep in the bosom of a lofty wood,
Near Coosawhatchie's slow revolving flood,
Where the blithe Mocking-bird repeats the lay
Of all the choir that warble from the spray;
Where the soft fawn, and not less timorous hind,
Beset by dogs, outstrip in speed the wind;
Where the grim wolf, at silent close of day,
With hunger bold, comes near the house for prey;
Along the road, near yonder fields of corn,
Where the soft dove resorts at early morn,
There would my breast with love of Nature glow,
And oft my thoughts in tuneful numbers flow;
While friendly George, by ev'ry Muse belov'd,
Smil'd his assent, and all my lays approv'd.

*Thomas Drayton (1758–1825) inherited both Ocean Plantation and Magnolia Plantation from his father, John Drayton (b.1715) in 1799. Ocean was probably named for a landing on the Coosawhatchie River once called Ocean Landing, now Dawson's Landing. Thomas Drayton married Mary Wilson, daughter of planter Algernon Wilson (d. 1774) of St.Paul's Parish. Davis mentions the three oldest Drayton children: William Henry, Sarah "Sally" Daniel, and Maria Sarah. Three more were born later (Taylor, "The Draytons of South Carolina and Philadelphia," 1–25).

About half way on the road from Charleston to Savannah, is situated a little
village called Coosawhatchie, consisting, of a blacksmith's shop, a courthouse,
and a jail. A small river rolls its turbid water near the place, on whose dismal
banks are to be found many vestiges of the Indians that once inhabited them;
and in the immeasurable forests of the neighborhood, (comprehended within the
district of Coosawhatchie) are several scattered plantations of cotton and of rice,
whose stubborn soil the poor negro moistens with his tears, and Whose sore task
/ Does not divide the Sunday from the week!

It was on one of these plantations that I passed the Winter of 1798, and the
Spring of the following year.

I lived in the family of Mr. Drayton, of whose children I had undertaken the
tuition, and enjoyed every comfort that opulence could bestow.

To form an idea of Ocean Plantation, let the reader picture to his imagination
an avenue of several miles, leading from the Savannah road, through a continued
forest, to a wooden house, encompassed by rice-grounds, corn and cotton-fields.
On the right, a kitchen and other offices on the left, a stable and coach-house: a
little further a row of negro-huts, a barn and yard: the view of the eye bounded
by lofty woods of pine, oak and hickory.

The solitude of the woods I found at first rather dreary; but the polite attention of an elegant family, a sparkling fire in my room every night, and a horse
always at my command, reconciled me to my situation; and my impulse to sacrifice to the Muses, which had been repressed by a wandering life, was once more
awakened by the scenery of the woods of Carolina. I indulged in the composition
of lyric poetry, and when I had produced an Ode, transmitted it to Freneau, at
Charleston, who published it in his *Gazette*. But planters have little disposition
for poetry, and the eye of the Carolina reader was diverted from my effusions, by
the more interesting advertisements for fugitive slaves; I was therefore apprehensive that my reputation would not become extended by the Muse.

The country near Coosawhatchie exhibited with the coming Spring a new and
enchanting prospect. The borders of the forests were covered with the blossoms
of the dog-wood, of which the white flowers caught the eye from every part; and
often was to be seen the red-bud tree, which purpled the adjacent woods with
its luxuriant branches; while, not infrequently, shrubs of jessamine, intermixed
with the wood-bine, lined the road for several miles. The feathered choir began
to warble their strains, and from every tree was heard the song of the red-bird, of
which the pauses were filled by the mocking-bird, who either imitated the note
with exquisite precision, or poured forth a ravishing melody of its own.

I commonly devoted my Sundays to the pleasure of exploring the country,
and cheered by a serene sky, and smiling landscape, felt my breast awakened to

the most rapturous sensations. I lifted my heart to that Supreme Being, whose agency is every where confessed; and whom I traced in the verdure of the earth, the foliage of the trees, and the water of the stream. I have ever been of opinion, that God can be as well propitiated in a field as a temple; that he is not to be conciliated by empty protestations, but grateful feelings; and that the heart can be devout when the tongue is silent. Yet there is always something wanting to sublunary felicity, and I confess, I felt very sensibly the privation of those hills which so agreeably diversify the country of Europe.

In my walk to Coosawhatchie I passed here and there a plantation, but to have called on its owner without a previous introduction, would have been a breach of that etiquette which has its source from the depravity of great cities, but has not failed to find its way into the woods of America. When I first beheld a fine lady drawn by four horses through the woods of Carolina in her coach, and a train of servants following the vehicle, clad in a magnificent livery, I looked up with sorrow at that luxury and refinement, which are hastening with rapid strides to change the pure and sylvan scenes of nature into a theatre of pride and ostentation. When Venus enchanted Æneas with her presence in the woods, she was not attired in the dress of the ladies of Queen Dido's court; but, huntress like, had hung from her shoulders a bow, and was otherwise equipped for the toils of the chase.

I remember, with lively pleasure, my residence in the woods of South Carolina. Enjoying health in its plenitude, yet young enough to receive new impressions; cultivating daily my taste by the study of polite literature; blest with the friendship of a George, and living in the bosom of a family unruffled by domestic cares; how could I be otherwise than happy, and how can I refrain from the pleasure of retrospection.

Coosawhatchie! thou shalt not be unknown, if, by what eloquence nature has given me, I can call forth corresponding emotions in the breast of my reader to those which my own felt when wandering silently through thy woods.

My pupils, in the woods of Coosawhatchie, consisted of a boy and two young ladies, William Henry was an interesting lad of fourteen, ingenuous of disposition, and a stranger to fear. He was fond to excess of the chase. His heart danced with joy at the mention of a deer; and he blew his horn, called together his dogs, and hooped and hallooed in the woods, with an animation that would have done honor to a veteran sportsman. O! for the Muse of an Ovid, to describe the dogs of this young Actoeon. There were Sweetlips, and Ringwood, and Music, and Smoker, whose barking was enough to frighten, the wood nymphs to their caves.—His eldest sister Maria, though not a regular beauty, was remarkable for her dark eyes and white teeth, and, what was not less captivating, an amiable temper. She was grateful to me for my instruction, and imposed silence on her brother when I invoked the Muse in school. But it was difficult to control her little sister Sally, whom in sport and wantonness they called Tibousa. This little girl was distinguished by the languish of her blue eyes, from which, however, she could dart fire when William offended her. Sally was a charming girl, whose beauty promised to equal that of her mother.—That I passed many happy hours in watching and assisting the progress of the minds of these young people, I feel no repugnance to acknowledge. My long residence in a country where honor and shame from no condition rise, has placed me above the ridiculous pride of disowning the situation of a Tutor.

Though the plantation of Mr. Drayton was immense, his dwelling was only a log-house; a temporary fabric built to reside in during the winter. But his table was sumptuous, and an elegance of manners presided at it that might have vied with the highest circles of polished Europe. I make the eulogium, or rather exhibit the character of Mr. Drayton, in one word, by saying, he was a Gentleman; for under that portraiture I comprehend whatever there is of honor. Nor can I refrain from speaking in panegyric terms of his lady, whose beauty and elegance were her least qualities; for she was a tender mother, a sincere friend, and walked humbly with her God. She was indeed deserving the solicitude of her husband, who would not suffer the winds of heaven to visit her face too roughly.

It is usual in Carolina to sit an hour at table after supper; at least it was our custom in the woods of Coosawhatchie. It was then I related my adventures, to Mr. and Mrs. Drayton, in the eastern section of the globe, who not only endured my tales, but were elated with my successes, and depressed by my misfortunes.

About ten I withdrew to my chamber and my books, where I found a sparkling fire of wood, and where I lucubrated, smoked segars, and was lost in my own musings. The silence of the night invited meditation; but often was I to be seen at three in the morning sitting before my chamber-fire, surrounded like Magliabechi* by my papers and my books. My study was Latin, and my recreation the Confessions of the eloquent Citizen of Geneva.[†]

But I was not without company. A merry cricket in my chimney-corner never failed to cheer me with his song.—A cricket is not to be contemned. It is related by Buffon[‡] that they are sold publicly in the Asiatic markets; and it is recorded of

---

*Antonio Magliabechi (1633–1714), librarian to Grand Duke Cosimo III, was a bibliophile with a prodigious memory who was famously a sloven.

[†]Confessions of J. J. Rousseau, Citizen of Geneva, published in 1791.

[‡]Georges Louis Leclerc Comte de Buffon (1707–1788), French scientist.

Scaliger * that he kept several in a box. I remember an Ode which I consecrated to my midnight companion.

Ode to a Cricket

LITTLE guest, with merry throat,
That chirpest by my taper's light,
Come, prolong thy blithsome note,
Welcome visitant of night.
Here enjoy a calm retreat,
In my chimney safely dwell,
No rude hand thy haunt shall beat,
Or chase thee from the lonely cell.
Come, recount me all thy woes,
While around us sighs the gale;
Or, rejoic'd to find repose,
Charm we with thy merry tale.
Say what passion moves thy breast:
Does some flame employ thy care
Perhaps with love thou art opprest,
A mournful victim to despair.
Shelter'd from the wintry wind,
Live and sing, and banish care;
Here protection thou shalt find,
Sympathy has brought thee here.

The country in our neighborhood consisted of lofty forests of pine, oak, and hickory. Well might I have exclaimed in the words of my poetical friend: "Around an endless wild of forests lies, And pines on pines for ever meet the eyes!"

The land, as I have before suggested, was perfectly level. Not the smallest acclivity was visible, and therefore no valley rejoiced the sight with its verdure.

The staple commodity of the State is rice, but cotton is now eagerly cultivated where the soil is adapted to the purpose. The culture of indigo is nearly relinquished. It attains more perfection in the East-Indies, which can amply supply the markets of Europe. It is to the crop of cotton that the Planter looks for the augmentation of his wealth. Of cotton there are two kinds; the sea-island and

*Joseph Justus Scaliger (1540–1609) was a French religious leader and scholar compared to Aristotle in his day. Scaliger so appreciated the "music" of hearth-crickets that he kept them in a box in his study.

inland. The first is the most valuable. The ground is hoed for planting the latter part of March; but as frosts are not infrequent the beginning of April, it is judicious not to plant: before that time. Cotton is of a very tender nature. A frost, or even a chilling wind, has power to destroy the rising plant, and compel the Planter to begin anew his toil.

The winds in autumn are so tempestuous, that they tear up the largest trees by the roots. Homer, some thousand years ago, witnessed a similar scene:

> Leaves, arms and trees aloft in air are blown,
> The broad oaks crackle, and the sylvans groan;
> This way and that, the rattling thicket bends,
> And the whole forest in one crash descends.

Of the feathered race, the mocking-bird first claims my notice. It is perfectly domestic, and sings frequently for hours on the roof of a log-house. It is held sacred by the natives. Even children respect the bird whose imitative powers are so delightful.

I heard the mocking-bird for the first time on the first day of March. It was warbling, close to my window, from a tree called by some the Pride of India, and by others the Poison-berry Tree. Its song was faint, resembling that of birds hailing the rising-sun; but it became stronger as the spring advanced. The premices of this mocking songster could not but delight me; and I addressed the bird in an irregular Ode, which Mrs. Drayton did me the honor to approve.

Ode to the Mocking-Bird

SWEET bird, whose imitative strain,
Of all thy race can counterfeit the note,
And with a burthen'd heart complain,
Or to the song of joy attune the throat;
To thee I touch the string,
While at my casement, from the neighb'ring tree,
Thou hail'st the coming spring,
And plaintive pour'st thy voice, or mock'st with merry glee,
Thou bringest to my mind,
The characters we find
Amid the motley scenes of human life;
How very few appear
The garb of truth to wear,
But with a borrow'd voice, conceal a heart of strife.
Sure then, with wisdom fraught,

Thou art by nature taught,
Dissembled joy in others to deride;
And when the mournful heart
Assumes a sprightly part,
To note the cheat, and with thy mocking chide.
But when, with midnight song,
Thou sing'st the woods among,
And softer feelings in the breast awake;
Sure then thy rolling note
Does sympathy denote,
And shews thou can'st of others' grief partake.
Pour out thy lengthen'd strain,
With woe and grief complain,
And blend thy sorrows in the mournful lay;
Thy moving tale reveal,
Make me soft pity feel,
I love in silent woe to pass the day.

The humming-bird was often caught in the bells of flowers. It is remarkable for its variegated plumage of scarlet, green, and gold.

The whip-poor-will, is heard after the last frost, when, towards night, it fills the woods with its melancholy cry of *Whip poor Will*! *Whip poor Will*! I remember to have seen mention made of this bird in a Latin poem, written by an early Colonist. *Hic Avis repetens, Whip! Whip! Will, vocejocosa, Quæ tota verno tempore nocte canit.* *

The note of the red-bird is imitated with nice precision by the mocking-bird; but there is a bird called the loggerhead that will not bear passively its taunts. His cry resembles *Clink, clink, clank;* which, should the mocking-bird presume to imitate it, he flies and attacks the mimic for his insolence. But this only incurs a repetition of the offence; so true is it that among birds as well as men, anger serves only to sharpen the edge of ridicule. It is observable, that the loggerhead is known to suck the eggs of the mocking-bird, and devour the young ones in the nest.

Eagles were often seen on the plantation. The encounter between one of them and a fish-hawk is curious. When the fish-hawk has seized his prey, his object is to get above the eagle; but when unable to succeed, the king of birds darts on him

*Thomas Makin (d. 1733), a Latin tutor and teacher in Philadelphia, was the author. Translated it reads: "Here's Whip-per-will; a bird, whose fancied name / From its nocturnal note imagin'd came."

fiercely, at whose approach the hawk, with a horrid cry, lets fall the fish, which the eagle catches in his beak before it descends to the ground.

The woods abound with deer, the hunting of which forms the chief diversion of the Planters. I never failed to accompany my neighbors in their parties, but I cannot say that I derived much pleasure from standing several hours behind a tree.

This mode of hunting is, perhaps, not generally known. On riding to a convenient spot in the woods, the hunters dismount, take their stands at certain distances, hitch their horses to a tree, and prepare their guns,—while a couple of negroes lead the beagles into the thickest of the forest. The barking of the dogs announces the deer are dislodged, and on whatever side they run, the sportsmen fire at them from their lurking places. The first day two bucks passed near my tree. I had heard the cry of the dogs, and put my gun on a whole cock. The first buck glided by me with the rapidity of lightning; but the second I wounded with my fire, as was evident from his twitching his tail between his legs in the agony of pain. I heard Colonel Pastell* exclaim from the next tree, after discharging his piece, "By heaven, that fellow is wounded, let us mount and follow him,—he cannot run far." I accompanied the venerable Colonel through the woods, and in a few minutes, directed by the scent of a beagle, we reached the spot where the deer had fallen. It was a noble buck, and we dined on it like kings.

Fatal accidents sometimes attend the hunters in the woods. Two brothers a few years ago, having taken their respective stands behind a tree, the elder fired at a deer which the dogs had started; but, his shot being diverted by a fence, it flew off and lodged in the body of his brother. The deer passing on, the wounded brother discharged his gun which had been prepared, killed the animal, and staggering a few paces, expired himself. This disaster was related to me by Colonel Pastell and his son; Major Warley,† and Captain Pelotte,‡ who lived on the neighbouring plantations, and composed our hunting party.

After killing half a dozen deer, we assembled by appointment at some planter's house, whither the mothers, and wives, and daughters of the hunters had got before us in their carriages. A dinner of venison, killed the preceding hunt, smoked before us; the richest Madeira sparkled in the glass, and we forgot, in our hilarity, there was any other habitation for man but that of the woods.

*Probably Col. James Postell (1745–1824), elected sheriff of Beaufort County in 1791, and senator from St. Luke's Parish in 1797.

†This was likely Felix Warley (1747–1814).

‡"Captain Pelotte" was probably Charles Pelot, militia captain and descendent of Swiss immigrant, Rev. Francis Pelot (d. 1774), one of the first settlers of Coosawhatchie. The Pelot and Postell families were intermarried (Moore, Rowland, and Rogers, *History of Beaufort County*, 134, 238, 271, and 299).

In this hunting party was always to be found my pupil William Henry, who galloped through the woods, however thick or intricate; summoned his beagles, after the toil of the chase, with his horn; caressed the dog that had been the most eager in pursuit of the deer, and expressed his hope there would be good weather to hunt again the following Saturday.

I did not repress this ardor in my pupil. I beheld it with satisfaction; for the man doomed to pass every winter in the woods, would find his life very irksome, could he not partake, with his neighbors, in the diversions they afford.

Wolves were sometimes heard on the plantation in the night; and, when incited by hunger, would attack a calf and devour it. One night, however, some wolves endeavoring to seize on a calf, the dam defended her offspring with such determined resolution, that the hungry assailants were compelled to retreat with the tail only of the calf, which one of them had bitten off.

Wild cats are very common and mischievous in the woods. When a sow is ready to litter, she is always enclosed with a fence or rails, for, otherwise, the wild cats would devour the pigs.

I generally accompanied my pupil into the woods in his shooting excursions, determined both to make havoc among birds and beasts of every description. Sometimes we fired in vollies at the flocks of doves that frequent the corn fields; sometimes we discharged our pieces at the wild geese, whose empty cackling betrayed them; and once we brought down some paroquets, that were directing their course over our heads to Georgia. Nor was it an undelightful task to fire at the squirrels on the tops of the highest trees, who, however artful, could seldom elude the shot of my eager companion.

The affability and tenderness of this charming family in the bosom of the woods, will be ever cherished in my breast, and long recorded, I hope, in this page. My wants were always anticipated. The family Library was transported without entreaty into my chamber; paper and the apparatus for writing, were placed on my table; and once having lamented that my stock of segars was nearly exhausted, a negro was dispatched seventy miles to Charleston, for a supply of the best Spanish.

I conclude my description of this elegant family, with an observation that will apply to every other that I have been domesticated in, on the Western Continent; —that cheerfulness and quiet always predominated, and that I never saw a brow clouded, or a lip opened in anger.

One diminution to the happiness of an European in the woods of Carolina, is the reflection that every want is supplied him by slaves. Whatever may be urged on the subject of negroes, as the voice of millions could lend no support to falsehood, so no casuistry can justify the keeping of slaves. That negroes are human beings, is confessed by their partaking with the rest of mankind the faculty of speech, and power of combination. Now no man being born a slave, but with his original rights, the supposed property of the master in the slave, is an usurpation and not a right; because no one from being a person can become a thing. From this conviction should every good citizen promote the emancipation of Negroes in America.

The negroes on the plantation, including house-servants and children, amounted to a hundred; of whom the average price being respectively seventy pounds, made them aggregately worth seven thousand to their possessor.

Two families lived in one hut, and such was their unconquerable propensity to steal, that they pilfered from each other. I have heard masters lament this defect in their negroes. But what else can be expected from man in so degraded a condition, that among the ancients the same word implied both a slave and a thief.

Since the introduction of the culture of cotton in the State of South Carolina, the race of negroes has increased. Both men and women work in the field, and the labor of the rice-plantation formerly prevented the pregnant Negroes from bringing forth a long-lived offspring. It may be established as a maxim that, on a plantation where there are many children, the work has been moderate.

It may be incredible to some, that the children of the most distinguished families in Carolina, are suckled by negro-women. Each child has its Momma, whose gestures and accent it will necessarily copy, for children we all know are imitative beings. It is not unusual to hear an elegant lady say, Richard always grieves when Quasheehaw is whipped, because she suckled him!

Of genius in negroes many instances may be recorded. It is true, that Mr. Jefferson has pronounced the Poems of Phillis Whately, below the dignity of criticism, and it is seldom safe to differ in judgment from the Author of Notes on Virginia.* But her conceptions are often lofty, and her versification often surprises with unexpected refinement. Ladd, the Carolina poet,† in enumerating the bards of his country, dwells with encomium on "Whately's polished verse;" nor is his praise undeserved, for often it will be found to glide in the stream of melody. Her lines on Imagination have been quoted with rapture by Imlay of

*Phillis Wheatley (1753–1784), a slave when she published *Poems on Various Subjects, Religious and Moral*, in London in 1773. In *Notes on the State of Virginia*, Jefferson refers to her poems as "below the dignity of criticism" (XIV).

†Dr. Joseph Brown Ladd (1764–1786), a young Rhode Islander who practiced medicine in Charleston 1783 to 1786, wrote poetry under the pseudonym, "Arouet." His work was widely reprinted in America throughout the 1780s. He introduced the name of Phillis Wheatley in one of his longest poems. Soon after, Ladd was killed in a duel in Charleston over the actress Perdita.

Kentucky,* and Steadman the Guiana Traveller;† but I have ever thought her happiest production, the Goliah of Gath.

Of Ignatius Sancho, Mr. Jefferson also speaks neglectingly; and remarks, that he substitutes sentiment for argumentation. But I know not that argumentation is required in a familiar Epistle; and Sancho, I believe, has only published his Correspondence.‡

Before I quit the woods of Coosawhatchie, it will be expected from me to fill the imagination of my reader with *the vengeful terrors of the rattlesnake,* that meditates destruction to the unwary. Were I really pleased with such tales, I would not content myself with the story of the fascinating power of a rattlesnake over birds, but relate how a negro was once irresistibly charmed and devoured.

Vegetation is singularly quick in the woods of Carolina. Of flowers, the jessamine and woodbine grow wild; but the former differs widely from that known by the same name in England, being of a straw colour, and having large bells. Violets perfume the woods and roads with their fragrance.

In bogs, and marshy situations, is found the singular plant called the flycatcher by the natives, and, I believe, *dionæ muscipula* by botanists. Its jointed leaves are furnished with two rows of strong prickles, of which the surfaces are covered with a quantity of minute glands that secret a sweet liquor, which allures the flies. When these parts are touched by the legs of a fly, the two lobes of the leaf immediately rise, the rows of prickles compress themselves, and squeeze the unwary insect to death. But a straw or pin introduced between the lobes will excite the same motions.

The honey of the bees in Carolina is exquisitely delicious, and these insects are very sagacious in choosing their retreats. They seek lodgings in the upper part of the trunk of the loftiest tree; but here their nests cannot elude the searching eyes

*Gilbert Imlay (1754–1828), army officer and author, the lover of British writer and feminist Mary Wollstonecraft (1759–1797) and the father of her daughter, Fanny. Imlay wrote of Wheatley's poem "On Imagination": "Indeed I should like to be informed what white has written more beautiful lines" (Brown, "Jefferson's Notes on Virginia," 469).

†John Gabriel Stedman (1744–1797) acknowledged the merit of Wheatley's "elegant" poetry in *Narrative of a Five Years' Expedition against the Revolted Negroes of Surinam: In Guiana on the Wild Coasts of South America from the Year 1772, to 1777,* first published in London in 1796.

‡Ignatius Sancho (1729–1780), the first black prose writer published in England, also published poetry, plays, a theory of music, and composed pieces for the violin, flute, and harpsichord, all anonymously. Two years after his death, his *Letters* appeared and became an immediate best-seller, proving "an untutored African may possess abilities equal to a European." Jefferson, in *Notes on the State of Virginia,* wrote: "Ignatius Sancho has approached nearer to merit in composition; yet his letters do more honor to the heart than the head" (XIV).

of the negroes and children. The tree is either scaled, or cut down, the bees are
tumbled from their honeyed domes, and their treasures rifled.

Sic vos non vobis mellificatis Apes!

These are the few observations that I made on the productions of nature before me; a study I have ever considered subordinate, when compared to that of
life. I have used, only the popular names, though without any labour I could have
dignified my page with the terms of the Naturalist, for I had all the Latin phrases
at the end of my pen. But I return from brutes to man, though many readers may
be of opinion that in exhibiting the cruelty and wantonness of planters over their
slaves, I change not the subject.

It appears to me that in Carolina, the simplicity of the first colonists is obliterated, and that the present inhabitants strive to exceed each other in the vanities
of life. Slight circumstances often mark the manners of a people. In the opulent
families, there is always a negro placed on the look-out, to announce the coming
of any visitant; and the moment a carriage, or horseman, is descried, each negro
changes his every day garb for a magnificent suit of livery. As the negroes wear no
shirts, this is quickly effected; and in a few moments a ragged fellow is metamor-
phosed into a spruce footman. And woe to them should they neglect it; for their
master would think himself disgraced, and Sambo and Cuffy incur a severe flogging.

In Carolina, the legislative and executive powers of the house belong to the
mistress, the master has little or nothing to do with the administration; he is a
monument of uxoriousness and passive endurance. The negroes are not without
the discernment to perceive this; and when the husband resolves to flog them,
they often throw themselves at the feet of the wife, and supplicate her mediation.
But the ladies of Carolina, and particularly those of Charleston, have little tenderness for their slaves; on the contrary, they send both their men-slaves and
women-slaves, for the most venial trespass, to a hellish-mansion, called the Sugar-
house:* here a man employs inferior agents to scourge the poor negroes: a shilling

---

*The "Sugar-House," an unfortunate term for the Charleston Work House, stood near
Magazine and Mazyck (now Logan) streets, next to the Old Charleston Jail. Slave owners
paid a fee for slaves to be "sweetened up." They were forced to operate a treadmill for grind-
ing corn by walking on a belt, and were whipped and otherwise tortured. The Work House
was severely damaged in the 1886 earthquake and torn down. An earlier workhouse stood on
the original site of a sugar refinery or sugar warehouse, which may have contributed to the
name. A "sugar house" once stood at the foot of Tradd Street, the site where Chisolm's Rice
Mill was later erected. For a description of the Sugar House, see "Recollections of Slavery by
a Runaway Slave," a narrative serialized in *The Emancipator*, August 23, 1838, Documenting
the American South, University of North Carolina Libraries, docsouth.unc.edu/neh/run
away/runaway.html (accessed April 3, 2012).

for a dozen lashes is the charge: the man, or woman, is stripped naked to the waist; a redoubtable whip at every lash flays the back of the culprit, who, agonized at every pore, rends the air with his cries.

Mrs. D—— informed me that a lady of Charleston, once observed to her, that she thought it abominably dear to pay a shilling for a dozen lashes, and, that having many slaves, she would bargain with the man at the Sugar-house to flog them by the year!

Of the understanding of negroes, the masters in Carolina have a very mean opinion. But it is obvious to a stranger of discernment, that the sentiments of black Cuffy who waits at table, are often not less just or elevated than those of his white ruler, into whose hand, Fortune, by one of her freaks, has put the whip of power. Nor is there much difference in their language; for many planters seem incapable of displaying their sovereignty, by any other mode than menaces and imprecations. Indeed, it must occur to every one, that were things to be re-organized in their natural order, the master would in many parts of the globe, exchange with his servant.

An Englishman cannot but draw a proud comparison between his own country and Carolina. He feels with a glow of enthusiasm the force of the poet's exclamation:*

> Slaves cannot breathe in England!
> They touch our country, and their shackles fall;
> That's noble, and bespeaks a nation proud
> And jealous of their rights?

It is, indeed, grating to an Englishman to mingle with society in Carolina; for the people, however well-bred in other respects, have no delicacy before a stranger in what relates to their slaves. These wretches are execrated for every involuntary offence; but negroes endure execrations without emotion, for they say, "when Mossa curse, he break no bone." But every master does not confine himself to oaths; and I have heard a man say, "By heaven, my Negurs talk the worst English of any in Carolina: that boy just now called a bason a round-something: take him to the driver! let him have a dozen!"

Exposed to such wanton cruelty the negroes frequently run away; they flee into the woods, where they are wet with the rains of heaven, and embrace the rock for want of a shelter. Life must be supported; hunger incites to depredation, and the poor wretches are often shot like the beasts of prey. When taken, the men are put in irons, and the boys have their necks encircled with a "pot-hook."

*From an anti-slavery poem (1784) by English poet William Cowper (1731–1800).

The Charleston papers abound with advertisements for fugitive slaves. I have a curious advertisement now before me.—"Stop the runaway! "Fifty dollars reward! Whereas my waiting fellow, Will, having eloped from me last Saturday, without any provocation, (it being known that I am a humane master) the above reward will be paid to any one who will lodge the aforesaid slave in some jail, or deliver him to me on my plantation at Liberty Hall. Will may be known by the incisions of the whip on his back; and I suspect has taken the road to Coosawhatchie, where he has a wife and five children, whom I sold last week to Mr. Gillespie. A. Levi."

Thus are the poor negroes treated in Carolina. Indeed, planters usually consider their slaves as beings defective in understanding; an opinion that excites only scorn from the philosopher. The human soul possesses faculties susceptible of improvement, without any regard to the color of the skin. It is education that makes the difference between the master and the slave. Shall the imperious planter say, that the swarthy sons of Africa, who now groan under his usurpation of their rights, would not equal him in virtue, knowledge and manners, had they been born free, and with the same advantages in the scale of society? It is to civilization that even Europeans owe their superiority over the savage; who knows only how to hunt and fish, to hew out a canoe from a tree, and construct a wretched hut; and but for this, the inhabitants of Britain had still bent the bow, still clothed themselves in skins, and still traversed the woods.

Cotton in Carolina, and horse-racing in Virginia, are the prevailing topics of conversation: these reduce every understanding to a level, and to these Americans return from the ebullitions of the humorist, as the eye weary of contemplating the sun, rejoices to behold the verdure.

Captain Pelotte, who, I have observed, composed one of our hunting party, having invited me to the review of the Militia of Coosawhatchie district, I rode with him to the muster-field near Bee's-Creek, where his troop was assembled. It was a pleasant spot of thirty acres, belonging to a school-master, who educated the children of the families in the neighborhood.

There is scarcely any contemplation more pleasing than the sight of a flock of boys and girls just let loose from school. Those whom nature designed for an active, enterprising life, will contend for being the foremost to cross the threshold of the school-door; while others of a more wary temper keep remote from the strife. A throng of boys and girls was just released from the confinement of the school, as I reached Bee's-Creek with Captain Pelotte. Our horses and they were mutually acquainted. The beasts pricked up their ears, and some of the children saluted them by name; while some, regardless of both the horses and their riders, were earnestly pursuing butterflies; some stooping to gather flowers; some chanting songs; and all taking the road that led to the muster-field. If ever I felt the nature that breathes through Shenstone's School poem,* it was on beholding this band of little men and little women:

> And now Dan Phoebus gains the middle skie,
> And Liberty unbars her prison-door,
> And like a rushing torrent, out they fly,
> And now the grassy cirque is cover'd o'er
> With boist'rous revel-rout and wild uproar;
> A thousand ways in wanton rings they run,
> Heav'n shield their short-liv'd pastimes, I implore!
> For well may Freedom, erst so dearly won,
> Be to Columbia's sons more gladsome than the sun!

Captain Pelotte having reviewed his soldiers, marched them triumphantly round a huge oak that grew in the centre of the parade, animated by the sound of the spirit-stirring drum; and afterwards laid siege to a dinner of venison in the open air, to which I gave my assistance. It was a republican meal. Captain, Lieutenants, and Privates, all sat down together at table, and mingled in familiar converse. But the troop devoured such an enormous quantity of rice, that I was more than once inclined to believe they had emigrated from China.

On the 7th of April, 1799, I accepted the invitation of a Mr. Wilson,[†] who was visiting the family at Ocean, to accompany him to Savannah; glad with the opportunity to extend my travels into Georgia, and not less happy to cultivate his acquaintance.

We left Ocean plantation at eight in the morning. Mr. Wilson drove himself in a sulky, and I rode on horseback, followed by a servant on another.

The 11th of April, I returned with Mr. Wilson to the woods of Coosawhatchie, which, I found Mr. Drayton and family, about to leave to their original tenants of raccoons, squirrels, and opossums.

My table was covered with letters that were truly Ciceronian, from elegant friend. Mr. George had left the sublime College of Charleston, for a seminary less famous, but more profitable, at George-town, at the confluence of the rivers

---

*From "The School-Mistress, A Poem In Imitation of Spenser" by English poet William Shenstone (1714–1763).

†Wilson was probably one of Mary Drayton's older brothers: Joseph, Thomas, Daniel, John, Jehu, or Algernon Wilson Jr.

Winyaw and Waccamaw. There, in concert with his uncle, an Episcopal Minister,* he enjoyed an elegant society, and indulged in his favorite Studies.

Picture of a Family travelling through the Woods.—Terror inspired by two
Snakes, and the gallantry of an American boy.—Residence at Ashley River.—Removal to Sullivan's Island.—

    It was in the month of May, 1799, that Mr. Drayton and his family exchanged
the savage woods of Coosawhatchie, for the politer residence of their mansion on
Ashley River. In our migration we formed quite a procession. Mr. Drayton occupied the coach with his lady and youngest daughter, and I advanced next with
my fair pupil in a chair, followed by William Henry, on a prancing nag, and half
a dozen negro fellows, indifferently mounted, but wearing the laced livery of an
opulent master. Thus hemmed in by the coach before, a troop of horsemen behind, and impenetrable woods on both sides, I could not refrain from whispering
in the ear of my companion, that her friends had put it out of my power to run
away with her that day.

    About three in the afternoon, our journey being suspended by the heat of the
weather, we stopped to eat a cold dinner, in a kind of lodge that had been erected
by some hunters on the roadside, and which now hospitably accommodated a
family travelling through the woods.

    Here we took possession of the benches round the table to enjoy our repast;
turning horses loose to seek the shade; and cooling our wine in a spring that
murmured near the spot. William Henry, having snatched a morsel, got ready his
fowling-piece, to penetrate the woods in search of wild turkies; and while we were
rallying him on his passion for shooting, the cry from a negro of a rattlesnake!
disturbed our tranquillity. The snake was soon visible to every eye dragging its
slow length along the root of a large tree, and directing its attention to a bird,
which chattered and fluttered from above, and seemed irresistibly disposed to fall
into his distended jaws. London, a negro-servant, had snatched up a log, and was
advancing to strike the monster a blow in the head, when a black snake, hastening
furiously to the spot, immediately gave battle to the rattlesnake, and suspended,
by his unexpected appearance, the power of the negro's arm. We now thought
we had got into a nest of snakes, and the girls were screaming with fright, when,
William Henry, taking an unerring aim with his gun, shot the rattlesnake, in the
act of repulsing his enemy. The black snake, without a moment's procrastination,

---

*Rev. Enoch George (1767–1828) distinguished himself as a Methodist circuit rider and
pastor before he was ordained both deacon and elder by Bishop Asbury. He was appointed
presiding elder of Charleston in 1796. He would be elected and consecrated a bishop in 1816.

returned into the woods, and profiting by his example, we all pursued our journey, except William Henry, who stopped with a negro to take out the rattles of the monster he had killed. My pupil presented me with these rattles, which I carried for three years in my pocket, and finally gave them to the son of a Mr. Andrews, of Warminster, who had emigrated to Baltimore, and had been to me singularly obliging.—*

[*Davis's note:* Much has been said by Travellers of the fascinating power of snakes in America. *Credat Judæus Apella, non Ego!* Things are best illustrated by comparison. It is known almost to every man who has, not passed his days in the smoke of London, Salisbury, or Bristol, but, incited by the desire of knowledge, has made a Tour into the country; I maintain it could not escape the observation of such a Tourist, that birds will flutter their wings, and exhibit the utmost agitation, at the approach of a fox near a tree on which they are perched. Filled with the same dread, a bird in America cannot refrain from fluttering over a snake; and the American snakes, however inferior in cunning to the English foxes, being endued with more perseverance; fear deprives the bird of motion, and it falls into his jaws. It is by thus tracing effects to their causes that truth is promulgated; and hence I am enabled to detect and expose the fallaciousness of the opinion, that there is any charm, or fascination in the eye of a snake.]

We stopped a few days at Stono, where we were kindly received by Mr. Wilson, my late travelling companion into Georgia. I expected that William Henry would receive the applause of his friends for the presence of mind he had displayed in killing the rattlesnake; but when the youngest sister recited the story to the family, they heard her without emotion, and only smiled at it as a trifling incident.

In the venerable mansion at Ashley River, I again directed the intellectual progress of my interesting pupils, and, enlarged the imagination of William, by putting Pope's version of the *Odyssey* into his hands, which I found among other books that composed the family library. He had before read the *Iliad;* but neither Patroclus slain by Hector, nor Hector falling beneath the avenging arm of Achilles, imparted half the rapture which Ulysses inspired with his companions in the cave of Polyphemus. I am of the opinion of Warton, that the great variety of events and scenes exhibited in the *Odyssey,* cannot fail to excite a more lively interest than the martial uniformity of the *Iliad.*

The garden of Mr. Drayton's mansion† led to the banks of Ashley River, which, after a rapid course of twenty miles, discharged itself into the Atlantic.

---

†This was the original house at Magnolia Gardens, burned by Union soldiers in 1865. The nineteenth-century house now on the property was originally the family's hunting lodge. Magnolia Gardens has been open to the public since the 1870s.

The river was not wanting in picturesqueness, and, once, while stretched at my ease on its banks, I meditated an ode:

Ode on Ashley River

ON gentle Ashley's winding flood,
Enjoying philosophic rest;
I court the calm, umbrageous wood,
No more with baleful care opprest.
Or, on its banks supinely laid,
The distant mead and field survey,
Where branching laurels form a shade
To keep me from the solar ray.
While flows limpid stream along,
With quick meanders through the grove,
And from each bird is heard the song
Of careless gaiety and love.
And when the moon, with lustre bright,
Around me throws her silver beam,
I catch new transport from the sight,
And view her shadow in the stream.
While Whip-poor-will repeats his tale,
That echoes from the boundless plain;
And blithsome to the passing gale,
The Mocking-bird pours out his strain.
Hence with a calm, contented mind,
Sweet pleasure comes without alloy
Our own felicity we find—
'Tis from the heart springs genuine joy.

An elder brother of Mr. Drayton was our neighbor on the river; he occupied, perhaps, the largest house and gardens in the United States of America.* Indeed I was now breathing the politest atmosphere in America; for our constant visitants were the highest people in the State, and possessed of more house-servants than there are inhabitants at Occoquan. These people never moved but in a carriage, lolled on sophas instead of sitting on chairs, and were always attended by their negroes to fan them with a peacock's feather. Such manners were ill-suited to an Englishman who loved his ease; and whenever their carriages were announced,

---

*Drayton Hall (ca. 1738) is today the finest example of Georgian architecture in the country. Still held in trust by the family, it has been open to the public since the 1970s.

I always took my gun, and went into the woods. Oh! for a freedom from the restraint imposed by well-bred inanity.

From Ashley River, after a short residence, we removed to Charleston, which was full of visitors from the woods, and exhibited a motley scene. Here was to be perceived a Coachee, without a glass to exclude the dust, driven by a black fellow, not less proud of the livery of luxury, than the people within the vehicle were of a suit made in the fashion. There was to be discovered a Carolinian buck, who had left off essences and powder, and, in what related to his hair, resembled an ancient Roman; but in the distribution of his dress, was just introducing that fashion in Charleston, which was giving way in succession to another in London. But he had an advantage over his transatlantic rival; he not only owned the horse he rode, but the servant who followed. To be brief, such is the pride of the people of Charleston, that no person is seen on foot unless it be a mechanic, or some mechanical Tutor. He who is without horses and slaves, incurs always contempt. The consideration of property has such an empire over the mind, that poverty and riches are contemplated through the medium of infamy and virtue. Even negroes are infected with this idea; and Cuffey shall be heard to exclaim, "He great blackguard that—he got no negur. Where his horse? He alway walk."

I found my friend Doctor De Bow in high repute at Charleston, and not without the hope that he should soon keep his carriage. *Scribimus docti indoctique.* He was busy in writing a piece for the *Medical Repository* at New-York; that is, he was communicating his thoughts in a letter to the great Doctor Mitchel.* His object was to undermine the fame, of the Charleston Physicians, by exposing the impropriety of their treatment in the Croup; a complaint uncommonly prevalent in the southern States of the Union. "This treatise," whispered the Doctor, "will make me be called in to children, and if I once get the child for a patient, I shall soon have the parents. Oh! that I could only express my thoughts on paper! I would carry every thing before me. But writing and talking require very different qualifications. Impudence will make an orator; but to write well requires reading digested by reflection."

The Doctor entreated I would lend him my assistance to write his Essay on the Croup. I begged to be excused, by professing my utter unacquaintance with the mode of treating the disease.

"No matter," said the Doctor. "How to treat the disease no man knows better than I; but treating it, and writing a treatise on it, are things widely different. Come! let me dictate to you the heads of the discourse, and do you *lengthify*

---

*Dr. Samuel Latham Mitchell (1764–1831), cofounder and editor of the *Medical Repository*, the first medical journal in the United States, founded in 1797.

and ramify them secundum artem into a treatise. Quote good deal of Latin, and dignify your style with all the hard words you can remember. But let the title be powerful; let it smite the eye of the reader with irresistible force. For the *Medical Repository!* New, but unanswerable, objections against the present mode of treating the Croup, by the Physicians of Charleston; communicated in a Letter to Dr. Mitchel, by W. De Bow, M. D.—*Nullius addictus jurare in "verba magistri!"*

The Doctor was here interrupted by a negro boy, who called him to attend his master in the last stage of the yellow fever. The Doctor immediately slipped on a black coat, put his enormous spectacles on his nose, and snatching up his goldheaded-cane, followed the negro down stairs.

Having leisure for some literary, undertaking, I issued a prospectus for the publication of Two Voyages to the East-Indies.* The work was to be comprised in an octavo volume, and delivered to subscribers for two dollars. Mr. Drayton, without hesitation, subscribed for ten copies; and in a few weeks I could boast a long list of subscribers from the circles of fashion.

To avoid the fever, which every summer commits its ravages at Charleston, Mr. Drayton removed with his family in July to a convenient house on Sullivan's Island. The front windows commanded a view of the Atlantic, whose waves broke with fury not a hundred yards from the door. It is almost superfluous to observe, that Sullivan's Island lies opposite to Charleston, at the distance of eight miles.

In the garden on our premises, I took possession of a neat little box, which served me for a seminary, and house of repose.—Here I was gratified with the company of Mr. George, who came to visit me from George-town. Not more joyous was the meeting of Flaccus and Maro, at the Appian Way: *O! qui complexus, et gaudia quanta fuerunt!*

He was received with every elegance of urbanity by Mr. and Mrs. Drayton; but he compared our situation to Æneas among the Greeks; *vadimus immixti Danais haud numine nostro.* So natural is it for a wit to ridicule his host.

Passage-boats are always to be procured from Sullivan's Island to Charleston, and I was introduced by my friend to an Irish Clergyman, of the name of Best,[†] who was attached to Mr. George, partly from his being an Irishman, and partly from esteem for his attainments.

Mr. Best communicated to me a few anecdotes relative to Goldsmith, which I minuted down in his presence.

*The book was never published.

[†]William Best, a schoolmaster and member of the faculty at the College of Charleston, was described as "much more than ordinary" as a pedagogue (Easterby, *A History of the College of Charleston*, 40–42).

Mr. Best related to me some anecdotes that would serve to illustrate the "Traveller," which I regret are not preserved, for the "Traveller" is a Poem that is ever read with new rapture. The mind can scarcely refrain from picturing Goldsmith in the capacity of an Adventurer; travelling with an expansion to his mental powers, and feeling the impulse of his poetical genius; observing with a philosophic eye the mingled scenes before him, and framing from their diversity the subject of his poem.

The stone of Sisyphus calling my friend back to George-town, I was once more left to the tuition of William Henry, and his sisters. My pupil was not, I believe, content with his insular situation, but sighed for the woods, his dogs, and his gun. Man laughs at the sports of children; but even their most trifling pastimes form his most serious occupations; and their drums, and rattles, and hobbyhorses, are but the emblems and mockery of the business of mature age.

No families are more migratory than those of Carolina. From Sullivan's island we went again to the mansion on Ashley River, where I had invitations to hunt, to feast and to dance. But nothing could sooth the despondency I felt on the approaching return of Mr. Drayton to the woods of Coosawhatchie. He guessed the cause of my woe-begone looks, and, rather than be deprived of my services, politely offered to pass the winter on the banks of Ashley River: Nay, he even proposed to send his son, when the war terminated to make with me the tour of the Continent of Europe. There are few men that in my situation would have resisted such allurements; but I dreaded the tainted atmosphere that had dispatched so many of my countrymen to the house appointed for all living; and, filled with apprehension, I left this charming family in whose bosom I had been so kindly cherished to seek another climate, and brave again the rigors of adversity.

The fifteenth of December, 1799, I rode from Ashley River to Charleston, with the design of proceeding to George-town, and visiting the academic bowers of my friend. I had again determined to travel on foot, and enjoy the meditations produced from walking and smoking amidst the awful solitude of the woods. Having provided myself with a pouch of Havannah segars, and put a poem into my pocket, which Mr. George had composed over the grave of a stranger on the road, I crossed the ferry at Cooper's-River, and began my journey from a spot that retains the aboriginal name of Hobcaw.

"Taming of the Shrew," 1780. Mrs. Mary Ann Wrighten (Pownall), 1780.
Mezzotint by Robert Laurie, engraver. Courtesy of the Victoria and Albert
Museum, London.

JOHN LAMBERT (1808)

"Look to the Right and Dress!"

Englishman John Lambert (1775–ca. 1816) sailed to the British American colonies in 1806 with his uncle, James Campbell, sanctioned by the London Board to promote the growth of hemp in Canada. When the hemp venture proved unsuccessful, Lambert traveled across Canada and to the United States. He accumulated facts, statistics, and anecdotes with the intention of publishing his travels. From New York, he sailed on the *Calliope* for Charleston. He arrived during the Embargo of 1807, which had closed American ports to trade and left the city stagnant; nevertheless he found much to amuse him, as his account reveals. When the 1813 edition of his published *Travels* was reviewed in England, a critic pointed to Lambert's description of Charleston as written with "particular vivacity," and called it "altogether the best account of this place we remember to have seen." Lambert's account discloses much of Charleston cultural life in the early 1800s, the theater and its stage performers, artists, and cultural institutions at that time. He notes the amusements and entertainments, including the races and the novelty "pleasure garden," Vaux Hall Gardens on Board Street. He satirizes an amusing militia muster he witnessed in a field outside Charleston, from a time when the militia system was in force throughout South Carolina.

Lambert returned to Quebec in 1809 and departed for England. The following year *Travels through Lower Canada, and the United States of North America, in the Years 1806, 1807, and 1808* was published in three volumes. Its great success led him to prepare a second edition in two volumes in 1813, a third one the next year, and a fourth in 1816. The book was a sensation in the absence of much competition immediately before and during the War of 1812.

Lambert mentions in his *Travels* that while he was in New York, Washington Irving, his brother William Irving, and James Kirke Paulding were publishing a satirical periodical called *Salmagundi, or the Whim-wham's and Opinions*

Taken from *Travels through Lower Canada and the United States of America in the Years 1806, 1807, and 1808*, vol. 2 (London: C. Cradock & W. Joy), 1814.

of Launcelot Longstaff, Esq. and Others, a series of essays and poems lampooning New York society and politics. *Salmagundi* was published in twenty paperbound numbers between 1807 and 1808 and was the talk of the Atlantic seaboard. In 1811, Lambert brought out a British edition of *Salmagundi,* which he considered a model of American literature and an example of American manners for an English audience. He edited the publication and wrote a long introductory essay. Nothing further is known of his life.

Lambert's depictions of Canada in his *Travels* turned out to be of real importance; therefore Canadian scholars have tried to uncover further information about his life. There has been an effort to tie him to Englishman Colonel John By (1779–1836), a military engineer in Canada who is identified in the *Travels* as Lambert's "schoolfellow" in England. Carl F. Klinck, a Canadian literary historian, has attempted to connect Lambert to another travel account, *Cursory Observations made in Quebec, Lower Province of Canada, in the Year 1811.* Written under the pseudonym, "Jeremy Cockloft the Elder, Esq.," it identifies a fictional character from Washington Irving's Cockloft family in *Salmagundi. Cursory Observations* bears a striking similarity to Lambert's writing style in his *Travels.* However, no one has yet solved the mystery of what happened to Lambert after around 1816.

SOURCES

Alderman, Ralph M. *Critical Essays on Washington Irving.* Boston: G. K. Hall & Co., 1990.

———, and Wayne R. Kime. *Advocate for America: The Life of James Kirke Paulding.* London: Associated University Presses, 2003.

Baigent, Elizabeth. "Lambert, John." *Oxford Dictionary of National Biography.* Ed. H. C. G. Matthew and Brian Harrison. Oxford, UK: Oxford University Press, 2004.

Fryson, Donald. "Tramping through Quebec of the Past." *Society Pages: The Magazine of the Literary and Historical Society of Quebec* 20 (Summer 2009): 3–5.

Klinck, Carl F. "Salmagundi in Canada." In *The Influence of the United States on Canadian Development: Eleven Case Studies,* ed. Richard A. Preston. Durham, NC: Duke University Press, 1972.

———, and Sandra Djwa. *Giving Canada a Literary History: A Memoir.* Ottawa: Carleton University Press, 1991.

"LOOK TO THE RIGHT AND DRESS!"

The site of Charleston nearly resembles that of New York, being on a point of land at the confluence of the rivers and about fifteen miles distant from the light-house.

The town is built on a level sandy soil, which is elevated but a few feet above the height of spring tides. From its open exposure to the ocean it is subject to storms and inundations, which affect the security of its harbor. The city has also suffered much by fires: the last, in 1796, destroyed upwards of 500 houses, and occasioned 300,000. sterling damage.

The number of dwelling-houses, public buildings, and warehouses, &c. at present in Charleston, is estimated at 3,500. With the exception of Meeting-street, Broad-street, and the Bay, the streets are in general narrow and confined. They are all unpaved; and in blowing weather whirlwinds of dust and sand fill the houses, and blind the eyes of the people. The foot paths are all constructed of bricks; but a few years ago not even this convenience existed. It is said that objections have been made to the paving of Charleston, under an impression that it would render the streets hotter: but this must surely be an erroneous idea; for a sandy soil imbibes the heat much quicker, and retains it longer, than a pavement of stone. Yet even if that were not the case, still the deleterious effect which the sand, exposed to the action of violent winds, must necessarily have upon the eyes and lungs of the inhabitants, would more than counterbalance the increase of heat that it is supposed would accrue from paving the streets. I should, however, rather suspect that it is the expense alone which is objectionable; since the paving of the streets in Philadelphia has rendered that city both healthy and cool, and its salutary effects are obvious to the inhabitants. The drains in Charleston are also too small to carry off the filth and putrid matter which collect from all parts of the town: these, and the numerous swamps and stagnant pieces of water, mud, &c. in the neighborhood, no doubt tend considerably to the unhealthiness of the place.

The houses in the streets near the water side, including that part of the town between Meeting-street and the street called East Bay, are lofty and closely built. The bricks are of a peculiar nature, being of a porous texture, and capable of resisting the weather better than the firm, close, red brick of the northern states. They are made in Carolina, and are of a dark-brown color, which gives the buildings a gloomy appearance. The roofs are tiled or slated. In this part of the town the principal shopkeepers and merchants have their stores, warehouses, and counting-houses. Houses here bear a very high rent: those in Broad and Church-streets for shops, let for upwards of 300l. per annum; those along the Bay with warehouses let for 700l. and more, according to the size and situation of the buildings. The shipping, as at New York, lie along the wharfs, or in small docks and slips along the town. The wharfs are built of a peculiar sort of wood, called the palmetto or cabbage tree, the trunk of which is of a spongy, porous substance, and has the quality of being more durable in water, or under ground, than when exposed to the air. This renders it particularly excellent for the construction of wharfs, piers, &c. The embargo had reached Charleston about a fortnight before I arrived; I had not, therefore, an opportunity of judging of its trade from appearances, as every thing was dull and flat, and all business except the coasting trade completely at a stand.

The houses in Meeting-street and the back parts of the town are many of them handsomely built; some of brick, others of wood. They are in general lofty and extensive, and are separated from each other by small gardens or yards, in which the kitchens and out-offices are built. Almost every house is furnished with balconies and verandas, some of which occupy the whole side of the building from top to bottom, having a gallery for each floor. They are sometimes shaded with Venetian blinds, and afford the inhabitants a pleasant cool retreat from the scorching beams of the sun. Most of the modern houses are built with much taste and elegance; but the chief aim seems to be, to make them as cool as possible. The town is also crowded with wooden buildings of a very inferior description.

Three of the public buildings, and the Episcopal church of St. Michael, are situated at the four corners formed by the intersection of Broad and Meeting-streets, the two principal avenues in Charleston. St. Michael's is a large substantial church, with a lofty steeple and spire. It is built of brick cased with plaster. At present it is not in the best state of repair, yet it is no bad ornament to the town. The Branch Bank of the United States occupies one of the other corners.* This is a substantial, and, compared with others in the town, a handsome building; but from the injudicious intermixture of brick, stone and marble, it has a motley appearance. The body is of red brick; the corners, sides, and front are ornamented and interspersed with stone; pillars of marble adorn the entrance, and a facing of the same covers the front of the ground story. The expense of this building, I understand, was enormous. Another corner of the street is occupied by the gaol, with a courtyard and armory.† This building is no great ornament to the place; but its situation, being nearly central in the city, is well adapted to further the regulations of the police. A guard of about fifty men is maintained by the city, and assembles every evening at the gaol, where it is ready to act in case of disturbance. The men are chiefly foreigners. The negro slaves and servants are not allowed to be out after the beating of the drum at eight o'clock; otherwise they are taken up by the guard when going its rounds, and confined in the gaol. The

*The Bank of the United States was built at 80 Broad Street between 1800 and 1804. The building sold in 1818 to City Council. It is now City Hall.

†From 1802 to 1939, police headquarters was located at the Town Guard House at Broad and Meeting streets, now the Federal Courthouse and Post Office.

master or mistress must pay a dollar before they can be liberated, else the offender receives a flogging at the sugar-house.

The fourth corner is occupied by a large substantial building of brick cased with plaster. The ground floor is appropriated to the courts of law; above that are most of the public offices, and the upper story contains the Charleston Library and Museum.* The lower parts of the building are much out of repair, but the upper apartments are kept in good order. During my stay, I was allowed free access to the library, having been introduced by a friend to Mr. Davidson the librarian.† It was open from nine in the morning till two in the afternoon, and I spent many an hour in it very agreeably. The library contains about 4,000 volumes, well selected and arranged. They are mostly modern publications.

The library contains Boydell's elegant edition of Shakespeare,‡ and the large prints are framed, and hung up round the room. The portraits of the king and queen, belonging to that edition, are placed on either side the doorway leading to the inner room. I was not surprised at the obscurity of their situation, but was astonished to find them exhibited at all; and it is said that some opposition was made to their being put up. There is a large painting, executed by a Mr. White, of Charleston, exhibited in the library, and it is considered a very favorable effort for a young artist.§ The subject is the murder of Prince Arthur. The countenances of the ruffians are scarcely harsh enough, and their figures are not well proportioned. It is, however, a more successful specimen than could possibly be expected in a place where the arts meet with no encouragement, and where genius must resort to agriculture or commerce, to law or physic, if it wishes to avoid starvation! Some new casts from the Apollo Belvidere, Venus de Medicis, Venus rising from the sea, &c. were deposited in the library to be exhibited for a short time. They

*From 1790 to 1835, the Charleston Library Society was located in three rooms on the third floor of the County Court House. From 1807, the collections of the Charleston Museum occupied the same area. An adjacent room housed the library of the Medical Society (Lounsbury, *From Statehouse to Courthouse*, 60).

†John Davidson was librarian for the Charleston Library Society from 1797 to 1813.

‡The Charleston Library Society subscribed to the Boydell engravings. Englishman John Boydell, publisher of reproductions of engravings, produced an edition of Shakespeare's plays with illustrations by the best artists and engravers in England. He raised a list of subscribers and opened the Shakespeare Gallery in London in 1789 to display the work. A nine-volume folio edition was published in 1802, and Boydell printed two-volume elephant folios the next year. By the time of Lambert's visit, the Boydell engravings were controversial due to dissatisfaction with the prints and financial problems (Friedman, "Some Commercial Aspects of the Shakespeare Gallery," 396–401).

§John Blake White (1781–1859) studied painting in London and returned to Charleston in 1802.

were the property of Mr. Middleton,* and had lately arrived from Paris. The library also contains a few natural curiosities, such as fossils, minerals, mammoth bones, snakes, armadilloes, poisonous insects in spirits, &c. and two remarkable deer's horns which were found locked in each other, so as to render it impossible to separate them without breaking. It is supposed that the two animals had been fighting, and had forcibly locked their horns together in the onset, and being unable to extricate themselves, they both perished. A Museum has been lately established by a gentleman, who occupies a room adjoining the library. His collection at present consists chiefly of birds; and I doubt whether the liberality of the inhabitants will enable him to increase it.

It is surprising that the inhabitants of Charleston, after what they have suffered from fevers, should allow so many stagnant pieces of water, and filthy bogs, to remain in different parts of the town and neighborhood, under the very windows of the dwelling-houses. Surely they might fill them up, and prevent such nuisances from affecting the health of the people, as they cannot fail to do in their present state. The salt marshes and swamps around the town, which are situate so low as to be overflowed at high water, or spring tides, cannot be avoided, though they emit a very disagreeable effluvium at night; yet the other nuisances which I have mentioned might be easily removed.

Another very extraordinary, indolent, or parsimonious neglect of their own health and comfort is the filthy and brutal practice of dragging dying horses, or the carcasses of dead ones, to a field in the outskirts of the town, near the high road, and leaving them to be devoured by a crowd of ravenous dogs and turkey buzzards. The latter are large black birds resembling a turkey both in size and appearance; but from their carnivorous nature they have a most offensive smell. They hover over Charleston in great numbers, and are useful in destroying the putrid substances which lie in different parts of the city: for this reason they are not allowed to be killed. The encouragement of these carrion birds, however useful they may be, is extremely improper; for the people, instead of burying putrid substances, or throwing them into the river, are thus induced to leave them upon dunghills, exposed to the action of a powerful sun in the hottest seasons, to be

*The casts likely belonged to John Izard Middleton (1785–1849), who grew up at Middleton Place. Educated at Cambridge, he traveled most of his adult life in France and Italy, where he married the daughter of a Naples banker. He was an amateur artist and archeologist attracted to the ancient sites of Italy, of which he executed drawings between 1808 and 1809. These sketches were published in 1997 in a folio-sized book, *Grecian Remains in Italy: a Description of Cyclopian Walls, and of Roman Antiquities* (Norton, "First American Classical Archaeologist," 8–9; Robert Behre, "Painting Has Ties to Local Plantation," [Charleston, S.C.] *Post and Courier*, June 8, 2009).

destroyed by those birds. The latter, though extremely quick in devouring their dainty morsels, yet do not demolish them before the air is impregnated with the most noxious effluvia, arising from the putrid carcasses of dead dogs, cats, horses, &c. I have frequently seen half a dozen dogs and above a hundred turkey buzzards barking and hissing in fierce contention for the entrails, eyes, and other delicate *morceaux* of a poor unfortunate horse, whose carcass would perhaps lie so near the side of the road, that, unless passengers were to windward, they ran no little risk from the infectious vapors that assailed their olfactory nerves. A part of the common at the back of the town is a perfect Golgotha; where piles of horses' bones serve the negro-washerwomen to place their tubs on.

Such neglect on the part of the municipal officers, respecting these nuisances, would be unpardonable in any populous town; but how culpable must it be in a large city, like Charleston, whose local situation is unavoidably unwholesome! Every year increases the fatal experience of its inhabitants; and yet they neglect the only remedies which are acknowledged to be effectual, viz. a clean town and a pure air. These might be obtained, if not wholly, at least in part, by paving the streets; cleansing and enlarging the common sewers; filling up bogs, ditches, and pools of stagnant filth, with earth; cutting down the poisonous trees which line the streets, and planting others possessed of more wholesome properties; draining the useless marshes in the neighborhood, and confining the tide within certain bounds; adopting useful regulations for the prevention of disease, and maintaining the streets and habitations in a constant state of cleanness. The inhabitants are rich enough to carry into execution these improvements, nor would their time and money be spent in vain; for, as the town increased in healthiness, so it would increase in population, wealth, and splendor, and rival, in trade and commerce, the richest cities of the north.

The principal public buildings, besides those which I have already enumerated, are the exchange, a large respectable building situated in the East Bay, opposite Broad street; a poor-house;* a college, or rather grammar-school; a theatre; and an orphan-house.† This latter building is worthy of the city of Charleston. It is built at the back of the town, on the site of an old fortification, which, in the American war, proved the chief defense of the town when besieged by Sir Henry Clinton. The house is an extensive and commodious building of brick, and was erected in 1792. The establishment resembles our asylum for female orphans,

*The Poor House, Charleston Jail, and Work House stood between Queen, Franklin, Magazine and Logan streets, which, with the Marine Hospital, represented a block of medical, penal, and charitable institutions.

†The Charleston Orphan House, which stood at 160 Calhoun Street, was the first municipal orphanage in the country. The building, remodeled in the 1850s, was one of Charleston's most beautiful and imposing buildings. It was demolished in 1951.

except that it is not confined to girls only. It contains about 150 children of both
sexes, and the annual expense for provision, clothing, firewood, &c. is about
14,000 dollars, which is defrayed by the legislature of the State of South Carolina. Since its institution, upwards of 1,700 boys and girls have been received
into the house. The boys are supported and educated to the age of fourteen, and
are taught reading, writing, and arithmetic: the girls are supported and educated
until twelve years of age, and are taught the same, besides sewing and spinning.
They are then bound out to some respectable citizen for a term of service, and
distributed into nine classes; one of which is assigned to each commissioner of the
orphan-house, who visits them occasionally, and sees that proper attention is paid
to them by the persons to whom they are indented. The girls of this institution
spin and card as much cotton (which is given to the institution by charitable persons) as supplies both the boys and girls with summer clothes. On every Sunday
morning a suitable discourse is read to the children, by one of the commissioners
in rotation, at which time they repeat their catechism; and in the afternoon of
that day divine service is performed by some one of the ministers of the gospel
from the city or parts adjacent, in a chapel erected adjoining the orphan-house,*
which is also open to the inhabitants. As there is no established form of worship
in the United States, the Episcopal, Presbyterian, and Independent ministers of
Charleston perform service alternately, in the form of their respective persuasions.
It was intended to have appointed a regular minister; but there was such a difference of opinion as to what sect he should be chosen from, that the subject was
dropped. Baptists and Methodists, &c. are, I believe, excluded from performing
service in the orphan-house chapel. I attended one Sunday, and heard Dr. Buist,
the Presbyterian minister.† The chapel is small, and was crowded with people: it
put me in mind of the Asylum, or Magdalen, in every thing, except paying for
admittance, which is dispensed with at Charleston.

The theatre is a plain brick building, situated at the top of Broad-street.‡ It
is about the size of our Circus or Surrey theatre, but not so handsomely fitted
up. The establishment seems to be at present upon a very indifferent footing,
particularly since the embargo, which in the course of a month reduced the performers to half-pay. The present manager is a Mr. Placide.§ He married one of the

*The Orphan House Chapel (ca. 1801) stood on Vanderhorst Street. It was razed in 1953.
†Rev. George Buist (1770–1808), pastor of First Scots Presbyterian Church.
‡The Charleston or New Theater stood at Broad and Savage streets. The building was designed by architect James Hoban, designer of the White House. The exterior was described
as unattractive, but the interior was said to be elaborate.
§Alexander Placide (1750–1812), dancer, pantomime, and acrobat, established a reputation in France and England before coming to the United States. He first appeared on the

daughters of Mrs. Wrighten, originally a favorite singer at Vauxhall. She went to America, with many others of our theatrical heroes and heroines, and, like several of them, found an untimely grave at Charleston.* Mr. Hatton of the Haymarket theatre was engaged by the Charleston manager, and arrived in that city early in 1807. In the course of the summer he sang at the Vauxhall gardens, and in a few weeks fell a victim to the yellow fever. Mrs. Hatton[†] had a benefit afterwards at the theatre, and returned home the following spring. Among the female performers Mrs. Woodham[‡] is considered in every respect as the best. She possesses youth, beauty, and talents, attractions which never fail to captivate an audience, and consequently she is a great favorite with the Charlestonians. Her husband died while I was in Charleston:[§] he was a performer in the orchestra, but had

---

Charleston stage in 1791 as "the first Rope Dancer to the King of France and his Troup." He returned in 1794 with his "wife," a beautiful and accomplished actress known as "Madame Placide," and a troupe of French comedians and pantomimes. Placide took over the management of the Charleston Theater from 1800 to 1825, which resulted in the most flourishing period of theater in the city's history (Hoole, *Antebellum Charleston Theatre*, 3–6; Rogers, *Charleston in the Age of the Pinckneys*, 112; Chevalley, "The Death of Alexander Placide," 63–66).

*Mary Ann (Wrighten) Pownall, English actress-singer and composer, had a successful career in England. In 1792 she came to America and participated in some of the earliest American performances of opera and oratorio. She performed French and English songs during the Charleston theatrical season of 1795, "the most brilliant music year that music-loving Charleston people has yet known." Her two young daughters made their theatrical debuts in Charleston. In 1796, her daughter, Charlotte Sophia Wrighten, eloped with Alexander Placide, who everyone assumed was already married. Pownall ran a notice in the Charleston newspaper cancelling a performance that, due to "an unforeseen and unnatural change" that had "taken place in her family," she was "rendered totally incapable of appearing." "Prostrate with shock," she died eight days later at the age of forty. Twelve days later, Charlotte Sophia's twin sister, pining for her mother, died (Glickman and Schleifer, eds., *Composers: Music through the Ages* 4: 205–16; Willis, *The Charleston Stage in the XVIII Century*, 36).

[†]Anne Julia Kemble Hatton (1764–1838), wife of the theater manager mentioned, was a member of a family of famous English actors. Her parents were Roger Kemble and Sarah Ward Kemble; her sister, the famous actress Sarah Siddons; her brother, John Philip Kemble; and her aunt, actress Fanny Kemble. In 1794, she premiered "Tammany: The Indian Chief" on Broadway, the first known opera libretto written by a woman. After her husband's death, she wrote popular novels in England under the pen name "Anne of Swansea."

[‡]Mrs. George Woodham was a successful comedian and dancer.

[§]Mr. George Woodham was one of a number of stage actors whose deaths occurred in Charleston. Among them were Mrs. Pownall and her daughter, Mary Wrighten; Mrs. Williamson, known as actress Louisa Fontenelle (1773–1799),who died of yellow fever at the age of twenty-six; Mr. Edward Jones; and theater owner John Bignall (Willis, *Charleston Stage in the XVIII Century*, 442; Lindsay, *Burn's Encyclopedia*, "Louisa Fontelle").

originally made his appearance on the stage. Mr. Sully* is a most excellent comic
actor, and trampoline performer. A young gentleman of considerable property,
and respectable family, is married to one of his sisters, who was also a performer
on the stage.

Mr. Cooper[†] generally performs at the Charleston theatre every summer, and
never fails to draw crowded houses even in the most sultry weather. He dashes
about in a curricle; and after remaining about a fortnight in the city, he returns
to the northward with replenished pockets, if they are not previously emptied by
extravagance. A good benefit is reckoned to produce about eight hundred dollars.
One side of the theatre is in the rules of the gaol; which is a very convenient circumstance for the ladies of easy virtue and others who are confined in durance vile.
I expected to find the Charleston stage well supplied with negroes, who would
have performed the African and Savage characters, in the dramatic pieces, to the
life; instead of which the delusion was even worse than on our own stage; for so
far from employing real negroes, the performers would not even condescend to
blacken their faces, or dress in any manner resembling an African. This I afterwards
learnt was occasioned by motives of policy, lest the negroes in Charleston should
conceive, from being represented on the stage, and having their color, dress, manners,
and customs imitated by the white people, that they were very important personages; and might take improper liberties in consequence of it. For this reason, also,
"Othello" and other plays where a black man is the hero of the piece are not allowed

*Actor Matthew Sully, Jr., (d.1812) was the son of Matthew Sully (1769–1815), a promi-
nent English Harlequin, tumbler, and singer at Sadler's Wells before he and his wife, Sarah,
brought their children to America in 1792. They settled in Charleston, where the entire family performed on the local stage. There were four sons and six daughters. Five actress-daugh-
ters married in Charleston. Julia Sully married Jean Belzon or "Zolbius," actor and theater
artist, French miniaturist, and drawing master. Charlotte Sully married the famous English actor-comedian Robert Chambers. Harriett Sully married Dr. Josiah Dupre Porcher, a
Charleston professor. Jane Sully married J. B. LeRoy of Charleston. Elizabeth Sully eloped
with Henry Middleton Smith, owner of a large Goose Creek plantation. Another son, Chester Sully (1781–1834), became a well known cabinet and furniture maker in Virginia. The
youngest member of the family, Thomas Sully (1783–1872), became the nationally known
artist (Rogers, *Charleston in the Age of the Pinckneys*, 112; Willis, *Charleston Stage in the
XVIII Century*, 188–91; Davidson, *The Last Foray*, 137; Highfill, Burmin, and Langhans, *Dictionary of Actors, Actresses, Musicians, Dancers, Managers & Other Stage Personnel in London*,
339).
†Thomas Abthorpe Cooper (1775–1849) was an English tragedian and the foremost inter-
preter of Shakespeare in the United States. He first appeared at the Charleston Theater in
1806 and became a favorite of Charleston audiences for the next thirty years. He befriended
many locals, who entertained him during his stays.

to be performed;* nor are any of the negroes or people of color permitted to visit the theatre. During my stay in Charleston the "Travellers" was performed for Mrs. Placide's benefit; the last act was converted wholly into an American scene, and the allusions and claptraps transferred from an English Admiral to an American Commodore. In this manner most of our dramatic pieces are obliged to be pruned of all their luxuriant compliments to John Bull, before they can be rendered palatable to American republicans. Some few, however, inadvertently escape the pruning-knife of the manager; and I was not a little amused sometimes to hear the praises of my country warmly applauded in the theatre, while whole coffee-houses of politicians would be up in arms at the bare mention of its name.

The garden dignified by the name of Vauxhall is also under the direction of Mr. Placide.† It is situated in Broad-street, a short distance from the theatre, surrounded by a brick wall, but possesses no decoration worthy of notice. It is not to be compared even with the common tea-gardens in the vicinity of London. There are some warm and cold baths on one-side for the accommodation of the inhabitants. In the summer, vocal and instrumental concerts are performed here, and some of the singers from the theatre are engaged for the season. The situation and climate of Charleston are, however, by no means adapted for entertainments *al fresco.* The heavy dews and vapors which arise from the swamps and marshes in its neighborhood, after a hot day, are highly injurious to the constitution, particularly while it is inflamed by the wine and spirituous liquors which are drunk in the garden. It is, also, the period of the sickly season when the garden is open for public amusement, and the death of many performers and visitors may be ascribed to the entertainments given at that place.

There are four or five hotels and coffee-houses in Charleston; but, except the Planters' hotel in Meeting-street,‡ there is not one superior to an English public-house. The

---

*According to Stanley Hoole, Thomas Cooper performed *Othello* during the 1808–9 seasons, and other actors played him later on the Charleston stage. In the South, *Othello* was performed more times than any Shakespearean play except *Hamlet,* although the Othello character appeared increasingly "oriental" over the years (Hoole, *Antebellum Charleston Theatre,* 8–9; for more on William Gilmore Simms, see Christy Desmet, "Confession; or, the Blind Heart: An Antebellum Othello," *Journal of Shakespeare and Appropriation* 1, no. 1 [Spring–Summer 2005]: 1–25).

†Around 1800, Alexander Placide opened Vauxhall Gardens, a "circus" or pleasure garden where music and pantomimes were performed and ice cream and cold baths were offered to the public. It was located at the present site of the Cathedral of St. John the Baptist on Broad Street (Fraser, *Reminiscences of Charleston,* 97).

‡Mrs. Alexander Calder and her husband operated the Planters Hotel at the corner of Meeting and Queen streets. In January 1809, she ran an ad in the *Charleston Courier* informing

accommodations at the Planters' hotel are respectable, and the price about twelve dollars a-week. There are several private boarding-houses, from seven to fourteen dollars per week, according to their respectability. A curious anecdote is related of a lady who keeps the best boarding-house in the city. Soon after she became a widow, an old Scotch gentleman, a merchant of Charleston, paid his addresses to her, and solicited her hand in marriage. The courtship proceeded for a decent length of time, in order that it might not be said she wished to marry before her first "dear man" was cold in his grave. She then very willingly consented to throw off her weeds, and put on the bridal dress. But whether the old gentleman repented of his hasty love, or had some private reason for declining the marriage, I know not: he, however, put off the nuptial ceremony from time to time until his fair *inamorata* became impatient, and demanded the fulfillment of his promise, which it seems the old gentleman had unluckily given. He was now under the necessity of coming to an *éclaircissement,* and positively refused to marry her, giving as a reason that he understood she was rather too fond of the bottle. This false and scandalous accusation highly incensed the lady; and finding that he was going to reside in England, she disposed of her house and property, and followed him to London, where she commenced an action against him for breach of promise, and for defamation. The damages were laid at several thousand pounds, and eminent counsel were retained for the cause. The old gentleman finding himself so closely pressed, and likely to be a great loser by his unfortunate courtship, would have willingly married her rather than have to pay such enormous damages. This would very likely have taken place, for the lady herself was by no means hard-hearted, and might perhaps have taken the old spark to her bed, had not a keen relation of his, who probably was looking forward to a snug little legacy, said to him: "Why, mon, would you disgrace the blood of the M'Cl——s?" and offered to settle the dispute with the spirited widow. Matters were accordingly adjusted in an amicable manner: the lady withdrew her action, and the old gentleman paid her 700l. and all expenses. She afterwards returned to Charleston, and opened a very handsome boarding-house, which is resorted to by all the fashionable strangers who arrive in the city. The old gentleman has visited Charleston several times since to recover his outstanding debts and property, and I dare say never passes her house without a sigh for the loss of both wife and cash.

----

her patrons that she had "purchased from Major John Ward the large and commodious house at the corner of Church and Queen streets." The Calders relocated the hotel to the site of what is now the Dock Street Theater at 135 Church Street (Robert Stockton, "Do You Know Your Charleston," *News & Courier,* July 16, 1973).

Charleston contains a handsome and commodious market-place, extending from Meeting-street to the water-side, which is as well supplied with provisions as the country will permit. Compared, however, with the markets of the northern towns, the supply is very inferior both in quality and quantity. The beef, mutton, veal, and pork, of South Carolina are seldom met with in perfection; and the hot weather renders it impossible to keep the meat many hours after it is killed. Large supplies of corned beef and pork are brought from the northern states. Though the rivers abound with a great variety of fish, yet very few are brought to market. Oysters, however, are abundant, and are cried about the streets by the negroes. They are generally shelled, put into small pails, which the negroes carry on their heads, and sold by the measure: the price is about 8d. per quart. Vegetables have been cultivated of late years with great success, and there is a tolerable supply in the market. The long potato is a great favorite with the Carolinians. There are two kinds, which differ in nothing but the color. When boiled, they eat sweet, and mealy, resembling very much a boiled chestnut. Apples, pears, and other fruit are very scarce, being only brought occasionally from the northern states. In summer Charleston is tolerably well supplied with the fruits peculiar to southern climates; and large quantities of pineapples, &c. are brought from the West Indies. Wild ducks, geese, turkeys, and other fowl, are brought to market by the country people, though not in very great abundance.

The expense of living at Charleston may be estimated from the following table of commodities, the prices of which are in sterling money. Bread about 3d. per lb., butter 7d., cheese 6d., beef 5d., mutton 6d., veal 8d., oysters 8d. per quart, Hyson tea 6s. per lb., coffee 1s. 6d., Havannah sugar 6d., Louisiana sugar 6 1/2d., loaf sugar 1s., brandy 7s. per gallon, Jamaica rum 7s., New England rum 3s. 6d., Hollands 7s., Malaga wine 5s. 10d., Claret 12s. per dozen, spermaceti oil 5s. 3d. per gallon, lamp oil 3s., Florence oil 3s. per pint. Bottled porter, from London, 2s. 3d. per bottle. House rent from 30l. to 700l. per annum, boarding at taverns and private houses from a guinea and a half to three guineas per week, washing 3s. 6d. per dozen pieces, a coat from 5l. 10s. to 8l., other apparel in proportion; hair-cutting 3s. 6d., hire of a horse for a couple of hours 5s., for the afternoon 10s., hire of a gig 15s. Though liquor and many other articles are reasonable when purchased in any quantity, yet they are retailed at the taverns and small spirits-shops at an exorbitant rate. Hence a glass of brandy or rum and water is never sold for less than half a dollar; and every thing else in proportion.

Charleston has been described as the seat of hospitality, elegance, and gaiety. Whatever it may boast of the former, it is certain there was very little of the latter on my arrival in that city, though it was the season for amusements. But the fatal fever which had prevailed the preceding autumn, and carried off great numbers of the people, added to the general stagnation of trade occasioned by the embargo, seemed to have paralyzed the energies and damped the spirits of the inhabitants, and prevented them from partaking of those entertainments and diversions to which they were accustomed at that season of the year.

Genteel society in Charleston is confined to the planters, principal merchants, public officers, divines, lawyers, and physicians.

The planters are generally considered as the wealthiest people in the state. This may be true with respect to their landed property and slaves: but they are not the most moneyed people; for, except upon their annual crops of rice and cotton, which produce various incomes from 6,000 to 50,000 dollars, they seldom can command a dollar in cash, and are besides continually in debt. The long credit which merchants and traders throughout Charleston are obliged to give the planters and other people of property in the state, is the subject of universal complaint among the former; and whatever credit the Carolinians may deserve for their "unaffected hospitality, affability, ease of manners, and address," so flatteringly mentioned in every edition of Morse's Geography,* yet the payment of their debts can never be reckoned among their virtues.

When they receive money in advance for their crops of cotton or rice, it is immediately squandered away in the luxuries of fashion, good eating and drinking, or an excursion to the northern states; where, after dashing about for a month or two with tandems, curricles, livery servants, and outriders, they frequently return home in the stage coach with scarcely dollars enough in their pocket to pay their expenses on the road. If their creditors of ten or a dozen years standing become very clamorous, a small sum is perhaps paid them in part, unless the law interferes, and compels them to pay the whole debt and as much for costs. Thus the planter proceeds in his career of extravagance, which in the midst of riches renders him continually poor. With an estate worth 200,000 dollars he has seldom a dollar in his pocket but what is borrowed upon an anticipated crop: hence it may be truly said that he lives only from hand to mouth.

In the town of Charleston, where they for the most part have handsome houses, they live for the time being like princes: and those strangers who visit the city at that period, and have the means of being introduced at their houses, are sure to meet a hearty welcome. Every article that the market can supply is to be found at their festive board. The wine flows in abundance, and nothing affords them greater satisfaction than to see their guests drop gradually under the table after dinner. Hospitality is indeed their characteristic as long as the cash lasts:

*Rev. Jedidiah Morse (1761–1826) wrote *American Universal Geography*, the earliest American geography, in which he made a few flattering remarks about Charleston.

but when that is gone they retire to their plantations. There they are obliged to dispense with the luxuries, and often with the comforts, which they enjoyed in town. Every thing is made subservient to the cultivation of cotton and rice for the next year's round of dissipation. With hundreds of slaves about them, and cattle of various kinds, they are often without butter, cheese, and even milk, for many weeks. Fodder is frequently so scarce, that the cows, horses, &c. look half starved, and are driven into the pine barrows and woods to pick up a few mouthfuls of rank grass. The habitations of many of the planters are also in a dilapidated state, and destitute of the comforts and conveniences of domestic life. As to their negro-huts, they frequently defy all description.

This mode of living among the planters, of which the brilliant side only is exposed to public view, is followed more or less by most of the gentry in Charleston, and has led strangers to give them the character of a free, affable, and generous people. Others, however, who have had better opportunities of judging of their real character, charge them with ostentation, and a haughty supercilious behavior. These opposite qualities, no doubt, attach individually to many of the inhabitants, and most perhaps to the planters, who, it is natural to suppose, consider themselves in a more elevated and independent situation than the merchants who dispose of their produce, or the traders who furnish them with the necessaries of life. Hence they may be somewhat tinctured with that pride and haughtiness with which they are charged. At the same time their free and extravagant style of living, their open and friendly reception of strangers and visitors at their table, have no doubt won the hearts of those who have partaken of their good cheer, and established that excellent character which is said to be predominant among them.

Unlike the farmer and merchant of the northern states, who are themselves indefatigably employed from morning to night, the Carolinian lolls at his ease under the shady piazza before his house, smoking segars and drinking sangoree; while his numerous slaves and overseers are cultivating a rice swamp or cotton field with the sweat of their brow, the produce of which is to furnish their luxurious master with the means of figuring away for a few months in the city, or an excursion to the northward.

Property thus easily acquired is as readily squandered away; and the Carolinian, regarding only the present moment for the enjoyment of his pleasures, runs into extravagance and debt.

Where there are numerous borrowers, there will always be plenty of lenders; and many of the more shrewd and saving moneyed people of Charleston are ever ready to accommodate the rich, the gay, and the extravagant, with loans upon good security. Even some of the divines in that city are not ashamed to take an active part in money lending; and while they are preaching to their creditors the necessity of laying up a store in heaven, "where neither moth nor rust doth corrupt," they are busily employed in laying up for themselves a store of the good things of this world. How seldom is it that precept and example are united in the same person!

The merchants, traders, and shopkeepers of Charleston are obliged to lay a profit, frequently of 150 or 200 per cent. and more, upon their goods, for the long credit which the gentry are accustomed to take. Where they meet with good payments, they seldom fail to realize an independent fortune; for they sell nothing under 50 per cent, even for ready money: but it often happens that, after they retire from business, they have a number of debts to collect in. I met with several Scotch gentlemen at Charleston and Savannah, who had retired from business at those places, and resided in their native country, but were obliged to make frequent voyages to America to recover the remainder of their property. This is the case with most of those who have been in business in the towns of the southern states; but where one succeeds, twenty are ruined. Captain Turner, my fellow-passenger in the packet, told me that he had debts owing to him of twenty years standing, even by parents and their children, whose dancing had never been paid for by either generation.

Notwithstanding the vast sums of money lavished away by the planters and gentry of South Carolina, their equipages do not equal those of the northern states. They have certainly a greater number of slaves to attend them, but their coaches, carriages, and chaises, are mostly old and shabby. They have some excellent horses; but in general they are badly broke in, and will start and fly at almost every object they meet. Horse-racing is a favorite amusement with the Carolinians, though more discountenanced than formerly, many families having suffered greatly by the gambling bets made at the races. The Charleston races were held during my stay in that city. They commenced on Wednesday the 17th of February, and finished on the Saturday following. The first day, seven horses ran for a purse of 600 dollars; the second day, five for 400 dollars; the third day, three for 300 dollars; and the last day, a handicap purse of about 500 dollars was run for by all the horses that were distanced the preceding days. The race-course is about a mile and half from the city, on a fine level piece of ground, a full mile in circumference.* Four-mile heats are run for, by American-raised horses, and generally performed in eight minutes, though on the second day of the races this year one of the heats was performed in seven minutes.

*In 1792, The S.C. Jockey Club opened the Washington Race Track at what is now Hampton Park. The Jockey Club was founded as part of a fifteen-track circuit of jockey clubs that existed in the state during the antebellum period.

The races are under the direction of a jockey-club, from whose fund the purses which are run for are prepared. The second day of the races was uncommonly hot for the month of February. The thermometer stood at 82° in the shade, and the number of horses and vehicles of every description, passing to and from the race-ground, made the dust and sand fly about in clouds. The admittance to the race course was half a dollar for horses, and a dollar for carriages. There was not so large a concourse of people on the race-ground as I expected to see, and I was told that the races were very thinly attended. From the dullness of the times, the planters were short of cash, and many would not come into town. The purses were therefore poor, and few bets were made. But the preceding year, a purse of 1,000 dollars was run for, and two or three young ladies entered into the spirit of horse-racing with as much eagerness as the men. They sent their own horses to run, and betted with each other to a considerable amount.

Several large booths were fitted up at one end of the race-ground, and handsome cold collations of meat, poultry, and salads, were laid out on long tables for the accommodation of those who chose to dine there after the races. The day I was there, there were only two four-mile heats, and they were over before two o'clock. The gentry then returned to town, and spent the day in dinner parties, and the evening in balls and concerts. The middling and lower classes of the people remained on the ground, and diverted themselves with some hack races; after which they repaired to the booths, and finished the day in humble imitation of their superiors. A number of sailors enjoyed themselves with their girls, in the smaller booths; and the negroes, with their dingy misses, came in for a share of the fun. At night they all came reeling into town, well charged with wine, rum-punch, gin sling, and sangoree.

The period of the races, though short, was the only time that Charleston appeared to be enlivened during my residence there. There were no public entertainments, except occasional plays, and a concert once a fortnight; and they were so slightly attended, that the performers at the theatre were put on half-pay, and the concerts were with difficulty maintained. Private parties were also greatly abridged, and the town seemed to be enveloped in gloomy despondence. This was the natural effect of the stagnation of trade created by the embargo, which compelled the planters to sell their produce for less than one-half the usual price; and it was not always they could find purchasers, even on those conditions; as none, except a few speculating individuals from New-York and Boston, would lay out their money in cotton and rice, which frequently became a mere drug in the merchants' stores.

Hunting, shooting, fishing, and riding, are more or less the diversions of the Carolinians throughout the state. They are generally excellent shots, and a good

rifleman will be sure of a deer, or wild turkey, at 150 yards. A huntsman with
a smooth-barrelled gun will kill a deer at his utmost speed at the distance of
near 100 yards. In the lower country, deer-hunting is the favorite amusement of
the country gentlemen. For this purpose they associate in hunting clubs once a
fortnight or month, besides their own private sport. The bays and woods afford
a great plenty of this game; and when the deer are roused by the hounds, they
are either shot down immediately by the gentlemen who are stationed on either
side the bays, or they meet their fate at the different stands by which the deer
direct their course, and to which the huntsmen had previously repaired. Double-
barrelled guns are mostly used in these cases, loaded with buck shot, and sometimes with single ball; and so excellent is the skill of many persons accustomed
to this mode of hunting, that a deer has been often killed by each barrel of the
gun, as soon as they could be successively discharged. Sometimes the deer are seen
in flocks of eight or ten in number; and as many as four or five have been killed
in a single hunting of a few hours. The country gentlemen do not enter much
into the sport of fowling, Carolinians generally preferring riding to walking; and
when game of this kind is wanted for family use, they for the most part send out
a servant to procure it.

In the upper part of the State, the young men are particularly expert at rifle-
shooting; and articles instead of being put up at vendue are often shot for, with
rifles, at a small price each shot, which is a more useful and honorable mode than
the practice of raffling adopted in the lower country. This method of disposing
of goods is worthy of imitation in England, and would soon render the people
excellent marksmen. Although a riding-master is little known in Carolina, yet the
people are generally good horsemen, and make their way through thick woods
with surprising dispatch. This is effected by allowing boys at the age of seven or
eight years to commence riding, either to school or elsewhere; and soon after
they are allowed the use of a gun, from which they in a few years become expert
huntsmen.

The Carolinians are all partial to riding, and even in Charleston few ladies
venture to walk. They are seldom seen out of doors, except in their coach or
chaise. This renders the streets of that city very gloomy to a stranger who has been
used to the Bond-street of London, the Rue St. Honoré of Paris, or the Broadway
of New York, where so many lovely forms continually fleet before his eye. Many
of the ladies of Charleston are, however, not inferior in beauty and accomplishments to the ladies of the Northern States, though they labor under the disadvan-
tage of an unhealthy climate. If the younger part of society have failings different
from others, they may be attributed to their unavoidable intercourse with the
slaves, by whose milk they are frequently nourished, and in the midst of whom

they are generally educated. Parents are often too indulgent, and will frequently suffer their children to tyrannize over the young slaves, one or two of whom are usually appropriated to the use of each of the planter's children, and become their property. Hence they are nurtured in the strongest prejudices against the blacks, whom they are taught to look upon as beings almost without a soul, and whom they sometimes, treat with unpardonable severity.

From having their early passions and propensities so much indulged, the young Carolinians are too apt to acquire a rash, fiery, and impetuous disposition, which renders them incapable of comprehending Shakespeare's admirable definition of honor: "Not to be captious, not unjustly fight; / Tis to confess what's wrong, and do what's right."

Private quarrels frequently disgrace the public prints: challenges are sent; and if refused, the parties are posted as "prevaricating poltroons and cowards." A few months before I arrived, a duel took place between two young gentlemen of respectable families, which terminated in the death of both. There is, perhaps, no country in the world where duels are so frequent as in the United States. During my short stay of six months in that country, there were upwards of fourteen fought which came to my knowledge; and not one of them in which the parties were not either killed or wounded. Since my departure, I heard of a duel having been fought with rifles at only seven paces distance, in which two young men, whose families were of the highest respectability, were both killed on the spot. Such acts of desperation would lead one to suspect that the Americans were a blood-thirsty people; for they might satisfy their false honor at a greater distance from each other, and with less determinate marks of revenge. Duels are frequent and disgraceful enough in England; but they are far exceeded in the United States, where young men are in the habit of training themselves up as duel-lists. The man who fights a duel is a coward, compared with him who braves the false opinion of the world.

The amusements in Charleston during the hot months of the year are very few. The Vauxhall garden is the only public place of recreation, and that by no means safe after a sultry day. For two or three months during the sickly season, the genteel people shut themselves up in their houses, or retire to Sullivan's Island, situate in the harbor about six miles below the city. On this island a settlement has been effected called Moultrieville, after Major-general William Moultrie, who from a fort on the island in 1776 frustrated the attempt of a British naval armament under the command of Sir Peter Parker. Its commencement was about the year 1791, when the legislature passed an act, permitting people to build there on half-acre lots; subject to the condition of their being removed, whenever demanded, by the governor or commander-in-chief. Almost every part of the island, which is nearly three miles long, is now occupied, and contains upwards of two hundred dwelling-houses, besides kitchens and out offices. This place is little resorted to during the winter and spring; but in the summer and autumn numbers of people reside there, for pleasure or health; and packet boats are plying, at all hours, between it and Charleston. Along the hard beach of this island, its inhabitants enjoy the amusements of riding or walking; while the ocean incessantly breaks its waves at their feet, and vessels pass within two or three hundred yards of the shore.

There are a great number of Jews settled in Charleston; and they live principally in Kingstreet, where their shops are crowded together, and exhibit as motley a collection of clothing and wearing apparel as can be found in Houndsditch or Rag-fair. They are sufficiently numerous to have a synagogue;* and one company of the volunteer militia is formed entirely of Jews. They are, as is the case in most countries, moneyed people: and on their sabbaths the young Jewesses walk out in fine flowing dresses that would better suit the stage or ball-room than the street.

I saw only one Quaker in Charleston, and he is as remarkable for the singular plainness of his dress as the large property which he possesses. Of the traders and shopkeepers settled in Charleston, a great number are Scotch, who generally acquire considerable property, by close and persevering habits of industry; after which, they most commonly return to their native country. There are also several Irish traders, but their number is far inferior to the Scotch.

At the period when the Americans were so much exasperated against Great Britain, in consequence of the attack upon the *Chesapeake* frigate, the British subjects throughout the States were in an awkward predicament, and for some time were under the necessity of keeping within doors, until the fury of the populace was somewhat abated.[†] In Charleston, the inhabitants committed great excesses; and it was not merely the lower order of people who were concerned in them, but many, otherwise respectable, house-keepers. All the American inhabitants wore pieces of crape round their arms, as mourning for the sailors killed in the action; and ducked under the pumps all who refused to comply with that mark of respect for their deceased countrymen. The Scotch people, however, held out firmly against their threats, and some were in consequence severely handled by

*The first congregation of Kahal Kadosh Beth Elohim was established in 1749.

[†]On June 22, 1807, off the coast of Norfolk, Virginia, a British warship, the *Leopard*, intercepted the U.S. frigate *Chesapeake*. The British demanded to board, to muster the crew and search for deserters of the Royal Navy. Refused entry on grounds of American independence, they attacked the *Chesapeake*. Three men were killed, eighteen wounded, and four American sailors removed. The United States was outraged and its military spirit roused. In Charleston, the Washington Light Infantry was formed as a direct result (Hatfield with Senate Historical Office, *Vice Presidents of the United States*).

the mob. The outrages went to such a length, that proscription lists were made out, and not only several Scotchmen, but many of the American federalists, who viewed the business more as an aggression on the part of the United States, than by England, were beset in their houses by the populace, and vengeance demanded upon their heads. The reign of terror commenced, and self-appointed committees were deputed to wait on suspected persons. One merchant and his son barricaded themselves in their house, while the rest of the family were employed in making cartridges. The populace surrounded their dwelling; but the gentleman and his son declared that, if they attempted to force the doors, they would immediately fire upon them.

This violent ferment at length subsided: but the Scotchmen are of opinion, that if the Intendant of Charleston had not been a federalist, most of them would have been put to death. The conduct of one of them was, however, extremely reprehensible. He dressed a dog and a goat up in crape, to ridicule the people. They could not catch him for some time, as he kept within doors; but one morning about six o'clock they knocked at his door, which being opened, they rushed in, dragged him into the street, and carried him to a pump, where they ducked him so unmercifully, that he took to his bed, and died in the course of the following month, it being then the commencement of the sickly season.

While I remained in Charleston, there was considerable alarm on account of the depredations which were said to be committed by the sailors at night. There were upwards of one thousand in the city, who since the embargo had become very riotous, having no employ; and several were absolutely destitute of lodging and food, their landlords having turned them out after their money was gone. They paraded the streets several nights in large bodies, and the city guard was obliged to be strengthened. Some robberies were committed, and two or three negroes murdered, so that it became dangerous to be out at dark. The corporation at length published a proclamation, forbidding, under pain of imprisonment, any sailor to be out of his lodging-house after seven o'clock: they also advertised, that any sailor who was destitute of employment might go on board the *Hornet* sloop, and gun-boats belonging to the United States, where they should receive provisions, and be at liberty to quit the vessel when they chose. Not above sixteen accepted the offer, and several of them soon returned on shore again, in consequence of some smart floggings which they met with on board the *Hornet.* In the course of a week or two, the English Consul advertising that British seamen might have a free passage home in the British ships that were going to Europe, upwards of four hundred availed themselves of the offer, and sailed for England.

There are no white servants in Charleston. Every kind of work is performed by the negroes and people of color. Those who are unable to give 500 or 600 dollars for a slave, which is the usual price of a good one, generally hire them, by the month or year, of people who are in the habit of keeping a number of slaves for that purpose. Many persons obtain a handsome living by letting out their slaves for 6 to 10 dollars per month. They also send them out to sell oysters, fruit, millinery, &c.; or as carmen and porters. The slaves who are brought up to any trade or profession are let out as journeymen, and many of them are so extremely clever and expert, that they are considered worth two or three thousand dollars.

The mulattoes, or people of color, are very numerous in Charleston. Many of them are free, but a much greater proportion are slaves. They are said to be more insolent and debauched than the negroes; which is perhaps owing to the knowledge of their origin, and the liberties they conceive they are entitled to take. Many of the mulatto girls are handsome, and good figures. They are fond of dress, full of vanity, and generally dispense their favors very liberally to the whites. The negroes who are natives of Africa are often indolent. They are, however, in general more robust and capable of field labor than those born in Carolina; and have less deceit and libertinism in their character. The negroes born in Carolina are much tinctured with European vices, particularly if they live in Charleston; but they make the best servants, being well acquainted from their childhood with household duties, and the business of a plantation or farm. They have also a high opinion of themselves, and look with contempt upon the new Africans. I heard one of them observe, on seeing a drove of newly-imported negroes going out of Charleston to a plantation in the country—"Ah! dey be poor devils, me fetch ten of dem, if massa swap me." Free blacks are also a step above those who are in bondage, and nothing offends them more than to call them negroes. The steward of the *Calliope,* who was one of these, was highly offended with Captain Turner, who out of joke would frequently call him a damned negro. "Negur, massa!" says the steward, "me be no negur—don't call me negur, massa." An old negro woman is called momma, which is a broad pronunciation of mama; and a girl, missy. I once happened to call a young negro wench momma.—"Me be no momma," says she, "me had no children yet." The negroes are also called by a variety of names; and the catalogue of the heathen mythology of ancient heroes and demigods, of saints and martyrs, is ransacked for that purpose. Notwithstanding the vicious mode of fighting common among the whites in the southern states of America, I always observed that the negroes boxed each other fairly; and if any foul play happened to take place, the negro by-standers would immediately interpose.

The old negroes, both men and women, are very attentive to their religious duties; and pews in the churches and chapels of Charleston are appropriated to their use. The majority of the negroes are Methodists, whose mode of worship seems to be a favorite with most of the blacks throughout the States. Unlike the American Indians, who are caught by the paraphernalia and mysterious ceremonies of the Roman Catholic religion, the negroes receive with enthusiasm the pleasing doctrine of faith without works; and if there is little religious ceremony in the service, its simplicity is amply compensated by the thundering anathemas of the preacher: this catches their attention, and in imitation of their more enlightened white brethren, they often fall down in divine ecstasies, crying, shouting, bawling, and beating their breasts, until they are ready to faint. Much of this extravagance is now done away, at least in Charleston, since some of the most vehement of the Methodist preachers were obliged to decamp, lest the meeting-houses should be pulled down upon them. Several were pelted and dragged out of their pulpits by some young men of the town in the very middle of their horrid denunciations, and the frantic gestures of their deluded congregation. These violences were winked at by the municipality, as it was found that the absurd doctrines broached by those fanatical preachers did much injury to the slaves. Calm, dispassionate religion, of whatever denomination it may be, has never been withheld from the negroes, but rather encouraged, and in general they are very orderly and devout in their demeanor on Sundays. The free negroes and people of color are then dressed out in their best, and feel exalted as much above the slaves as the whites do above them. They pull off their hats, bow, scrape, and curtsey to each other, and the younger part seem to treat their elders with much respect and attention. The meeting-houses are crowded with all colors, and many of the slaves frequently sit on the steps outside the door.

Funerals are conducted much in the same style as at New York, except, that in Charleston the women attend. I have seen two or three hundred men, women, and children, walking arm in arm, in pairs. The corpse is placed on a sort of hearse, or rather cart, and covered with a pall, above which is a roof supported by four pillars; the whole is very mean, and drawn by only one horse, driven by a negro shabbily dressed. The relations, or particular friends, wear mourning, with crape hatbands and scarfs; the rest of the company are in colored clothes. Previous to setting out; refreshment is served round, and sprigs of rosemary or lavender are given to each. The negroes imitate the whites in their funerals, and it is curious to see a negro parson and clerk attending them. The bells never toll in Charleston at funerals. A few months before the yellow fever raged in that city, in 1807, an undertaker made his appearance, which was so great a novelty to the inhabitants that he was obliged to explain what was meant by the term *undertaker* in an advertisement. Before this carpenters were employed to knock up a coffin, and the deceased's friends were obliged to provide every necessary for the funeral, either at their own houses or at different shops. Military funerals are conducted with much parade and ceremony.

The charitable societies in Charleston, besides the Orphan-house, are the South Carolina Society, St. Andrew's, Fellowship, German Friendly, Mechanic, Mount Sion, Hibernian, Gemilut Hasadim, and Free Masons. The grand lodge of the latter is self-constituted, and threw off the yoke of the grand lodge of England. It does not possess a fund of more than a thousand dollars, and its charitable donations are but small. A remarkable proposition was once made in this lodge, that all its members should profess Christianity; it was, however, over-ruled; nor indeed could it have been admitted, as free-masonry was established with a view to embrace every denomination of religion in the world. Several of the new lodges in the United States are said to have degenerated from the pure principles of free-masonry, and are too apt to be influenced by politics.

The militia of South Carolina is divided into two divisions, each commanded by a Major-general. These divisions comprehend nine brigades, thirty-nine regiments of infantry, eight regiments and a squadron of cavalry, and one regiment and a battalion of artillery, besides artillery companies which are attached to some of the regiments of infantry. The brigades are commanded by as many Brigadier-generals; and the regiments are commanded by Lieutenant-colonels. The Governor is commander-in-chief of all the militia of the State, both by sea and land.

Every able-bodied white male citizen, between the age of eighteen and forty-five, is enrolled in the militia, and free people of color are enrolled as pioneers. One-third of the militia may be marched out of the State by order of the executive of the United States, on particular emergencies, and under certain conditions; and treated in every respect the same as the regular troops, except that in cases of court-martial the court is to be selected from the militia of the State. Officers rise by seniority; and no election exists except in the first appointment of subaltern. The number of effective militia in South Carolina is about 40,000, of whom 2,000 are cavalry.

In Charleston, the inhabitants have formed themselves into volunteer corps, armed and clothed at their own expense. One half consists of cavalry and artillery. The uniform of the latter is a long blue coat, with red facings, and large cocked hat and red feather; it has a heavy appearance, and is but ill adapted to such a corps, whose chief perfection is in celerity of movement. The little company of Jews wear a similar dress, which, with their peculiarity of features, renders them grotesque-looking soldiers. I was present at a review, on the race-ground, of the different corps, and the new levy of militia, forming a part of the 100,000 men ordered by Congress to hold themselves in readiness for the defense of the country. They appeared to be very ill disciplined, and the new levy, which mustered about 1,000 men, was out of uniform, and had no other arms than their own rifles or fowling-pieces. The volunteer companies were dressed in a variety of uniforms, and made a respectable appearance. The emblem upon the colors of the artillery corps was apt enough to the situation of the country at the period of the revolution: it was an artilleryman standing by the side of a cannon, and a serpent upon the ground near his feet, looking up in the man's face, with the motto, "Don't tread on me." The militia in the United States is for the most part badly disciplined. In the towns, some show of a military force is kept up by the volunteers, who are fond of captivating the ladies with their smart uniforms and nodding plumes; but throughout the country places the militia meet only to eat, drink, and be merry. I met with an excellent satire upon one of these meetings while I was at Charleston. As it may afford my readers some amusement, I have taken the liberty to lay it before them.

I happened not long since to be present at the muster of a captain's company, in a remote part of one of the counties; and as no general description could convey an adequate idea of the achievements of that day, I must be permitted to go a little into the detail, as well as my recollection will serve me. The men had been notified to meet at nine o'clock, "armed and equipped as the law directs," that is to say, with a gun and cartouch box at least; but as directed by the law of the United States, "with a good firelock, a sufficient bayonet and belt, and pouch with a box to contain not less than twenty-four sufficient cartridges of powder and ball." At twelve o'clock about one-third, perhaps half, the men had collected; and an inspector's return of the number present would have stood nearly thus: one captain, one lieutenant, ensign none, sergeants two, corporals none, drummers none, fifers none, privates present 25, ditto absent 30, guns 15, gunlocks 12, ramrods 10, rifle pouches three, bayonets none, belts none, spare flints none, cartridges none, horsewhips, walking canes, and umbrellas, twenty-two.

A little before one o'clock, the captain, whom I shall distinguish by the name of Clodpole, gave directions for forming the line of parade. In obedience to this order, one of the sergeants, the strength of whose lungs had long supplied the place of a drum and fife, placed himself in front of the house, and began to bawl with great vehemence, "All Captain Clodpole's company to parade there! come, gentlemen, parade here! parade here!" says he, "and all you that hasn't guns, fall into the lower eend." He might have bawled till this time, with as little success as the Syrens sung to Ulysses, had he not changed his post to a neighboring shade; there he was immediately joined by all who were then at leisure, the others were at that time engaged either as parties or spectators at a game of fives, and could not just then attend: however, in less than half an hour the game was finished, and the captain was enabled to form his company, and proceed in the duties of the day.

"Look to the right and dress!"

They were soon, by the help of the non-commissioned officers, placed in a straight line; but as every man was anxious to see how the rest stood, those on the wings pressed forward for that purpose, till the whole line assumed nearly the form of a crescent.

"Whew! look at 'em!" says the captain: "why, gentlemen, you are all crooking here at both eends, so that you will get on to me by and by: come, gentlemen, dress! dress!"

"This was accordingly done; but impelled by the same motive as before, they soon resumed their former figure, and so they were permitted to remain.

"Now, gentlemen," says the captain, "I am going to carry you through the revolutions of the manual exercise, and I want you, gentlemen, if you please, to pay every particular attention to the word of command, just exactly as I give it out to you. I hope you will have a little patience, gentlemen, if you please, and I'll be as short as possible; and if I should be a-going wrong, I will be much obliged to any of you, gentlemen, to put me right again, for I mean all for the best, and I hope you will excuse me if you please. And one thing, gentlemen, I must caution you against, in particular, and that is this, not to make any mistakes if you can possibly help it, and the best way to do this, will be to do all the motions right at first, and that will help us to get along so much the faster, and I will try to have it over as soon as possible. Come, boys, come to a shoulder.

"Poise foolk!

"Cock foolk!—Very handsomely done.

"Take aim!

"Ram down cartridge!—No! No! Fire. I recollect now, that firing comes next after taking aim, according to Steuben;* but with your permission gentlemen, I'll read the words of command just exactly as they are printed in the book, and then I shall be sure to be right." "O yes! read it, Captain, read it," exclaimed twenty voices at once, "that will save time."

"'Tention the whole then: please to observe, gentlemen, that at the word fire! you must fire! that is, if any of your guns are loaden'd, you must not shoot in year-nest, but only make pretence like; and all you gentlemen fellow-soldiers, who's armed with nothing but sticks, and riding switches, and corn stalks, needn't go through the firings, but stand as you are, and keep yourselves to yourselves.

"Half coch foolk!—Very well done.

---

*Fredrich Wilhelm Augustin, Baron von Steuben (1730–1794), a Prussian officer who served in the American Revolution. A superb drillmaster, he helped discipline the Continental Army and wrote *Regulations for the Order and Discipline of the Troops of the U.S.*, which became the army's standard drill manual.

"S, h, u, t, (spelling) shet pan!—That too would have been very handsomely done, if you hadn't have handled the cartridge instead; but I suppose you wasn't noticing. Now, 'tention one and all, gentlemen, and do that motion again.

"Shet pan!—Very good, very well indeed, you did that motion equal to any old soldiers; you improve astonishingly.

"Handle cartridge!—Pretty well, considering you done it wrong eend foremost, as if you took the cartridge out of your mouth, and bit off the twist with the cartridge box.

"Draw rammer!—Those who have no rammers to their guns need not draw, but only make the motion; it will do just as well, and save a great deal of time.

"Return rammer!—Very well again—But that would have been done, I think, with greater expertness, if you had performed the motion with a little more dexterity.

"Shoulder foolk!—Very handsomely done, indeed, if you had only brought the foolk to the other shoulder, gentlemen. Do that motion again, gentlemen, and bring the foolk up to the left shoulder.

"Shoulder foolk!—Very good.

"Order foolk!—Not quite so well, gentlemen; not quite all together: but perhaps I did not speak loud enough for you to hear me all at once; try once more if you please; I hope you will be patient, gentlemen, we will soon be through.

"Order foolk!—Handsomely done, gentlemen! very handsomely done! and all together too, except that a few of you were a leetle too soon, and some others a leetle too late.

"In laying down your guns, gentlemen, take care to lay the locks up, and the other sides down.

"'Tention the whole! Ground foolk!—Very well.

"Charge bagonet!" (Some of the men)—"That can't be right, Captain, pray look again, for how can we charge bagonet without our guns?"

(Captain) "I don't know as to that, but I know I'm right, for here it is printed in the book c, h, a, r, yes, charge bagonet, that's right, that's the word, if I know how to read; come, gentlemen, do pray charge bagonet! Charge, I say! Why don't you charge? Do you think it an't so? Do you think I have lived to this time of day, and don't know what charge bagonet is? Here, come here, you may see for yourselves; it's as plain as the nose on your fa—stop—stay—no!—halt! no, no! 'faith I'm wrong! I'm wrong! I turned over two leaves at once. But I beg your pardon, gentlemen, we will not stay out long; and we'll have something to drink as soon as we've done. Come, boys, get up off the stumps and logs, and take up your guns, and we'll soon be done; excuse me if you please.

"Fix bagonet!

"Advance arms!—Very well done, turn the stocks of your guns in front, gentlemen, and that will bring the barrels behind; and hold them straight up and down if you please. Let go with your left hand, and take hold with your right just below the guard. Steuben says the gun must be held up p, e, r, perticular: yes you must always mind and hold your guns very perticular. Now, boys, 'tention the whole!

"Present arms!—Very handsomely done! only hold your guns over the other knee, and the other hand up, turn your guns round a leetle, and raise them up higher, draw the other foot back! Now you are nearly right. Very well done, gentlemen; you have improved vastly since I first saw you: you are getting too slick. What a charming thing it is to see men under good discipline! Now, gentlemen, we are come to the revolutions: but Lord, men, how did you get into such a higglety-pigglety?"

The fact was, the shade had moved considerably to the eastward, and had exposed the right wing of these hardy veterans to a galling fire of the sun. Being but poorly provided with umbrellas at this end of the line, they found it convenient to follow the shade, and in huddling to the left for this purpose, they had changed the figure of their line from that of a crescent to one which more nearly resembled a pair of pothooks.

"Come, gentlemen," says the captain, "spread yourselves out again into a straight line, and let us get into the wheelings and other matters as soon as possible."

But this was strenuously opposed by the soldiers. They objected to going into these revolutions at all, inasmuch as the weather was extremely hot, and they had already been kept in the field upwards of three quarters of an hour. They reminded the captain of his repeated promise to be as short as he possibly could, and it was clear he could dispense with all this same wheeling and flourishing if he chose. They were already very thirsty, and if he would not dismiss them, they declared they would go off without dismission, and get something to drink; and he might fine them if that would do him any good; they were able to pay their fine, but could not go without drink to please any body; and they swore they would never vote for another captain who wished to be so unreasonably strict.

The captain behaved with great spirit upon this occasion, and a smart colloquy ensued; when at length, becoming exasperated to the last degree, he roundly asserted, that no soldier ought ever to think hard of the orders of his officer; and finally he went as far as to say, that he did not think any gentleman on that ground had any just cause to be offended with him. The dispute was at length settled by the captain's sending for some grog, for their present accommodation, and agreeing to omit reading the military law, as directed by a late act, and also all the military manoeuvres, except two or three such easy and simple ones as could be performed within the compass of the shade. After they had drunk their grog, and "spread themselves," they were divided into platoons.

"'Tention the whole!—To the right wheel!" Each man faced to the right about.

"Why, gentlemen, I didn't mean for every man to stand still and turn nayturally right round; but when I told you to wheel to the right, I intended for you to wheel round to the right as it were. Please to try that again, gentlemen; every right hand man must stand fast, and only the others turn round."

In a previous part of the exercise, it had, for the purpose of sizing them, been necessary to denominate every second person a "right hand man." A very natural consequence was, that on the present occasion those right hand men maintained their position, and all the intermediate ones faced about as before.

"Why look at 'em now!" exclaimed the captain in extreme vexation. "I'll be d—d if you can understand a word I say. Excuse me, gentlemen, but it rayly seems as if you couldn't come at it exactly. In wheeling to the right, the right hand eend of the platoon stands fast, and the other eend comes round like a swingle tree. Those on the outside must march faster than those on the inside, and those on the inside not near so fast as those on the outside. You certainly must understand me now, gentlemen; and now please to try once more."

In this they were a little more successful.

"Very well, gentlemen; very well indeed: and now, gentlemen, at the word wheel to the left, you must wheel to the left.

"'Tention the whole! To the left—left no—right—that is the left—I mean the right—left, wheel! march!"

In this he was strictly obeyed; some wheeling to the right, some to the left, and some to the right, left, or both ways.

"Stop! halt! let us try again! I could not just then tell my right hand from my left; you must excuse me, gentlemen, if you please; experience makes perfect, as the saying is; long as I've served, I find something new to learn every day, but all's one for that: now, gentlemen, do that motion once more."

By the help of a non-commissioned officer in front of each platoon, they wheeled this time with considerable regularity.

"Now, boys, you must try to wheel by divisions, and there is one thing in particular which I have to request of you, gentlemen, and it is this, not to make any blunder in your wheeling. You must mind and keep at a wheeling distance; and not talk in the ranks, nor get out of fix again; for I want you to do this motion well, and not make any blunder now.

"'Tention the whole! By divisions! to the right wheel! march!"

In doing this, it seemed as if Bedlam had broke loose; every man took the command—"Not so fast on the right!—How now! How now!—Haul down those umbrellas!—Faster on the left!—Keep back a little in the middle there—Don't crowd so—Hold up your gun, Sam—Go faster there!—Faster!—Who trod on me?—D—n your huffs, keep back! keep back!—Stop us, captain, do stop us—Go faster there—I've lost my shoe—Get up again—Ned, halt! halt! halt!—Stop, gentlemen! stop! stop!—"

By this time they got into utter and inexplicable confusion and so I left them.

"Samuel F. B. Morse Self-Portrait," 1818.
Courtesy of Ruthmere Museum, Elkhart, Indiana.

Samuel F. B. Morse (1818–20)

"Hospitably Entertained and Many Portraits Painted"

Samuel Finley Breeze Morse (1791–1872) was born in Charlestowne, Massachusetts, a sixth-generation Yankee Puritan. His clergyman father, Jedidiah Morse, authored the first American geography books. His mother was Elizabeth Ann Breeze Finley, the granddaughter of Calvinist minster Samuel Finley, founder and first president of Princeton University. Morse graduated from Yale in 1810 and returned to Massachusetts, where he worked as a bookseller's apprentice. In 1811, he left for London with his mentor, South Carolina native artist Washington Allston, to study art at the Royal Academy and receive instruction from Benjamin West, considered the leading artist in Europe. Morse wrote home to his parents: "My ambition is to be among those who shall reveal the splendor of the fifteenth century; to rival the genius of a Raphael, a Michelangelo, or a Titian; my ambition is to be enlisted in the constellation of genius now riding in this country; I wish to shine, not by a light borrowed from them, but to strive to shine the brightest." He achieved some success in Europe with historical painting; however, his father, who had financed his son's art studies for four years, was not impressed and ordered him home to Massachusetts. He returned to America in 1815 to find little public interest in historical pictures; therefore he was "forced" to paint portraits. He soon embarked on a portrait-painting tour through New England to New Hampshire, where he met his future wife.

At the time, the demand for portraiture in Charleston was greater than any city south of Philadelphia. Northeast artists were in demand and were migrating south in great numbers. Morse had a number of advantages when he considered he might join them. Through Washington Allston, he had procured a patron in planter John Ashe Alston, an avid art collector, who lived on the Waccamaw River near Georgetown, South Carolina. Further, from 1809 to 1810 Morse's parents had lived in Charleston, where they befriended such prominent locals as

Taken from the Samuel F. B. Morse Papers, Manuscript Division, Library of Congress, Washington, DC.

Charles Cotesworth Pinckney and members of the Legare, Palmer, Beach, Barn-well, and Ball families, who might now grant him commissions and sponsorship. When his great-uncle, James E. B. Finley, a well-connected Charleston physician, offered the young artist further introductions if he chose to travel south, Morse sailed for Charleston, confident of commissions. He arrived in late January of 1818 and set up a studio. He waited a few tenuous weeks for clients before he secured many commissions, for which he received four times what he had earned in the North.

Morse returned to Charleston for three subsequent social seasons. His last season coincided with an economic depression that was spreading through the South. As Charleston's seaport lost business to New Orleans and New York ports, the value of imports and exports was down. Lowcountry crop failures further contributed to the financial panic. Planters were overextended, and Morse was forced to lower his prices. After this difficult season, he did not return to Charleston. A partial list of his Charleston clients gives the names of fifty-five sitters, and the prices he received for these portraits alone totals over four thousand dollars, a hefty sum in that day.

Over his four seasons in Charleston, Morse wrote to his parents and his fiancée (then wife), Lucretia Pickering Walker. He received letters from his patron, Colonel John Ashe Alston in Georgetown, which provides the most extant collection of material available concerning the life and art patronage of Alston (unfortunately, Morse's replies to Alston have not survived). His further correspondence includes letters to and from Morse from a difficult client, Mrs. Caroline Ball.

Samuel Morse ended his painting career in 1837, frustrated in his attempts to paint significant historical subjects and make a living through his art. While working as a professor at New York University, he invented the American electro-magnetic telegraph, which eventually became the Western Union telegraph and transformed the nation. He sought a patent and, in 1844, built the first telegraph line between Baltimore and Washington. He was also a pioneer photographer and introduced the daguerreotype to America. He was a candidate for Congress and twice ran for mayor of New York. A biography of Morse had not been published for sixty years when, in 2003, author Kenneth Silverman published *Lightning Man: The Accursed Life of Samuel F. B. Morse*.

SOURCES

"The Fortnightly Club of Redlands, California." December 19, 1996. Meeting 1578 at www.redlandsfortnightly.org/papers/morse.htm (accessed March 23, 2012).

Kloss, William. *Samuel F. B. Morse*. New York: Harry N. Abrams, 1988.

Lipton, Leah. "William Dunlap, Samuel F. B. Morse, John Wesley Jarvis, and Chester Harding: Their Careers as Itinerant Portrait Painters." *American Art Journal* 13, no. 3 (Summer 1981): 34–50.

Morse, Samuel F. B. Papers. Manuscript Division, Library of Congress, Washington, DC.

Staiti, Paul. "Samuel F. B. Morse in Charleston 1818–1821." *South Carolina Historical Magazine* 79 (April 1978): 87–112.

"Hospitably Entertained and Many Portraits Painted"
1818 Social Season

[S. F. B. Morse to Lucretia Walker]
Feb. 17th 1818, Charleston, So. Carolina
My Dearest Lucretia,
The climate here is delightful, as mild as our May or June. Many days it has been comfortable without fire, and with the windows open. I am growing fleshy, for this weather agrees with me well. I think it would be of an advantage to you also, dear. The people of Charleston are very hospitable and social and I have very many kind and warm friends here already. This will make it pleasant to you. I have as much as I can do at portrait painting in this place at 60 or 70 dollars a head, at this rate I should be able to lay up something handsome every year.

Sunday, Feb 22nd 1818
A great press of business, dearest Lucretia, broke me off in my letter but I have a moment on this sacred day while I can converse with my dearest. Oh, what a different Sabbath from our quiet, heavenly Sabbaths in New England. All here is noise and confusion, scarcely a place to be found where one can have a moment's solitude. The slaves employ this day in visits to one another; they are in a manner their own this day. The people of fashion also employ this day in visiting and dinner parties. It is the most common day for paying calls; the result of all this is that the *day of rest* is a day of reunion & bustle in Charleston. This is an objection to living in this place, the greatest that can be waged; but still, dearest, there are *some Christians* here. Some that mourn the degraded and low state of our blessed Redeemer's kingdom in this region, some that pray, and strive against the torrent of dissipation, and unGodliness, but alas! They are few I fear and the observation you make, dear, in your letters, that when God withdraws the visible influence of his Sprit from any place, religion languishes in the hearts of his children, is powerfully exemplified here.

Monday, Feb. 23rd

Yesterday I heard two most excellent sermons, one from Dr. Flinn* and the other from an Episcopal minister by the name of Phillips, a sound and—pious man.

This morning, dear, I commence painting again; a sitter at 9, at 11, & at 4—do you see I am completely full of business? I rec'd two notes yesterday & Saturday from two of the wealthiest and most influential men of Carolina, Gen. Pinckney† and Hon. John Alston;‡ the former wishing I believe a *full-length* of his brother, the latter two portraits in *full-length* and *half-length* of his daughter, this commission alone will put 6 or 700 in my pocket. Besides this I have not time to fulfill all the engagements of the different applicants, and I hear every day of more who have determined to sit for their portraits. I have enough, or shall have, to employ me another season, perhaps for two or three more. I think, dear, that Providence is making the way plain to our union this next summer or fall. My profession is abundantly productive, for with application I can make a fortune in a few years.

[John Alston to S. F. B. Morse Esquire]

Georgetown February 28th 1818

Sir,

I have the pleasure to acknowledge the receipt of your favor of the 23rd and will thank you to take a half-portrait of my daughter with hands,§ and to have it framed. I wish the dress to be white, but should you think any light color handsomer, I would prefer it. She is at the boarding school of Mrs. Colcock¶ and will

*Andrew Flinn, founder and first pastor of Second Presbyterian Church, known for many years as "Flinn's Church."

†Charles Cotesworth Pinckney, first mentioned as a young lawyer in the Josiah Quincy account.

‡John Ashe Alston (1780–1831), from the Allston/Alston family of planters on Waccamaw Neck in Georgetown County, owned vast expanses of land and rice fields, and numerous plantation houses around Georgetown. He was the son of Col. William Alston (1756–1839), one of the richest men in South Carolina, and his first wife, Mary Ashe (1756–1788). He graduated from Princeton in 1799. An art collector, Alston owned works by artists Benjamin West, Gilbert Stuart, Thomas Sully, and John Vanderlyn. Alston commissioned at least sixteen portraits from Morse, including six of his daughter, Sally (Egbert, "Two Portraits by Thomas Sully," 11–16; Taylor, *Antebellum South Carolina*, 108).

§Morse charged more to include the hands of the sitter in a portrait.

¶Millescent Jones Colcock (1743–1829), "whose mother was a Pinckney," was the widow of lawyer John Colcock (1744–1782). She ran a girl's boarding school in Charleston at Tradd and Lamboll streets, which was very successful ("The Autobiography of William Colcock," unpublished papers, Manuscripts Department, Library of the University of North Carolina

attend you upon your application. I prefer to have a specimen of your painting in the half-portrait of my daughter, before I conclude as to the portraits of my other children who are also in Charleston. Should you be unwilling to make an extraordinary exertion of your talents, which I am told are very great, for so small a sum as eighty dollars, being the sum mentioned by you for half-portraits with hands, I am very willing to add more. I wish you to *add as superb a landscape as you are capable of designing and painting.* An answer when convenient would oblige me. I am sir, with great respect,

Your Obedient Servant,

John A. Alston

[S. F. B. Morse to His Parents]

Charleston, So. Carolina March 23rd

My Dear Parents,

I have not had one moment's time to answer your other letters. I can hardly spare the time now to write you. I am completely occupied. I have finished and begun 27 portraits large and small, and have upwards of 40 more engaged, who have placed their names on a list. Those I cannot finish I will leave till next season, when I must return early (say Nov.). I have contrived to prepare some canvas for my immediate use but feel much in want of some from England.

I have a field opened here for making my fortune in a short time. I have become the fashion, and every one says that I am sure of a fortune. I shall apply myself with all my might and use the utmost economy; all that I can collect (for most of my pictures are not paid for) I will send to you as soon as I can.

Religion is at a low ebb here. I intend to bring with me to Charlestown [Massachusetts], some of the portraits to finish such as the full-length of Washington and the half-length of Gen. Thomas Pinckney* and the original portrait of some I have to copy. This will give me employment enough till I return to Carolina,† at a greater price by *one half* than I could expect in Maine.

March 26th. I send you in this letter a Post note on the Branch Bank of Philadelphia which will be paid in Boston, for Five Hundred Dollars; please write me

---

at Chapel Hill, Southern Historical Collection, #2986; Hagy, *People and Professions of Charleston*, 12).

*Thomas Pinckney was first mentioned as a young lawyer in the 1773 Quincy account.

†Morse would concentrate on the face and features of the sitter, then on the general composition and body proportions, and save completion of facial shading, body dress, and details of landscape, still life, and architecture, and so forth for the summer months back in New England.

immediately as you receive it. I have taken 20 dollars of Mrs. Keith* and 5 of Mrs. Gilchrist,† and given receipts.

In great haste I must close, not one minute's time for anything. I have 80 on my list, and daily increasing; I have many engaged for next season.

[S. F. B. Morse to Lucretia Walker]
Charleston, So. Car. March 29th 1818
My Dearest Lucretia,
I have portraits engaged to the amount of between 6. & 7000 dollars and every day brings more to the list. I have already done to the amount of 1300 dollars and am constantly in my room from 8 in the morning until dark. Everyone tells me my fortune is sure (this, however, as God pleases). I must return next November (God willing) for I shall not be able to finish half that are engaged before I must return to Boston. This climate in the winter is delightful; with all my constant application I have never felt better, and my friends tell me I am growing more ruddy, and fleshy. My friends are numerous, and increasing. There are many inquires after you. For they seem acquainted with you already. I have some pretty cousins‡ here who sally me now and then, "What," (say they) "not a letter yet? Why she can't love you much." You will find, dear in Charleston, a fine climate for the winter and a good society.

[John Alston to S. F. B. Morse Esquire]
Waccamaw, near Georgetown May 19th 1818
My dear Sir,
Among the paintings which I have not yet mentioned to you & which I intend to request you to execute for me; there is none which of all others I am the most interested in. I have an original miniature of my deceased wife§ & I wished you to take a *portrait* copy of it; I mean your copy to be executed in oil colors, as I do not wish any paintings but such are done in oil. I did not wish your try to be in minia-ture, but of such size as you should think best-suited to preserve the fidelity of the features. I had indulged the hope of having it in my possession and to *deliver* it to

---

*This was probably widow Jane Keith (1773–1849), last of the three wives of Rev. Dr. Isaac Keith, pastor of the Circular Congregational Church until his death in 1813. While they were in Charleston from 1808 to 1809, Morse's parents had stayed at the house of Rev. Keith.

†Mrs. Adam Gilchrist, widow of a wealthy merchant who died in 1816. She was the mother of Maria Gilchrist Cogdell, whose husband, John Cogdell, was Morse's good friend (O'Neall, *Biological Sketches of the Bench and Bar*, 215–18).

‡Morse's pretty cousins were Dr. Finley's young daughters, Mary and Ann Finley (Mabee, *American Leonardo*, 177).

§Alston's wife, Sarah McPherson Alston, had died in 1812.

you for that purpose, but I fear our early departure will prevent me. It is now in the possession of a painter who has had it for 20 mos. this past, & who has during this time been engaged in taking copies of it. One copy he has executed as large as life. He is now engaged on the fifth miniature copy. If by *chance* I should have it in my power to deliver it to you, I hope you will take & *finish* a copy of it during your absence this summer. I had also another copy of this picture taken by a painter who is celebrated both in Europe & in this country—the painting was such as was to be expected from the splendor of his talents but the young gentlemen attempted it as large as life and by that *mean* failed in the resemblance. Should I be fortunate enough to obtain it in time I hope you will take it with you. The politeness of your letter & particularly the friendly one last received has induced me to trouble you more than I otherwise would have taken the liberty to do.

I remain, Dear Sir, with great consideration & respect,

Yr. Most obt. Servant

John A. Alston

[S. F. B. Morse to His Parents]

Charleston, S. Car. May 25th 1818

My Dear Parents,

I have just rec'd your letter of the 13th. I have finished in Charleston for the season. All things are on board the Sch[ooner] *Fenwick,* Capt. Daggett, for Boston in which vessel I have taken my passage. We were to have sailed yesterday, the wind only prevents, shall probably sail tomorrow.

I enclose a draft on the Branch Bank of the U. States in Boston for $2150.00, making in all that I have remitted to you $3050.00. This with about 50 dollars in specie, which I bring with me, will be my clear earnings for the winter. Not a cent is due me in Charleston. Nor do I owe a cent.

1818–1819 Season

On October 1, 1818, Morse married Lucretia Walker (1799–1825), daughter of Mr. and Mrs. Charles Walker, Esq., in Concord, Massachusetts. She accompanied him to Charleston for his second winter season.

[S. F. B. Morse to His Parents]

SCHOONER TONTINE, AT ANCHOR OFF CHARLESTON LIGHTHOUSE, THURSDAY, November 19, 1818, 5 o'clock P.M.

We have arrived thus far on our voyage safely through the kind protection of Providence. We have had a very rough passage attended with many dangers and more fears, but have graciously been delivered from them all. It is seven days since we left New York. If you recollect that was the time of my last passage in this same vessel. She is an excellent vessel and has the best captain and accommodations in the trade. Lucretia was a little seasick in the roughest times, but, on the whole, bore the voyage extremely well. She seems a little downcast this afternoon in consequence of feeling as if she was going among strangers, but I tell her she will overcome it in ten minutes' interview with Uncle and Aunt Finley* and family.

She is otherwise very well and sends a great deal of love to you all. Please let Mr. and Mrs. Walker know of our arrival as soon as may be. I will leave the remainder of this until I get up to town. We hope to go up when the tide changes in about an hour.

Friday morning, 20th, at Uncle Finley's
We are safely housed under the hospitable roof of Uncle Finley, where they received us, as you might expect, with open arms. He has provided lodgings for us at ten dollars per week. I have not yet seen them; shall go directly.

[John Alston to S. F. B. Morse Esquire]
Georgetown December 11th 1818
Sir,
I wish to obtain the favor of you, to paint in oil on canvas a small half-portrait of my two sons. I am the more desirous of it as I have the engraved likenesses of two gentlemen whose attitudes I admire exceedingly. If you will execute them I will send you the engravings, and also a small portrait which will show you the exact size that I wish them. I wish your answer in a few days as I shall have a good opportunity of sending by water the portrait & engravings, if you consent. My three children† are now in the country, but will return to Charleston the beginning of January, when I will have the pleasure to write to you. I remain, Sir, most respectfully,
Your obt. Servt.
John A. Alston

*James Edward Burr Finley (1758–1819) was the uncle of Morse's mother. Born in Maryland, he attended the College of Philadelphia, then pursued medicine. He was made a regimental surgeon in the Continental Army. After the Revolution, he practiced medicine at Willtown in Colleton County and in Beaufort. In 1798, he married Mary Peronneau Young (1775–1852) of Colleton County. They moved to Charleston in 1813, and Dr. Finley was president of the South Carolina Medical Society from 1816 to 1818. Never financially successful as a doctor, he was also a planter. The Finleys lived at 10 Meeting Street (Brunhouse, "David Ramsay, 1749–1815 Selections," 143, 8n).
†Alston's children were William, Thomas, and Sarah (Sally).

[S. F. B. Morse to His Parents]

December 22nd 1818

My Dear Parents,

I was detained a long time from commencing my painting from various causes. My things did not arrive until after we had been here 10 days, and I had not then obtained a room. I found difficulty in obtaining one. I have at last found one.* I was obliged to have some alteration made in the light which would have taken three or four hours for our northern workmen to have completed, but it took six days. I have commenced painting again with success. I have five or six new sitters and more applying every day; I have not yet collected any money but expect to soon.

Lucretia is well and contented. She makes many friends and we receive as much attention from the hospitable Carolinians as we can possibly attend to. She is esteemed quite handsome here; she has grown quite fleshy and healthy, and we are as happy in each other as you can possibly wish us.

There are several painters arrived from New York,† but I fear no competition; I have as much as I can do.

General Pinckney is out of town, but will be in town in January or Febr. Mr. Allston [sic]‡ of Georgetown has written me, and wishes me to paint 2 more pictures of his sons beside those I have painted which I shall finish as well as I can from the boys when they come to town. I have an order to paint a copy of General Pinckney's small at half the price of the great one, that is 150 dollars. It is very much admired.

[John Alston to S. F. B. Morse Esquire]

Georgetown December 28th 1818

Sir,

I am infinitely obliged to you for consenting to execute the last two pictures I requested. You will herewith receive the 9th Volume of the *Analectic Magazine* which contains an engraved likeness of Chief Justice Marshall,§ & I wish my son

---

*For a second season, Morse stayed at the boarding house of Mrs. Margaret Monro, probably at 36 Church Street, although she also owned a boarding house at 95 Church. It was a short walk from Church through St. Michael's Alley to Morse's studio, located in back of the Barelli, Torres & Co. store at 35 Broad Street (Mabee, *American Leonardo*, 72; *Charleston Courier*, December 17, 1818; Hagy, *Charleston S.C. City Directories for the Years 1816, 1819, 1822, 1825, and 1829* [see 1819]).

†There were now thirteen seasonal artists competing in town.

‡John Ashe Alston, not "Allston."

§Supreme Court Chief Justice John Marshall (1755–1835) had presided over the 1807 trial of former Vice-President Aaron Burr for treason, which resulted in an acquittal. Burr was

Thomas represented in this attitude. I have chosen it on account of the fine view presented of the face, but I could wish the eyes represented as looking *directly* at one. It has also another advantage, that of exhibiting a large part of the body—but it is not my wish that my son should be dressed like the Chief Justice. I wish him dressed in a black coat & white waistcoat, no cravat, but a handsome ribbon in his shirt collar, but if you think the ribbon better left out, you can do so. He must also be seated in a beautiful chair, & the pen & paper held in his hands must rest on a handsome table. In the back view, I *earnestly* beseech you to introduce an appropriate & *magnificent* scenery, & let your canvas be enlarged, if you please, to make room for it. My feelings with regard to this boy are unutterable; he is enveloped in the fervor of my affection. "Et vitae & morti gloria justa mea." I will not trespass further upon your attention with regard to his picture, than to say that, while I am desirous to pay for every touch of your pencil, I *entreat* it may be executed in such a measure as will induce me to exclaim when I see it, "Tu Marcellus eris."

You will also receive the 3rd volume of the *Analectic Magazine* containing an engraved likeness of Fisher Ames.* I wish my son William represented in this attitude with an appropriate landscape also. A small portrait of the Reverend Samuel Stanhope Smith† will also be handed to you in order to show you the size I wish you to paint the above likeness. I wish them executed in *oil* on canvas, but if you judge the face too small for you, then make it as near the size as you can—I leave it *entirely* to you. After you have sufficiently examined the size of the Smith's picture be pleased to return it to Mssrs. Kershaw & Lewis.‡

I know not how to thank you sufficiently for the fine portrait you have been pleased to execute of my daughter. Its frame had reached me long before your

---

the father of Theodosia Burr Alston (1783–1813), the wife of Alston's brother, Joseph Alston (1778–1816), governor from 1812 to 1814. Not long after the death their young son in 1812, Theodosia sailed from Georgetown to meet her father in New York and the ship was lost at sea. Joseph Alston, overwhelmed by loss, died a few years after his wife disappeared (Groves, *The Alstons and the Allstons*, 54–55).

*Fisher Ames (1758–1808), U.S. congressman from Massachusetts. The Gilbert Stuart engraving appeared in *Analectic Magazine* 3 (April 1814), facing page 309 (Staiti, "Samuel F. B. Morse's Search for a Personal Style," 275).

†Rev. Samuel Stanhope Smith (1751–1819), the son of Rev. Robert Smith of Charleston, was a Presbyterian minister and professor who served as seventh president of Princeton University. He was founder of Hampden-Sydney College in Virginia.

‡The firm of Kershaw & Lewis (Charles Kershaw and John Lewis) were Alston's rice factors. The extended Alston family of planters sent enormous quantities of rice to this firm in Charleston, which later became Kershaw, Lewis and Robertson (Childs, *Rice Planter and Sportsman*, 67).

letter. Upon its arrival it shall be placed at the head of my little collection. The full-size half-portrait of Mrs. Mary Wollstonecraft, afterwards to Mrs. Godwin, painted by Mr. Opie, so long & so justly idolized by me,* shall give place to it. My fine original head of Mr. Fox,[†] and even my "Venus & Cupid" painted by Mr. West will no longer possess charms for me. I am overpowered by my anxiety to see it, & will be obliged to you to have it *most beautifully* framed when finished. As soon as you are ready to deliver three you took to the North to finish, be pleased to forward me your accompt. by mail & I will instantly request Messrs. Kershaw & Lewis to receive the pictures & pay the accompt.

The rest of the pictures, as you have not yet began them, had better from the second accompt. You were kind enough to assure me on your departure the last spring, that you would take a full size half-portrait of my daughter as soon as you returned this winter. She will return to Mrs. Colcock's in fifteen days, & I would wish you to prepare immediately for it. I would value a likeness taken immediately on her return while her countenance was fresh in my memory much more than I would one taken some time after. The countenance of young persons alter almost every month, & it would not be much gratification to receive a likeness I have in substance never seen in my children. I take the liberty of applying this observation with regard to my two sons, but particularly with regard to Thomas. If you could finish *all* of the heads, I would wait with great pleasure for all the rest, as *long* as you choose.

I had nearly forgotten to say to you that in your *small* portrait of my son William, I wish you to represent him looking directly at one; in the engraved likeness of Mr. Ames from which the attitude is to be taken, it is not quite so. I regret most extremely I have not, at this moment, the miniature of my wife which you have permitted me to consider you as engaged to take a copy of. Had I thought its absence at this moment *could* have occurred, it should not have left me; however, I hope to receive it in time before you leave here. I have ever been desirous to have three copies more taken from it, one from yourself, from Wm. Vanderlyn,[‡]

---

*Cornish painter John Opie (1761–1807) painted Mary Wollstonecraft, who had married social philosopher and author William Godwin (1756–1834). Mary Shelley, author of *Frankenstein*, was their daughter. Opie's portrait of Mary Wollstonecraft later hung in the National Portrait Gallery in London (Earland, *John Opie and His Circle*, 124).

[†]Charles Fox (1749–1806), controversial British Whig statesman whose last great achievement was the abolition of the British slave trade. Busts, portraits, and statues of Fox were popular with the English aristocracy. It is curious that Alston, a slave owner, had a bust of Fox in his art collection.

[‡]This was not William but John Vanderlyn (1775–1852), a portrait artist from Kingston, New York, who created landscapes in the neoclassical style including "Falls of Niagara,"

& from Mr. Stuart.* As you informed me you could not spare time to take your copy of it the last summer, I sent it in the interim by one of my young half brothers, to Mr. Vanderlyn, whose extraordinary politeness & kindness I can never sufficiently compensate. Not being sufficiently satisfied with his copy on which he bestowed unlimited attention, he has proceeded to take a second, which I expect with the original shortly. As soon as I receive them I will send you the original and the copy with my remarks, so that I am sure of enjoying all the advantages that talent can afford on a subject; of all others in the world, the most interesting to me. I remain, Sir, with perfect respect & consideration,
Your Obt. Servt.,
John A. Alston

[John Alston to S. F. B. Morse Esquire]
Georgetown Jan 6th 1819
Sir,
My son Thomas will have the honor to present you this letter & I will be very much obliged to you to finish the face of his small portrait as soon as you can conveniently, but with regard to the other parts of it I would prefer your taking a long time. Let his *hair* be beautifully disposed of & give with perfect fidelity a fair expression to his animated eye. Having said so much to you about his portrait I will close this part of my letter by again praying you to let the rays of you genius converge on this little picture, & you charge a proportionate price. I offer you for it my eternal gratitude.

My son William will also attend to your commands. I beg the favor of you to take a small portrait of the same size as these two last ones of my sons, of my friend W. Benj. F. Dunkin,:† if you will make known my request to him he will

a popular subject in early nineteenth-century America. He was a protégé of Aaron Burr. (Rumor had it Vanderlyn was the lover of Theodosia Burr, but that's another story.) He would exhibit canvases in Charleston, principally "Versailles Panorama" between 1822 and 1823, and frequent Charleston until 1836. Vanderlyn's portrait of Andrew Jackson hangs today in the art collection of Charleston City Hall (Marsh, "John Vanderlyn, Charleston and Panorama," 217–429; Avery, *John Vanderlyn's Panorama*, 25–26).

*Gilbert Stuart (1755–1828), a native of Rhode Island, studied painting at the Royal Academy with Benjamin West. He found patronage in the Manigault family of Charleston. First an itinerant painter, before his death Stuart painted over a thousand American political and social figures. He is now considered one of America's foremost portraitists.

†Benjamin Faneuil Dunkin (1792–1874) served in Alston's Third Regiment Militia during the War of 1812. Born in Philadelphia, he graduated from Harvard and was admitted to the Charleston bar in 1814. He owned Midway Plantation on the Waccamaw River near George-

sit for it immediately; I am too lazy to write to him but he will not refuse me anything. Paint it if you please with *hands.*

I have a sister & am extremely desirous that you should take a full size half-portrait of her w[ith] hands. She resides on this place* & has at length yielded to my solicitations for it. She will go to Charleston for the sole purpose if you will consent to take it, but cannot remain but for a few days. Could you not take a sitting morning & afternoon & finish the *face* in a short time, the rest you might finish at you leisure. I am Sir, with great consideration

Your humble servt.,

John A. Alston

[John Alston to S. F. B. Morse Esquire]

Georgetown Jan 11th 1819

Sir,

My brother William Alston[†] leaves here today for Charleston & intends to look at your paintings. I am extremely desirous to get you to take a full size half-portrait of him with hands. He has partly promised me to attend you for that purpose tho' his stay in Charleston will be but a very few days. I am afraid he will disappoint me, & I will therefore consider it a great favor if you will assist me in persuading him to sit. You will probably have an opportunity of doing so. The face could be completed while he remains in town & the rest of the portrait finished at your leisure. If I remember right, you informed me that your price for such work with a plain back would be eighty dollars. I wish it executed in the same manner as you did my father's. I will wish it represented in such an attitude as to admit of the face looking directly at one. In that of my father's, it is not quite so.

I avail myself of this opportunity to acquaint you that my daughter will soon return to Charleston & will attend you, but as her portrait is to be painted in your *best manner* & with an *elegant landscape,* I agreed the last thing to pay you one hundred and fifty dollars, it is to be a full size half-portrait with hands. You

---

town. The next year, he would marry Washington Sala Prentiss (1800–1870), whose portrait Morse also painted. Dunkin would later serve as chancellor and chief justice of South Carolina (Davidson, *Last Foray*, 194; Easterby, "South Carolina Through New England Eyes," 127–36).

*Alston's sister, Lady Maria Nisbet (b. 1778), estranged from her husband, Scotch Baronet Sir John Nisbet (1775–1827), had returned home in 1810. After Nesbit's death, she married Dr. John Murray (Groves, *The Alstons and the Allstons*, 54; Côté, *Theodosia Burr Alston*, 350).

[†]William Algernon Alston (1781–1860).

would much oblige me if you would take it as soon as she attends you. I mean the face, for the rest I would rather have done when you are at leisure. I would also be much obliged to you to represent her in as handsome an attitude as you can design.

I am, Sir, with great respect & consideration
Your humble servt.,
John A. Alston

[John Alston to S. F. B. Morse Esquire]
Georgetown January 28th 1819
Dear Sir,

I have the honor to receive your letter of the 22 instant. I am very much flattered & gratified with the attention you have been pleased to show me. It has *always* been my intention to procure from you some *first rate* prices & I have been deterred *only* by the consideration of your being too much engaged to bestow that attention upon one of them, on *which alone* I would be willing to receive it. I hope you will excuse this liberty I take, and the trouble I now give you, it is the tax which distinguished citizens must pay the community for the honors they receive. I wish to engage you to paint a full length portrait as *large as life*, of a very young & small person, with the "richest display of scenery" that it is in *your power* to design and execute, the scenery to be *very extensive* and *large*, to allow room for a *full display* of your genius. A small part, say the head and *hands only* to be immediately painted & *no other part* of it to be touched until you return to the Northward, & the picture not to be delivered to me until the expiration of twelve months or longer if you choose. When you deliver the picture you are to pledge me the honor of a gentleman that it is the *finest you ever painted,* & in the execution of the landscape you have exhausted all the powers of your invention.

This is requiring a great deal of you, & I would disdain to say so much were I not fully determined to give you a price equal if not far beyond the magnitude of my request. But for particular reasons I wish you to name a price at which you would be satisfied, in your answer, which I beg will be *immediate,* as there is an extraordinary occasion for it. I request you *will not* impart any part of this letter to any person *whatever.* I cannot be satisfied unless I obtain your price first. I shall *insist* upon your receiving as soon as the face and hands are finished a part of the payment in advance say two hundred dollars of it. It is unnecessary to say more until I hear from you when I will explain myself *fully* & I beg you will gratify me in this request, with that hope, I remain Dear Sir, most respectfully
Yr obt. servt.,
John A. Alston

[S. F. B. Morse to His Parents]
Charleston So. Car Jan. 30th 1819
My Dear Parents,
After trying hard to collect a little money for you I have been able to get the sum of 400 dollars, as you will see by the above bill which I hope will arrive safe and be a relief to you. Money is very scarce here and those who owe me are principally out of town. I will send you all as fast as I can collect it. We are all well and I am constantly employed and have constant additions to my list. I have more than I can do this season already. Mr. Alston of Georgetown is making continual application to me and giving me more to do for him. I have added to my list to the amt. of about 1000 dollars since I have been here, and there is no probability of its stopping. Three or four whom I considered doubtful last season, have declined sitting; in consequence, I believe, of the scarcity of money. But no others have followed their example, and they may comply before I leave Charleston finally.

I have scarcely a moment's time to write. I snatch a moment now while waiting for dinner.

[John Alston to S. F. B. Morse Esquire]
Georgetown January 30th 1819
Dear Sir,
Your letter of the 29th inst. was duly received & I write to you in such a state of mind & heart that I can with *reason* beg that no part of this letter may be made known to *any one*. I shall, as much as I am able endeavour to repress the feelings under which I am labouring, & communicate my ideas with betraying as little of my weakness as the nature of the case will permit me. The portrait alluded to in my last letter is a full-length one as large as life of my beloved daughter whose existence in this world will very soon terminate. She is in a deep consumption, her frame is wasting *very fast* & the destroying hand of this incurable disease has at length reached her face which is generally the last part it touches. In two days after you receive this you will either find her at Mrs. Colcocks or learn there where she may be found. I will give you the price you require for the picture, say six hundred dollars, and pay you two hundred dollars of it as soon as you finish the head. The arms & hands you must not attempt to finish but only take a sketch of, as it will be impossible for you to determine the *attitude* (*on which my very soul is fixed*) without the most mature deliberation, & the finishing of them at this moment would be injurious. You perceive the necessity of finishing the head with as little delay as the difficulty of it will admit. In accomplishing it, I trust it is unnecessary for me to say that no consideration whatever ought to hurry you in the least but that you ought to take as much time *literally* as if you

had nothing else to do. I trust you will perceive the importance of what I have at stake. If you fail I have no appeal. I wish I could write as I feel. I trust that on such an occasion you will put forth all your powers—that you will make the canvas speak. I have seen several of your portraits before one of which I often sit & admire. But I will not have you believe that I admire it as *it is, far from it,* I admire only in it the genius which tells me what it could perform were it *pressed.* In the countenance of my daughter you must give all the *animation* in your power; you must let "from her expressive eye her soul *distinctly speak*"—"Every muscle of her face must be full of *motion* and *expression.*" Instead of the flat & commonly expressive likenesses that are taken & which are usually denominated (though falsely) striking ones, you must exhibit a picture *truly animated.* It is not possible for you to have such another opportunity of placing me under such obligation to you as the present, & is there a spectacle more interesting to humanity than that of a father imploring from your genius an image of his departing & only daughter, & that daughter too the representative of his deceased wife? As soon as you will inform me that the head is *perfectly finished* & that you have no further occasion for her attendance I will call to see it. The *extent* of the landscape I have already described. Next to the countenance it is the attitude which interests me. It must be divine. May you exhibit in this picture the learning of Michael Angelo [*sic*], the grace of Correggio, the coloring of Titian, but *above all,* I invoke the spirit of "the divine Raphael" to inspire you with the *attitude.* How often shall I leave the grave of my child for the society of this picture.* It shall be placed in a room where none shall enter but myself. There prostrate & alone I shall offer you the humble tribute of my gratitude. Little did I think when a youth while I hung with rapture on the eloquent accents of your father that I should ever receive such consolation from *his* son.† I had nearly forgotten to say that I wish you to paint your name under one of the feet of this picture, & the year.

The half-portrait with hands as large as life of my daughter I wish you to execute also. If you will execute the head perfectly so as never more to have occasion

---

*"Sally" or Sarah McPherson Alston (1807–1878) recovered. She later married John Izard Middleton, had seven children, and lived to age seventy-one. Morse was paid eight hundred dollars for the finished full-length portrait of Sally wandering amid the ruins of a gothic abbey. It was his most expensive and, six feet high, his largest portrait. In 1819, the portrait was described in the *New England Galaxy and Masonic Magazine*: "The whole canvas is filled with the ruins of a venerable architecture—gothic, crumbling, and falling, encumbered with ivy, and festooned with the luxuriance of nature—with glimpses of blue sky between." The portrait has not survived.

†Over the years, Jedidiah Morse had preached many times from Charleston pulpits, where John Alston likely heard him.

for her, I will wait as long as you choose for the rest of this picture also. I will delay going to Charleston until I hear from you that both of the heads are finished, as I wish to see both at the same time. As this is an important letter will you oblige me by saying that you have received it, as I shall be uneasy until I hear you acknowledge the *date*. I am Sir, with the greatest respect and consideration

Your humble servt.,

John A. Alston

[John Alston to S. F. B. Morse Esquire]

Georgetown March 7th 1819

Dear Sir,

Your favor of the 4th ulto. was duly received & I cannot find words sufficient to expressing my gratitude for it. To have *such an assurance* from *you,* on a subject of such importance to my feelings, is more gratifying & acceptable to me than anything else in the world that *could be offered to me* upon the reception of this picture (the full-length likeness of my daughter as large as life, of such a description as to the size of the canvas & landscape). It will only remain for me to testify my gratitude *in a manner* worthy your pencil & *my honor.* I have already said to you, that in order to give you full time to accomplish my object, the picture is not to be delivered until twelve months from the time I made application for it, or longer if you choose. My daughter is at the boarding school of Mrs. Fraser* & will attend you at any time, & should you experience any difficulty in her attendance I request you will acquaint me and I will have it removed. You have been good enough to promise to execute a full size half-portrait of each of my sons with hands & landscape, & I am to pay you for each of them 150 dollars. It is proper form to apprize you that my sons will return to the country on the first of April and will remain during that month & very probably may not return to Charleston until the end of May. Your time may then be too limited to take their pictures. The object of this letter is to beg the favor of you to finish the heads of each during the present month, *so perfectly* as *never again* to require their *attendance.* I shall send them to the North this spring to remain for some years & I do not think you will have another opportunity of seeing them. As they may never return to me I feel extremely unhappy about these pictures & beg the favor of a line from you about them as soon as convenient; will you finish them before you leave Charleston or take them to the North to complete? Should you intend to take them with you, I beseech you to finish the *heads perfectly* as you perceive you

---

*Miss Fraser's Ladies School at 1 St. Philip Street (Hagy, *Charleston, S.C. City Directories for the Years 1816, 1819, 1822, 1825, and 1829*, 9).

cannot again see them. I wish the heads finished at any rate as soon as possible, for should you conclude to take them with you & they are executed late, upon being packed up soon after & excluded from the air so long, they will certainly turn yellow & get otherwise injured. Excuse, my Dear Sir, this freedom, & impute it *only* to the affection of a father. You had hardly reached Charleston bar last year before my youngest son was given over by the physicians; he was near expiring in convulsions to *which he is subject,* & should this again occur I may lose this picture. The first thing I thought of when he was in peril was the likeness you had taken of him, and this, on account of your desire to gratify me, you have commenced; so that had he died I should not have had a fine likeness of him. *I wish to be insured against this misfortune.* I wish you to let me know what will be your price for each of the small portraits of my sons which I hope you will finish before you leave here. I make the request merely because it will be necessary for me to give any factors directions as to their payment. I have forgotten to request the price of the small portrait of Mr. Dunkin which I beg you will not *fail* to execute. My sister will attend you in a few weeks. I thank you for the impression of the seal you sent me; it will probably be the subject of a communication some time hence.

Accept, Dear Sir, the assurance of my respect & regard,

John A. Alston

As soon as the heads of the two portraits of any daughter are completed I hope to hear from you.

[S. F. B. Morse to His Parents]

Charleston So. Car. March 26th 1819

My Dear Parents,

I will just say that Lucretia is just recovering from a *severe bilious fever,* which has confined here to her bed for several days.

It is necessary I should visit Washington, as the President will stay so short a time here that I cannot complete the head unless I see him in Washington (by the by, the City Council have passed a unanimous vote to request me to paint it for the City Hall, and have agreed to give me more than I asked, 750 dollars).* I

---

*When President James Monroe announced plans to tour Charleston in 1819, the city requested that Morse paint his portrait to commemorate the occasion. Monroe arrived in April and was fêted at balls and parties, and attended the theater, military reviews, and a firework display. He was so busy he was unable to sit for a portrait. Therefore it was arranged that Morse would travel to Washington and paint Monroe's portrait, which the artist did later that year (Morse to Elizabeth Morse, December 17, 1819, Samuel F. B. Morse Papers, Library of Congress).

therefore propose leaving here for Baltimore by water; leave Lucretia in the care of Nancy at Baltimore and go on to Washington to complete my business there; then proceed to Baltimore—and go on to Philadelphia by steamboat and stage, stay a few days there, or a day as may be; then to New York by steamboat and stage, a day or two there; then by packet to Providence; from there *home* by easy stage. There can be no danger but rather benefit by such a plan. There will be very little land carriage, and plenty of time to rest, after every short journey. *Aunt Finley* thinks there will be no danger rather benefit, and she, you know, is a good judge in these matters.

I have not received any money lately of sufficient importance to send you, but hope to send a remittance soon. I shall not make so much this season as last, from a variety of causes all of which I cannot explain in a letter. One is that Lucretia's illness has caused a considerable expenditure to me and there have been several pictures which I painted last year that I have redeemed by painting them over again.

[John Alston to S. F. B. Morse Esquire]
Georgetown April 10th 1819
Dear Sir,
Your favor of the 31st ulto. was duly received, & I would have answered it immediately but was desirous of seeing your portrait of my daughter before I did so; four days ago I had the pleasure to view it & have been since then *too ill* to write to you. I hope you will deem the apology sufficient. I wrote immediately upon the receipt of your favor to Mssrs. Kershaw & Lewis, and requested them to pay you two hundred dollars, according to my promise, as part payment for the full-length portrait you are to execute of my daughter as large as life; and I also requested them to pay you sixty-six dollars for the frame of the small portrait you have just sent me, both of which payments I suppose they have by this time made you. The account you have been pleased to give me of the painting of the head of my daughter, together with the numerous reports of others on the same subject, has so completely overwhelmed me that I *shall not* express to you my feelings or my gratitude. My obligations are eternal; they shall long, *very long,* be *substantially* expressed to you. There is nothing I have, *or can have,* so near my heart as this picture. My soul hovers over it even in imagination, & should it meet my expectations, it will cling to it as to the Angel of Mercy. Your first letter consenting to undertake this picture shall always be preserved by me; it reflects as much credit to your head & heart, as any of your productions will to your pencil. Let the suitableness of the drapery, the variety, the contrast, be beautiful in perfection—but, above all, so graceful, that it may never be equaled by any one. Whenever you will inform me of any of the rest of the pictures being ready

for delivery, I will direct Mssrs. Kershaw and Lewis to receive such and pay you for them. Is it your intention to take any of them to the North to finish & if so which of them? I ask this because I shall in such case insist upon paying half of the price before your departure; as there is to be a beautiful landscape to the full sized half-portrait of my sons, & also to the full sized half-portrait of my daughter. I fear its being done here for want of time—but this I leave to yourself. Though my letters are dated at Georgetown I reside eight miles from that place. Your portrait of my daughter was left in Georgetown at the house of a friend; nearly all of the citizens have seen it & I really think it will occasion you some applications. I found several looking at it & even His Honor the Judge who happened at that time to be holding the circuit court. Everyone thought himself at liberty to make remarks. Some declared it to be a good likeness, while others insisted it was not so, and several who made such remarks, I knew had never seen my daughter. At last a rich Jew gentleman observed, "it was the richest piece of painting he had ever seen." This being so much in character that I assure you, sir, I could contain myself no longer, which, spreading among the audience occasioned not an unpleasant moment. I am extremely pleased with it. There is certainly very considerable likeness, & the more I examine it the better pleased I am but do not think the likeness quite as striking as I could have wished. With regard to the painting, you know, nothing could exceed it. As a painting alone I would have given much more than it cost me, & considered myself fortunate in meeting with it. Some of my friends think the likeness extremely strong. I am satisfied it is the best ever taken of my daughter. I should be much gratified to see the fine picture of Mr. Washington Allston,* but must decline the purchase of it. It has always been my intention to procure a piece of Mr. Allston's painting & I am sure I shall do so even though it cost more than the present one—but I would greatly prefer some of his figures to a landscape, & I would wish moreover to have one of his last productions as every one will constantly improve. I certainly shall at some future day apply to him. I assure you sir, I feel much flattered and gratified at your kind letter in assisting me to procure these fine paintings. It will induce me to take the liberty of getting your assistance at some time hence, which otherwise I would not have ventured upon with regard to Mr. Fisher's painting of the falls of

*Washington Allston (1779–1843), known as the "American Titian," was worshipped as an artist in his day. He was a cousin of John Ashe Alston. Born at Brookgreen Plantation (now Brookgreen Gardens) into the Alston/Allston family of planters, Allston attended prep school in Rhode Island, graduated from Harvard in 1800, and studied art at the Royal Academy in London under Benjamin West. He was Morse's principal teacher at the Royal Academy from 1811 to 1815. Allston later made his home in Boston. He and Morse remained friends until Allston's death (Staiti, "Samuel F.B. Morse in Charleston 1818–1821," 87–112).

Niagara.* I wish you when you next write, to have the goodness to state to me his price probably and the length and breadth of the picture & will then determine upon it. In the mean time receive my very best thanks for the preference you have been pleased to give me. His fame has reached me; it is as loud as that cataract. Believe me Dear Sir, with much respect & consideration—
Your obliged servant,
John A. Alston

[John Alston to S. F. B. Morse Esquire]
Georgetown May 28th 1819
Dear Sir,
I have just had the pleasure of receiving your kind favor of the 22nd instant, & have directed Mssrs. Kershaw & Lewis to pay you immediately the $636, being the amount of the accompt. you enclosed—and to receive from you the pictures.

I beg you will procure the frame of my daughter's large picture *at the North,* it will be more splendid that any one that could be gotten here, & I am much interested about the frame, which I wish to be as *superb as can be bought.*

I thank you very sincerely for your benevolence & friendly sentiments with regard to my son Thomas. This is the fourth time the physicians have pronounced him to be "in articulo mortis," indeed he appeared to be even in the last stage of death, in this last attack, & I in truth despair of ever raising him, which I believe I have already mentioned to you. A year ago you began a picture of him which you informed me you had condemned; if it [is] of no further use to you, you *will much oblige me* if you will send it to me with the rest. The least resemblance of him would afford me happiness. It will be hung only in my chamber & not seen by anyone else. As it is unfinished I do not wish it framed, I will give you for it what sum you may require. I do not intend to send him to the North as I expected as I cannot consent to part with him. He is just recovering, & I trust will live long enough for you to have another touch at him.[†] My Mother-in-law has delighted me with the description of the dress and drapery you intend to adopt

---

*Alvan Fisher (1792–1863), portrait artist, landscape and animal painter from Boston, was an itinerate painter in Charleston beginning in 1819. Fisher's scenes of Niagara now hang at the Smithsonian, the New-York Historical Society, the National Museum, and the Farnsworth Art Museum in Rockland, Maine.

[†]Thomas survived his father. He married his first cousin, Josephine Alston. However, he died at the age of nineteen in 1835, four years after his father's death. Alston's son, William, did not survive his father. William graduated Princeton in the class of 1825 and married Caroline Thomas of New Jersey in 1826. He died in 1829 (Groves, *The Alstons and the Allstons,* 55–56; Egbert, "Two Portraits by Thomas Sully," 11–16).

for my daughter. Let it be *splendid* beyond description. You cannot imagine my anxiety at this subject. I assure you, Dear Sir, that, wherever you go, you will be followed by my best wishes & feelings, & that I am
Most Respectfully Your's
John A. Alston

[John Alston to S. F. B. Morse Esquire]
June 3rd 1819
Dear Sir,
I am truly sorry I did not receive your kind letter until late tonight, & I beg you will believe it does not put me to the *smallest inconvenience* to pay the little sum I owe you; be pleased therefore to call on Mssrs. Kershaw & Lewis & you will now receive it. I have sent them by this mail an order for the money. Could anything add to the respect & esteem I have always entertained for you, it would be the sentiments you have expressed. Those only who are blessed with them *can* appreciate them. They justify the opinion I had of you. Could you instill such into the minds of my sons I would value them even more than the productions of your genius.

A neighbor who had borrowed a sum of me, returned to me with *convenience* to himself, as much of it as was necessary to pay you. Mssrs. Kershaw & Lewis are truly good & worthy men, but their customers are all pressing upon them for money & they are unable as they express themselves to "turn round" which is the reason your payment has accidentally been delayed. I regret the circumstances but we must expect now & then such slaps. They had rice of mine on hand which it appears they were unable to sell, & they had also the care of a very large quantity more at Mr. Paul Trapier's Mill, not yet pounded out, by the time this last arrives in Charleston, I hope we may all exclaim, "Redeunt saturnia regna." For your present of the old portrait of my son Thomas I thank you sincerely, it shall be noted in its proper place. Accept, Dear Sir, the assurances of my respect and regard,
John A. Alston

1819–1820 Season

[S. F. B. Morse to His Wife]
Charleston, S. Carolina January 12th 1820
My dear Lucretia,
We got to Georgetown at 5 o'clock and set out immediately again; rode all night, very cold, but clear and pleasant, and arrived without accident or sickness safely at Charleston yesterday at 9 o'clock.

I went immediately to Aunt Finley's. The moment they saw me they all burst into tears & were silent.* I have never felt more depressed than at this time; jaded out by a long, fatiguing sleepless ride, finding Aunt and little cousins in a different house; in black; Aunt so altered I should scarcely have known her, everything reminding me of Uncle's absence. This too compared with the absence of my dear Lucertia. At Mrs. Munro's† the room where we slept, and dined, and supped; the places where we walked; all, all made me, dear wife, feel most miserable. I felt the anticipation of what might take place were we taken from each other by death. Oh! I went early to bed, slept soundly 12 hours & waked entirely refreshed and well.

I have got excellent rooms over Dr. Buxbaum's apothecary's shop.‡ It is as we had heard; he, his wife and partner in business and was at death's door, himself with yellow fever. The rooms are very convenient and large. I pay 33 dollars per month for them. I am very busy in getting all things ready, so dearest, excuse the brevity of this letter. I have every thing to say but must defer them till next letter.

[John Alston to S. F. B. Morse Esquire]
Georgetown Jan. 24th 1820
My Dear Sir,
It gives me great pleasure to hear of your safe arrival in Charleston. The late storm made me somewhat uneasy on your account. The account you have been pleased to give me of the superb portrait of my daughter is more gratifying than you can imagine. It only remains that you should be equally well-satisfied with the price. I will not say—it is my *wish*—to compensate you for your *extra* labour, but shall take care that *you shall be satisfied*. Whatever sum we conclude you shall receive, shall be immediately paid upon your answering this letter. You have tried your best and you therefore know the pains it has cost you. I beg to know your opinion of the extra price—my reply shall be immediate. If I could for a moment suppose that you think me capable of imposing upon your delicacy, I would instantly name the extra price, but I have too high an opinion of you, to do such an injustice. My object is merely to have some idea of what you suppose is

---

*Morse refers to the sudden death of Dr. Finley. Summoned late at night to the bedside of a charity patient on James Island, he had contracted country fever and died.

†Morse boarded again at Mrs. Munro's in Church Street, where he and Lucretia had boarded the prior winter.

‡His studio for the season was over 101 Broad Street (*Charleston Courier*, January 19, 1820).

sufficient. It may not entirely govern my decision. I will also thank you to let me know the price of the frame. I will direct Mssrs. Kershaw & Lewis to make you immediate payment. One of the vessels that attend at my plantation will, in eight or ten days, call on Messrs. Kershaw & Lewis for the picture. I am unwilling that so good an opportunity should be lost, or I will cheerfully agree to its remaining longer with you. As the vessel is now at my plantation, the time of her calling may be sooner, or perhaps a few days longer than the time I have mentioned. I was much disappointed the last winter in not obtaining the portrait of my friend Mr. Benjamin F. Dunkin; will you please be so obliging as to assure me in your answer that you will *immediately* commence it. I wish this portrait to be a very neat one. I lately saw a beautiful portrait of that valiant officer Lieutenant James Dudly, represented in his regimental. I wish just such a one of Mr. Dunkin. Paint him dressed in his regimentals, the epaulette & sword to be exposed. Lieutenant Dudly's was a *reduced half*-portrait or rather a little more than a half-portrait in order that the body should appear to advantage. The painting extended to about half way down the thighs—the color of the pantaloons being thus introduced, it afforded a handsome contrast with the coat which was of a different color. He was in the act of walking, his *left arm* being extremely exposed & the left hand with the *glove on,* resting on the hilt of the sword. The coat was buttoned; no part of the *right arm* was seen but the *right hand* was *fully* exposed. One of the buttons about the middle of the breast of the coat, was unbuttoned & the right hand placed resting partly in it; the figure a little turned to the left as if to observe one, but the *face fully exposed* to you. But a small part of the sword was seen, only the hand as the left hand rested on the hilt of the sword; the *left arm* was consequently nearly draped, the sword being hung on the left side at the usual place. It was, as I have said, of a reduced but *beautiful size*—for example, had the whole figure been painted suppose it would have been thirty-two inches. No hat was seen. It was painted on a small piece of board, but I assure you it was *truly elegant.* Let Mr. Dunkin's be of *this size,* and a plain back will be sufficient. You will receive from Mssrs. Kershaw & Lewis the two large portraits of my sons, which have been injured from being kept from the air; please to repair them as possible so that they may have time to dry before their removal. I shall insist upon making you full compensation for this trouble. Is it your intention to go to the North next spring, & to return to Charleston next winter—I am thinking of a new portrait I wish to execute which is the reason of my inquiry. With respect & esteem I am, Dear Sir,

Your most obt. Servt.

John A. Alston

[John Alston to S. F. B. Morse Esquire]
February 4th 1820
My Dear Sir,
I did not receive your letter of the 25th ulto. until yesterday. I reside about ten miles from Georgetown; my father much nearer, & his servant receives my letters & newspapers from the office there. He brings them across the river & delivers them to my servant who conveys them to me. Your letter covering the extracts from the papers was mistaken by my father's servant who thought it contained money & according to his instructions, declined the delivery of *such letters* to anyone but myself. He duly acquainted me of having a letter of this sort, but being engaged with the company of two gentlemen from the North who did not leave my house until yesterday, I was unable to receive your letter before then. I have been this particular in my apology for this delay of my answer as I would not have you wait a moment for payment, even if I knew it a matter of no consequence. Messrs. Kershaw & Lewis will hand you this & will pay you immediately $250 for the frame—and $600 for the picture—also $10 more for the boxing & freight. I will then have paid you for the picture but $800—two hundred dollars having been already paid you in part for it. *I know* that $1000 is the least sum I ought to have paid for it; two hundred is too small a sum for your extra labour, it does not come up to the spirit of any voluntary observations on the subject. I would have made $400 the extra price did I not believe I should have occasion for a picture from you, now & then. I shall *always* consider you engaged to me for such pictures as I may annually want. We will now begin with one of them. I wish another *small whole length* portrait of my daughter—the *face only* to be finished in Charleston, all the rest to be painted at your leisure, next summer, at the North, to be delivered to me the next winter—half of the price to be paid when the head is finished, & the other half when the picture is delivered. What is your price? It must be nearly the size of the little picture you first painted of her, but somewhat *larger*, perhaps the length of the figure, maybe about *thirty-two* inches. I always objected to your first little portrait of her because it is rather *too small.* *The face is not sufficiently large to give a fair likeness.* Make the next just sufficiently large to affect this purpose. I should suppose that a figure of thirty-two inches would answer. Let the landscape equal any of the little pieces of Guido.* I wait with impatience for your answer with this assurance. I want words to express my anxiety for the *attitude* of this portrait. It is the *attitude* which marks a great genius—by this Raphael became entitled to the appellation of "The Devine" & I

---

*Guido Reni (1575–1642), early Italian Baroque painter noted for the classical idealism of his mythological and religious subjects.

confess I would sooner have a fine attitude than a fine painting. Do me the favor of making the attitude the subject of your profound study & could you give me some knowledge of it before you leave Charleston it would be very acceptable. I have a place quite sufficiently large to receive the large portrait. It will be sent to a *fine* new dwelling house on one of my plantations that I have hitherto not frequented as often as my interest required. It will be therefore advantageously placed as my visits will henceforth be more frequent. At present I reside in my kitchen, while my house at my residence is finishing. When finished, it will be the permanent place of the picture. I lately had the misfortune to be burnt out. Hence the goodness to say to Mr. Dunkin that I have not yet received his answer to my letter—& believe me to be, Dear Sir, most Sincerely,
Your obliged & humble servant,
John A. Alston

[S. F. B. Morse to His Wife]
Charleston S. Car. February 17, 1820
My Dearest Lucrece,
I know of nothing new to tell you that will interest you. I don't know that I told you that young Ramsey the lawyer who was lame from a wound in his hip received in a duel some time ago, fought another duel only a day or two before I arrived in Charleston with Hunt the lawyer, and was severely wounded again in the hip.* From all accounts he was entirely to blame on the whole affair; how dispiriting this must be to his sisters and Miss Futerill,† and what a grief would it be to his good mother were she alive. Dr. Flinn is not expected to live from day

---

*This was likely lawyer David Ramsay Jr. (1795–1826), the son of Dr. David Ramsay and Martha Laurens Ramsay, who first trained as a doctor. His opponent was Benjamin Hunt (1792–1854) from Boston, the cousin of Benjamin F. Dunkin. Hunt "was said to have fought a duel with one of the Ramsays, in which he wounded his opponent and generally led quite a stormy life." A graduate of Harvard, Hunt was a lawyer and member of the South Carolina General Assembly, 1818–53, who served in the state militia. He was referred to as "Bully Hunt" for his involvement in frequent disputes and quarrels. A 1913 *New York Times* article gives the date for the duel as 1824, or perhaps they dueled again (Morison, *Life and Letters of Harrison Gray Otis*, 276n; Carson, *Life, Letters and Speeches of James Louis Petigru*, 64; Gillespie, *Life and Times of Martha Laurens Ramsay*, 222. 282–83, 312; J. C. Hemphill, "Charleston's Old Race Course as a Duelling Spot," *New York Times*, January 28, 1913).

†Catherine Futerill (sometimes spelled Futerull) was the daughter of a jailer in the Tower of London, where Henry Laurens was imprisoned for fifteen months by the British in 1780. After Laurens was exchanged for Lord Cornwallis, she returned with the Laurens family to Charleston. She remained a close friend of Martha Laurens Ramsay, lived with her family, and served as governess and tutor to her children. She later returned to England. Dr. David

to day, he has been very ill ever since I have been here; his complaint is dropsical combined with many other diseases. From what I can learn, he appears to be in a happy frame of mind. Dr. Palmer* has been quite unwell with rheumatic fever, dangerously so, but has entirely recovered so as to preach again.

The weather here is delightful, there has been no frost since I arrived, and but two or three days in which we have required fire, for some days past it has been as warm as summer. The *trees are in bloom* and everything wears the cheerful aspect of spring.

Aunt and cousins are well and send a great deal of love to you. We often talk of you. I visit a good deal with the Perroneaus, I am much pleased with them; they always inquire affectionately after you and desire to be remembered to you when I write, as do the Misses Lightwoods.[†] The latter gave a splendid ball a few nights since, 200 invitations. I was not invited, as I was informed, because I did not attend *such places*. I am proud of this distinction and am glad it is known sufficiently to prevent even the invitation. Mrs. Munro & daughter desire also to be remembered to you.

I am engaged constantly in painting and have as much as I can do: did I tell you in my last letter that Col. Alston insisted on giving me *200* dollars more than I asked for the picture of little Sally Alston commission to paint her again full-length next season, smaller than the last, & larger than the first portrait, for which I shall receive 400 dollars & and he intimates also that I am to paint a picture *annually* for him. Is not he a strange man? (as people say here). I wish some more of the great fortunes in this part of the country *would* be as strange and encourage other artists, who are men of genius and starving for want of employment.

Good-bye, my dear wife. I am in momentary expectation of a sitter, so must close in haste.

[John Alston to S. F. B. Morse Esquire]
Georgetown February 25th 1820
My Dear Sir, Your favor of the 9th instant was duly received. At that time I was at the bedside of a dying friend who has at last paid the debt of nature. I could not sufficiently collect my mind to write to you sooner. I thank you for all the kind things you have been pleased to say of me, but it is I who am under obligations to you, not you to me. I shall never think otherwise. If you have not already began

---

Ramsay Jr. named one of his children for her (Brunhouse, "David Ramsay, 1749–1815: Selections," 106, 5n; Calhoun, *Circular Church*, 44).

*Rev. Benjamin Morgan Palmer (1780–1847), pastor of the Circular Congregational Church for many years.

[†]The Lightwoods, related to Aunt Mary (Peronneau) Finley, lived on Meeting Street.

the new full-length portrait of my daughter, *thirty two inches in length,* I beg you will begin it *immediately.* It will require much time to dry. You were so kind to promise you would only finish the face in Charleston; the rest is to be done this summer, at your leisure, at the North. As soon as the *face* is *perfectly finished,* be pleased to inform me of it. I shall wait with impatience to—of it. Let the face be *completely done before you leave Charleston* and by no means require to be re-touched on your return. I pray let this be done as my daughter may die before you get back to Charleston. I take the liberty of begging you *not* to introduce the black servant into this picture. I can not approve of it. But could you in-troduce some beautiful animal or other into the picture it would gratify me ex-cessively. When I consider that the canvas is to be two sizes larger than the two large portraits of my sons, together with the beautiful landscape, I am sure that the price you have fixed, say four hundred dollars, is reasonable enough. The attitude, the drapery, the scenery, and fine painting is certainly highly gratifying to me; but be pleased to recollect that the likeness is even more acceptable to me. My daughter may possibly die before long. Of how much value then would the likeness be to me: but even was she to live, would not a *striking likeness* of her be a source of never-ending happiness to me. I therefore pray your utmost exertion in the likeness. I beg to hear from you very soon as I shall be uneasy until I know you have gotten this letter. When you write please let me know how you come on with Mr. Dunkin's portrait. The portrait you have sent me of my daughter is truly superb; I am delighted with it beyond description. May your fame be immortal.

Accept, Dear Sir, the assurances of my profound respect & esteem,
John Ashe Alston

Have you the condemned portrait of my son?

I do not wish you to take the full-size half-portrait of my daughter which I requested of you to do the last year. The above mentioned likeness of her I mean as a *substitute* for the *half-portrait.*

[S. F. B. Morse to His Wife]
Charleston S. Car. Feb. 27th 1820 Sunday
My Dearest Wife,
I am full of business but hope to get away by the latter end of April; tell me when you shall be in N. Haven at farthest.

Henry* is a steady good boy and helps me a great deal. He discovers daily more genius; I think uncommon genius. My former pupil Mr. Hinckley has learnt out,

*Henry Cheever Pratt (1803–1880) from New Hampshire was employed as an errand boy in the parsonage of Rev. Morse when Samuel saw his paintings on a barn door and enrolled

so much so that he is now able to keep a shoe store. He finds it more profitable to measure feet rather than noses and pays more regard to the understanding of his customers, than to paint their faces.

I wrote you in the last that Dr. Flinn was not likely to live; he is since dead. And was buried on Saturday. I trust he is in heaven. Aunt Finley and cousins are well, and thank you for the remembrance you make of them. They all send a great deal of love to you. Mrs. Munro & daughter, Mr. & Mrs. McCall, Mr. & Mrs. Cogsdell, Mr. & Mrs. Willington, the Perroneaus, Mrs. Judy Colcock, & many others send a great deal of love to you & always ask after you when they see me.

[John Alston to S. F. B. Morse Esquire]
Georgetown March 15th 1820
Dear Sir,
Will you let me know the price for the portrait of Mr. Dunkin? Be good enough to direct a frame to be made for it. In your next letter will you assure me that the new portrait of my daughter shall be well painted, together with its landscape, as the large picture of her which you have just sent me. I shall expect this assurance. The interest I entertain on the subject is more than I can express to you. I wish you to picture at the North as splendid a frame for it as you can possibly have made. In your next letter will you trace with your pen, or a part of it, the attitude of her face; having began to paint the face the attitude of it is already accomplished. Let the drapery be as beautiful as possible. In the lower part of your little painting of my daughter, there is something very superb. I was enamored with it in the moment I saw it. I regret to find that your name is not painted on the large picture. In the new portrait pray do not fail to have it painted. I expect to have a portrait executed by Mr. Sully* & Mr. Vanderlyn. In my little collection I wish to have the names of the different artists painted in each piece. I wrote, in December last, to Mr. Stuart, of Boston, about a piece, but have not received a reply. If you will be so obliging to let me know Mr. Fisher's price for a view of the falls of Niagara; and the size of the proposed view; and whether there will be two views or one, I will write you then immediately, if I will become a subscriber.

---

him in art classes. He was now Samuel's painting assistant. He would return to Charleston as a portrait artist, and was later renowned for his landscapes, particularly of the American Southwest (Mabee, *American Leonardo*, 78).

*Thomas Sully's portraits of Alston's son, William, and his wife, Caroline Thomas Alston, were bequeathed to Princeton University by a descendant in 1960 (Egbert, "Two Portraits by Thomas Sully," 11–16).

With regard to Mr. Vanderlyn's views of the falls of Niagara, I must decline the purchase of them; though I confess I decline with considerable reluctance. For the last three years I have ardently wished to purchase these very views and if I had known they could have been bought I would long since have been the owner of them. I recollect the very time he painted them—it has been a good while since—no one can more highly estimate the genius of Mr. Vanderlyn than myself, but I must select some other subject from him & have moreover the advantage of some later production of his pencil. Which of my friends was it who lately observed to you that I had a picture mania? You made, I understand, a most excellent reply; you wished I "would come to town, then, and bite a dozen." Indeed, my very good sir, was it in my power to excite in them a just admiration of your talents, I would readily come to town and bite the whole community. The man who is insensible to the productions of your pencil is deprived of one of the finest pleasures this world can afford; & should you not have the greatest encouragement, I would hesitate whether to blame the ignorance or the villainy of my fellow creatures. As for myself, the genius of painting has ever been the Goddess of my idolatry. I am, Dear Sir, with sincerity,
Your obliged & obt. Servant,
John A. Ashe

P.S. I understand that my daughter has lately had some irruption on her face, but that the spots have nearly disappeared; should any such marks or spots, be still visible, they must not, I beg, be represented in the picture, as they will soon go away.

[John Alston to S. F. B. Morse Esquire]
April 3rd 1820
Dear Sir, I understand you have lately painted a small but excellent likeness of Mr. Pinckney Alston,* and only a small part of the body is represented; your price has been for it, but forty dollars. You have now with you my father's picture, and I am *expressly desirous* that you should take for me a copy of my father's likeness before you part with his picture. It will be perhaps the only chance of my ever getting a copy, as from the distance, the picture could never be sent back to you for the purpose—as I wish it only to be in every respect exactly the same size as that of Mr. Pinckney Alston, representing no more of the body. I shall expect to pay you the same price, say forty dollars. Will you be so obliging to let me know that you will *immediately* commence this copy for me. I shall be much indebted to you for your politeness. On the honor of a gentleman *no one* has the remotest idea of my having such a desire. I request therefore you will not impart or disclose this

*Thomas Pinckney Alston (1795–1861), Aston's younger half-brother.

desire to *anyone*—it must not be placed on your list. You can detain my father's portrait for this purpose as long as you choose, under an excuse of its requiring time to dry, if it should be called for. I am more interested in getting this copy than you can well imagine. It is very near to my heart; & I trust you will immediately gratify me. Excuse the pressing manner of my request, on such occasion I cannot but be pressing. My father is now old & I know not how soon he may be called to pay the debt of nature. I earnestly beg you will take *uncommon pains* in making the copy as *correct* as is in your power. If I am misinformed as to the price, I will pay you whatever price you required for Mr. Pinckney Alston's portrait. If your business would permit you, I beg your answer by the *next mail.*

Messrs. Kershaw & Lewis have been instructed to pay you your price for Mr. Dunkin's portrait & frame. I instructed those gentlemen to let this picture remain with you for twenty or thirty days until it is perfectly dry. You will also receive from them two hundred dollars being in part payment for my daughter's new portrait.

Please to inform Mr. Fisher that I am extremely happy to avail myself of the opportunity of possessing a specimen of his painting, & that I will readily give him the next winter, on his return to Charleston, the two hundred dollars for each of his two views of the fall of Niagara.

In your answer, please to say, if I am to consider that I am to receive the two views of the falls, the next winter. I am, My Dear Sir, with esteem

Your most obt. Servt.,

John A. Alston

[S. F. B. Morse to Mrs. Ball]
Charleston, S. Car. April 21, 1820
Mrs. J. Ball *
Dear Madam,
You may recollect that just before you left town for the country, you promised to send me a check for *$600* in advance for the full-length portrait to be completed

*Martha Caroline Swinton Ball (1786–1847) was the widow of John Ball Sr. (1760–1817), a member of a family of planter-merchants whose rice estates were numerous. By 1810, John Ball and his brother Elias operated Limerick, Kensington, Hyde Park, Quinby, Midway, and Jericho (otherwise called Backriver) plantations. John and Caroline, his second wife, married nine months after the death of his first wife, when he was forty-four years old and Caroline was nineteen, younger than two of his sons. She gave birth to eleven children by Ball. She later married Louis Augustin Taveau (1790–1856) and had five more children. (Dethloff, "Colonial Rice Trade," 231–43; Schantz, "'A Very Serious Business,'" 1–22; Cody, "There Was No 'Absalom' on the Ball Plantations," 563–96; Ball, *Slaves in the Family*, chap. 14).

this summer for you. In consequence of this expectation I had so arranged my funds as to pay my existing debts in Charleston from this sum. The disappointment I experienced in not securing this fund, and learning you had left town, was such to embarrass me. I have the happiness to say that I have at length so arranged my affairs, as to be only under the necessity of requesting the favor of you to honor an order for *One Hundred Dollars,* which I have taken the liberty to give to Mrs. Munro, in part payment of my bill. This will leave *Five Hundred* to be paid when I have completed the picture. The circumstances that you were packing up to leave town is in itself a sufficient apology for overlooking this business, as I well know by experience that such a time above all others is the most perplexing to one's memory. I shall sail tomorrow for N. York in the *President,* and expect to visit Charleston again say next November and shall then hope to present you your picture completed. With sentiments of respect & esteem,
I oblige myself
Your mo. obt. hum. servt.,
Sam. F. B. Morse

1820–1821 Season

[S. F. B. Morse to His Wife]
Charleston So. Car. Dec. 27th 1820
My Dearest Wife,
I shall return by early Spring, unless I have a press of business as shall make it greatly for my interest to stay a little later, I wrote you, dear wife, from the steamship acquainting you with my having attained rooms for 80 dollars for 6 months. *I am occupied fully* so that I have no reason to complain. I have not a *press* like the *first* season or like the *last,* but still I can say I am all the time employed. I find it good to trust in Providence, the promise is sure, I feel perfectly easy. Mr. Shiels* is the only competitor I have in Charleston, and he is not a rival. My President's pleases very much; I have heard no dissatisfaction expressed; it is placed in the great Hall† in a fine light and place. I have not yet received the money; the Council do not meet till the first of January 1821. I have not yet heard from Col. Alston, expect a little next mail. Mrs. Ball wants some alterations, that is to say every five minutes she would like it to be different. She is the most

---

*William Shiels (1785–1857) from Edinburgh was active in New York before he came to Charleston as a portrait artist in the 1820s. He served as a director of the short-lived South Carolina Academy of Fine Arts.

†Morse's portrait of President James Monroe still hangs in Council Chambers at City Hall.

unreasonable of all mortals; derangement is her only apology. I can't tell you all in a letter, must wait till I see you. I shall get the rest of the cash from her shortly.

I find you are remembered, my dear wife, with much affection by a great many in this place. Mrs. & Dr. Wagner* and all that family enquired particularly after you. On Christmas day I dined with them that day; their little son is not so thriving as little Sue,[†] though months older he cannot walk firmly yet. You ask "how I like Perroneau Finley." I am very much pleased with him; he is totally the reverse of Rush, sedate and studious, and very kind and affectionate to his mother and sisters.[‡] I do not mean that Rush is not the latter but he is certainly not the former. Rush by the way is a midshipman in the Navy. He left the law and wrote on for a warrant, which he obtained a few days since. All are well at Aunt Finley's; Mary is in the country to spend the holidays.

[S. F. B. Morse to His Wife]
Wednesday January 10th 1821
I have been making an arrangement, which I think you will all approve of. I found on calculation, that I am paying whole of Charleston at the least $22. per week. I have, therefore, determined to leave Mrs. Munro's and live in Batchelor's Hall.[§] I purchase my own tea & sugar, have contracted to have my dinner brought to my room for me & Henry at $1.00 per day, and I have purchased a moss mattress, pillow and blanket, and shall sleep at my room, by this arrangement. I find I shall save $6.50 per week, which will be something in 5 months. I also save at least 4 hours, in the day, of time, & if I can only find constant employment, I shall do well. So you see, notwithstanding Mother sometimes thinks I have but little fore-sight, I show in this instance at least that like an experienced seaman I can foresee storm, and when the weather is squally can get all things *snug*. I cannot say my prospect is bright this season. I am in good spirits, however, and am determined to *trust,* for I know in whom I have believed. We may not be rich, but we will

---

*Dr. John Wagner (d. 1841) graduated from Yale and studied medicine in New York and abroad before settling in Charleston. He rose to eminence as a surgeon at the South Carolina Medical University, which he helped bring into existence.

[†]Susan Walker Morse (1819–1885), their first child.

[‡]William Peronneau Finley (1803–1876) and Rush Finley (b. 1801), the latter named for Philadelphia physician Benjamin Rush (1746–1813), a relative.

[§]"Batchelor's Hall" refers to men lodging together without women. The term originated in inns, once segregated with men sharing a large hall. Arriving back in town for the season, Morse had discovered a financial change in the complexion of the city; therefore he reduced his portrait fees and his expenses, by living in his studio with his assistant.

never want. I have received the $365 from Col. Alston, but have not received a line or word from him; he has not got the pictures yet. He may be waiting to see them before he writes, but I am preparing (without having any reason, however) for a discontinuance of his patronage. This may or may not be; I am trying to be indifferent which way it goes; Mrs. Hayne,* has made me a present of a beautiful *fawn,* which they are keeping for me until I return home. I shall bring it with me.

[S. F. B. Morse to His Wife]
January 28th 1821
I wish I could write encouragingly as to my professional pursuits, but I cannot. Notwithstanding the diminished price and the increase of exertion to please, and although I am conscious of painting much better portraits than formerly (which, indeed, stands to reason if I make continual exertion to improve), yet with all I receive no new commissions, cold and procrastinating answers from those to whom I write and who had put their names on my list. I give less satisfaction to those whom I have painted; I receive less attention also from some of those who formerly paid me much attention, and none at all from most.

[Mrs. Ball to S. F. B. Morse]
Feb. 1, 1821
Mrs. Caroline Ball's compliments to Mr. Morse, is keenly sorry that she was out of town when his other note came, and intended calling on him since her return, but was prevented so doing by business.

Mrs. B. regrets extremely not having it in her power to settle for the whole of the portrait this year, having been much disappointed with her crop, which has received considerable damage by the gale. Will consider it a great favor if Mr. M. will be contented with half the sum, and wait for the other half, which she will positively pay with the proceeds of the next crop. Had the picture could have been completed last year, she could have paid in whole as she had laid up the cash for that express purpose, but supposing she could command the same this year, she laid out that for the payment of Negroes that she purchased.

*Rebecca B. Alston Hayne (1792–1853) was John Alston's sister. She was married to Robert Young Hayne (1791–1839), Morse's cousin by marriage. Morse's Aunt Finley was Robert Hayne's aunt by her earlier marriage to Robert Young.

As soon as the rice is sold, which she expects will be in a few days, she will call on him with three hundred dollars, one hundred being already paid.

[S. F. B. Morse to his Wife]
Wednesday 7th Feb.
Dearest wife, I have been prevented by a variety of circumstances from continuing the letter on Monday, and until now; all the leisure time I get being devoted to our new-born academy.* They have made me a principle in this business and I am now one of the committee to draw up the laws of the academy, which engages all my attention that I can spare from my profession. I think the infant looks healthy, and promises well.

Mrs. Ball paid me 300. There is still due 400 which she wishes me to wait for till next season. I will take her note however with interest, and raise the money on it before return if possible. Mr.Cogdell[†] is at my elbow and says write down much regard from him and his wife. Goodbye.

[S. F. B. Morse to His Parents]
Feb. 8th 1821
My Dear Parents,
I am happy in remitting you the above sum of 800 dollars. Out of this sum, I wish strictly paid the moment it is received 259 dollars to Mr. Doggett for his frame bill. The rest 541 may be set down to my credit. This money I have just received from Mr. John Alston who *insisted* that I should receive *200 dollars* more than *I asked,* is he not a liberal minded man? At the same time he has given me a commission to paint his daughter again full-length, not so large as the last nor so

---

*This was the Academy of Fine Arts. On December 27 Morse wrote Lucretia: "Since writing this there has been formed here an Academy of Arts to be erected immediately. J. R. Poinsett, Esq., is President, and six others with myself are chosen Directors. What this is going to lead to I don't know. I heard Mr. Cogdell say that it was intended to have lectures read, among other things. I feel not very sanguine as to its success; still I shall do all in my power to help it on as long as I am here." The academy died out in 1830 due a lack of public patronage and finances (Morse to Lucretia, December 27, 1821, Morse Papers, Library of Congress).

†John S. Cogdell (1778–1847) was invited to Morse's room so often that he demanded to pay a share of the rent. A lawyer, banker, and state representative, he was appointed comptroller general of the state in 1818. However, he was a painter and sculptor by avocation. He wanted to paint and sculpt professionally but was dissuaded by artist Washington Allston, who felt Cogdell needed a more viable means of support for his family. Cogdell's artwork was exhibited at the Boston Athenaeum, the National Gallery of Design, the Pennsylvania

small as the first, for which I shall charge him perhaps 400 dollars. He intimates in his letter that he shall wish pictures of me annually and that I must pledge myself always to him for the pictures he may wish; which of course I shall & without mush hesitation.

[S. F. B. Morse to His Wife]
Charleston So. Car.
Wednesday the 14th morning 7 o'clock
I promised you an account of the way in which we live in our new mode. We rise a little after daylight; say 1/2 past six, and Henry makes a fire and puts on the tea kettle. By the time we are dressed and have our beds out of the way, and the room in order, our tea is ready (for we have tea for breakfast). We then have prayers (by no means the least advantage we enjoy in our new manner of living). Then comes the business of the forenoon until 3 o'clock, when one of the negroes brings up our dinner in a large wooden box, sets it down, and makes his exit. Our dinner consists of *beefsteak,* or perhaps a *roast fowl,* a little rice and some *Irish potatoes.* With this we contrive to get along in excellent health and in good trim for study after dinner; then comes the afternoon's study and the night. We have our tea, *simple bread* and butter and tea. Our milk breakfast is a pint brought to us at night, which allows me a tumbler of bread & milk at 10 o'clock just before we go to bed. Prayers close the day, and we get out of our beds again, and active. So you have particularly all the *varieties* in our mode of living; I never enjoyed my health better. I feel that I have enough, and I am consoled under some considerable self-denials with the thought that I am laying up the more for my dear family at home, and can sooner be able to remain with them altogether.

[S. F. B. Morse to His Wife]
Charleston February 18th 1821
My Dearest Wife,
I begin to feel a little anxious to hear from you now; it is a fortnight since I heard by letter from you, but the mails continue so irregular that I attribute the delay entirely to them. I am quite tired of seeing before the post office door *"no mail north of Raleigh."* Raleigh seems to be the *sticking* place.

Academy of Fine Arts, and the Charleston Library Society. His diary (six volumes) is in the collection of the Winterthur Museum, Joseph Downs Collection of Manuscripts and Printed Ephemera, Winterthur, Delaware (Mabee, *American Leonardo,* 78; Rutledge, "Artists in the Life of Charleston," 144).

I sent you yesterday, to father, from the (*Courier*) Feb. 17th in which you will see the notice of our Academy of Arts. The rules were drawn up principally by myself. It looks *prosperous now* but I am not sanguine as to its success; still I mean to *act* as if I was *sure* whilst I am here, which will be but a *short time*. My plan of a school of painting in New Haven strikes me as eligible the more I think of it. Providence I think is indicating to me a removal from Charleston for the present. I find no increase of sitters. I complete the *last sitting* of my *last sitter* tomorrow. I wait with submission the direction of Providence. I know he will direct to the best course; if it is his will that I stay longer, it will be shown me in the proper time. If it is to return home, that also will be shown in the proper time. I feel perfectly easy in either event.

But this is the Sabbath, my dear Lucrece, and I would not take up its scared hours in looking at my worldly concerns.

I have heard an excellent sermon from Dr. Palmer, text "Quench not the spirit." There is some attention in the congregation; I hope an increasing attention. I have endeavored to be faithful to my dear cousins here, by talking plainly & realizing plain things to them, but as yet without effect. I have felt much for them, of late, and have felt a boldness and confidence in conversation with them, which I never had before. May not God be intending blessings for them? I hope so with all my heart. Mary is peculiarly situated, surrounded by temptation. She has been invited to a ball which she attended, but she said she did not like it. This might be expected at first but a love of flattery and attention, and fondness of admiration, and consciousness of beauty, are powerful temptations; and might cause a stronger heart than hers to fall before them. Do, dear Lucrece, just sit down after you have received this and write her a letter of good advice. She loves you, I believe next to her Mother, and a word from you would have great effect. Tell her your own experience of the vanities of worldly pleasures, and in your way allure her into the consideration of these things. I particularize Mary because she has just "*come out,*" as the world has it. But lest your letter should seem partial direct it to both cousin Mary & Anna. Just enclose the letter to me in another to me, and I will deliver it when I think it will have the best effect. Do comply with this without delay.

[S. F. B. Morse to His Wife]
Monday morning February 26th
Circumstances have occurred since this morning has opened that renders it somewhat doubtful, whether I shall return on the steamship; two new sitters have called this morning, and one more on Saturday last makes 3 new ones to commence. These may detain me, especially as it is not improbable that more may

offer. I shall paint however all my might will; and if possible still come but don't expect me. Spring has opened here, asparagus in the Market. Jessamine flowers are gone. The peach trees are all in bloom, and the fig trees putting forth their fruit and leaves.

[S. F. B. Morse to His Wife]
Charleston, S. Car. March 5th 1821
Monday morning
My dearest Lucrece,
I did not begin my letter to you as usual on Sunday, as yesterday was communion Sabbath and the intermission short. We had a very interesting meeting; it will rejoice you to learn that even in Charleston there is a revival of religion. Yes, dear wife, the Lord has heard the prayers of his children in this place and is visiting them in mercy. Dr. Palmer has been for some time much engaged, and the church also has roused in some degree from her slumbers. The prayer meetings are well attended, solemn and impressive, and some sinners are awakened and anxiously inquiring, "What shall we do to be saved?" It is "the day of small things," but how thankful ought we to be for a single drop in such as place as Charleston. God has not forsaken this city, great and crying as their sins are, he remembers that there is a remnant of his children here, and for this he will bless the place. Oh! That this work just commenced may go on with power in this stronghold of Satan, until the assertion shall be proved, that the word of God is mighty to the pulling down of strongholds and till the whole aspect of this city shall be changed, from blasphemy, and profanity, to prayer & praise.

As to my profession, I am fully employed from morning till night, and shall be kept here probably longer than I expected. As this is the last season in Charleston, I may as well make the most of it. Among other portraits, I am painting Bishop Bowen,* as a present from some of his people to him, which is also to be engraved; it is as large as the one of General Thomas Pinckney for which I shall get $300. This picture I shall take home to finish, & exhibit in N. York when the Bishop is well known, so I shall in this way be introduced to the N. York public.

Goodbye, dear wife, business calls me. Spring has opened delightfully; peach and plum trees all in bloom and all the fields clothed in green; the weather almost uncomfortably warm. I think you will have an early spring in the North. In the

*Nathaniel Bowen (1779–1839), born in Boston and reared in Charleston, was consecrated third Episcopal bishop of South Carolina in 1818. He became rector of St.Michael's. His portrait by Morse now hangs in Grace Church in New York, where he was first rector.

latter part of April or May, you may expect me home, as soon as I can finish my press of business.

[Mrs. Ball to S. F. B. Morse]
16th March 1821
Mrs. Ball's compliments to Mr. Morse and thinks it proper to inform him that no one sees any likeness at all in the portrait, or would ever suppose it was taken for her, and the general opinion is, that she should return it again to him, but she not feeling disposed to hurt his feelings on doing so, yet having no satisfaction in the picture, thinks he is in duty bound, as a man of honor, and more especially as a Christian to make an abatement on the price of it, which she, and everyone else thinks, exorbitant—but which (did it give any satisfaction) she would have paid with pleasure.*

[S. F. B. Morse to Mrs. Ball]
March 16th 1821
Answer to Mrs. J. Ball
Mrs. J. Ball
Madam, I dare not trust myself to write the state of my feelings on receiving your note of this morning. Suffice it to say that I can neither take the picture back, make any alteration in it, or abate one iota of price.

As the charge of exorbitancy, I must repel that by the following facts. I have painted the portrait of the President for the City Hall, charged the Council 700 dollars; they voted me 750 exclusive of the frame. I painted a portrait of Miss Alston for her father, nearly the same size with yours and charged him 800 dollars; he sent me 1000 and a commission to paint three more pictures. I painted another for him only one third the size of yours and charged him 400 dollars,

---

*Caroline Ball puts the blame for her inability to pay on her crop but she was said to be a lavish, frivolous spender and a clotheshorse. When her husband died in 1817, the inventory of his estate lists 669 slaves and nine plantations. Each of his heirs, including Caroline, received ten percent of his estate. Caroline sued three times for a larger portion of the estate. Her stepson, John Ball, Jr. (1782-1834), retained ultimate authority over his father's money and what was dispersed to Caroline and her children; therefore she was obligated to submit her bills for his approval. To the Ball descendents, Caroline was posthumously named "Buzzard's Wing," said to have placed a curse on the subsequent Ball line. Her first Ball sons were lavish playboys, who both died relatively young and tragically. Cody, "There Was No 'Absalom' on the Ball Plantations," 563–96; Dethloff, "Colonial Rice Trade," 231–43; Schantz, "'A Very Serious Business,'" 1–22; Ball, *Slaves in the Family*: see Chapter 14, "The Curse of Buzzard Wing."

which he promptly paid with many thanks. You are the first, madam, that ever made that charge against me, and must be the only one.

I am exceedingly hurt madam that I am obliged to write in this way you have compelled me to do; and lest I lose my self command, shall proceed no further. Yr. Mo. Ob. Servt.

Sam F. B. Morse

[S. F. B. Morse to Mrs. Ball]
Sunday evening
18th March 1821
Since writing the note I sent you, in answer to yours I have taken the subject into prayerful consideration, and under the influence of this frame of mind, have thought it my duty, in the first place, to ask your pardon for any thing in yesterday's note which is expressive of passion or any other feeling inconsistent with a Christian spirit; and in the next place (since you appealed in the note in question to me as a Christian) to state in as concise a manner as possible and with a Christian disposition the following facts. You must very well recollect the circumstances under which your portrait was commenced in the winter of 1819. It was contrary to my wish to begin it at the time I did, and that I commenced it entirely at your desire; and that the price and the size of the picture was known to you and agreed upon before I began it. You must also recollect that I had more sittings for the head than usual in order to make various alterations, which you wished, and which I protested against at the time; and that after the head was finished, your children down to the smallest and your friends generally and those who know you, endorsed the picture. I acquainted you at the time of the causes that prevented my completing the picture in the summer following.

You must recollect that when I returned the next winter you took another sitting at your request (in accordance also with my wish) to retry the face, and that you then expressed your satisfaction with it & at the arrangement of the background which I had chalked out and explained to you, and apparently as the result of this feeling offered me the price of the picture in advance which I declined in part, offering to receive one half at the time. You know that you promised to send me the check for the half that afternoon. It was Saturday. You were to leave town on Monday, the same time you requested me to procure a frame for the picture, the price not to exceed 200 dollars. You also recollect the inconveniences I was put to by relying on the receipt of the sum you promised, which you forgot to send me. I completed your picture in the summer with two others; which have given, as far as I can learn, entire satisfaction. Yours was painted with the same attention and with the same ability as the others, and admired as a picture after it was finished by some as the others and more by many. Among those latter were the celebrated Col. Trumbull* and Vanderlyn, paint-ers from N. York. My parents, brother's wife, and many friends in New Haven will bear testimony to the frequency from the many of this sentiment: "I am sure she must be pleased with it." When I open[ed] the picture at my room in a very unfavorable light & [saw] so large a picture, I was witness to the favorable attention it met with from visitors, by whom it was known as your likeness, with scarce an exception. You cannot but recollect, Madam, that when you yourself with your children visited it, notwithstanding you expressed yourself before them in terms so strong against it and so wounding to my face, yet all your children dissented from you, the youngest saying it was "Mama" and the oldest, "I am sure, Mother, it is very like you." It must be fresh in your recollection also that you wished certain parts altered, which you "could not bear." The curtain, the guitar, &c. and that I preceded to alter them at your request, and contrary to my own judgment avowed to you at the time. You must know also that during all this time, no complaint was made to me of exorbitancy in price. You wrote me since you saw the picture (which I have on file) in which you beg of me to wait until another year for the payment of one half the sum, and though it was very inconvenient to me to wait, yet I placed myself and my father and family in a temporary difficulty to accommodate you, and agreed to wait your time for the 400 dollars. In view of all these facts, madam, you cannot be surprised, if I was a little off my guard on receiving your note of Friday.

I have stated all the facts above related from a clear recollection of them, aid-ing in many of them by the corroborating testimony of others.

My next duty suggested under the influence of the feelings avowed in the commencement of this communication is to recall the question [and answer] that I will not make any diminution in the price. If under all these circumstances, you can consciously offer me less the price I have asked, just so much as your conscience allows you to give, I will receive and ask no more. At the same time, madam, let me observe that my honor and conscience will feel perfectly easy should you pay me the remaining 400 dollars with the interest from the day the picture was delivered.

Your picture from the day I commenced it has been the source of one of my greatest trials, and if it has taught me any degree of patience & forbearance, I shall have abundant reason to be thankful for the affliction.

With respect

Yr. Mo. Ob. Serv.

S.F.B.M.

---

*John Trumbull (1756–1843), renowned artist who, in 1792, completed a portrait of George Washington for Charleston.

[S. F. B. Morse to Mrs. Ball]
March 28th 1821
Mrs. C. Ball
Madam,
I have just received a letter from my father in which he requests a remittance of as much as I can collect in receipts from the notes of mine on interest. Not wishing to put you to inconvenience in the immediate payment of what is due me, if you will sign an accompt. note payable in 6 months, I can probably raise the money on it and be relieved from much embarrassment. I leave town in ten days for the North and wish a definite arrangement of this debt.
With respect Madam
Y Mo. Obt. Serv.
S.F.B.M.

[Mrs. Ball to S. F. B. Morse]
March 28th 1821
Dear Sir,
As you have referred it to my conscience & to pay you what I thought proper for the picture: I delayed writing until I had weighed it well in my mind, the result of which was taking in consideration the time and labor which you had devoted it, & expense attending it. I think the real value of it is $400 (without the frame). I now therefore make you the offer of two hundred cash which I would endeavor to spare, so as to bring the matter to a final conclusion.
    Had I not have made a very short crop this year, the consequences of which have involved me very much in debt, I would not hesitate to pay you the whole charge of portrait—atho' not done to my satisfaction. Should you feel disfavor to accept of the above proposition, I will send you an order of Mathews and Bonn for the money. If you will not, I am sorry to say that I cannot pay the four hundred until this time next year, as the whole crop is not gathered until March.
Yours in Christian bonds,
Caroline Ball

[S. F. B. Morse to Mrs. Ball]
March 28th
Mrs. C. Ball
Dear Madam,
As you can spare but 200 dollars at the present time, I will be content to take the 200 you offer now and give you my receipt. And though it puts me to much inconvenience, I will, to accommodate, wait as you request for the remaining 200

until next year. I have therefore enclosed a blank note for 200 dollars payable in a year, which you will please to sign. Thus by giving the order you promise on Mssrs. Matthews & Bonneau,* and signing the note on the remaining 200, this unpleasant business will be amicably and finally adjusted.

Yrs. Respectfully,

S. F. B. Morse

[S. F. B. Morse to Mrs. Ball]

Thursday 29th March 1821

Madam,

Supposing that I was dealing not only with a woman of honor, but (from her professions) with a Christian, I ventured in my note of the 18th inst., to make an appeal to your conscience in support of the justness of my demand of the four hundred dollars still due from you for your portrait. By your last note, I find, you are disposed to take an advantage of that circumstance of which I did not suppose you capable. My sense of the justness of my demand was so strong, as will appear from the whole tenor of that note, that I venture [an] appeal, not imagining that any person of honor, of the least spark of generous feeling, and more especially of *Christian principle,* could understand [I was doing] anything more than the enforcing my claim by an appeal to that principle which I knew should be the strongest in a real Christian. Whilst, however, you have chosen to put a different construction on this part of the note, and supposed that I left you to say whether you would pay me anything or nothing, you have (doubtless unconsciously) shown that your conscience has decided in favor of the whole amount which is my due, and which I can never voluntarily relinquish.

Although you affirm in the first part of your note that, after due deliberation, you think the real value of the picture is four hundred dollars (without the frame), yet, had your crop been good, your conscience would have adjudged me the remaining four hundred dollars without hesitation. And again (if your crop should be good) you could pay me the four hundred next season. Must I understand from this, Madam, that the goodness or badness of your crop is the scale on which your conscience measures your obligation to pay a just debt, and that it contracts or expands as your crop increases or diminishes? Pardon me, madam, if I say that this appears to be the case from your letter.

My wish throughout this whole business has been to accommodate the time and terms of payment as much to your convenience, as I could consistently with

---

*Mathews & Bonneau, Factors on Martin's Wharf (Hagy, *Charleston, S.C. City Directories for the Years 1816, 1819, 1822, 1825, and 1829*, 52).

my duty to my family & myself. As a proof of this you need only revert to my note of yesterday, in which I inform you that I am paying interest on money borrowed for the use of my family which your debt if it had been promptly paid, would have prevented. My wish is still to accommodate, and if you will give me your note for 400 dollars on interest for six months, or even for one year, I will take it although even this is not justice to my family, or myself as I shall make a great sacrifice in so doing.

I must request a decisive answer today as I shall leave town in a few days, when all uncollected accounts will be given to my attorney for collection.
With respect, Madam,
Yr. obt. Serv.

[Mrs. Ball to S. F. B. Morse]
March 29th 1821
Mr. Morse,
The reason for writing that I would have paid for your full price for the portrait, was not that my commission was at all governed by the crop which I had made; but in order to prevent the dispute which I *foresaw* would take place between us in making the facts which I did, and which to me was very painful so to do, but supposing that as a *Christian* you might be convinced of the *injustice* of charging a full price for a picture that you heard gives *no satisfaction* and which you might have seen throughout the whole sitting, altho' I did not say any thing, hoping that when it was finished it would be to my wish.

However I wish to say no more on the subject, as I do not make money my God, and you will continue to demand—or rather enforce the remaining four hundred, it will be paid with interest according to the time appointed.

[S. F. B. Morse to His Wife]
March 31, 1821
I just drop you a hasty line to say that, in all probability, your husband will be with you as soon, if not sooner than this letter. I am entirely clear of all sitters, having outstayed my last application; have been engaged in finishing off and packing up for two days past and contemplate embarking by the middle or end of the coming week in the steamship for New York. You must not be surprised, therefore, to see me soon after this reaches you; still don't be disappointed if I am a little longer, as the winds most prevalent at this season are head winds in going to the North. I am busy in collecting my dues and paying my debts.

"Margaret Hall" (née Hunter), by Sir Francis Leggatt Chantrey. Pencil.
1820s or 1830s. Copyright National Portrait Gallery, London.

MARGARET HUNTER HALL (1828)

"The Dowdies and their Clumsy Partners"

Margaret Hunter Hall (1799–1876) was born in Edinburgh and reared in Spain, where her father, Sir Jon Hunter, was British consul-general. In 1825, at the age of twenty-six, she married Captain Basil Hall (1788–1844), a retired British Royal Navy officer and author of voyages and adventures. He was the son of Fourth Baronet Sir James Hall, an eminent geologist, and Lady Helen Hamilton Hall. Their family mansion was on the site of an ancient castle at Dunglass, Scotland, said to have been the inspiration for "Ravenswood Castle" from the novel *Bride of Lammermoor* by Sir Walter Scott, a close friend of Basil and Margaret Hall. The Halls moved in high society circles in both London and Edinburgh, and were friends with many distinguished figures of their day.

While making plans to embark on a fourteen-month tour of North America, Basil met John James Audubon, in Liverpool with a portfolio of bird paintings he hoped to exhibit in Europe and make a name for himself. Audubon complained that Hall "exhausted him with hundreds of questions about America." However, he wrote to his wife of Margaret Hall: "Few women ever attracted my notice more forcibly at first sight, although by nature thou knowest well I am dearly fond of amiable ones. But her fine face was [possessed] of something more than [the ordinary] and her [demeanour] had a power that I cannot describe to thee. Her youth and form all unite to [cause] a liking."

Beginning in May of 1827, armed with over a hundred letters of introduction, the Halls set off with their fifteen-month-old daughter, Eliza, and her Scots nursemaid, Mrs. Crownie. During her travels, Margaret wrote a series of private letters to her sister, Jane Hunter Guthrie, in which she expressed her distress at much that she witnessed in America. She disparaged Americans of both sexes who smoked cigars, chewed tobacco, and spit, even in courts and churches. She observed members of a church choir "blacken the floor" spitting, "ejection after

Taken from Margaret Hunter Hall Papers, 1827–28, Manuscript Division, Library of Congress.

ejection, incessant from the twenty mouths." She was stunned at the common vulgarity, and observed Americans eating with knives. She did not like the food, dirt, or smells of America, and wrote that she was received at American inns with "unbending, frigid heartlessness." She found the act of handshaking odd, and missed the deference she took for granted in Britain.

In South Carolina from February to March of 1828, the Halls traveled from Columbia to Charleston, where they were introduced to Dr. Philip Tidyman, who Margaret found a grand bore. At Charleston balls and dances, she was unimpressed with "the dowdies and their clumsy partners." However, Margaret Hall's account allows us to peer into the society of Charleston in the 1820s. It also recounts the experience of travel in that day, as she and her family journey through South Carolina. On leaving Charleston, they make their way into the surrounding region, visiting plantations as they make their way to Savannah.

On leaving America, Margaret Hall wrote her sister: "We had a gay setting-out as there was no one there whom it cost us a tear to part with." Basil published his *Travels in North America in the Years 1827 and 1828,* which caused a "moral earthquake" in this country with its criticism of America. It was banned by American booksellers, and he was derided in the American press. Had his wife's letters been published in that day, they would have caused a worse tremor.

In the ensuing years, the Halls lived in Edinburgh and Italy before they settled in Southsea, a seaside resort near Portsmouth, England, a well-known naval base. Basil continued to publish illustrated accounts of innumerable exotic travels and to write for scientific journals. In his fifties, he was diagnosed as insane and committed to an institution, where he died in 1844. Margaret lived decades after her husband's death. She remained an aristocratic member of European circles for the rest of her life. Her grandson, foremost British Japanologist Basil Hall Chamberlain (1850–1935), wrote:

> What I have a keen recollection of is my grandmother, Mrs. Basil Hall's house at Southsea, where I used to come spend happy holidays. There was a library, in which I made acquaintance with Lyell's books on geology & many others, while munching maple-sugar. I think the maple-sugar was a recollection, or rather a taste cultivated by her in old American days; for Captain Basil Hall and she had travelled all over the United States taking with them my mother then an infant in arms. My grandmother was not at all "an old goodie," despite the sugar, but a very keen and clever old lady, extremely fond of society. Her house was a centre for half the navy, as they successively passed through Portsmouth. She had also known many interesting people, among others Sir Walter Scott, one of whose novels she possessed [in] the original manuscript.

Over a century after Margaret Hall wrote her travel letters, Una Pope-Hennessy (1876–1949) purchased the originals. She published an edited version entitled *An Aristocratic Journey: Being the Outspoken Letters of Mrs. Basil Hall. Written During a Fourteen Month's Sojourn in America 1827–1828* (1931). Pope-Hennessy's unedited, typed transcript of the original letters now resides at the Library of Congress. The following account is taken verbatim from that transcript, offering a new edition of Hall's original lively letters written in South Carolina. They are published here courtesy of Michael Mallon, literary executor of the Sir John Pope-Hennessy estate.

SOURCES

McCarthy, James. *That Curious Fellow: Captain Basil Hall, R.N.* Scotland, UK: Whittles Ltd., 2011.

Millar, Alexander Hastie. *Roll of Eminent Burgesses of Dundee, 1513–1866.* Dundee, Scotland: John Leda and Co., 1887.

Mulvey, Christopher. *Anglo-American Landscapes.* Cambridge, UK: Cambridge University Press, 1983.

Ota, Yuzo. *Basil Hall Chamberlin: Portrait of a Japanologist.* Richmond, Surrey, UK: Curzon Press Ltd., 1998.

Townsend, Peter, ed. *Burke's Peerage Baronetage and Knightage.* 105th edition. London: Burke's Peerage Ltd., 1970.

"THE DOWDIES AND THEIR CLUMSY PARTNERS"

Charleston, South Carolina, February 26

MY DEAREST JANE,

We were invited to a ball this evening and until two hours ago had resolved to go, but neither of us have yet got over the fatigue of our late journey, and the nearer time approached the more reluctant did we feel to encounter the additional labor of dressing, going out, and, most especially, talking. So we put on our dressing gowns and sat down to write, which many persons perhaps would consider the great fatigue of all, but I find it quite refreshment. We are at length at Charleston which for so many months we have talked of visiting, but whilst we were still at so great a distance I always felt we would never get there, as if it were a place beyond our reach, which feeling was not lessened by the alarming accounts everyone gave of the discomforts, miseries, and I may almost say dangers, of a journey to Charleston, but all of this was much exaggerated. That is if you choose to make the best instead of the worst of the little distresses to be met with, and here we are all safe, well and happy, as if we had merely posted down in a comfortable carriage from London to Edinburgh.

My last date I wrote to you was the 23rd from the little inn where we slept that night. We accommodated with two rooms, tho' neither of them spacious dimensions, but we were comfortable on the whole and fell into a sound sleep from which we were awakened by the most tremendous peal of thunder I have ever heard in my life. Every pane of glass shook as if it would tumble out. There was no more but the rain fell in torrents, and continued pretty violently till morning. We were dressed and at breakfast by six, at which hour the stage, with the stage proprietor and his brother, arrived. We had provided ourselves with a good basket full of provisions, three cold chickens, a tongue, two loaves, tea and sugar, biscuits, apples, oranges, and a little box of jelly for Eliza. The whole of the road from Norfolk to Charleston you get nothing except Indian corn bread except at the towns, and as none of us have learnt to eat it, we take care to provide ourselves with wheaten bread wherever it is to be had.

Away we went on the morning of the 24th under the same pelting rain that had fallen during the night, but at length it ceased, the clouds dispersed, and the sun shone out brilliantly and beautifully. The appearance of the various little creeks that we passed make the driver doubt the propriety or possibility of crossing a certain swamp called Four Holes Swamp, which after such rains as had fallen is wont to be rather deeper than is convenient. On this account we had to wind our way through the forest by little paths which to the inexperienced eye looked hardly wide enough to allow of the passage of a gig, but our driver knew every little turn and threaded his course through with our mammoth of a stage behind him without any accident. Indeed we found the road better than we should have done the proper one; the only inconvenience attending it was that we were obliged to travel thirty miles with the same team of horses, instead of changing them. We also missed the dinner house by this arrangement, but that was no subject of regret and when we stopped halfway to water the horses, we pulled out our basket and had a hearty meal.

By seven o'clock we reached our resting place, Snell's Tavern. Here we found a large party of gentlemen and I began to have some fears of wont of accommodation; this was removed when I was taken upstairs. That is to say there were beds enough, but then the rooms were by no means numerous and I suspected we should have to endure the inconvenience of being put in the same room, or bed I believe, with so many companions, for the lady in waiting ushered us into a room with six beds in it, all packed so close together that they did not look unlike a large one. A little remonstrance however did away with this difficulty and we were put in possession, neither of them to be sure as large as this piece of paper but people can reduce themselves wonderfully in size when it is necessary, and by the time we return home I think Basil and I will be able to put up in an oyster shell. The bed was very comfortable, but alas we were allowed but a short time to enjoy it, for before three, up drove another stage and the passengers: more especially one man who was very drunk made such a row that sleep was soon banished. We were so thoroughly roused up, we thought it as well to be jogging, so we dressed by the remains of our tallow candle and mounted our stage and went trundling along eighteen miles of bad road to the breakfast house. Off again, and rumbled over worse roads for thirty miles to the dinner house. On both those days however the interest of the scenery was much enlivened by the beautiful shrubs with which the swamps were filled, yellow Jessamine, pink and red honeysuckle, laurustinus, and near Charleston, hedge rows of what is called in England I think the dog rose, large single-leafed wild white roses in such luxuriant abundance that they looked like bushes covered with snow. The weather too is enchanting, perfect summer, and everything so green and fresh.

This evening Basil brought us in bananas, for fruit shops are full of West Indian fruits. We had but fifteen miles to drive after dinner to Charleston, and arrived an hour after sunset, guided by a bright moon. We had some time before we were to secure lodging at Mrs. Kerrison's boarding house, 131 Church Street, and found it all ready for our reception. We are very comfortably lodged and have our meals in our own parlor except dinner. We had an immense number of letters of introduction which we sent out last night and this morning, and have had numerous calls in consequence. Some of our visitors we saw, but the greater part of the morning we denied ourselves that we might enjoy reading our letters undisturbed. I went to see one sight today which I had not before had an opportunity of witnessing, an auction of slaves. There was an immense collection of them gathered together near the Post Office, from the balcony of which I saw it.* A table was placed in the centre on which stood the auctioneers and the different lots as they were set up and knocked down to the highest bidder like so many books, chairs or bullocks. There were multitudes of infants, little unconscious things sleeping on their mother's arms or smiling and laughing merrily quite unaware of their own degradation. They were sold in families which so far it was pleasant to see, but still it was a horrible sight. Close by were auctions of horses and carriages going on, so near indeed it was impossible to distinguish whether the last bid was for the four footed or the human animal. There was an expression

*The Old Exchange and Custom House served as post office from 1815 to 1896.

of dogged indifference about the poor blacks, but I am told they do not at all like to be removed from the place where they have been brought up.

We took a walk this evening thro' Charleston, a very pretty place it is. All the houses are built, apparently in reference to hot weather only, with deep verandahs round. Some of the verandahs are fitted the whole way round with Venetian blinds, but altogether the houses look very pretty.

Charleston, 2nd March:—Whilst Mrs. Crownie was at church this afternoon Basil and I carried Eliza to visit a gentleman and lady, Dr. and Mrs. Tidyman,* who had invited her to walk in their garden. Into the garden accordingly we went and a very curious sight it was to me to see so many flowers in full bloom, orange trees in flower, peas just at a proper stage for eating, and we actually gathered two ripe strawberries which Eliza got, and remember this is only the 2nd March but the season we are told is at least a month or six weeks ahead of what it usually is. Today the thermometer has been at 72, and those who are not so fond of heat as we are find the weather quite oppressive. The natives are groaning sadly at having been deprived of their usual portion of bracing weather, which they imagine fits them better to bear the summer heats, tho' this I believe is considered mistaken doctrine by the physicians, as the stronger and more braced anyone is, the more subject they are to take the yellow fever, and to have it severely.

We did not go to the ball to which we were invited on the 26th, but on the 27th we went to the races where there was but a small show of company, and I did not admire the free use the gentlemen made of their whips in trying to keep the course clear. I am sure that an Englishman would not have submitted to one half that the foreign people put up with very quietly. I know nothing whatever about horses, so that the interest I take in a race is not very great and I never have any wish to return. Consequently I have not been again. In walking that evening we strolled into some of the fruit shops where we saw all sorts of West Indian fruits and sweetmeats and great lumps of sugar cane. We have had bananas every day since we came here and yesterday where we dined, asparagus and peas. The asparagus is very poor certainly compared to what is to be had in London this season. The peas were excellent.

*Dr. Philip Tidyman (1776–1850), the son of an English immigrant jeweler and goldsmith who made a fortune in Charleston, was educated at the University of Edinburgh and received a PhD at Gottingen, the first American to receive doctorate at a German university. He returned to Charleston in 1801, where he was a physician and a planter. He served in the South Carolina House of Representatives and published anonymous articles and essays on various subjects. His wife at the time of Hall's visit was Susannah Somers Tidyman. Their house in downtown Charleston was a scene of much socializing (Krumpelmann, "Duke Bernard of Saxe-Weimar," 201–3 (Dr. Tidyman 9b. 1777); Davidson, *Last Foray*, 119, 255).

On the 28th we took a family dinner at Mr. Stephen Elliott's, the editor of the *Southern Review* in this country,* of which you have probably never heard, altho' the good folks of Carolina say that has made a good deal of noise in England. It would be totally out of the question to make them understand the degree of ignorance and want of interest that prevails in England regarding everything in America, indeed I always feel that it is uncivil to tell them of it, altho' truth obliges one to do so sometimes. The party at Mr. Elliott's consisted of four in his own family, the Attorney-General, Mr. Petigru,† Judge Huger,‡ Mr. Legare,§ one of the writers in the said *Southern Review*, and Mrs. Nott, an unfortunate little French woman, whose unlucky stars have transplanted her from Paris to Columbia! She, in a mistaken hour, having married an American, who is now Professor of Belles Lettres in the College of Columbia.' And most bitterly does she feel the change; indeed, I cannot fancy one more intolerable, and she has no hope of ever bettering herself. A family dinner in Charleston is a very plain affair, if we are to judge by the specimen we had at Mr. Elliott's, there was not a bit of second course of any kind, not a pie nor a pudding, and no apology for the absence of it, so I suppose it is the usual style, for people in this country are apt enough to make apologies for what ought to be there, instead of letting the deficiency pass without comment.

On the 29th there was a ball given by the Jockey Club,** to which we were invited and went. The room is good and was well lighted; nevertheless, it was a very

*Stephen Elliott (1771–1830), a founder, coeditor, and contributor to *Southern Review*.
†James Louis Petigru (1789–1863).
‡Judge Daniel Elliott Huger (1779–1854).
§Hugh Swinton Legare (1797–1843).
'Caroline Amelie Oules Nott (1809–1837), the wife of Prof. Henry Junius Nott (1797–1837), was not French but Belgian. The couple was known for a well attended salon in Columbia. He was a professor at South Carolina College and author of *His Novellettes of a Traveller; or, Odds and Ends from the Knapsack of Thomas Singularity, Journeyman Printer* (2 vols., 1834). Born in Union District, Nott worked on a biography of Revolutionary War hero, Maj. Joseph McJunkin (1755–1846)—incidentally, the great-great-great-great-grandfather of this author—that was never completed. In October of 1837, the Notts were sailing from New York to Charleston abroad the steamboat *Home* when it was shipwrecked off Cape Hatteras in a hurricane. The Notts were among the many causalities. The event was much publicized in the press for the famous that were on board (Hale, *Authentic Account of the Loss of Steam Packet Home*, 1–20; O'Neall, *Biological Sketches of the Bench and Bar*, 12, 513).
**At the time of Hall's visit, the Jockey Club and St. Cecilia balls were held at St. Andrew's Hall located at 118 Broad Street. It was destroyed in the fire of 1861. Basil Hall wrote of the same event: "The room was large, the ball handsomely got up, and every thing ordered in the best style, with one small exception—the ladies and gentlemen appeared to be entire

dull ball, much too thinly attended, and too small a proportion of gentlemen. They do not invite any of the gentlemen of this State except those belonging to the Club, and many of the ladies whose husbands or brothers are not members do not choose to go. There were awful pauses between the dances, and the music was really insufferably bad. I had thought the young men much more gentlemanlike when I saw them in the morning, than those generally to be seen in this country, but in the evening they looked very second-rate, indeed more vulgar I think than most I have seen elsewhere. As for the female part of the company, I never in my life saw so many ugly women gathered together. There were but three pretty women in the room, two of them from Philadelphia, the other a French girl. There was a supper, a very handsome one as far as quantity and quality went, but such an absence of taste, such a contrast to be sure from Mr. Vaughan's beautiful set out at Washington,* such heavy ornaments and great lumbering, long, two-pronged forks to eat one's rice with.

Yesterday March 1st we had another stroll about the town, which I admire the more I see of it. It is a remarkable cheerful looking place, Charleston. We went today to St. Michael's Church and had a very good sermon on the religious education of children from Dr. Bowen Bishop of South Carolina. But I am forgetting the dinner party of yesterday the 1st. The dinner at Mr. Petigru's consisted of (the company I mean) thirteen gentlemen and three ladies: Mrs. Petigru,[†] Mrs. Nott, who is living in the house, and myself. The others were all gentlemen without their wives, according to the fashion of the place, and of many other places in the Union. Women are just looked upon as house-keepers in this country and as such are allowed to preside at the head of their own table, that they may see that

---

strangers to one another. The ladies were planted firmly along the walls, in the coldest possible formality, while the gentlemen, who, except during the dance, stood in close column near the door, seemed to have no fellow-feeling, nor any wish to associate with the opposite sex" (Hall, *Travels in North America*, 133–50).

*The Halls had dined in Washington with Charles R. Vaughan (1774–1849), from 1825 the envoy extraordinary and minister plenipotentiary to the United States at the British Embassy. He had served as private secretary to the British embassy in Madrid from 1810 to 1820, and was well known by Margaret from her youth in Spain. Vaughan lived in style in Washington, where he was known for his *recherché* dinners.

†Jane Amelia Postell Petigru (1795–1868), the wife of James Petigru. She was later addicted to alcohol and morphine. For more on the Petigru's wife and daughters, see Jane H. Pease and William H. Pease, *A Family of Women: The Carolina Petigrus in Peace and War* (Chapel Hill: University of North Carolina Press), 1999; and William H. Pease and Jane Pease, *James Louis Petigru: Southern Conservative, Southern Dissenter* (Athens: University of Georgia Press), 1995.

all goes right. The evening party was at the house of a Mrs. Thomas Lowndes,* and I think there was a greater number of pretty women than on the preceding evening, but most of them dressed so ill that they would mar even real beauty. I must in justice say one thing in favor of the South Carolinians; they are remarkably hospitable, not only in inviting strangers into their houses, but lending their carriages, which is a much less common piece of hospitality. By the by, I was asked by one of the lodgers in this house the other day one of those puzzling questions that the Americans are so apt to put, how the American ladies compare in point of information and acquirements with those of Edinburgh. I was obliged to refuse to make a comparison, as I should have been obliged to sacrifice either conscience or my politeness in comparing them with any ladies that I know, English, Scotch, or Irish.

MARCH 5:—Tomorrow is our day of starting and as we go at eight in the morning, of course all our business must be finished tonight. For this reason we mean to cut a ball we were invited to tonight in order to have good time to finish our preparations. I begin to find that the only time of rest for us is when we are actually on the roads, travelling some forty or fifty miles a day. One is so fatigued when one only stops for a week or ten days by the multitude of parties, the innumerable visits to be returned and here, I mean in America, harassed by the tiresome way they press you to prolong your stay, even after demonstrating that by doing so whole weeks of plans would be deranged and the risk of encountering the unhealthy season be incurred. This is very different from the kind, considerate letter we had since coming here from Mr. Couper of St. Simon's Island,[†] the old Scotch gentleman whom I have so frequently mentioned. We had been hesitating about going to visit him, but the style of his letter is so considerate and shows him to be a man of so much sense and real kindness that we at once resolved upon it. Instead of being hurried along by the public stage we have engaged a private carriage with four horses to take us on leisurely. We have made the bargain only as far as Savannah with the understanding that if we are mutually satisfied and all things suit, we are to go on. The person who is to drive us is a certain Mr. Wallace, the civilest of all civil people, whom we met in the capacity of stage proprietor

---

[*]Sarah Ion Lowndes (1778–1840) was the wife of retired lawyer and congressman Thomas Lowndes (1766–1843). They lived at Oakland Plantation and owned a house downtown, where they frequently entertained. Their daughter, Harriett (1812–1892), would marry future South Carolina governor William Aiken (1806–1887) in 1831 (Chase, "The Lowndes Family of South Carolina," 156).

[†]John Couper (1759–1850), a leading agriculturist internationally, was a famous host in St. Simons, Georgia. The Halls visited the Couper Plantation after leaving Charleston and Savannah, as did other travelers.

last year at Saratoga, from whence he forwarded us to Albany. I knew that he could not be an American, that was a moral impossibility. There was a civility about him—and above all a perseverance and steadiness of his going on in his own particular line, without the smallest pretensions to wish to be thought a gentleman, tho' much more of one than many who pretend to be so—that bespoke anything rather than an American. The Americans boast of their independence, but it is not independence of character; at least what I consider such. Instead of being content to be respectable in their own line of life, they all ape being gentlemen, and such a burlesque it is to be sure! Mr. Wallace is an Englishman, a very enterprising man who resides here in winter and at Saratoga in summer, following his profession of letting out stages and horses. Once or twice since we have been here we have had a carriage from him to go out at night, and generally Mr. Wallace has jumped out behind and acted as footman. An American would have scorned such a thing, but for my part I feel infinitely more respectful for a man who thinks his dignity not compromised by making himself useful than for one who is so jealous as to be constantly in dread of lowering himself, not by bad conduct, drinking brandy or the like, but by appearing for a moment to put himself in a lower rank than those who are inside the carriage.

The 3rd we dined with a party of twenty at Dr. Tidyman's—the proportions were fifteen gentlemen and five ladies. We had a very grand dinner as could possibly be and heaps of it, as there always is. Everything however was really handsome and there was less appearance of effort than usual. Dr. Tidyman was long in Scotland, but returned from there many years ago. He was intimate with Baron Hume,* the MacKenzies,† and many others. He has been remarkably kind and attentive to us, really most particularly so, and therefore it is with pain that I am obliged to confess to myself and you that he is one of those intense bores who make life a burden to those on whom they bestow their company. The Americans are all given more or less to speak in parentheses, but this man's parentheses are so numerous and so involved that it is almost impossible to connect the different parts of his sentence, and to disentangle the substance from the branches right and left and in every direction. We went after the dinner to a military ball given by the officers belonging to the different militia corps. There was no one present without uniform except Basil, but I don't think the change of dress improved the appearance of our friends here, who may for aught I know be very effective

---

*Baron Hume (1757–1838), professor of Scots law at the University of Edinburgh, regarded as the founder of modern Scottish criminal law. He was nephew of Scottish Enlightenment philosopher, historian, and economist David Hume (1711–1776).

†Like Hume, Henry Mackenzie (1745–1831), eminent Scottish lawyer and novelist, was a notable figure of Edinburgh society.

in the field but they are certainly not drawing room soldiers. I thought however we were to have been favored with a specimen of their fighting powers in a little civil war springing up, for the manager had taken rather more brandy or whisky or some such gentleman-like liquor than his head was competent to bear, and he became most extremely overbearing and ordered about the republican gentlemen and ladies in a way that would not have been quietly submitted to in England. We did not remain to see the issue of the contest and have not heard anything of it since. I must do the Charlestonians the justice to say that I have not seen any chewing amongst them, nor spitting. I am *told* that even smoking is in disrepute. They are very hospitable and make you as welcome to their carriages as to their dinners, but there is the same apparent coldness of character and feeling as about all their countrymen, an absence of heartiness and cordiality which is the chief charm of such attentions. The fact is they hate the English and there is no sincere feeling of friendship or kindliness towards them and all the attention is merely a sort of bribe to make us speak well of them.

Last night the 4th at a party I met an English woman, Mrs. Butler Clough,* the wife of an English merchant. She has been in this country about five years and speaks of it in exactly the same terms as we do. It is a sad banishment for an English lady to have her lot cast in America. We did up all the sights in Charleston yesterday, Work House, Poor House, Jail, Orphan Asylum, and Rice Mill, which was the only thing much worth seeing. All the others are much inferior to the establishments of the same kind in the Northern States.

Charleston to Savannah—Jacksonburough, South Carolina

March 6, 1828

MY DEAREST JANE,

It was only last night that I dispatched a long letter to you and it will be long before I dispatch another, and therefore until tea is ready I shall employ myself in writing to you. We breakfasted between seven and eight this morning, but it

---

*Mrs. James Butler (Anne Perfect) Clough lived at 188 East Bay. Her husband was a cotton merchant representing Liverpool in Charleston from 1822 to 1836, when they returned to England. They were the parents of English poet Arthur Hugh Clough (1819–1861) and Anne Jemima Clough (1820–1892), a luminary of nineteenth-century education for women in England. Born in England, the Clough children lived in Charleston until they were sent to school in England (Arthur from the age of four). A brother, George Augustus Clough, died in Charleston of "stranger's fever" in 1843, at the age of twenty-two. He is buried in St. Michael's Church graveyard (Clough, *A Memoir of Aunt Jemima Clough by Her Niece*, 6; Hagy, *Charleston, S.C. City Directories for the Years 1816, 1819, 1822, 1825, and 1829*, 140).

was nine before we first got off. We shall probably use the carriage we now have for a month, and therefore it is of considerable consequence that it should be as comfortable as we can make it. You know Basil's genius for contrivances, and of course he adapts many a one to increase our comfort in travelling. We have a multitude of small things too which require sorting at first setting out. Mr. Wallace in his short tight jacket worked away on his province and at nine as I said before, we left Mrs. Kerrison's boarding house, and I must confess that with one exception I should not care though I did not see any of the Charlestonians again. That exception is Mr. Petigru, the Attorney-General of the State. He sat a couple of hours with us last night and is a very intelligent, sensible man, tho' he has never in his life been out of South Carolina. There surely is a greater want of interest in American society than in that of any other country I ever was in or heard of. My conscience too smites me for speaking so of persons who have shown us so much attention and civility, for somehow I cannot call it kindness, but I cannot help it. I cannot like their society and I cannot like themselves. Mrs. Cough, the English lady I met the other night says there is no tenderness in this country.

I forgot to mention that at all balls and dances at Charleston a favorite dance is the Spanish dance, as they call it, and in *plan* it certainly is a Spanish country dance, but in execution, Oh Heavens! To me it was actually excruciating to witness such barbarism and to remember the contrast of beautiful Spanish women with their graceful figures and sparkling eyes, instead of the dowdies and their clumsy partners I now saw, handling and elbowing each other about, for their propriety will not allow them to waltz, so they *poussette* and hold each other by the elbow instead of the side. I respect all scruples on the score of propriety and if people don't like to waltz they are quite right to let it alone, but why murder a pretty dance by substituting most ungraceful alterations for the prettiest part of it? Why not leave it undone?

A mile from Charleston to-day we crossed the Ashley River in a horseboat. It is a very fine wide river, of whose existence I had never heard till within three or four miles of Charleston. After that we travelled thirty miles. On each side of the road for the greater part of the way there were well cultivated looking farms, and we saw the slaves forming the ground into ridges with large hoes, in place of having horses to plough it. Varieties of beautiful flowers were in the swamps and numerous live-oak trees in every direction. We passed through but little pine barren. Within a mile of our destination we crossed the Edisto River, the most rapid we have seen since we left the St. Lawrence. Before arriving at the ferry, the road was covered for about a quarter of a mile with water about a foot and a half deep. At times it is so deep that people are obliged to go the whole way in a flat, as you may remember we had to be boated over part of the high road at

Richmond some years ago when the Thames got so high. It must look so strange to be ferried through the forest. We arrived at Jacksonburgh between five and six, having stopped an hour on the road to rest the horses. We dined in the carriage upon provisions of our own supplying.

Mr. Skirving's Plantation on the Combahee River (Pronounced Cumbee) Fifty Miles W. of Charleston, March 8

This place is well worthy of being noted in as particular a manner as possible, as you will allow when I tell you of all the comforts we have found here. Mrs. Skirving* is a lady with whom we made acquaintance in Charleston, and when we talked of travelling to Savannah she begged that we would make use of her house as an inn, and as we were desirous of seeing some plantations we resolved to accept her offer, altho' it increased our journey several miles by taking us off the direct road. Accordingly yesterday morning we left Jacksonburgh at eight o'clock, after having breakfast. It was a lovely morning and the hoar frost which had covered the ground gradually melted beneath the hot sun. The road was very interesting partly through forests of pine and live-oak and partly through nicely cultivated fields and the whole way covered with innumerable beautiful flowers and shrubs. After a drive of eighteen miles we found ourselves at Mr. Skirving's gate. We had no idea of what sort of a place a plantation house might be, and not having conjured up anything very delightful in our own minds, our plan was to take some dinner, walk a little, and then go on five or six miles further to another plantation, the owner of which was, we understood, at home. At the door of the house we were met by the head man, or driver as he is called, a black man of the name of Solomon. The overseer is always a white man, but there is none at present and it was to Solomon that Mrs. Skirving directed us to apply. The more we saw of the house, the more did our inclination to remain increase. Everything looked so clean and comfortable. The bed rooms especially were such

*Bethia Price Skirving (d. 1842) and her maiden sister, Miss Mary Price (d. 1854), owned Llandovery Plantation on Cuckold's Creek, a branch of the Combahee. Bethia was the widow of William Skirving Jr. (1773–1805); however, Llandovery was left to the Price sisters by their father, William Price (1738–1823), who was born in Wales. After the death of Bethia and Mary Price, the property was sold innumerable times. In 1888, it was purchased at auction by an African American farmer, Benjamin Garrett, whose family retained the property for almost a century. In 1984, it was sold to two corporations, Westvaco and TiAun, although Garrett's descendants continue to own houses on a portion of the land (Linder, *Historical Atlas of the Plantations of the Ace Basin*, 61; Fisher, Middleton, and Harrison, *Best Companions*, 257).

as we have not been used to of late, with their snow-white quilts and draperies, delightful arm chair and sofa, nicely set out toilet tables, and in short everything that is luxurious, and before we had been here an hour we had resolved to remain all night. The house is small but very comfortable. On the first floor is a small drawing-room and dining room opening upon a deep piazza as they call them here. From this piazza a few steps lead down to a delightful garden filled with all sorts of flowers in full bloom and close to the piazza is an orange tree covered with the flower and fruit in all stages. They are bitter oranges, the sweet do not ripen here.

Having settled ourselves a little we proceeded with Solomon to see the Negro huts about five hundred yards from the house. They are twenty-nine in number, very neatly arranged. In each hut there are two apartments, one for sleeping in. Some of the huts had windows but very few, most of them having no light but what was admitted by the open door, or an occasional separation between logs. In one of the largest were assembled all the children under the age of fourteen whom they consider too young to work. They were under the charge of one woman who prepares their meals for them and takes care of them whilst their parents are at work in the fields. The children as well as the men and women are fed upon Indian corn, which is served out to them at the beginning of each week; to each man and woman a peck in the week. The children have their allowance measured daily. After dinner we went to see them at their work, making a dam to prevent the Combahee from overflowing the rice fields to a greater degree than is wished, for they are always kept under water, which is what makes a rice plantation so peculiarly unhealthy during the hot weather. Indeed even at this season when there is no such danger, it is quite easy to imagine how deadly it must be to inhale the noxious vapors rising from such immense beds of stagnant water. All the way that we have come from Norfolk, were we to travel it in the months of May and so on, we should meet with certain and sudden death, for the swamps are as pernicious as the rice fields. Along with those at work there were two other drivers, each with his wand of office in his hand, that is to say a cart-whip with which to keep their human cattle under subjection. The slaves on this plantation are I believe as well used as any that we could see. They have a doctor to attend them when they are ill, and tho' not sumptuously fed and clothed, they have both food, clothing, and weather-tight houses, but still it makes one melancholy to see them even at their best. There was no laughing or talking in the field, no sign whatever of merriment or happiness; they seemed to work on mechanically, aware that the slightest relaxation was watched by the driver and would be followed by the infliction of his cart whip. The scene looked out of place on such a heavenly day when everything looked smiling and happy except the human beings. Solomon is an intelligent man, for his caste, and we have asked him many questions, but frequently he stops and says that he does not like to answer such and such a question, a man may get into trouble by saying too much. He told us that he has belonged to four masters in succession. It sounded very strange to hear a man tell that formerly he used to sell for from six to seven hundred dollars but that now he does not suppose he would fetch more than four hundred. Mrs. Cownie and Eliza walked about the place with him whilst we were writing this morning, and he spoke more freely to them than to us. He told Mrs. Cownie that he cannot read nor write, but that his wife who can is teaching him, but when he hears his mistress coming he hides the book, because he knows she would be so angry if she detected him. Of course the policy of the planters is to keep their slaves in a state of ignorance that they may not come to knowledge of their own degraded situation. In the meantime Solomon keeps all his accounts in his head.

But I must now tell you of our own treatment. At two o'clock we found a most admirable dinner prepared for us, boiled turkey, roast chicken, asparagus, peas, potatoes, rice custard, and sweetmeats, all admirably dressed and nicely served. Tea was brought in the same good order and the whole establishment is apparently under the most excellent management; all are servants altho' slaves, born and bred, a race whom understand their business perfectly. Mrs. Skirving is an English woman; altho' she has been long in this country, she still speaks of England as home, and certainly the arrangements of her house and household have a very English air. We slept sound in our beds till seven o'clock, but if the dinner was good, what shall I say of the breakfast! Such a breakfast! Such admirably boiled rice, such hashed turkey, broiled quails, and Indian corn flour which heretofore I have thought so bad, made into cakes of every description, each one more delicious than the other. I am sure you must think us very great epicures, but if you had been exposed for as many months as we have been, to wallowing in grease, you would know how to value a clean and good meal when put within your reach.

Mr. Nathaniel Hayward's Plantation, March 8

This is the gentleman's house I mentioned we had thought of coming to last night from Mr. Skirving's, before the comfort of everything there tempted us to remain. We left our excellent quarters about eleven o'clock, and with a guide to show us the way proceeded to Mr. Hayward's.* I ought to mention however that

*Nathaniel Heyward (1766–1851) lived at the Bluff Plantation but owned sixteen other plantations, where he conducted the state's largest rice-growing operation. At his death,

at the door of Mrs. Skirving's all the house servants and Solomon were assembled to bid us good-bye. Solomon shook hands most cordially with each of us, as did likewise an old woman who keeps the keys, and the others all bowed and smiled and looked quite pleased with us. I believe we treated them with more civility and kindness than they are used to, and this gained their goodwill I think much more than the dollars and half dollars that we gave them. We had only five miles to come to this place, and on stopping at the door, found that we were expected altho' the master was out to superintend the work. Whilst we were sauntering about in the garden (for altho' the 8th of March it is a day for sauntering) Mr. Hayward made his appearance, and with him we proceeded to walk about the grounds, the rice fields that is to say, for his whole plantation is rice with the exception of the corn that he cultivates to feed his slaves upon. His plantation is considered one of the best regulated in this State. At dinner we were joined by one of his sons who had been out hunting. We were not much the better of his conversation, nor that of his brother who came in the evening, neither of them spoke a word.* I have heard of sisters being no greater use at a party than to fill two chairs, but I never saw the case so completely identified as in the case of those two brothers. The old gentleman himself is much more willing to talk, but nei- ther is he a man of much information, and when we had got all out of him that we could relative to the cultivation of rice and the treatment of slaves, the conver- sation flagged so much that we were glad to make our escape to our own room.

We walked to the slave huts and looked into one or two of them, each of which consisted of two sleeping apartments and one hall, as they call it. Here as at Mr. Skirving's, one old woman was employed in looking after the children, whilst the parents were at work. Mr. Hayward does not interfere with his slaves in any way further than is necessary for the good of his own interest. They may have two or three wives apiece so long as they do not quarrel about them, but if they quarrel he interferes. He says they have no morals nor principles whatever, and are all the most notorious thieves. The masters have power of life and death

---

his estate included forty-five thousand acres of lowcountry plantations, over two thousand slaves, and nine Charleston houses. His wife, heiress Henrietta Manigault (1769–1827), died not long before the Halls' visit. Heyward owned nearby White Hall Plantation, from which Basil Hall produced drawings in his published travels.

*Heyward's only surviving sons, Charles Heyward (1802–1866) and Arthur Manigault Heyward (1805–1852). Charles left Princeton in 1824 to assist his father in operating the family plantations. Arthur Heyward did not attend college but also became a successful rice planter (Scarborough, *Masters of the Big House*, 9; Davidson, *Last Foray*, 209; Heyward, "The Heyward Family of South Carolina," 157).

over them. If a slave were for instance to be caught on Mr. Hayward's plantation cutting our portmanteaus from the back of our carriage, his master would call together two magistrates and five freeholders and if it were proved that he was guilty, they would forthwith string him up to the nearest tree. We have been very well used here, but on the whole commend me to the house where the mistress is absent. I still think Mrs. Skirving's English education is seen in the arrangements of her establishment which is vastly superior in all respects to this one, altho' the proprietor here is by much the richer of the two.

This pretty place is quite on the Combahee River. The weather already is almost sultry, altho' in the morning there has once or twice been frost. We crossed the Ashepoo River yesterday, the seventh; all the rivers we come to now retain their Indian names.

Coosawhatchie, S. Carolina, March 9

This is a little bit of a village on a river of the same name. We left Mr. Hayward's this morning at ten o'clock, crossed the Combahee, and stopped here between one and two, after a drive of eighteen miles, to rest the horses and to dine, as we thought upon our own provisions, but at the tavern we found a roast joint of venison and upon that we made an excellent dinner.

Old House, 10 1/2 Miles of Coosawhatchie, March 9

On leaving Mr. Nathaniel Hayward's this morning he gave us a letter for his relation, Mr. William Hayward, whose house he said was a good distance for a day's journey, and that the owner would be most happy to receive us.* Accordingly on we came, altho' at Coosawhatchie we were told that Mr. Hayward was from home. However by the time we reached his gate it was half past five o'clock and there was no place where we could put up short of nine miles further on, which would have obliged us to travel in the dark, so we boldly drove up to the door. The servant told us that his master was from home, but that he could with ease accommodate us for the night. This was too hospitable to be rejected, so we had our things taken out of the carriage, walked in, had fires lighted in the sitting room and two bedrooms, and in half an hour were as much at home as if we had

---

*Old House Plantation was once the country seat of Nathanial Heyward's father, Daniel Heyward (1720–1777). Nathaniel's brother, William Heyward (d. 1786), had inherited the property. His son, William, was proprietor at the time of Hall's visit. The site is in Jasper County (South Carolina Department of Archives and History, National Register of Properties in S.C., October 6, 1997).

lived all our lives in South Carolina. But only imagine our luck and our delight in finding ourselves in full possession of a gentleman's establishment without the *germe* of the company of the gentleman himself! Imagination could not have conceived a more perfect piece of luck. Assuredly we must allow the virtue of hospitality to its full extent to these planters, for it is quite common for strangers to go to their houses in the way we have come here. Dick, the head servant, has given us tea and is to give us breakfast to-morrow before we start for Savannah, which is still about thirty miles distant.

A TRUE ACCOUNT OF THAT

FATAL DUEL

Which took place on Tuesday morning 26th March,
1822. beween, Sir Alexander Boswell Bart. and
James Stuart Esq. in Fife when Sir Alexander
was mortally wounded, and died on Wednesday.

WE are deeply concerned to state, that a meeting took place on Tuesday
morning about ten o'clock, at Auchtertool. in Fife, between Sir Alexander Boswell, Bart. of Auchinleck, attended by the Honourable John Douglas,
brother to the Marquis of Queensberry, and James Stuart, Esq. of Dunearn,
attended by the Earl of Rosslyn. The parties both fired by signal, when Sir
Alexander was mortally wounded in the right shoulder, the ball shattring the
collar bone; but on the most minute examination, its course fterwards could
not be discovered.

Sir Alexander was carried to Balmuto house, where he died on Wednesday
afternoon at three o'clock.

An erroneous account having appeared of the manner in which Mr Stuart
got possession of some papers, proving that Sir Alexander Boswell was the
author of the numerous attacks in the Glasgow Sentinel against Mr Stuart, we
are desired to state, that Mr Stuart some time ago raised an action of damages against Messrs Bothwick and Alexander, the proprietors of the Sentinel.
On one of the last days of the Session, a gentleman from Hamilton, (the
country agent of Mr Bothwick) came to Mr Stuart, and stated that Mr Bothwick was extremely desirous of having the action settled, and asked Mr Stuart
if he was inclined to do so. Mr Stuart answered, that would depend on the
communications made to him. The gentleman said Mr Bothwick was in jail
in Glasgow, for a debt which he (the agent) was going to discharge, and that
Mr Bothwick would produce all he papers in his possession. Mr Stuart
did not agree to any settlement of the action, but having been long extremely
anxious to find out The Authors of the attacks upon him, he went to Glasgow ; and Mr Bothwick after being liberated from prison, brought a number
of papers and put them into the hands of his Edinburgh agent, who was then
at an hotel along with Mr Stuart. Among these that gentleman and Mr
Stuart to their utter astonishment, found in the hand writing of Sir Alexander
Boswell (who had never been suspected,) the papers which led to the fatal
reneountre. Mr Stuart neither paid, nor agreed to pay, any part of the debt
for which Mr Bothwick was imprisoned ; he neither paid, nor agreed to pay,
Mr Bothwick any money: and he never was in the office of the Sentinel from
which he understood the papers were brought. We understand that Mr Stuart
has given notice ,that he is ready to appear to stand his trial.

Broadside entitled "A True Account Of That Fatal Duel," 1822.
Courtesy of the National Library of Scotland, Edinburgh.

James Stuart, Esq. (1830)

"Devil in Petticoats"

James Stuart (1775–1849) was born in Fifeshire, Scotland, the son of Dr. Charles Stuart, a minister and physician descended from the third Earl of Moray, and Mary Erskine, the daughter of Reverend John Erskine, the famous Scottish divine. Stuart studied at the University of Edinburgh and was admitted to the Society of Writers to the Signet in 1798. He endeavored in agriculture and bred beef cattle; and as a deputy-lieutenant and justice of the peace, took an active part in business in his county in Scotland. However, his Whig enthusiasm offended authorities, and he was often involved in disputes. In 1822, he killed his cousin, Sir Alexander Boswell, the son of biographer and diarist James Boswell, in a duel after the young Boswell ridiculed him in articles published in the *Glasgow Sentinel*. Stuart fled to France but returned to be tried for murder as "art and part in a duel." The trial was a sensation in the international press. Stuart was defended by the greatest lawyers of the Scots Bar, and he was accompanied to trial by relatives, the Earl of Moray and his uncle, David Erskine, and other figures in the higher circles of Scotland. He pled not guilty and was acquitted. Nevertheless there remained a good deal of controversy surrounding him, more so after Sir Walter Scott reproduced the duel in one of his Waverley novels, *St. Ronan's Well*, published in 1824.

After the trial, Stuart engaged in extensive land speculation until he was bankrupted, his Edinburgh estate and effects sold at a well-publicized auction that lasted fourteen days. Sir Walter Scott wrote in his journal on February 9, 1829: "At twelve I went to Stuart of Dunearn's sale of pictures. This poor man fell a victim to speculation. And though I had no knowledge of him personally, and disliked him as the cause of poor Sir Alexander Boswell's death, yet 'had he been slaughterman to all my kin,' I could but pity the miserable sight of his splendid establishment broken up, and his treasures of art exposed to public and unsparing sale." Stuart, forced to resign a position he had in "the collectorship of the

Taken from *Three Years in North America* (Edinburgh: Printed for R. Cadell, 1833), 2.

widows' fund" and seeking to flee publicity, left Scotland. He boarded the packet *William Thomson* with his wife, Eleanor, and traveled in the United States from 1828 to 1831. He toured the South during the first half of 1830. In Charleston, he lodged at the Planters Hotel, where he found his proprietress to be "a devil in petticoats." Like so many travelers, Stuart was escorted around town by Dr. Tidyman, the unofficial host of the city. Unlike Margaret Hall, he was quite taken with Tidyman.

In 1833, Stuart published his travels in *Three Years in America*. It was highly controversial due to the author's notoriety, and a best seller. Two more editions appeared in the following year. Stuart became editor of the London *Courier*, a Whig newspaper. In 1836, he was appointed an inspector of factories for the north of England and Scotland, a position he held until his death in London.

SOURCES

Anderson, William. *The Scottish Nation*. Vol. 3. Edinburgh: A. Fullerton & Sons, 1863.

Anonymous. *The Trial of James Stuart, Esq., Younger of Dunearn, Before the High Court of Justiciary, at Edinburgh, on Monday, June 10, 1822*. Edinburgh: George Ramsay and Co., 1822.

Burke, Peter, Esq. *Celebrated Trials Connected with the Aristocracy in the Relations of Private Life*. London: William Benning & Co., 1849.

Lodge, Edmund. *The Peerage of the British Empire*. London: Saunders and Oatley, 1851.

Moss, Michael S. "Stuart, James (1775–1849)." *Oxford Dictionary of National Biography*. Ed. H. C. G. Matthew and Brian Harrison. Oxford, UK: Oxford University Press, 2004.

Scott, Sir Walter. *The Journal of Sir Walter Scott*. Vol. 2. New York: Burt Franklin, 1890.

Stephen, Sir Leslie, and Sir Sydney Lee. "James Stuart 1775–1849." In *Dictionary of National Biography*. Vol. 55. London: Smith, Elder & Co., 1898.

———

"DEVIL IN PETTICOATS"

March 1830.

I had heard on the way to Charleston, that this was the week of the Charleston races, and I was therefore not much surprised when I found that I could not be accommodated at the Carolina coffee-house, kept by Stewart,* or at Jones's

---

*Carolina Coffee-house or Stewart's Coffee House, kept by Angus Stewart, was located at 20 Tradd Street. It was frequented by businessmen and planters, and offered limited accommodation (Schackleford, *Directory and Stranger's Guide*, 1825; "Carolina Coffee House, Tradd Street," advertisement in *The* [Charleston] *Times*, January 8, 1821, 4).

hotel,* which I had been desired first to try. From thence I went to the Plant-ers' hotel. On my mentioning that I required a room for myself, the landlady protested that the house was so full, that it was impossible to let me have one. I pressed my suit, however, so long and so earnestly, that she at last became propitious, and told Mr Street, her husband,† who happened to come in at the moment, what she had done, but that she was persuaded that I was at least a colonel. I got possession of a small apartment; and after the races were over, I was comfortably enough accommodated.

The ordinary at this hotel was very good. It being the race week, the table was full, and there were several ladies. The dinner consisted of turtle-soup, fish, and abundance of food. Mrs Street sat at the head of the table, and her husband at the foot. I lost no time in walking about the town, which is as different as possible from any of the American cities I have yet seen. The population is somewhat above 30,000. The fine houses are very large, many of them inclosed like the great hotels in Paris, and all of them covered with verandas, and situated in gardens neatly dressed, and at this season not only adorned with the fairest evergreen shrubs, but with a great variety of beautiful roses, jonquils, and summer flowers. On the other hand, many of the streets, though not all of them, were dirty and unpaved, and the houses in some parts of the town had a filthy appearance. It was at once obvious, from the style of the town, and the appearance of the people, many of them but meanly apparelled, and from the great number of coloured people, that I was now in a state where there was a far greater inequality of condition than in the American cities which I had yet seen, and that I was in a slave-holding state. In fact, the coloured population is larger than the white population.

*Jones Hotel, a fashionable resort hotel for whites, was operated by Jehu Jones (b. 1769), a "free man of color." It was said to have been unsurpassed in cuisine and service. Jones, first a tailor, bought the property (originally the William Burrows House) for thirteen thousand dollars in 1815. It was later operated by John and Eliza Seymour Lee and was afterward known as the Mansion House. In subsequent years, the hotel declined to a rooming house, unten-anted in its last two years. Declared unsafe, the building was dismantled in 1928 to be reerected elsewhere. When that did not happen, its drawing room was saved and installed at the Win-terthur Museum in Delaware (Simons and Simons, "The William Burrows House," 155–76).

†Horatio Gates Street (1777–1849), a "sea captain, store and hotel-keeper" from Con-necticut, was manager of the Planter's Hotel. He also operated a tavern or coffee house in Charleston at Queen and Church streets. He was described as "six feet, four inches tall" and "like Abraham Lincoln, in height and strength, with a kind face, friendly-eyes and manner." His wife, Lois B. Holt (1780–1855), also from Connecticut, was described as "a large woman of commanding presence." The Streets spent their last years on Edisto Island, where they are buried (Nelson and Carhart, *Genealogy of the Morris Family*, 163; William L. King, *The News-paper Press of Charleston*, 55).

I went to the theatre on the evening I arrived at Charleston. It is a clean-looking house both without and within,—particularly within. I was surprised to see it, so ill attended, especially in the race week. When I returned to the hotel in the evening, I found the streets totally deserted. I hardly met a person of whom I could ask my way home. This is owing to a regulation, which requires that none of the coloured people,—that is about one-half of the population,—shall be out of their houses or residences after nine o'clock in the evening. On opening the hotel door, the male servants of the house were, I found, already laid down for the night in the passages with their clothes on. They neither get beds nor bedding here, and you may kick them or tread upon them as you come in with impunity.

On the following morning, I had a delightful walk in the city and its environs, and was very much confirmed in the opinion which I had formed at first sight. There is obviously a great distinction of classes here. Some of the houses are worth L.10,000, and are real palazzos, surrounded with orange trees, magnolias, pal-mettos, and other trees almost of a tropical climate. The streets are lined with the pride of India tree. The whole appearance is far more that of a city where luxury abounds, than what I have previously seen in the United States. Early in the fore-noon, I went to the race-ground, which is on a piece of very fine turfy about two miles from the city. Many alterations in the manners of the people were obvious. The equipages were much handsomer. Coaches with coats of arms painted on the doors were not uncommon; and there were several servants in livery.

The race was very well attended by gentlemen and by the nobility, but the number of ladies was comparatively small. There is a jockey club here, from whom the stewards of the races are chosen. The stewards wear roses of crimson ribbon in their breasts to distinguish them, and top-boots, and white corduroys, and seem disposed to exert their little brief authority to the utmost. Although there are constables at the starting-post to prevent the people from coming on the course, one of the stewards appeared very much to envy them their calling, for no sooner did a man of colour appear on the course, and within his reach, than he struck him with his horse-whip. No wonder that these people thirst for vengeance. Here, on the race-course, there were at least two men of colour for every white person, yet they were obliged to submit to treatment which the white man dared not even to have threatened to a person of his own colour. The race turned out a very good one, as the horses, though of no great swiftness, were well matched. There were four heats. The riders were all boys of colour. The thermom-eter is at present here above 70°. I saw no mosquitos, but the flies were exceed-ingly troublesome, and are kept off the provisions, while on the table, by slaves with palmetto fans. Oranges, shaddock, bananas, and other fruits of a tropical country, are very abundant here. Oranges are sold for a halfpenny each. There is frequent communication with the Havannah.

On returning to the hotel, I found a gentleman had in my absence called for me, and left a note asking me to dine with him next day. Having written my answer accepting the invitation, I went to the bar-room to beg Mr Street to send it by one of the boys, of whom there were several about the house, but he at once told me, that he could not send any of his slaves out of the house. The bar-keeper, Mr Ferguson, from Golspie, in Sunderland, North Britain, seeing my dilemma, offered to carry my note, and the landlord consented. Ferguson, however, afterwards told me, that the landlord had been very ill pleased with him for showing me so much civility, because he knew that his presence was always necessary in the bar-room. Ferguson at the same time told me, that the slaves were most cruelly treated in this house, and that they were never allowed to go out of it, because, as soon as they were out of sight, they would infallibly make all the exertion in their power to run away. Next morning, looking from my window an hour before breakfast, I saw Mrs Street, the landlady, give a young man, a servant, such a blow behind the ear as made him reel, and I afterwards found that it was her daily and hourly practice to beat her servants, male and female, either with her fist, or with a thong made of cow-hide.

I dined with a large party this day in a very handsome house of some antiquity, the rooms fitted up with figured wainscot in the old English style. Twenty persons sat down to dinner at about half-past four o'clock. We had a most abundant feast, of which I mention the particulars merely to show the style of such a dinner here. It was attended by an upper servant and three servants in livery, all of course slaves. The table was covered with turtle-soup, fish, venison, boiled mutton, roast turkey, boiled turkey, a ham, two boiled salted tongues, two tame ducks, two wild ducks, some dressed dishes, boiled rice, hominy, potatoes, cauliflower, salad, &c. The whole of this dinner was placed on the table at once before we sat down. When it was removed, a complete course of pastry and puddings succeeded, and then a most excellent dessert of oranges, shaddocks, bananas, and a variety of West India fruits, with iced cream in profusion. The liquids consisted of Champagne, Madeira, sherry, port, claret, porter, lemonade, &c. The ladies left the table soon after the dessert appeared, and the gentlemen broke off one by one, and always went out by the outer passage, and not by the stair to the drawing-room, from which, and from coffee not being announced, I presumed that it was not understood that the dinner party were expected again in the drawing-room. I took my leave before eight o'clock, when only three or four of the party remained.

Dr. Tidyman of Charleston, to whom I had been made known by Colonel Burn,* was at great pains to show me the objects worthy a stranger's attention here, although my visit happened to be at a time not very convenient for him. He could not see me at first when I called, but he applied to one of his friends within an hour or two afterwards to take me to the race, and who came to the hotel for me in his carriage. He took me to his seat in St Michael's Church on the following Sunday forenoon. This is a very handsome church, of the Episcopalian persuasion, with as respectable and genteel-looking a congregation as one would see anywhere in Britain. I afterwards went to his house, where I met many of the principal inhabitants of the city. It seemed to be the fashion for them to come for a few minutes on a Sunday forenoon to drink a glass of wine, and take a bit of cake. The custom seems to be the same here as in the northern parts of the United States, that when two gentlemen are introduced to each other, they shake hands. I have found this custom to be universal in every part of the United States, instead of the formal bow in great Britain. The persons made acquainted with each other uniformly shake hands. I afterwards again and again partook of Dr. Tidyman's hospitality. His dinner was very much in the English style. Venison is on the table at every dinner here, and although not so dry as in the northern states, is very inferior to the wild venison of Scotland, or even to a good leg of Scotch Highland mutton.

Dr Tidyman had four livery servants, of course slaves, who, by their obvious attachment to him and his family, and the alacrity with which they attended to every instruction that was given them, showed their sense of the kindness with which they were treated.

Dr Tidyman, in a late publication, relating chiefly to the establishment of the recent tariff, states the expense of providing clothing, food, &c. for a slave, on a well-managed plantation, to be about thirty-five dollars per annum. He also states the amount of the wages of a labourer, a white man, in the United States, to be three times as great as in Europe. Now, supposing the price of a slave to be 400 dollars, and 40 dollars a year's interest at ten per cent on his price, the prodigious saving of employing slaves is obvious. The wages of a white man cannot be reckoned at less than 500 or 600 dollars. Dr Tidyman mentions that, with kind masters, the condition of slaves is rendered as happy as a state of slavery can admit of. This is unquestionably true. Indeed I myself have seen instances of quite as strong, if not stronger attachment, on the part of a slave, than I ever saw on the part of a white man to his master,—but the master may, at pleasure,

---

*Earlier in his travels, Stuart visited Col. Burn in Frankford, Pennsylvania. An American who had lived in England, Burn owned land in Scotland.

be guilty of abuse of power to his slave; and it is quite notorious in the southern parts of America, that even the greatest slave proprietors, whose interest ought to lead them to treat their slaves well, treat them the worst. I could easily refer to many instances. One, however, is so well known, that there is no impropriety in mentioning it, viz. that of General Hampton,* one of the greatest, if not the very greatest, slave proprietor in the United States, a South Carolinian, with, however, the chief part of his property situated in Louisiana. He not only maltreats his slaves, but stints them in food, overworks them, and keeps them almost naked. I have seen more than one of his overseers whose representations gave a dreadful account of the state of slavery on his plantations, and who left his service because they would no longer assist in the cruel punishments inflicted upon his slaves; but I do not mention such a fact as this merely on such authority. General Hampton's conduct towards his slaves is matter of notoriety.

Dr Tidyman has a large plantation; his overseer's salary is 1000 dollars a-year.

Dr Tidyman carried me round the environs of Charleston in his carriage, to the orphan hospital, in the front of which is a statue of the great Lord Chatham, who was justly popular in this country, on account of his opposition to the war with the colonies. The whole hospital is clean, and well kept. The top of the hospital affords the best view which there is of the city and neighhourhood of Charleston, and of the bay and adjoining rivers.

Dr Tidyman also took me to a rice-mill, the whole arrangements of which are very conveniently and beautifully managed. The process is shown,—beginning with the conveyance of the rice from the schooner into the cart, until it is ground and ready for packing.

There is at Charleston a guard of soldiers, who patrole the city during the night.

During part of the summer months, so dangerous a fever prevails here, that a great part of the inhabitants leave the city,—Dr Tidyman and his family go regularly to the vicinity of Philadelphia.

I took a long drive on the 4th March, in an open carriage, to see the country in the neighbourhood of Charleston, great part of which is of a very sandy soil. The roads are in some places very bad, owing to the great weight of the waggons bringing cotton to be shipped at Charleston. The scenery here would be very tame, if it were not for the fine rivers on both hands,—but the inland part of South Carolina is in many places mountainous, and very beautiful.

My driver was a free man of colour. He gave a frightful account of the treatment to which he and all the people of colour, whether free or slaves, are subject

*Gen. Wade Hampton (1751–1835).

in this state. He had been accustomed formerly to go every season to the State of New York during the period when, owing to the inhabitants leaving the city, business was almost at a stand; but, by an act passed a few years ago, it is declared that a free person of colour leaving the state, though merely crossing the boundary, shall never be allowed to return; and as this person driving me has a wife and family, he feels himself really and truly a prisoner in the State of South Carolina.* The same law declares, that it shall not be lawful for free persons of colour to come from another state into this. If they should be brought in a vessel, they are immediately confined in gaol, till the vessel is ready again to proceed to sea,—the captain paying the expenses of their detention. It is now contrary to law that even free persons of colour should be educated;—they are incompetent witnesses in any case where the rights of white persons are concerned; and their trials are conducted by a justice of the peace and freeholders, without the benefit of a jury. So far as respects the slaves, they are even still in a worse situation; for, though their evidence is in no case admissible against the whites, the affirmation of free persons of colour, or their fellow-slaves, is received against them. I was placed in a situation at Charleston which gave me too frequent opportunities to witness the effects of slavery in its most aggravated state. Mrs Street treated all the servants in the house in the most barbarous manner; and this, although she knew that Stewart, the hotel-keeper here, had lately nearly lost his life by maltreating a slave. He beat his cook, who was a stout fellow, until he could no longer support it. He rose upon his master, and in his turn gave him such a beating that it had nearly cost him his life; the cook immediately left the house, ran off, and was never afterwards heard of,—it was supposed that he had drowned himself. Not a day, however, passed without my hearing of Mrs Street whipping and ill using her unfortunate slaves. On one occasion, when one of the female slaves had disobliged her, she beat her until her own strength was exhausted, and then insisted on the bar-keeper, Mr. Ferguson, proceeding to inflict the remainder of the punishment.—Mrs Street in the meantime took her place in the bar-room. She instructed him to lay on the whip severely in an adjoining room. His nature was repugnant to the execution of the duty which was imposed on him. He gave a wink to the girl, who understood it and bellowed lustily, while he made the whip crack on the walls of the room. Mrs Street expressed herself to be quite

*Laws in the early 1820s prohibited manumission of slaves by their masters and the immigration of free blacks. Free persons who ventured outside of the state were restricted from returning home. When Jehu Jones, the aforementioned owner of Jones Hotel, left and tried to reenter the state in the 1820s, he was not allowed to return, despite innumerable petitions attesting to "his irreproachable character."

satisfied with the way in which Ferguson had executed her instructions; but, unfortunately for him, his lenity to the girl became known in the house, and the subject of merriment, and was one of the reasons for his dismissal before I left the house;—but I did not know of the most atrocious of all the proceedings of this cruel woman until the very day that I quitted the house. I had put up my clothes in my portmanteau, when I was about to set out, but finding it was rather too full, I had difficulty in getting it closed to allow me to lock it; I therefore told one of the boys to send me one of the stoutest of the men to assist me. A great robust fellow soon afterwards appeared, whom I found to be the cook, with tears in his eyes;—I asked him what was the matter? He told me that, just at the time when the boy called for him, he had got so sharp a blow on the cheek bone, from this devil in petticoats, as had unmanned him for the moment. Upon my expressing commiseration for him, he said he viewed this as nothing, but that he was leading a life of terrible suffering;—that about two years had elapsed since he and his wife, with his two children, had been exposed in the public market at Charleston for sale,—that he had been purchased by Mr Street,—that his wife and children had been purchased by a different person; and that, though he was living in the same town with them, he never was allowed to see them;—he would be beaten within an ace of his life if he ventured to go to the corner of the street. Wherever the least symptom of rebellion or insubordination appears at Charleston on the part of a slave, the master sends the slave to the gaol, where he is whipped or beaten as the master desires. The Duke of Saxe Weimar, in his travels,* mentions that he visited this gaol in December 1825; that the "black overseers go about everywhere armed with cow-hides; that in the basement story there is an apparatus upon which the negroes, by order of the police, or at the request of the masters, are flogged; that the machine consists of a sort of crane, on which a cord with two nooses runs over pulleys; the nooses are made fast to the hands of the slave and drawn up, while the feet are bound tight to a plank; that the body is stretched out as much as possible,—and thus the miserable creature receives the exact number of lashes as counted off." The public sale of slaves in the market- place occurs frequently. I was at two sales, where especially at one of them, the miserable creatures were in tears on account of their being separated by their relations and friends. At one of them a young woman of sixteen or seventeen was separated from her mother and father, and all her relations, and every one she had formerly known. This not

---

*Bernhard, Duke of Saxe-Weimar-Eisenach (1757–1828), author of *Travels by His Highness Duke Bernhard of Saxe-Weimar-Eisenach through North America in the Years 1825 and 1826*, published in 1828.

infrequently happens, although I was told and believe that there is a general wish to keep relations together where it can be done.

The following extract of a letter from a gentleman at Charleston, to a friend of his at New York, published in the New York newspapers while I was there, contains even a more shocking account of the public sales of slaves here.—"Curiosity sometimes leads me to the auction sales of the negroes. A few days since I attended one which exhibited the beauties of slavery in all their sickening deformity. The bodies of these wretched beings were placed upright on a table,—their physical proportions examined,—their defects and beauties noted.—'A prime lot, here they go!' There I saw the father looking sullen contempt upon the crowd, and expressing an indignation in his countenance that he dare not speak;—and the mother, pressing her infants closer to her bosom with an involuntary grasp, and exclaiming, in wild and simple earnestness, while the tears chased down her cheeks in quick succession, 'I can't leff my children! I wont leff my children!' But on the hammer went, reckless alike whether it united or sundered for ever. On another stand, I saw a man apparently as white as myself exposed for sale. I turned away from the humiliating spectacle.

"At another time I saw the concluding scene of this infernal drama. It was on the wharf. A slave ship for New Orleans was lying in the stream, and the poor negroes, handcuffed and pinioned, were hurried off in boats, eight at a time. Here I witnessed the last farewell,—the heart-rending separation of every earthly tie. The mute and agonizing embrace of the husband and wife, and the convulsive grasp of the mother and the child, were alike torn asunder—for ever! It was a living death,—they never see or hear of each other more. Tears flowed fast, and mine with the rest."

Charleston has long been celebrated for the severity of its laws against the blacks, and the mildness of its punishment towards the whites for maltreating them. Until the late law, there were about seventy-one crimes, for which slaves were capitally punished, and for which the highest punishment for whites was imprisonment in the penitentiary.

A dreadful case of murder occurred at Charleston in 1806. A planter, called John Slater, made an unoffending, unresisting slave, be bound hand and foot, and compelled his companion to chop off his head with an axe, and to cast his body, convulsing with the agonies of death, into the water. Judge Wild, who tried him,* on awarding a sentence of imprisonment against this wretch, expressed his regret that the punishment provided for the offence was insufficient to make the law respected,—that the delinquent too well knew,—that the arm, which he had

---

*Judge Samuel Wilds (1775–1810) of Darlington.

stretched out for the destruction of his slave, was that to which he alone could look for protection, disarmed as he was of the rights of self-defence.* But the most horrible butchery of slaves which has ever taken place in America, was the execution of thirty-five of them on the lines near Charleston, in the month of July 1822, on account of an alleged conspiracy against their masters.†

The whole proceedings are monstrous. Sixty-seven persons were convicted before a court, consisting of a justice of the peace, and free-holders, without a jury. The evidence of slaves not upon oath was admitted against them, and, after all, the proof was extremely scanty. Perrault, a slave, who had himself been brought from Africa, was the chief witness.‡

He had been torn from his father, who was very wealthy, and a considerable trader in tobacco and salt on the coast of Africa. He was taken prisoner, and was sold, and his purchaser would not give him up, although three slaves were offered in his stead. The judge's address, on pronouncing sentence of death on this occasion, on persons sold to slavery and servitude, and who, if they were guilty, were only endeavoring to get rid of it in the only way in their power, seems monstrous. He told them that the servant who was false to his master would be false to his God,—that the precept of St Paul was to obey their masters in all things, and of St Peter, to be subject to their masters with all fear,—and that, had they listened to such doctrines, they would not now have been arrested by an ignominious death.

The proceedings of this trial made some noise at the time. An official account of it was published, in which the execution of so great a number of persons was

---

*Under South Carolina law, killing a black, free or slave, did not constitute murder but a misdemeanor, and Slater was merely fined. The jury was appalled at the leniency of the law. In his sentencing the trial judge, Wilds, informed Slater he hoped "eternal punishment" would make up for the failure of the legal system, a speech that ran in newspapers throughout the country. Regardless, it was another fifteen years before the law was changed (Dale, "Getting Away with Murder," 96–97).

†Stuart refers to the Denmark Vesey slave conspiracy. Vesey, a free black carpenter, led a number of free blacks and slaves in a plot to kill whites (and blacks who protested), free the slaves, and exodus in mass to Haiti. The revolt was never acted out; however, thirty-five blacks involved were tried and hanged and another thirty-two convicted were sold out of the region. Because Vesey was a free black, his involvement brought free blacks under tighter scrutiny and new laws were adopted for the regulation of all blacks. The laws were unevenly invoked but curtailed freedoms and were sharp reminders of white domination in the city. Blacks would experience the aftershock of the Vesey conspiracy for the next 30 years (Pearson, *Designs Against Charleston*, 61, 307; Johnson and Roark, *Black Masters*, 41–46).

‡Perault (or Peirault), a blacksmith owned by John Strohecker, was a witness in court against his coconspirators. As a result of his testimony, he was sentenced to transportation outside the country.

justified by the precedent of George the Second, who executed fifty-four of the first men in Britain for the rebellion of 1745.

The existence of slavery in its most hideous form, in a country of absolute freedom in most respects, is one of those extraordinary anomalies for which it is impossible to account. No man was more sensible of this than Jefferson, nor more anxious that so foul a stain on the otherwise free constitutions of the United States should be wiped away. His sentiments on this subject, and on the peculiar situation of his countrymen in maintaining slavery, are thus given in a communication to one of his friends:—"What an incomprehensible machine is man! who can endure toil, famine, stripes, imprisonment, and death itself, in vindication of his own liberty, and the next moment be deaf to all those motives whose power supported him through his trial, and inflict on his fellow men a bondage, one hour of which is fraught with more misery than ages of that which he rose in rebellion to oppose. But we must await with patience the workings of an overruling Providence, and hope that that is preparing the deliverance of these our suffering brethren. When the measure of their tears shall be full,—when their groans shall have involved Heaven itself in darkness,—doubtless a God of justice will awaken to their distress, and, by diffusing light and liberality among their oppressors, or at length, by his exterminating thunder, manifest his attention to the things of this world, and that they are not left to the guidance of a blind fatality."

Harriet Martineau by Richard Evans. Oil on canvas. Exhibited 1834.
Copyright National Portrait Gallery, London.

HARRIET MARTINEAU (1835)

"Many Mansions There Are in This Hell"

Harriet Martineau (1802–1876), feminist, social reformist, and abolitionist, was one of the first female professional writers of her century, and the first English-woman to write systematically on economics and politics. The daughter of a Norwich textile manufacturer who gave all of his children an excellent liberal education, Martineau began to go deaf at the age of twelve and could hear only with the use of an ear trumpet. After her father's death in 1826, she supported her mother and herself by stitching needlepoint and publishing articles on economic topics with a political economy cast, for which she achieved success, and as a writer of popular journalism in newspapers, magazines, and books. She attained fame and financial success with *Illustrations of Political Economy,* a series of novellas on economic topics, which sold more copies than the novels of Charles Dickens. *Illustrations* includes her some of her earliest attacks on slavery. She built her arguments on two grounds: immorality and economic inefficiency. Her fourth story in *Illustrations,* "Demerara," exposed the human suffering that resulted from slave systems "that waste both capital and labor." It was published not long before she traveled to the United States, and had been widely read when she arrived.

She arrived in America with her traveling companion, Louisa Jeffery, and letters of introduction from prominent Englishmen. These letters—along with Martineau's fame as an author, well-known Unitarian beliefs, and views on social reform and slavery—allowed her to meet famous Americans. Aware that Americans were beginning to feel betrayed by "blatant misrepresentations" in British travel accounts, she did not divulge her intention to publish her travels until she returned to England—although some suspected her intent.

Martineau traveled in this country at a time of increased agitation between North and South due to the Nullification crisis. Further, by 1835, the controversy over slavery had rekindled throughout the nation. She wrote in her *Autobiography* that in Washington, once it became apparent she intended to tour the

Taken from *Retrospect of Western Travel* (London: Saunders and Otley), 1838, vol. 2.

southern states, "intimations . . . came to me in all manner of ways." And: "I was specially informed of imprisonments for opinions the same as are found in 'Demerara,' which indeed might well be under the laws of South Carolina, as I found them in full operation. Hints were offered of strangers with my views not being able to come away alive. But the most ordinary cunning or sensitiveness of the slave-holders would account for attempts like these to frighten a woman from going where she might see slavery for herself. I wrote friends and my family that I went into the danger warily: and I requested that my letter might be kept in evidence of this, in case of my not returning."

They stayed with Reverend Samuel Gilman (1791–1848), minister of the Unitarian Church, and his wife, Caroline Howard Gilman (1794–1888), a poet and later the author of *Recollections of a Southern Matron* and other books. The Gilmans, transplants from New England, moved to Charleston in 1819 and had become well-loved local figures. From their house, Martineau convened with key Charlestonians.

As a result of her travels, Martineau first published *Society in America*. At the request of her publishers, she made further drafts upon her journals for a second book, *Retrospect of Western Travel*. It was intended "to communicate more of my personal narrative, and of the lighter characteristics of men, and incidents of travel" than the first. The book won a greater popular success. Charlestonians, however, felt betrayed by her comments, such as "many mansions there are in this hell."

Martineau claimed to have witnessed fanaticism from both the North and South over the question of slavery. In later life, she was not at all sympathetic with the South. At the end of the Civil War in 1865, she wrote: "The difficulty is with the thousands of shiftless, barbarous, helpless white refugees, who have never worked, & hate & dread work,—though they arrive barefoot & hungry. The planters are eager to let & sell the greater part of their estates to Northern men, who know how to make the land answer; & the poor whites,—the younger ones at least, will soon learn to work & thrive, like the Yankees. Their most universal complaint is that they never were asked about secession,—never wished it,—never knew anything about it."

From England, Martineau continued her prolific output of work and promoted causes, published tracts, and wrote books of history, biography, philosophy, sociology, and fiction. Volumes of her works continue to be published and studied, including scholarly analyses, reprint editions, and collections, among them *Harriet Martineau's Writing on the British Empire* (2004), *Harriet Martineau's Writing on British History and Military Reform* (2005), and *The Collected Letters of Harriet Martineau* (2007).

SOURCES

Johnson, Paul. "Lady of Letters: Review of *The Collected Letters of Harriet Martineau.*" *Literary Review* (November 2007): 9–10.

Klaver, Claudia. "Imperial Economics: Harriet Martineau's *Illustration of Political Economy* and the Narration of Empire." *Victorian Literature and Culture* 35 (2007): 21–40.

Logan, Deborah, ed. *The Collected Letters of Harriet Martineau.* Vol. 5. London: Pickering & Chatto, 2007.

Martineau, Harriet. *Autobiography.* Boston: James R. Osgood Co., 1877.

"Many Mansions There Are in This Hell"
City Life in the South

We were to have arrived at the city about six p.m. of the 10th of March, when every object would have looked bright in the sunshine of a spring evening. As it was, we reached the railroad station at ten minutes past four the next morning. There was much delay in obtaining our luggage and getting away from the station. We could not think of disturbing the slumbers of the friends whose hospitality we were about to enjoy, and we therefore proceeded in the omnibus which was in waiting to the Planter's Hotel. We were all hungry, having scarcely tasted food since noon the day before; and very weary, having travelled the whole of two nights, and enjoyed no sufficient rest since we left Richmond, nine days before. Every little event became a great one to persons so exhausted. The omnibus jolted and stopped, and we were told that an accident had happened. The gentlemen got out, but the darkness was total. A light was brought from a private house, and it appeared that a wheel had touched the kerbstone! It seemed as if horses were never backed in Charleston, so long were we in proceeding. When I afterward saw what the streets of Charleston are like, I do not wonder at any extreme of caution in a driver. The soil is a fine sand, which, after rain, turns into a most deceptive mud; and there is very little pavement yet. The deficiency of stone is, however, becoming supplied by importation, and the inhabitants hope soon to be able to walk about the city in all weathers, without danger of being lost in crossing the streets. They told me, as an *on dit,* that a horse was drowned last winter in a mudhole in a principal street.

At the hotel all was dark and comfortless. We made a stir among the servants; the gentlemen got two men to light a fire, and fetch us wine and biscuits; and we persuaded two women to make up beds and warm some water. We were foolish enough to be tempted to take wine and water, as we could have neither tea or coffee; and when we rose from our unrefreshing sleep an hour after noon, we formed such a dismal group of aching heads as could hardly be matched out of a hospital.

Two of us proceeded, in a light pretty hack-carriage, to the friend's house where we were expected. Nothing could be more considerate than our reception. A pile of English and American letters and newspapers awaited us, and our hostess knew that we must be fatigued; a fire was therefore immediately lighted in my chamber, and we were told that the day was our own; that our dinner would be sent up to us, and that we should not be expected in the drawing-room till we chose to join the family. I shall not soon forget the refreshment of lingering over family letters and London newspapers; of feeling that we were not liable to be called up in the dark for a fortnight at least; and of seeing my clothes laid in drawers, for the first time, I think, since I landed. A chest of drawers is seldom to be seen in the chambers, or, at least, in the guest-chambers of American houses. We were favoured in the article of closets with rows of pegs, but I believe I had the use of a chest of drawers only two or three times during my travels.

A circumstance happened this day which, as being illustrative of manners, may be worth relating. The day before I left Richmond, Virginia, two companions and myself had employed a hack-carriage, driven by a black, for some hours; and, on dismissing it, had paid the fare, which we thought reasonable, two dollars and a half. The proprietor of the carriage and master of the driver had by some means heard who it was that had been his customer. Finding that I had left Richmond, he took the trouble to send the two dollars and a half down to Charleston, five hundred miles, with a message that it was not for the honor of Virginia that I should pay carriage hire! and the money was awaiting me on my arrival.

I had soon reason to perceive that Charleston deserves its renown for hospitality. A lecturer on phrenology sent us tickets for his course;* six carriages were immediately placed at my disposal, and the servants came every morning for orders for the day. The difficulty was to use them all and equally; but, by employing one for the morning drive and another for the evening visiting, we contrived

*In 1832, the Charleston *Mercury* noted that J. G. Spurzheim, "the famous Lecturer on Phrenology," arrived in America. However, it was one of his disciples, Dr. Jonathan Barber, who "took the gospel to Charleston." Phrenologists believed the shape of the head or skull determined intellect and character, a subject that stimulated considerable interest among Charlestonians in the next years. The Medical College exhibited a collection of phrenological skulls and hosted several lecture series on the topic. It was discussed at meetings of Charleston's Literary and Philosophical Society. Phrenology would later lose favor in the South due to the large participation of phrenologists in the abolition movement (McCandless, "Mesmerism and Phrenology in Antebellum Charleston," 199–230).

to show our friends that we were willing to avail ourselves of their kindnesses. I believe there was scarcely a morning during our stay when some pretty present did not arrive before I rose; sometimes it was a bouquet of hyacinths, which were extremely rare that year, from the lateness and severity of the frosts; sometimes it was a dish of preserve or marmalade; sometimes a feather fan, when the day promised to be hot; sometimes a piece of Indian work; sometimes of indigenous literary production. One morning I found on my window-seat a copy of the *Southern Review*, and a bouquet of hyacinths from General Hayne;* and the next a basket of wafers from Mrs. P.; and the third a set of cambric handkerchiefs, inimitably marked with complimentary devices, from Mrs. W.

In the midst of all this there was no little watchfulness, among a totally different set of persons, about my proceedings with regard to the negroes. I had not been in the city twenty-four hours before we were amused with ridiculous reports of my championship on behalf of the blacks; and, long after I had left the place, reported speeches of mine were in circulation which were remarkably striking to me when I at length heard them. This circumstance shows how irritable the minds of the people are upon this topic.

I met with no difficulty, however, among my associates. I made it a rule to allow others to introduce the subject of slavery, knowing that they would not fail to do so, and that I might learn as much from their method of approaching the topic as from anything they could say upon it. Before half an hour had passed, every man, woman, or child I might be conversing with had entered upon the question. As it was likewise a rule with me never to conceal or soften my own opinions, and never to allow myself to be irritated by what I heard (for it is too serious a subject to indulge frailties with), the best understanding existed between slaveholders and myself. We never quarrelled, while, I believe, we never failed to perceive the extent of the difference of opinion and feeling between us. I met with much more cause for admiration in their frankness than reason to complain of illiberality. The following may serve as a specimen of this part of our intercourse:

The first time I met an eminent Southern gentleman, a defender of slavery, he said to me (within the half hour), "I wish you would not be in such a hurry away. I wish you would stay a year in this city. I wish you would stay ten years, and then you would change your opinions."

"What opinions?"

"Your opinions on slavery."

"What do you know of my opinions on slavery?"

"Oh, we know them well enough: we have all read 'Demerara.'"

*Robert Young Hayne.

"Very well: now we shall understand each other; for I must tell you that I think about slavery exactly as I did when I wrote that story. Nothing that I have seen shows me that I have anything to qualify of what is said there. So now you do know my opinions."

"Oh, yes. I don't want to know anything more of your opinions. I want you to know mine."

"That is exactly what I want. When will you let me have them?"

We had engaged to dine with this gentleman the next week; it was now arranged that our party should go two hours earlier than the other guests, in order to hear this gentleman's exposition of slavery. He was well prepared, and his statement of facts and reasons was clear, ready, and entertaining. The fault was in the narrowness of his premises, for his whole argument was grounded on the supposition that human rights consist in sufficient subsistence in return for labor. Before he began I told him that I fully understood his wish not to argue the question, and that I came to hear his statement, not to controvert it; but that I must warn him not to take my silence for assent. Upon this understanding we proceeded, with some little irritability on his part when I asked questions, but with no danger of any quarrel. I never found the slightest difficulty in establishing a similar clear understanding with every slaveholder I met.

Some of the reports of my championship of the negroes arose from a circumstance which occurred the day after my arrival at Charleston. Our host proposed to take us up a church steeple, to obtain a view of the city and its environs.* The key of the church was at the Guardhouse opposite, and our host said we might as well go for it ourselves, and thus get a sight of the Guardhouse. One of the city authorities showed us over it, and we stayed a few moments in a room where a lady was preferring a complaint against two negro boys for robbing a henroost. They were proved guilty, and sentenced to be flogged at the place of punishment at the other end of the city.

The view from the church steeple was very fine; and the whole, steeped in spring sunshine, had an oriental air which took me by surprise. The city was spread out beneath us in a fanlike form, in streets converging towards the harbor. The heat and moisture of the climate give to the buildings the hue of age, so as to leave nothing of the American air of spruceness in the aspect of the place. The sandy streets, the groups of mulattoes, the women with turbaned heads, surmounted with water-pots and baskets of fruit; the small panes of the house windows; the yucca bristling in the gardens below us, and the hot haze through

*St. Michael's Church steeple.

which we saw the blue main and its islands, all looked so oriental as to strike us with wonder. We saw Ashley and Cooper rivers, bringing down produce to the main, and were taught the principal buildings—the churches and the Custom-house, built just before the Revolution—and the leading streets, Broad and Meeting streets intersecting, and affording access to all that we were to see. It would be wise in travellers to make it their first business in a foreign city to climb the loftiest point they can reach, so as to have the scene they are to explore laid out as in a living map beneath them. It is scarcely credible how much time is saved and confusion of ideas obviated by these means. I gained much by mounting the State House at Boston, Pennsylvania Hospital at Philadelphia, the new hotel at Baltimore, the Capitol at Washington, the high hills about Cincinnati, the college at Lexington, the hill where the Statehouse is to be at Nashville, the Cotton-press at New Orleans, and this church steeple at Charleston.

Another care of the traveller should be to glance at the local newspapers. This first morning I found a short newspaper article which told volumes. It was an ordinance for raising ways and means for the city. Charitable and religious institutions were left free from taxation, as were the salaries of the clergy and schoolmasters. There was a direct levy on real property, on slaves, and on carriages, and a special tax on free people of color; a class who, being precluded from obtaining taxable property and luxuries, were yet made to pay by means of a polltax.

Our mornings were divided between receiving callers and drives about the city and in the country. The country is flat and sandy, and the only objects are planters' mansions, surrounded with evergreen woods, the gardens exhibiting the tropical yucca, and fenced with hedges of the Cherokee rose. From the lower part of the city glimpses of the main may be had; but the intervening space is very ugly, except at high tide; an expanse of reeking slime, over which large flocks of buzzards are incessantly hovering. On the top of each of the long row of stakes discovered at low water sits a buzzard.

The houses which we visited in returning calls were generally handsome, with capacious piazzas, rich plants and bouquets, and good furniture. The political bias of the inhabitant was often discoverable from the books on the table, or the prints and casts on the walls. In no society in the world could the division of parties be more distinct, and their alienation more threatening than in Charleston at the time I was there. The Union gentlemen and ladies were dispirited and timid. They asked one another's opinion whether there was not some mysterious stir among the nullifiers; whether they were not concerting measures for a new defiance of the general government. This anxious watchfulness contrasted strangely with the arrogant bearing of the leading nullifiers. During my stay

Mr. Calhoun* and his family arrived from Congress; and there was something very striking in the welcome he received, like that of a chief returned to the bosom of his clan. He stalked about like a monarch of the little domain; and there was certainly an air of mysterious understanding between him and his followers, whether there was really any great secret under it or not. One lady, who had contributed ample amounts of money to the nullification funds, and a catechism to nullification lore, amused while she grieved me by the strength of her political feelings. While calling on her one morning, the conversation turned on prints, and I asked an explanation of a strange-looking one which hung opposite my eye; the portrait of a gentleman, the top of the head and the dress visible, but the face obliterated or covered over. She was only too ready to explain. It was a portrait of President Jackson, which she had hung up in days when he enjoyed her favor. Since nullification she had covered over the face, to show how she hated him.[†] A stranger hardly knows what to think of a cause whose leaders will flatter and cherish the perpetrators of a piece of petty spite like this; yet this lady is treated as if she were a main pillar of the nullification party.

Some of our mornings were spent in going with the Hayne and Calhoun families to the public library, to a panorama, and to the arsenal.[‡] The library is supported by private subscriptions, and is very creditable to the city, whose zeal about its books might well have been exhausted by the repeated destruction of the library by fire and in the war. We amused ourselves with files of newspapers which have survived all disasters; old *London Gazettes* and colonial papers extending as far back as 1678.

*Martineau referred to Senator John C. Calhoun (1782–1850) as the "cast-iron man," who "looks as though he had never been born." He had served as Congressman, U.S. secretary of war and vice-president twice before being elected to the U.S. Senate. Initially a nationalist, he had changed course during nullification toward extreme states' rights. He was now leader and spokesman for slavery and the southern states.

[†]President Andrew Jackson (1767–1845) signed the Tariff of 1832. When South Carolinians refused to pay the tax and threatened to withdraw from the Union if it was enforced, they fully expected Jackson to side with the Nullifiers as he was born in South Carolina. However, Jackson felt the Constitution established "a single nation," not a league of states. He called nullification an "abominable doctrine," and South Carolinians "unprincipled men who would rather rule in hell than subordinate in heaven." When he denied South Carolina the right to secede and threatened the state with force during the crisis, he was forever after vilified by the Nullifiers.

[‡]The Arsenal (Citadel Square) was built in 1829 in response to the 1822 Vesey conspiracy. In 1832 at the height of the Nullification crisis, South Carolina dismissed federal troops there and installed state militia troops as a message that the state meant to defend itself against "federal tyranny."

We visited the arsenal twice; the second time with Mr. Calhoun and Governor Hayne,* when we saw the arms and ammunition, which were not visible the first time, because "the key was not on the premises;" a token that no invasion was immediately expected. There were two bombs brought in by Governor Hayne, and all the warlike apparatus which was made ready during the nullification struggle. It is difficult to believe that Mr. Calhoun seriously meant to go to war with such means as his impoverished state could furnish; but there is no doubt that he did intend it. The ladies were very animated in their accounts of their State Rights Ball,† held in the area of the arsenal, and of their subscriptions of jewels to the war fund. They were certainly in earnest.

The soldiers were paraded in our presence, some eleven or twelve recruits, I believe; and then Mr. Calhoun first, and Governor Hayne afterward, uncovered and addressed them with as much gravity and effusion of patriotic sentiment as if we had been standing on the verge of a battlefield. Some of our party were of Union politics, and they looked exceedingly arch during the speechifying. It will be too sad if this child's play should be turned into bloodshed after all, for the gratification of any man's restless ambition, or in the guilty hope of protracting slavery under the reprobation of the whole of society except a small band of mercenaries.

My chief interest in these expeditions was in the personages who accompanied me. Governor Hayne's name is well known in England from his having furnished the provocation to Webster's renowned speech, exhibiting the constitutional argument against nullification;‡ and from his being afterward the leader of the struggle in South Carolina, while Mr. Calhoun fulfilled the same function in Congress. He is descended from the Haynes whose cruel sufferings in the Revolutionary War are notorious, to the disgrace of the British; one of the two brothers having perished through the miseries of a British prison-ship, and the other having been hanged by Lord Rawdon and Colonel Balfour, under circumstances which, I believe, justify the horror and reprobation with which the act is viewed by all who have heard the story.§ It is one of the most dreadful tales of the

---

*Robert Y. Hayne was the prior governor of South Carolina (1832–34).

†The "State Rights Ball" was held at the C. C. Pinckney Mansion on East Bay Street in March of 1831. The "Volunteer Ball" took place at the arsenal on March 27, 1833, to celebrate the "victory" of Nullification (*Niles' Weekly Register*, April 20, 1833, 128; McInnis, *Politics of Taste in Antebellum Charleston*, 80–82).

‡As U.S. senator, Hayne was famous for an 1830 senatorial debate with Daniel Webster on nullification, in which he spoke in defense of the South against New England. The subsequent Hayne-Webster debates were featured in newspapers far and wide.

§Robert Y. Hayne was a great-nephew of Isaac Hayne (1745–1781), hanged by the British during the Revolution. Isaac Hayne was executed by joint order of Col. Nesbit Balfour

Revolutionary War, and the English have not been behind the Americans in their feeling with regard to the case.

Such stories are very painful, but they ought not to be forgotten. The horrors of colonial war may not be over; and it is well that the conflicts of duty and affection which can take place only in wars of this character should be remembered, while Great Britain has colonies which she may oppress, and noble subjects, like Colonel Hayne, whom she may be even now alienating, and whose contrariety of affections she may be yet again driven or tempted to solve in blood.

The present representative of the family was made speaker of the South Carolina House of Representatives at the age of twenty-seven. He was afterward attorney-general of the state, a senator in Congress, and governor of the state. During the preparations for war in 1832, he was the soul of every movement. He is now considered to be deeply involved in the Southern transactions relating to the acquisition of Texas, whatever these may in reality be, and to have linked his fortunes with the slavery question. When I saw him he was, forty-four years of age, with a robust, active frame, a lively, pleasant countenance, and very engaging manners, with much of the eagerness of the schoolboy mixed with the ease of the gentleman. He can do everything better than reason, as appeared in the senatorial conflict, in which he was ground to powder by the tremendous weight and force of Webster's constitutional argument and sound declamation. Governor Hayne can state clearly, enforce ardently, illustrate gracefully, and boast magnificently, but he cannot reason. His best friends are probably the most anxious to admit this; for there is such want of reason in his present course of opposition to the first principles on which society is founded, and in his attachment to wornout feudal institutions, that the observer, however friendly, finds himself reduced to the alternative of supposing this busy mind perverted by unholy passions or by an unbalanced imagination.

Governor Hamilton* is less known at a distance, but he is, perhaps, a yet more perfect representative of the Southern gentleman. He is handsome, and his manners have all the grace without much of the arrogance of the bearing of his class. I was much struck, too, with his generous appreciation of the powers and virtues of the great men of every party at Washington; a moral grace which I should have been glad to see shared in a greater degree by some of his neighbors. Governor

---

(1744–1823), commandant of the garrison at Charleston, and Francis Rawdon-Hastings or Lord Rawdon (1754–1826), supernumerary aide-de-camp to Sir Henry Clinton. It was not Isaac Hayne's brother who died on a British prison ship but his cousin, Abraham Hayne, the grandfather of Robert Y. Hayne.

*James H. Hamilton Jr. (1786–1857) had been governor from 1830 to 1832.

Hamilton has done what he could to impair the favorable impressions he makes upon all who know him by the atrocious report he issued in 1835, as chairman of a committee of the South Carolina Legislature appointed to consider what steps should be taken in defense of "the peculiar domestic institutions of the South."* This report is unconstitutional in its requisitions, and savage in its spirit towards the abolitionists.

With these gentlemen, their friends, and the ladies of their families, we saw many sights and passed many pleasant hours; and with gentlemen and ladies of the opposite party we spent other portions of our leisure. I was told much of the Poorhouse, rather in a tone of boasting; and I was anxious to see what a poorhouse could be in a region where all laborers were private property, and where pauperism would therefore seem to be obviated. Infirmity, vice, and orphanhood keep up a small amount of pauperism even here, reducing capitalists to a state of dependence. There were about one hundred and twenty inmates when I visited the institution, and the number was soon to be reduced by the periodical clearance made by sending the children to the Orphan-house, and the insane to the State asylum at Columbia. The intemperate and vagrants were employed in coffin-making and stone-breaking. By a slight stretch of the law, persons found drunk are sent here and locked up for a month. We saw two respectable-looking men who had been brought in intoxicated the day before, and who looked duly ashamed of their situation.

The Orphan-house has been established about forty years, and it contained, at the time of my visit, two hundred children. As none but whites are admitted, it is found to be no encouragement to vice to admit all destitute children, whether orphans or not; for the licentiousness of the South takes the women of color for its victims. The children in this establishment are taught reading, writing, and arithmetic, and the girls sewing; but the prejudice against work appears as much here as anywhere. No active labor goes on; the boys do not even garden. No employment is attempted which bears any resemblance to what is done by slaves. The boys are apprenticed out to trades at fourteen, and the girls to mantuamaking, almost the only employment in which a white Southern woman can earn a subsistence. The children are taken in from the age of two years, but they generally enter at the ages of four, five, or six. I was rather surprised to see them badged, an anti-republican practice which had better be abolished; but I wondered the

*As chairman of the Committee on Federal Relations in the State Senate, Hamilton introduced and carried resolutions influential in committing South Carolina to the independence and annexation of Texas. This was a contentious political issue of the era, with southerners lobbying to add Texas as a slave state (Texas Legislature, *Obituary Addresses on the Occasion of the Death of James Hamilton*, 23).

less when I observed the statue of Pitt still standing in the courtyard, with the right arm shot off in the war, however. There is a good-sized church connected with this establishment, which was well filled on the afternoon when I went with the family of a friend, who was taking his turn with his brother clergy to preach.

Charleston is the place in which to see those contrasting scenes of human life brought under the eye which moralists gather together for the purpose of impressing the imagination. The stranger has but to pass from street to street, to live from hour to hour in this city, to see in conjunction the extremes between which there is everywhere else a wide interval. The sights of one morning I should remember if every other particular of my travels were forgotten. I was driven round the city by a friend whose conversation was delightful all the way. Though I did not agree in all his views of society, the thoughtfulness of his mind and the benevolence of his exertions betokened a healthy state of feeling, and gave value to all he said. He had been a friend of the lamented Grimke;* and he showed me the house where Grimke lived and died, and told me much of him; of the noble-ness of his character, the extent of his attainments, and how, dying at fifty-four, he had lived by industry a long life. My mind was full of the contemplation of the heights which human beings are destined to reach, when I was plunged into a new scene; one which it was my own conscientious choice to visit, but for which the preceding conversation had ill-prepared me.

I went into the slave market, a place which the traveller ought not to avoid to spare his feelings. There was a table on which stood two auctioneers, one with a hammer, the other to exhibit "the article" and count the bids. The slaves for sale were some of them in groups below, and some in a long row behind the auc-tioneers. The sale of a man was just concluding when we entered the market. A woman, with two children, one at the breast, and another holding by her apron, composed the next lot. The restless, jocose zeal of the auctioneer who counted the bids was the most infernal sight I ever beheld. The woman was a mulatto; she was neatly dressed, with a clean apron and a yellow head-handkerchief. The elder child clung to her. She hung her head low, lower, and still lower on her breast, yet turning her eyes incessantly from side to side, with an intensity of expectation which showed that she had not reached the last stage of despair. I should have thought that her agony of shame and dread would have silenced the tongue of every spectator; but it was not so. A lady chose this moment to turn to me and

*Thomas Grimke died of cholera on October 12, 1834. A legal educator and reformer, he had been an advocate of absolute nonresistance, even given defensive warfare. He remained well loved, even though he was the brother of the abolitionist Grimke sisters, with whom he managed to remain on speaking terms. Grimke was married to Sarah (Sally) Drayton, the daughter of Thomas Drayton, mentioned as a child in the John Davis account.

say, with a cheerful air of complacency, "You know my theory, that one race must be subservient to the other. I do not care which; and if the blacks should ever have the upper hand, I should not mind standing on that table, and being sold with two of my children."* Who could help saying within himself, "Would you were! so that that mother were released!" Who could help seeing in vision the blacks driving the whites into the field, and preaching from the pulpits of Christian churches the doctrines now given out there, that God has respect of persons; that men are to hold each other as property, instead of regarding each other as brethren; and that the right interpretation of the golden rule by the slaveholder is, "Do unto your slaves as you would wish your master to do unto you if you were a slave!" A little boy of eight or nine years old, apparently, was next put up alone. There was no bearing the child's look of helplessness and shame. It seemed like an outrage to be among the starers from whom he shrunk, and we went away before he was disposed of.

We next entered a number of fine houses, where we were presented with flowers, and entertained with lively talk about the small affairs of gay society, which to little minds are great. To me every laugh had lost its gayety, every courtesy had lost its grace, all intercourse had lost its innocence. It was a relief to think of Grimke in his grave, escaped from the hell in which we were pent. If there be a scene which might stagger the faith of the spirit of Christianity itself; if there be an experience which might overthrow its serenity, it is the transition from the slavemarket to the abodes of the slavemasters, bright with sunshine, and gay with flowers, with courtesies, and mirth.

If the moral gloom which oppresses the spirit of the stranger were felt by the residents, of course this condition of society would not endure another day. Much trouble is experienced, and there are many sighs over the system; but the anxiety is not to any great number what it was to the sisters of Grimke;[†] such a poisoner of life as to induce them to sacrifice property, home, friends, and repose, in order to obtain ease of mind for themselves, and to do something towards destroying the curse by which their native region is blighted. Every day shows how many mansions there are in this hell; how variously the universally allowed evil visits minds of different strength and discernment. All suffer, from the frivolous and sophisticated child to the far-seeing and disciplined saint. The difficulty is to

*According to Martineau, this remark was made by her hostess, Caroline Gilman (*Autobiography*, 344).
[†]Sarah Grimke (1792–1873) and Angelina Grimke Weld (1805–1879), early advocates of abolitionism and women's rights, were Quakers, educators, and writers who traveled throughout the North lecturing about their firsthand experiences growing up with slavery in Charleston. They were hated in the South for their abolitionist beliefs.

have patience with the diversity, and to wait, as God waits, till the moral gloom strikes upon every heart, and causes every eye to turn for light where some already see it. At the same hour when the customary sins of the slavemarket were being perpetrated, hundreds of the little people of Charleston were preparing for their childish pleasures—their merry dancing-schools, their juvenile fancy balls—ordering their little slaves about, and allowing themselves to be fanned by black attendants while reposing in preparation for the fatigues of the evening; ministers of the Gospel were agreeing to deprive persons of color of all religious education; a distant Lynch mob was outraging the person of a free and innocent citizen; elegant ladies were administering hospitality, and exchanging gossip and sentiment.

Our evening engagements were as strangely contrasted as those of the morning. We were at parties where we heard loud talk of justice and oppression; appeals to the eternal principles of the one, when the tariff was the subject, and expressions of the most passionate detestation of the other, which might, but for the presence of black faces in the rooms, lead a stranger to suppose that he was in the very sanctuary of human rights. We were at a young heiress's first ball, where every guest was presented with a bouquet on entering; where the young ladies waltzed, and the young gentlemen gave loose to their spirits, and all who were present had kindly greetings for the stranger. Nothing could be gayer than the external aspect of these entertainments; but it is impossible for the stranger to avoid being struck with the anxiety which shows itself through it all. I think I never was in society in any of the Southern cities without being asked what I would do if I had a legacy of slaves, or told, in vindictiveness or sorrow, that the prosperity of the North was obtained at the expense of the South. I was never in Southern society without perceiving that its characteristic is a want of repose. It is restlessly gay or restlessly sorrowful. It is angry or exulting; it is hopeful or apprehensive. It is never content; never in such a state of calm satisfaction as to forget itself. This peculiarity poisons the satisfaction of the stranger in the midst of the free and joyous hospitality to which he would otherwise surrender himself with inconsiderate delight. While everything is done that can be conceived of to make you happy, there is a weight pulling at your heartstrings, because you see that other hearts are heavy, and the nobler the heavier. While the host's little child comes to you at first sight, and holds up her mouth for a kiss, and offers to tell you a story, and pours out all her mirth and all her generosity upon you, the child's father tells you that there is a dark prospect before these young creatures, and Heaven knows what lot is in store for them. Your vigilance is kept active by continual suggestions that society is composed of two classes, which entertain a mortal dread of each other. If ever you forget this for an hour, it is recalled by the sight of a soldier at the corner of a street, of a decaying mansion or deserted estate, or of some anti-republican arrangement for social or domestic defense. You reproach yourself because you are anxious and cannot be deceived; and feel as if it were ingratitude to your entertainers not to think them the secure and happy people which, in alternation with their complaints of all the external world, they assure you they are.

Our evenings were diversified with attendance upon phrenological lectures— which, however, soon ceases to be a variety, from the absolute sameness of all courses of lectures on that subject—with readings at home, and with a visit to a scene which I was strongly urged not to omit, the Saturday night's market held by the slaves.

I should have been sorry to miss this spectacle. The slaves enjoy the amusement and profit yielded by this market. They sit in rows, by lamplight, some with heaps of fruit and vegetables before them, or surrounded by articles of their own manufacture: boxes, bedsteads, baskets, and other handiworks, very cheap, and of good workmanship. The bananas, pines, imported apples, and oranges, which are seen in great abundance, are usually the property of the master; while the manufactured articles, made at spare hours, are nominally the slave's own. Some are allowed to make use of their leisure in preparing for the market, on condition of bringing their masters six dollars each per week, retaining whatever surplus they may gain. I could not learn the consequence of failing to bring in the six dollars per week. They enjoy the fun and bustle of the market, and look with complacency on any white customers who will attend it. Their activity and merriment at market were pointed out to me as an assurance of their satisfaction with their condition, their conviction that their present position is the one they were made for, and in which their true happiness is to be found.

At the very same moment I was shown the ruins of the church of St. Philip, destroyed by fire, as they frowned in the rear of the lamplight; and I was informed that the church had once before been on fire, but had been saved by the exertions of a slave, who "had his liberty given him for a reward."*

"A reward!" said I. "What! when the slaves are convinced that their true happiness lies in slavery?"

The conversation had come to an awkward pass. A lady advanced to the rescue, saying that some few, too many, were haunted by a pernicious fancy, put into

*In February of 1835, a fire broke out in a boarding house (and brothel) for sailors at the corner of State and Lingard streets. The fire destroyed over sixty dwellings, St. Philip's among them. In 1796, St. Philip's had been saved after a slave risked his life to put out a fire. For his bravery, he was given his freedom and took the name Will Philip Lining (Rutledge, "The Second St. Philips," 112–13).

their heads by others, about liberty; a mere fancy, which, however, made them like the idea of freedom.

"So the benefactor of the city was rewarded by being indulged, to his own hurt, in a pernicious fancy?"

"Why, yes."

My impressions of Charleston may easily be gathered from what I have said. It seems to me a place of great activity, without much intellectual result; of great gayety, without much ease and pleasure. I am confident that, whatever might be the reason, the general mind was full of mystery and anxiety at the time of my visit; and that some hearts were glowing with ambitious hopes, and others sinking in fears, more or less clearly defined, of the political crisis which seems to be now at hand. These are the influences which are educating the youth of Charleston, more powerfully than all schools and colleges, and all books; inducing a reliance on physical rather than moral force, and strengthening attachment to feudal notions of honor and of every kind of good; notions which have no affinity with true republican morals. The prospects of the citizens are "dark every way," as some declared; for the rising generation must either ascend, through a severe discipline and prodigious sacrifices, to a conformity with republican principles, or descend into a condition of solitary feudalism, neither sanctioned by the example nor cheered by the sympathy of the world; but, on the contrary, regarded with that compassion which is precisely the last species of regard which the feudal spirit is able to endure.

We left Charleston in company with Mr. Calhoun and his family. The great nullifier told me many and long stories of his early days. Not being aware of my strong impressions respecting his present views and purposes, he could have no idea of the intense interest with which I listened to his accounts of the first kindling of his burning mind. He was five years old, standing between his father's knees, when his first political emotions stirred within him, awakened by his parent's talk of the colony and of free times just after the Revolution. If some good angel had at that moment whispered to the parent, inspiring him to direct that young ambition to the ultimate grandeur of meek service, to animate that high spirit to a moral conflict with all human wrongs, we might already have owed to a mind so energetic the redemption of the negro race from the affliction, and of the republic from the disgrace of slavery, instead of mourning over the dedication of such powers to the propagation and exasperation of the curse. I feared how it would be; what part he would take in the present struggle between the two principles of greatness, physical force with territorial conquest, and moral power shown in self-conquest. I feared that Mr. Calhoun would organize and head the feudal party, as he has done; but I never had any fears that that party would prevail. When we parted at Branchville he little knew—he might have been offended if he had known—with what affectionate solicitude those whom he left behind looked on into his perilous political path. I am glad we could not foresee how soon our fears would be justified. Mr. Calhoun is at present insisting that the pirate colony of Texas shall be admitted into the honorable American Union; that a new impulse shall thereby be given to the slave-trade, and a new extension to slavery; and that his country shall thereby surrender her moral supremacy among the nations for a gross and antiquated feudal ambition. He vows, taking the whole Union to witness, that these things shall be. The words have publicly passed his pen and his lips, "Texas shall be annexed to the United States." His best friends must hope that the whole world will say, "It shall not."

"City of Charleston, South Carolina, Looking across Cooper's River."
Engraving and aquatint, with watercolor. Painted by G. Cooke; engraved by
W. J. Bennett, ca. 1838. Courtesy of the Library of Congress, Washington, DC.

JOHN BENWELL (1838)

"July the 4th"

John Benwell first published his account in 1852 in England as *Incidents of Travel: Being a Narrative of Four Years in the United States, and Territories of America*. The next year, the account was published in the United States as *An Englishman's Travels in America*. It is unclear when the author actually traveled through the country; however, dates of key events he describes indicate it occurred from the late 1830s to 1840. He chronicles that he sailed from Bristol to America and remained for four years. He traveled from New York to Ohio and down the Missouri and Mississippi rivers to Louisiana. He crossed the Gulf of Mexico to Florida, where he witnessed a campaign against the Seminole and Cherokee Indians. At Fort Anderson he met General Zachary Taylor, leader of American forces in a campaign against the Seminoles (1837).

From Tallahassee, Benwell took a stage to Macon, Georgia, and traveled by railway to Charleston. He arrived on July 4 to witness festivities on King Street. Among his experiences in town, he met a free black man from a contingent of wealthy, interconnected free blacks who owned successful businesses and real estate in the city. This encounter provides a rare glimpse into the life of a free black in Charleston in that day.

The identity of John Benwell has never been fully established. There is some evidence that he was the grandson of John Benwell (1749–1824), founder and headmaster of the Quaker school, Sidcot, and author of *Extracts from a Diary Kept by the Late John Benwell of Sidcot* (1825). Another grandson, Joseph Austin Benwell (1816–1886), was a well-known English artist and illustrator of Oriental landscapes. Joseph had a brother named John Benwell (b.1814), but there is little information available concerning him. A cousin, William Arnee Frank (1808–1897), was also a recognized artist. His brother, John Frank (1809–1900), was a schoolmaster and editor. The Benwell and Frank families were long active in the

Taken from *An Englishman's Travels in America: His Observations of Life and Manners in the Free and Slave States* (London: Binns and Goodwin), 1853.

Society of Friends in England. Quakers were the first corporate body to condemn slavery, and John Benwell was vehemently anti-slavery in his account. However, a few sources, including William Cushing in *Initials and Pseudonyms: A Dictionary of Literary Disguises* (TY Crowell & Co., 1885), claim "John Benwell" is a pseudonym. Even so, it remains probable his true identity is one of the Benwell/Frank family members already mentioned.

After his account was published in this country in 1853, numerous editions followed. Benwell wrote in his preface: "Some of the incidents related in the following pages will be found to bear upon, and tend forcibly to corroborate, the miseries so patiently endured by the African race, in a vaunted land of freedom and enlightenment, whose inhabitants assert, with ridiculous tenacity, that their government and laws are based upon the principle, 'That all men in the sight of God are equal.'"

SOURCES

Benwell, John. Papers, 1846–52. Library of Congress, Washington, DC.
Fant, Jennie Holton "Re: Benwell family." Message to Dee Murray, Benwell descendant. July 19, 2013. Private e-mail.
Knight, Francis Arnold. *A History of Sidcot School: A Hundred Years of West Country Quaker Education.* London: J. M. Dent & Co., 1908.

"July the 4th"

After numerous stoppages, the train at length reached Charleston. After leaving my ticket at the terminus, I disposed of my baggage by hiring a negro to carry it to my boardinghouse, and slowly wended my way into the city.

A spacious public square at the end of King-street, through which I had to pass to my table *d'hote,* presented an animated view, the citizens being assembled to celebrate the anniversary of the Independence conferred by Washington and his compatriots by the solemn declaration of the 4th July, 1776. Long tables, under gay awnings, to shield the company from the burning rays of the sun, which at the time were intense, groaned with every luxury the climate afforded; but the banquet was not furnished by this alone, for Cuba and some of the neighboring islands, it was stated, had been ransacked for delicacies. Crowds of elegantly-dressed ladies (in general of very sallow look and languid air) and spirit-like children, with swarthy-looking men, many of whose visages bore evident traces of exposure to the ill effects of the climate and of dissipation, crowded the festive board. The negro attendants in dozens moved about with automatic order, as is characteristic of all the race on such occasions, for the negro is a "model waiter" at a banquet. Their snowy costumes contrasting strongly with their black visages and the jovial scene around. The merry peals of laughter, as some unlucky wight upset a dish, or scattered the sauce in everybody's face within reach, indicated lightness of heart, and merriment and conviviality seemed the order of the day.

The imposing scene before me, after a long absence from social meetings in civilized life, was very cheering, and, had it not been for the inertia I felt at the time, arising from a fatiguing journey and the tertian ague,* I should have felt disposed to participate in the day's enjoyment. Other considerations might, however, have prevented this: I was a stranger to all around, and knew that I should be either subjected to impertinent interrogations, or become the object of invidious remark—this, in my debilitated state of health, I felt anxious to avoid, as calculated to impede my restoration. My joining the assembled party might also have involved the chance of surveillance during my stay, which, before my departure for Europe, I intended should be rather protracted. I may have been mistaken in this view, but, from the character I had heard of the place, I felt justified in giving way to the suspicion.

I was beguiled into the erroneous idea that a sense of happiness and security reigned in the assembled multitude, a notion quite fallacious, from attendant circumstances, as I shall directly explain. Troops were stationed at a guard-house in the vicinity, and the sentinels paced in front of the building, as if in preparation for, or in expectation of, a foe, affording a great contrast to the apparent security of the inhabitants assembled in the square. Before reaching Charleston, I had been apprised of the state of jeopardy the citizens were in from the possibility of a recurrence of those scenes of anarchy enacted at the insurrection of the slaves some time before.—Still, there was a strong lurking suspicion that the émeute of the negroes had only been temporarily suppressed, and awful forebodings of fire and of blood spread a gloom on the minds of all.

As I passed up the long range of tables, the health of the President of the Republic was responded to by the company. The cheers were deafening, and, what most surprised me was, that the negro waiters joined heartily, I may say frantically, in it, and danced about like mad creatures, waving their napkins, and shouting with energy. Some of the elder ones, I noticed, looked mournfully on, and were evidently not in a gay humor, seeming a prey to bitter reflections.

Notwithstanding the curse of slavery, which, like a poisonous apse, taints the very air they breathe with the murdered remains of its victims, the white citizens of the south are extremely sensitive of their civil and political rights, and seem to

*Malaria.

regard the palladium of independence secured by their progenitors as an especial benefit conferred by the Deity for their good in particular. Actuated by this mock patriotism (for it is nothing less), the citizens of the south omit no opportunity of demonstrating the blessings they so undeservedly inherit, and which, if I am not mistaken, will, ere many years elapse, be wrested from them, amidst the terrible thunders of an oppressed and patient people, whose powers of endurance are indeed surprising.

Leaving the square, I passed up King-street, at the top of which was my intended boarding-house. The shops in this fashionable resort are fitted out in good style, and the goods are of the best description. After sunset the streets are often lined with carriages. The city lies flat, like the surrounding country, and, owing to this, is insalubrious; stagnant water collects in the cellars of the houses, and engenders a poisonous vapor, which is a fertile source of those destructive epidemics, that, combined with other causes, are annually decimating the white population of the south of the American continent in all parts.

At the top of King-street, facing you as you advance is a large Protestant Episcopal church. I went there to worship on the following Sunday, but was obliged to leave the building, there being, it was stated by the apparitor, no accommodation for strangers, a piece of illiberality that I considered very much in keeping with the slave-holding opinions of the worshippers who attend it. This want of politeness I was not, however, surprised at, for it is notorious, as has been before observed by an able writer, that, excepting the Church of Rome, "the members of the unestablished Church of England—the Protestant Episcopalian, are the most bigoted, sectarian, and illiberal, in the United States of America. Vital piety, or that deep sense of religious duty that impels men to avoid the devious paths of sin, and to live "near to God," is, I am inclined to believe (and I regret it, as a painful truth), by no means common in America. There are, however, many pastors who faithfully warn their flocks of the dangers of the world, and who strenuously advise their hearers to take warning lest they be over-captivated with the "Song of the Syrens." These, however, I must say, are chiefly in the free states, for I cannot regard southern ministers in any other light than pharisaical, while they continue openly (as is their constant practice) to support from their pulpits the institution that is the main stay of the southern states; I mean slavery.

I afterwards went into a large Independent chapel in another part of the town, where I was more courteously treated. Here was a very eloquent and noted preacher, a Dr. Groyard, from Mobile. He was delivering a very eloquent harangue, interspersed with touches of pro-slavery, sentimentalism and rhetorical flourish, the former especially directed to the negroes in the gallery, when, suddenly, a cry of "Fire! fire!" was raised in the street. The learned Doctor stood as if electrified, and the instant after his hearers rushed pell-mell out of the chapel, amidst the shrieks of the females, and the consternation of the men, caused, without doubt, by a lurking suspicion of impending evil from the negroes which I have before referred to. On ascertaining that the alarm was caused by a house being on fire in the vicinity, the service was abruptly terminated.

The following day I continued my perambulations; to the left of the Episcopal church I have already mentioned, and surrounded by umbrageous trees in a park-like enclosure, is the Townhall. I entered this building, where I found a bench of magistrates, the mayor of the city being amongst them, adjudicating on the cases brought before them. These consisted chiefly of negroes apprehended in the streets after nine o'clock the previous night; they were in all cases, except where their owners paid the fine, sentenced to receive from ten to twenty lashes, which were administered at once by the city gaoler, in a yard at the rear of a building, near which officers were in attendance for the purpose. So heinous in a negro, is the crime of lifting his hand in opposition to a white man in South Carolina, that the law adjudges that the offending member shall be forfeited. This is, or was, quite as inexorable as the one I have before spoken of, and when in Charleston, I frequently, amongst the flocks of negroes passing and repassing, saw individuals with one hand only. Like the administration of miscalled justice on negroes in all slave-holding states in America, the process was summary; the offender was arrested, brought before the bench of sitting magistrates, and on the *ex parte–*statement of his accuser, condemned to mutilation, being at once marched out to the rear of the building, and the hand lopped off on a block fixed there for the purpose. I noticed a block and axe myself in the yard of a building near the town-hall, and on looking at them closely, saw they were stained almost black, with what I have little hesitation in saying was human blood. My conductor, however, tried to divert my attention from the object, and knowing I was an Englishman, refused to enter on the subject.

Another of the many cruel laws put in force after the émeute of the negroes, was to prohibit any colored person from walking on the pavements, and forcing all males to salute every white they met. These distinctions, although falling into disuse, are not even yet abolished, but still, with many others equally odious, disgrace the Carolinian statute book. I saw several negroes from the plantation districts, walking in the road instead of on the pavement, in accordance with this law, touching their hats to every white passer-by; they were consequently obliged to be continually lifting their hands to their heads, for they passed white people at every step. Although I believe no punishment is now enforced for the omission of this humiliating homage to color, the men I have referred to were doubtless afraid to disregard the ceremony.

The general appearance of the majority of the coloured people in the streets of Charleston denoted abject fear and timidity, some of them as I passed looking with servile dread at me (as they did at almost every one who happened to pass), so that I could read in many of their looks a suspicion of interference, which, commiserating their condition as I did, was quite distressing.

It is impossible to form a correct estimate of what the perpetuators of slavery have to expect, if once the coloured population obtain a dominant position. The acknowledged gradual depopulation of the whites in the slave states, through sickness, exhaustion of the land, and consequent emigration, united with other causes, there is no doubt will eventually result in a great preponderance of coloured people, who, aroused by the iniquitous treatment they undergo, will rise under some resolute leader, and redress their wrongs. I was quite struck to see in Charleston such a disproportion of the colours, and, without exaggerating, I can say, that almost if not quite three-fourths of those I met in the streets were, if not actually of the negro race, tinged in a greater or less degree with the hue.

Pursuing my perambulations, I came to the slave and general cotton place of vendue,* to the left of the General Post-office, which building is a very substantial edifice of stone. Here a dozen or twenty auctioneers were loudly holding forth to the assembled crowds, and cracking up their wares in New York style. The most indescribable scene of bustle and confusion prevailed, the whole street being covered with open bales and boxes of goods. In one part of the street was a slave warehouse, and advertisements were placarded outside of the particulars of the various lots to be offered for competition, and now on view. As the privilege of viewing in this instance was confined to those who possessed tickets, I did not apply for one, as I knew that the wish would be attributed to curiosity, and possibly a worse construction be put upon it, through my being a stranger in the place.

Passing onwards through the assembled throng, I got into a more secluded part of the city, and came upon a large burial-ground, in which many of the monuments erected to the memory of the dead were of a very expensive description. One in particular attracted my notice; this, on inquiry of a gentlemanly-looking man, who, like myself, was inclined to "meditate among the tombs," I ascertained had been erected by the relatives of a planter, who had resided in an adjoining state, but who had several cotton plantations within ten miles of Charleston; these he occasionally visited, but in general confided to the care of an overseer, who lived with his family on one of them. The season anterior to his last visit had been a very unpropitious one, and he was much dissatisfied with the management. To prevent a recurrence of this loss, and, under the strong impression that

*Vendue Range.

the hands were not worked as they should be, he resolved to inspect the plantations himself, and administer some wholesome discipline in *propria persona;* for
this purpose, he visited one of the plantations, intending afterwards to proceed
to the others in rotation. It so happened that he arrived when not expected; and,
finding his overseer absent, and many of the hands not as closely engaged as he
wished, he became violently enraged. Summoning the overseer, he ordered all
hands in front of the house to witness a punishment, and causing eight or ten
of those whom he pointed out to be tied up at once and well whipped, stood by
the while in uncontrollable anger to give directions. In the midst of the scene,
and while urging greater severity, he was seized with a fit of apoplexy, which was
of such a nature, that it at once closed his career, and he died instantaneously.
Directly the man fell, the negroes collected round him and uttered cries and lam-
entations, and the poor wretch who was at the moment the victim of his brutality,
on being untied, which was immediately done, joined in it. Notwithstanding that
my companion had a decided leaning towards the extinction of slavery (although
he started various objections to its abolition), I was quite inclined to believe his
relation, having, when in Florida, met with a somewhat similar instance of the
devotedness of the negro race, in an old woman who was bitterly bewailing the
loss of her deceased mistress. The latter was an English lady, but not over kind to
her, and reflected no credit on her countrywomen. The poor creature in touching
strains enlarged upon her beauty and accomplishments, but when I questioned
her as to her treatment of the negroes in general belonging to the estates, would
say little on the subject, and shook her head; in it was plain that, like most females
living in the south, she was a pampered worldling, entirely engrossed by principles of self-interest, and little regarding the welfare of her dependents, if not, as I
have before observed, very severe towards them. She died prematurely, from the
effects of one of those virulent fevers, that in southern latitudes are so often fatal
to the inhabitants, especially to those who have been nurtured in Europe. Her
encoffined remains were shipped on board a vessel, to be conveyed to England
for burial, in accordance with her expressed wish. When the poor creature came
to that part of her piteous tale, when, as she called her, her "beautiful angel of a
mistress" was put in the coffin, and the estate hands were called in to take a last
view of her (a custom in vogue there sometimes), she was overpowered with grief,
and her utterance was so choked, that she could scarcely proceed.

During my stay in Charleston, I became acquainted with a gentleman of colour, who followed a lucrative business as a dealer of some kind, and who had
formerly been a slave. The introduction arose in rather a singular way, it being
through a proposition made to open a school for the education of coloured children, in which I took an interest.

Great opposition was offered to the scheme by the white rulers of the place, who declared the project illegal, the enactments passed subsequent and prior to the insurrection stringently forbidding it, or any attempt to impart secular knowledge to the slaves.* Notwithstanding the violent threats used to prevent it, a meeting was however convened to be held at the house of the gentleman referred to, and which I resolved, though not unaccompanied with danger to my person, to take an active part in. I accordingly went to his home on the evening appointed; this was a spacious house, furnished in sumptuous style, with extensive premises adjoining, contiguous to the north end of the levee. I noticed that the walls were hung with good oil paintings gorgeously framed, principally family portraits, but the most prominent in position was that of the unfortunate Haytian chief, Toussaint L'Ouverture, whose cruel end, at the instigation of the vindictive Bonaparte, will for ever reflect shame on the French name as long as a sense of justice and love of virtue and probity exists in the bosom of mankind. The misfortunes of Toussaint L'Ouverture have indeed with justice been pronounced the "history of the negro race," for, in almost every instance where coloured men have pushed themselves above the common level, they have incurred the envy of white men, and, in too many instances, have been crushed by their overbearing tyranny.[†]

The meeting was conducted with religious decorum, most, if not all, of the coloured gentlemen present being members of the Wesleyan connection.[‡] I was pleased with the temperate spirit in which their wrongs were discussed; and, after drawing up the rules, forming a committee, and arranging other necessary preliminaries, the meeting broke up.

*In 1834, a state law was passed that made it illegal for free persons of color to maintain schools either for free blacks or for their slaves. Thomas Bonneau, a free black teacher, taught at a private school for free blacks from 1803 to 1831. Daniel Alexander Payne (1811–1893), who studied under Bonneau, opened a school for both slaves and free blacks until the South Carolina General Assembly closed it down in 1835.

[†]Toussaint L'Ouverture (1743–1803) raised a slave army and drove Napoleon out of St. Domingue (Haiti) in 1791. Napoleon eventually agreed to terms of peace but betrayed L'Ouverture as he was arrested, taken to France, and imprisoned in a dungeon in the mountains, where he died.

[‡]The Wesleyan Connection was officially formed in 1843 when a group split from the Methodist Episcopal Church, primarily in protest over their objections to slavery. Founder John Wesley once called the slave-trade "that execrable sum of all villainies." The Methodist General Conference of 1836 officially acknowledged the evils of slavery while at the same time condemning abolition. Charleston's African Methodist Episcopal Church, to which many free black men belonged, was in keeping with the Methodist Church's philosophy. However, many free blacks in Charleston owned slaves, and it is probable some men at the meeting Benwell attended were themselves slave owners.

On reaching my hotel on my return, I was at once waited upon by the land-lord, who, in certainly a respectful manner, informed me that the interest I had the day before incautiously expressed regarding the school, had led to my being watched to the house where the meeting was held; and that, to avoid the unpleas-antness which would result from my continuing to take any steps in the matter, and which might ensue, he said, from the suspicions excited, he strongly advised that I should the next day address a letter to the editor of the principal newspaper in the city, repudiating all connection with a movement calculated, he said, to disturb the public mind, and, perhaps, cause disturbance. This I refused to do, but told him I did not intend to figure prominently in the matter, and that my stay in the city would be very limited. He then related several instances of mob law, which had been enacted—within the twelve months preceding, which, he said, were quite necessary to maintain southern rights, and which he did not fail to let me know he fully concurred in. After this hint, conveyed, I must say, in a friendly spirit, whatever my private opinion was as to the occasion of it, I mingled, during the remainder of my stay, very little with the frequenters of his establishment—a policy which I considered necessary from personal considera-tions; and, owing to this cautious behaviour, I was not afterwards interfered with, though often eyed with suspicion.

The school was opened during my stay, but continued so but a short time, the virulent conduct of the constables, supported by some of the citizens and the civil authorities, compelling its discontinuance. This is not to be wondered at, when it is remembered that the old statute law of South Carolina prohibits the edu-cation of negroes, bond or free, under a penalty of fine and imprisonment; and, although before the recent émeute it was falling into disuse, that event revived its enforcement with ancient malignity.

The free negro gentleman, at whose house the preliminaries for opening the school referred to were gone through, informed me, on a subsequent occasion, that the constant vexations and annoyances he was subjected to, owing to the prejudice in the minds of southern people regarding colour, would compel him to relinquish his business, and proceed either to Canada or to the free states. He deplored the alternative much, as he had been born and bred a slave in Carolina, and, by untiring assiduity, had saved money enough to emancipate himself and his wife; "In fact," he added, "I feel this is my country, and leaving it will come hard." He had a numerous family, which he maintained in great respectability, and his business being a profitable one made him more reluctant to abandon it and the advantages that otherwise would attend his continuance in Charleston. He hospitably entertained me at his home, and appeared highly gratified at meet-ing with a white man who felt disposed to regard him with equality.

After dining at his house one day, he took me for a ride round the suburbs of the city, which I noticed were flat and exceedingly uninteresting. We returned by way of the Marine Parade, which is certainly a *chef d'oeuvre* of its kind. This is on the south side of the city, and commands a magnificent sea-view. It is raised far above the sea, and laid out with carriage-drives and paths for pedestrians. Far out is a fort on an island; this is always garrisoned by a detachment of U.S. troops, and of late years has been used as a receptacle for those daring chiefs among the Indians, who, by their indomitable courage, have been the terror of the United States frontier. Here that hero Osceola, chief of the Seminoles, died not long before, in captivity, from excessive grief, caused by the treachery of certain American officers, who, under a pretended truce, seized him and his attendant warriors.*

Below us in the bay we could see the fins of several sharks, ploughing the waves in search of prey; while the constant sailing to and fro of Cuba fruit-boats, laden with bananas, pawpaws, pine-apples, and every luxury that and contiguous islands afford, enlivened the scene, which altogether was one of extraordinary beauty.

There was a large assemblage of ladies and gentlemen promenading, and, as I rode with my friend, I had some very furtive glances from the crowd, which were intended, no doubt, to remind me that my keeping such company was *infra dig*, if not open to suspicion. There was in truth no little hazard in riding about in public with a man against whose acquaintance I had a short time before been cautioned, and I felt my position rather an uncomfortable one.

Had some of the young blood of Charleston been up, there is little doubt but that I must have left the place sans ceremonie. Possessed of a natural urbanity, or, what in elevated society amongst white people, would be termed true politeness, the manner of the well-bred negro is prepossessing. This was very remarkable

---

*Osceola was naturally against the U.S. government in 1835 concerning the westward migration of the tribe, which precipitated warfare between the Seminoles and the U.S. He was seized in 1837 and imprisoned with members of his tribe, first at St. Augustine, then at Fort Moultrie, where he died in 1838. In 1895, Mr. R.B. Simms of South Carolina recalled attending, many years before, a performance by actor Edwin Forrest (1806–1872) in Charleston. Osceola, imprisoned at Ft. Moultrie at the time, was allowed to attend the theater along with "half a dozen of his braves" being held with him. Forrest, in the midst of his performance noticed this odd group in the audience and let out an Indian war whoop from the stage, whereupon Osceola and his tribesmen jumped out of their seats and "gave an answering whoop that rent the air with its mighty roar and fairly chilled the blood of many a nervous hearer." Two or three ladies fainted. Forrest claimed it was the "greatest compliment ever paid to his powers as an actor" ("Osceola, the Chief, at the Play," *New York Times*, May 28, 1895, 15).

in my coloured friend, who was well informed, and possessed a refinement and intelligence I had never before met with in any of his race. On the subject of enslavement he would at first venture few observations, confining himself to those inconveniences and annoyances that affected him individually; he, however, became, after a time, more communicative.

On the whole, at first, I was not a little apprehensive that my coloured acquaintance was under the impression that my friendship was not sincere, although he did not say as much in his conversation; the impression, however, soon left me, after a further intimacy. I considered then, and do now, that the suspicion was quite excusable, the Jesuitical practices and underhand trickery descended to by the white population in the slave states, in order to ascertain how individuals stand affected, are so numerous, that the coloured people are obliged to be wary of those they either suspect, or of whom, being strangers, they know little.

I remember well, whilst riding with him on the occasion I have already referred to, we drove past a white man on horseback, who (as is common in Charleston), was correcting his negro in the street. The poor fellow was writhing under the cruel infliction of a flagellation with a raw-hide, and rent the air with his cries. This only increased the rage of his master, who seemed to take delight in striking his face and ears. I eagerly watched the scene, and, as we passed, leaned over the back of the gig. My companion, fearing, I suppose, lest the sight might provoke in me some exclamation, and thus get us into notice, nudged me violently with his elbow, saying at the same time, hurriedly, "Don't heed, don't heed." My blood was getting hot, and but for my companion, my passion would, in all probability, have got the better of my discretion, and I should without remedy have been involved in a dispute, if not immediately apprehended. As we rode on, I adverted to this barefaced exhibition of tyranny in an open thoroughfare, which, I remarked, was sufficient proof of the iniquity of the system, in spite of the assertions made by the southerners to the contrary. In reply to this, all my companion remarked was, "Did you never see that done before?" My answer was, I had seen negroes cruelly treated on estates, and elsewhere, but that this scene was the more revolting from its being enacted in the open highway. Seeing that he was anxious to avoid the subject, and that the observations he had made were drawn from him by my remarks, I remained silent, and, wrapped in deep reflections on the outrage we had witnessed, at length reached his dwelling. The occurrence I suppose somewhat affected my spirits, for soon after we got into the drawing-room, no one else being present, my friend addressed me, no doubt observing my depression, nearly as follows. "Sir, you seem to have a tender compassion for my poor countrymen; would to God white men were all as feeling here. The system is an accursed one, but what can we do but bear it patiently? Every hand seems against us, and we dare not speak for ourselves." I told him I deeply sympathised with his oppressed countrymen, and lived in hope that before long the public mind in America would be aroused from its apathy, and the accumulated wrongs of the race be redressed. His only reply was, "God grant it, I hope so too."

In Charleston there exist several charitable institutions, but these, I believe, with only one exception, are for the benefit of poor white people. The innate benevolence of the human heart is thus, in the midst of dire oppression, wont to hold its sway, notwithstanding the poisonous influences that surround. But the pro-slavery business neutralizes these would-be benefactors, and taints all their endeavours, under the cloak of benevolence, to remove the odium it so justly incurs. "Liberate your slaves, and then I will talk to you about religion and charity," were the emphatic words of an eminent northern divine in his correspondence with the committee of a benevolent institution in the south, some years ago, and the admonition speaks as forcibly now as it did then.

As you walk the streets of Charleston, rows of greedy vultures, with sapient look, sit on the parapets of the houses, watching for offal. These birds are great blessings in warm climates, and in Carolina a fine of ten dollars is inflicted for wantonly destroying them. They appeared to be quite conscious of their privileges, and sailed down from the house-tops into the streets, where they stalked about, hardly caring to move out of the way of the horses and carriages passing. They were of an eagle-brown colour, and many of them appeared well conditioned, even to obesity. At night scores of dogs collect in the streets, and yelp and bark in the most annoying manner. This it is customary to remedy by a gun being fired from a window at the midnight interlopers, when they disperse in great terror. I should remark that this is a common nuisance in warm latitudes. Some of these animals live in the wilds, and, like jackals, steal into the towns at night to eke out a scanty subsistence. At first my rest was greatly disturbed by their noisy yelpings, but I soon became accustomed to the inconvenience, and thought little of it.

The warmth of the climate induces great lassitude and indisposition to exertion, alias indolence. I began to experience this soon after arriving in the south. This, which in England would be called laziness, is encouraged by the most trifling offices being performed by slaves. The females in particular give way to this inertness, and active women are seldom to be met with, the wives of men in affluent circumstances being in general like pampered children, and suffering dreadfully from ennui. On one occasion an English gentleman at Charleston, with whom I became acquainted, and whose hospitality I shall never forget, when conversing on the subject, addressed me thus: "Good, active wives are seldom to be met with in this state, amongst the natives; I may say, hardly ever; the females are nurtured in indolence, and in seeking what they term a settlement, look more to the man's means than the likelihood of living happily with him. There is no disguising it—the *considera*—with them is a *sine qua non*. Few girls would refuse a man who possessed a goodly number of slaves, though they were sure his affections would be shared by some of the best-looking of the females amongst them, and his conduct towards the remainder that of a very demon." These sentiments I very soon ascertained to be in no way libellous. A southern wife, if she is prodigally furnished with dollars to "go shopping," apparently considers it no drawback to her happiness if some brilliant mulatto or quadroon woman ensnares her husband. Of course there are exceptions, but the patriarchal usage is so engrafted in society there, that it elicits little notice or comment. Nor, from what I gleaned, are the ladies themselves immaculate, as may be inferred from the occasional quadroon aspect of their progeny.

The Jews are a very numerous and influential body in Charleston, and monopolize many of its corporate honours. They were described as very haughty and captious; this, however, is saying no more of the stock of Israel than is observable all over the world, when they are in prosperous circumstances, although, when this is not the case, perhaps none of the human family are so abject and servile, not excepting slaves themselves. In process of time, these people bid fair to concentrate in themselves most of the wealth and influence of Charleston. If their perseverance (which is here indomitable) should attain this result, they will be in pretty much the same position there that Pharaoh occupied over their race in Egypt in olden time, and, if reports speak true, will wield the sceptre of authority over their captives in a somewhat similar style. Avarice is the besetting sin of the Israelite, and here his slaves are taxed beyond endurance. To exact the utmost from his labour is the constant aim, and I was informed that many of the slaves belonging to Jews were sent out, and compelled on the Saturday night to bring in a much larger sum than it was reasonably possible the poor creatures could earn, and if not successful, they were subjected to the most cruel treatment.

Not long after my arrival in Charleston, I several times met a young coloured man, who was of so prepossessing an appearance, that I felt desirous to become acquainted with him, and, as I was at a loss to find my way to the residence of the mayor, a good opportunity one day offered, and I addressed him. He very courteously took me to the street in which the house was situated, and we talked on general topics as we went—in the course of which he stated, he was saving money for his ransom, and in two years intended to proceed to Montreal, in Canada. I could see, however, that the free manner in which we conversed attracted the attention of three or four individuals as we passed them—these would stop as if to satisfy their curiosity, some even took the trouble to watch us out of sight;

looking back, I several times saw one more impertinent-looking than some others eyeing us intently, and once I fancied I saw him turn as if to overtake us. This curiosity I had often perceived before, but, as disagreeable results might follow, I invariably made a practice to take no notice of it when in the company of a coloured individual. A smile played upon the features of my dusky companion, as I turned to observe the inquisitive fellows I have referred to; perhaps I was taken for a negro-stealer, but, as I treated my companion with equality, I was most likely set down as one of those dangerous personages, who, through zeal in the cause of emancipation, sometimes penetrate, into the slave districts, and are accused (with what degree of justice I cannot tell) of infusing into the minds of the slaves discontented notions and agrarian principles.

As I met, on the occasion I have just referred to, an individual who knew I had felt an interest in endeavouring to establish the school for the education of negro children, the result of which I have already mentioned, I was apprehensive that the contretemps would have exposed me to the unpleasantness of at least being shunned afterwards as a man entertaining principles inimical to southern interests—and, however resolute I felt to pursue an independent course while I remained in Charleston, I could not shake off a fear I vaguely entertained of a public recognition by a deeply prejudiced and ignorant populace, who, once set on, do not hesitate to proceed to disagreeable extremes. This fear was enhanced in no little degree by the operation I had witnessed, of the tarring and feathering process practised by enraged citizens in the Missouri country.

The most degrading phrase that can be applied in the south to those white individuals who sympathize in the wrongs inflicted on the African race, I soon found to be, that "he associates with niggers." Thus a kind-hearted individual at once "loses caste" among his fellow citizens and, invidious though it certainly is, many slave-owners are deterred by this consideration, blended with a politic regard for their own safety, from exercising that benevolence towards their dependents which they sincerely feel; placed, as it were, under a sort of social ban, such men artfully conceal their sentiments from the public, and, by a more lenient treatment of their own hands, quiet their consciences; while, at the same time, they blunt their sense of what is honest, upright, just, and manly. Instances have occasionally occurred where men of correct principles have so far succumbed to this sense of duty, as to liberate their slaves. These are, however, rare occurrences, and, when they do happen, are usually confined to men of sterling religious principles, who, like that great exception, the respectable class of people called Quakers, in America, refuse, from a conviction of the enormity of the evil, to recognize as members those who hold or traffic in slaves.

It is through the influence of such men that the iniquities of the system become exposed to public view, and remedies are sometimes, in flagrant cases of
cruelty, applied. The legislatures of the several slave states, however, have given
such absolute dominion, by a rigorous code of laws, to the owner, that the greatest enormities may be committed almost with impunity, or at least with but a
remote chance of justice having its legitimate sway.

The mass of slave-owners are interested in concealing enormities committed
by their fellows, and are backed by a venal press, which, whether bribed or not
(and there is every reason to suspect that this is often the case), puts such a construction on outrage by garbled reports, as to turn the tide of sympathy from the
victim to the perpetrator. No editor, possessing the least leaven of anti-slavery
principles, would be patronized; and it not infrequently happens that such men
are mobbed and driven perforce to leave the slave, for the more northern or free,
states. Here they stand a better chance, but, in many instances, the prejudice, it
is said, follows their course, and southern influence occasions their bankruptcy or
non-success.

The practice, so common in the slave states, of the citizens congregating at
the bars of hotels or cafes in the towns and cities to while away the time, renders
attendance at such places the readiest means of ascertaining the state of the public
mind on any engrossing subject, opinions being here freely discussed, not, however, without bias and anger; on the contrary, the practice is most sectarian, and
frequently involves deadly feuds and personal encounters, these latter being of
every-day occurrence. Ever since I had been in the southern states, my attention
had been attracted to the swarms of well-dressed loungers at cafes and hotels.
At first, like many other travellers, I was deluded by the notion that these idlers
were men of independent means, but my mind was soon disabused of this fallacy. I ascertained that the greater portion of these belong to that numerous class
in America known as sporting gentlemen; in plainer terms, gamblers. Some of
these men had belonged to the higher walks of life; these were the more "retiring
few" who (probably through a sense of shame not quite extinguished) felt rather
disposed to shrink from than to attract attention. The majority of these idlers
were impudent-looking braggarts, who, with jaunty air and coxcombical show of
superiority, endeavoured to enforce their own opinions, and to silence those of
every one else.

There was also another class of frequenters at such places; this consisted of
tradesmen who pass much of their time hanging about at such resorts, to the
great detriment of their individual affairs; and, lastly, such travellers as might be
stopping in the town, who, through ennui and inveterate habit, had left their

hotels, and sauntered "up town" (as they call gadding about), to hear the news of the day.

Soon ascertaining that such places were the best, and, excepting the public prints, the only resort to ascertain the latest intelligence, and to collect information respecting the movements of the black population, and the company, however exceptionable, being termed there respectable, I adopted the plan, on several successive evenings, of quietly smoking a cigar and listening to passing observations and remarks. Some of these were disgusting enough; so much so, that I will not offend my readers by repeating them. Suffice it to say, that any individual possessing the slightest pretensions to the name of gentleman, in any hotel I had visited in England, on indulging in the indecorous language I heard at these places, would, by a very summary process, have met with ejectment, without ceremony. Here, however, a laxity of moral feeling prevails, that stifles all sense of propriety; and scurrility, obscene language, and filthy jests, of which the coloured population are, I suppose, per force of habit, the principal butts, form the chief attractions of such places of resort to their vitiated frequenters.

In the course of these visits I was present at some angry altercations; one of these referred to the recent visit of an individual who was termed by the disputants an "incendiary abolitionist," and who, it appeared, had been detected in the act of distributing tracts, which had been published at Salem, in Massachusetts, exposing the disabilities the African race were labouring under. Extracts from one of these tracts were read, and appeared very much to increase the violence of the contending parties, one of whom insisted that the publication contained nothing but what might be read by every slave in the sacred Scriptures, and that, therefore, it could not be classed as dangerous, although he admitted that it contained notions of "human rights" that were calculated to imbue the mind of the "niggers" with unbecoming ideas. These sentiments did not at all accord with those of the company, and several expressions of doubt as to the soundness of the speaker's own pro-slavery principles, together with the increasing excitement, caused him to withdraw from the contest. His immediate antagonist, who was evidently the leading man on the occasion, enlarged on the danger attending the sufferance of such men at large in the slave states, and proceeded, with great volubility, to quote various passages from the Black Code* to show that the Legislature had contemplated the intrusion of such pestilent fellows, and had, in fact, given full power to remedy the evil, if the citizens chose to exercise it; and went on to observe, that the rights of southern people were now-a-days invaded on every hand,

*Before 1865 these laws were known more familiarly as Slave Codes, although they included free blacks and mulattos.

and it behoved them to stand in their own defence, his advice, he said, was, if the municipal authorities let the fellow go, to form a committee of justice to adjudicate on the case, and if it was considered conducive to the public weal, to administer salutary punishment. This proposal was uproariously applauded, and four of the citizens present, with the last speaker for chairman, were named on the spot to watch the case. "And now," added this gentleman, "we'll have a gin sling round for success." I heard the day following that the individual who was the subject of the foregoing proceedings, was accused before the mayor, who dismissed the case with a caution, advising him to leave the city with all dispatch, to avoid disagreeable consequences. This the man, by the aid of a constable, managed to do, that functionary, no doubt for a consideration, taking him to the city prison, and locking him up until nightfall, when he was assisted to leave the place, disguised as a soldier. This, I was informed by a friend, to whom I afterwards related it, was one of those commotions that occur almost daily in southern towns and cities.

Such lawless frequenters of hotels, taverns, and cafes, form a kind of social police, and scarcely a stranger visits the place without his motives for the visit being canvassed, and his business often exposed, much to his great annoyance and inconvenience.

So accustomed do American travellers in the south appear, to this system of internal surveillance, that I several times noticed strangers at the hotel or cafe counters openly explaining the object of their visits, and if there is nothing to conceal, however annoying the alternative appears, I am convinced the policy is not had, a host of suspicions being silenced by such a course.

In my travels on the whole route from New York to Charleston, I discovered a most unjustifiable and impertinent disposition to pry into the business of others. If I was questioned once, I am sure I was at least fifty times, by my fellow-travellers from time to time as to my motive for visiting America, and my intended proceedings. I found, however, that a certain reserve was an efficient remedy. Captain Waterton, of South American celebrity, as an ornithologist, and who visited North America in his travels,* mentions that if you confide your affairs and intentions when questioned, the Americans reciprocate that confidence by relating their own. My own experience, however, did not corroborate this view of the case, for, though loquacious in the extreme, and gifted, so that to use a Yankee phrase, they would "talk a dog's hind-leg off," they are in general cautious not to divulge their secrets. To say the least of it, the habit of prying into the business

---

*Charles Waterton (1782–1865), explorer, naturalist and satirist, famous for *Wanderings in South America, the North-West of the United States, and the Antilles in the Years 1812, 1816, 1820 & 1824*, which was published in many editions after 1825.

of others, is one totally unbecoming a well-ordered state of society, which the American, speaking generally, is decidedly not. It is extremely annoying, from the unpleasant feeling it excites, that you are suspected if not watched (this applies forcibly to the slave districts); and it is a habit that has arisen purely from the incongruity of society at large on the American continent, and a want of that subdivision of class that exists in Europe.

During my visits to the various hotels while I remained in Charleston, for the purpose of collecting information, I was several times interrogated in a barefaced manner by the visitors who frequent those places, as to my politics, and especially as to my principles in regard to the institution of slavery; now, as I was not unaware that my intimacy with the gentleman of colour, which I have already referred to, had got abroad, I was obliged to be extremely guarded in my replies on such occasions. It was on one of these that I felt myself in great hazard, for two individuals in the company were discussing with much energy, the question of amalgamation (that is, marriage, contracted between black and white men and women), and I was listening intently to their altercation, when suddenly one of them, eyeing me with malicious gaze, no doubt having noticed my attention to the colloquy, said, "Your opinion, stranger, on this subject; I guess you understand it torrably well, as you seem to be pretty hard on B——'s eldest daughter." This unexpected sally rather alarmed me, for the name he mentioned was that of my coloured friend I have before alluded to, and whose daughter I had only met once, and that at her father's house.

I scarcely knew what to reply, but thought it best to put on a bold face, so facing the man, I thanked him with much irony for the inuendo, and said, it was a piece of impudence I thought very much like him from what I had overheard.

This was said in a resolute tone, and the fellow quailed before it, his reply being, "Now stranger, don't get angry, I saw you the other day at B——'s house, and could not tell what to make of it, but I hope you don't think that I was in arnest."

I replied to this, that I knew best what business I had at B——'s house, and that his plan was to mind his own business. I then left him, apparently highly indignant, but in fact glad to make my escape. Like bullies all the world over, the southern ones are cowards; there is, however, great danger here in embroiling yourself with such characters, the pistol and bowie knife being instantly resorted to if the quarrel becomes serious. I saw this braggart on several occasions afterwards, but he evidently kept aloof, and was disinclined to venture in the part of the room I occupied. I ascertained that he kept a dry goods store in King-street, and was a boisterous fellow, often involved in quarrels.

The discussion on amalgamation, which is a very vexed one, was again introduced on a subsequent occasion; a planter from the north of the state having (as is
sometimes the case) sold off everything he possessed, and removed to the State of
Maine, taking with him a young quadroon woman, with the intention of making
her his lawful wife, and living there retired. After the expression of a variety of
opinions as to what this man deserved, some being of opinion that the subject
ought to be mooted in the legislature at Washington—others, that his whole
effects ought to be escheated, for the benefit of the public treasury—and by far
the greater number that he ought to be summarily dealt with at the hands of the
so-considered outraged citizens, which, in other language, meant "lynched,"—it
was stated, by a very loquacious Yankee-looking fellow present, who made himself prominent in the discussion, that it was the opinion of the company, that
any man marrying a woman with negro blood in her veins, should be hanged, as
a traitor to southern interests and a bad citizen. This sentiment was loudly applauded, and, had the unfortunate subject of it been in Charleston or near it,
he would, in all probability, have been called to account. To me it appeared remarkable, that men, who are always boasting of the well-ordered institutions of
their country (slavery being a very important one, be it remembered), should be
ever ready to set aside all law, and, as it were, by ex parte evidence alone, inflict
summary vengeance on the offender; I was, however, always of opinion, when
amongst them, that four-fifths of the men would rejoice if all law were abrogated,
and the passions of the people allowed to govern the country, thus constituting
themselves judges in their own case, and trampling under foot every semblance
of justice, equity, and common propriety. As it is, in many parts of the Union,
the judges and magistrates are notoriously awed by the people, and the most per-
fidious wretches are suffered to escape the hands of justice. A full confirmation of
this is to be found in the frequent outrages against law and order reported in the
newspapers, and which there elicit little regard.

Walking for a stroll, a day or two after, in the vicinity of the Marine-
promenade, I saw a strange-looking cavalcade approaching. Two armed overseers
were escorting five negroes, recently captured, to the city gaol. The poor creatures were so heavily shackled, that they could walk but slowly, and their brutal
conductors kept urging them on, chiefly by coarse language and oaths, now and
then accompanied by a severe stroke with a slave-whip carried by one of them.
The recovered fugitives looked very dejected, and were, no doubt, brooding over
the consequences of their conduct. The elder of the party, a stout fellow of about
forty-five years old, of very sullen look, had a distinct brand on his forehead of the
initials S.T.R. I afterwards inquired what these brand-marks signified, supposing,

naturally, that they were the initials of the name of his present or former owner. My informant, who was a by-stander, stated that he was, no doubt, an incorrigibly bad fellow, and that the initials S.T.R. were often used in such cases. I inquired their signification, when, to my astonishment, he replied it might be, "Stop the rascal," and added that private signals were in constant use among the inland planters, as he called them, who, he said, suffered so much by their hands running away, that it was absolutely necessary to adopt a plan of the kind for security. He further stated, that such incorrigibles, when caught, were never allowed to leave the plantations, so that if they ventured abroad, they carried the warrant for their immediate arrest with them. "But," he went on, "people are beginning to dislike such severity, and a new code of regulations, backed by the Legislature, is much talked of by the innovators, as we call them, to prevent such practices." I have no doubt this man owned slaves himself.

I said I thought myself that the policy of kindness would answer better than such severities, and it would be well if slave-holders generally were to try it.

"Ah, stranger," he replied, "I see you don't understand things here, down south. Don't you know that people who are over kind get imposed on? This is specially the case with slaves; treat them well, and you'll soon find them running off, or complaining. The only way to manage niggers is to keep them down, then you can control them, but not else."

It has been urged a thousand times in defence of the upholders of slavery in its various ramifications, that they are in reality, as a body, opposed to the system, and would readily conform to any change that would be sufficiently comprehensive to indemnify them from present and future loss. From conversations heard in South Carolina, and other slave districts, I am quite satisfied that this is a misrepresentation, and that the generality of proprietors regard any change as a dangerous innovation, and that, far from reluctantly following the occupation of traders in flesh and blood, it is quite congenial to the vitiated tastes of the greater portion of southern citizens, whose perverted notions of justice and propriety are clamorously expressed on the most trivial occasions. In whatever sphere of society amongst them you go, you find the subject of "protecting their rights" urged with impetuosity; the same rancorous feeling towards men of abolitionist sentiments, and the same deprecation of the slave race. To decry the negroes in public opinion is one of their constant rules of action, and if an individual attempts to assert their equal rights with mankind at large, he is considered as disaffected towards southern interests, and, if not openly threatened, as I have before observed in this work, is unceremoniously talked down. It is thus often dangerous to broach the subject, and if an individual, more daring than people generally are when in the plague-infected latitudes of slavery, attempts to repudiate the views so unhesitatingly expressed by the pro-slavery advocates, that the negro race is but the connecting link between man and the brute creation, he is looked upon with disgust, and his society contemned. This overbearing conduct is so ingrained, that it shows itself on the most trifling occasions, in their intercourse with their fellow-citizens.

Argumentative facts might be produced ad infinitum to prove that the legal enactments for the government of the slave states of America have been framed so as to vest in the proprietor as much control over the lives and persons of those they hold in servitude as any animal in the category of plantation stock.

It is the practice of the inhabitants of Charleston, in common, I believe, with all owners of slaves in towns or cities in the slave states, who have not employment sufficient for them at home, or when the slave is a cripple, to send them out to seek their own maintenance. In such cases the slave is compelled to give an account of what he has earned during the week, at his owner's house, where he attends on Saturday evenings for the purpose. A fixed sum is generally demanded, in proportion to the average value of such labour at the time. I was informed that it frequently happens, that the master exacts the utmost the slave can earn, so that the miserable pittance left is scarcely sufficient to sustain nature; this, no doubt, accounts for the haggard, care-worn appearance of such labourers, for, with few exceptions, I found hands thus sent out, more miserably clad and less hale than the common run of slaves. On the other hand, if a slave is a good handicraftsman, he is able to earn more than his master demands; such instances are, however, rare. These are the men who, by dint of hard work and thrifty habits, accumulate sufficient eventually to obtain manumission. There is, in most cases, a strict eye kept on such hands, and if the boon is attained, it is in general by stealthy means.

At my boarding-house in Charleston, I often saw negro laundresses who called for linen; one of these in particular, I noticed, seemed to be in habitual low spirits; on one occasion she appeared to be in unusual distress, in consequence of one of the boarders leaving the house in her debt. She said that her owner would certainly punish her if she did not make up the required sum, and where to procure it she could not tell. I was touched by her tale, and immediately opened a subscription amongst the boarders in the house, and succeeded in collecting a trifle over the amount she had lost; this I handed her, and she went on her way rejoicing.

I was told by a Carolinian who lodged at this house, that the practice of sending out slaves to earn money in the way I have described, has been in vogue from time immemorial, and that it was such a profitable mode of realizing by slave labour, that it was followed more extensively in that state now than formerly.

I will conclude this part of my narration, by quoting the words of a powerful writer on the subject of slavery as I have witnessed its operation in America.

"Amongst the afflicting ills which the wickedness of man has established upon earth, the greatest beyond compare is slavery. Indeed, its consequences are so dreadful, the sins which it engenders are of such gigantic proportions, and all its accompaniments are so loathsome and hideous, that the minds of benevolent persons revolt from contemplating it, as offering a spectacle of crime and cruelty, too deep for a remedy, and too vast for sympathy. Slavery is an infinite evil, the calculations of its murders, its rapine, its barbarities, its deeds of lust and licentiousness, though authenticated by the most unquestionable authorities, would produce a total of horrors too great to be believed; and to narrate the history of these cruelties which have been perpetrated by American slave-masters within the last five years alone, would be to tell idle fables in the opinions of those who have not deeply studied the tragical subject. If we take the United States of America, where the outcry against slavery is greater than in any other country under heaven, and where we hear more of religion and revivalism, more of bustle and machinery of piety, a country setting itself up as a beacon of freedom; then does slavery amongst such a people appear transcendently wicked; a sin, which, in addition to its usual cruelty and selfishness, is in them loaded with hypocrisy and ingratitude. With hypocrisy, as it relates to their pretensions to liberty, and with ingratitude, as it relates to that God who gave them to be free. This, indeed, makes all the institutions of America, civil and religious, little better than a solemn mockery, a tragical jest for the passers-by of other nations, who, seeing two millions and a half of slaves held in fetters by vaunting freemen and ostentatious patriots, wag the head at the disgusting sight, and cry out deridingly to degraded America, 'The worm is spread under thee, and the worms cover thee.'"

"Fredrika Bremer," by Johan Gustaf Sandberg, 1840.
A replica or study of Sandberg's famous portrait of Bremer.
Courtesy of the Library of Congress, Washington, DC.

Fredrika Bremer (1850)

"The Lover of Darkness"

Fredrika Bremer (1801–1865) was born in Finland (then a part of Sweden), the daughter of a wealthy ironmaster whose family estate, Arsta, was in Stockholm. She was reared to marry into the aristocracy but in 1828 she anonymously debuted as a writer with a series of novels published until 1831, soon followed by others. Written from the viewpoint of an independent woman, her novels empowered female readers and were highly successful. By the 1840s, she was an acknowledged part of cultural life in Sweden, and her work was translated into many languages. When she journeyed in in the United States between 1849 and 1851, seven of her books had been translated into English. *The Neighbors,* published in 1843, sold 175,000 copies and was on the U.S. best-seller list. Newspapers and magazines distributed articles about her all over America, and her eccentricities were well reported. Once she arrived in New York, crowds queued outside her hotel "to shake her hand, ask for an autograph, or invite her home." She was welcomed in New England because of her antislavery views and gained entrée into intellectual circles, where Nathaniel Hawthorne described her as "a little fairy person, worthy of being the maiden aunt of the whole universe" and "a withered brier rose, still retaining the freshness of morning."

During her travels, the country was rife with contention. Congress had passed the Compromise of 1850, which abolished the slave trade in the District of Columbia but avoided a fundamental decision as to the right of slavery to exist under the Constitution. The Fugitive Slave Act of 1850 obligated law officers as well as private citizens in free states to participate in the capture and return of slaves to whatever southern slave owner claimed possession, making free states complicit with slavery. Non-slaveholding states were fighting compliance. The foremost statesmen of the day like Henry Clay and Daniel Webster were vehemently debating the Fugitive Slave Bill and the Compromise of 1850. Undeterred, Bremer, ready to embark from Boston, wrote "And now—to the South! to the

Taken from *The Homes of the New World; Impressions of America* (New York: Harper Bros.), 1853.

South!" She wrote to her sister, "Mrs. W.H., of Charleston, has written to me and kindly invited me to her house there. But I must see her first to know whether we can get on well together. I shall therefore, in the first instance, go to an hotel in the city, and remain there for a few days in the most perfect quiet, and in the enjoyment of freedom and solitude. Then we shall see!"

Bremer arrived in Charleston in late March 1850. She had tea with Mrs. W.H., found this lady's mansion and company acceptable, and moved from her hotel to Mrs. H.'s house. She met a number of Charlestonians. Whether by accident or intention, she observed the funeral cortege of John C. Calhoun, the largest gathering ever witnessed in Charleston. Just weeks earlier, Calhoun had read his "disunion" speech on the Senate floor, predicting the dissolution of the Union if the North did not stop "agitating" the slavery question. Now his body was paraded through Charleston. With him gone, Bremer felt there was no southern leader forceful or powerful enough to keep secessionist hotheads in check. Aware that Calhoun's death bode ill for the future of the South, Bremer wrote, "The prospects of the citizens are 'dark every way.'"

From her travels, she wrote letters home to her younger sister, Agatha (who died before Fredrika returned to Sweden). Bremer edited and published the letters as *The Homes of the New World: Impressions of America.* Some American readers were shocked at her candor, and the book's reception in this country was mixed.

Bremer became a leader of the women's movement. Her last two novels, *Hertha* (1856) and *Father and Daughter* (1859), led to changes in the legal status of unmarried women in Sweden and to the founding of a women's rights journal. She remained active in reform and philanthropic endeavors. However, she claimed her greatest source of happiness in life was the abolition of slavery in the United States.

SOURCES

Benson, Adolph, ed. *America of the Fifties: Letters of Fredrika Bremer.* New York: American-Scandinavian Foundation, 1924.

Pearson, Lennart. "When Fredrika Bremer Came to Charleston." *Swedish-American Historical Quarterly* 56 (October 2005): 214–30.

"THE LOVER OF DARKNESS"

LETTER XIII

Charleston, April 12th, 1850.

I SEE a feeble Southern beauty reposing upon a luxurious bed of flowers in a nectarine grove, surrounded by willing slaves, who at her nod bring to her the most precious fruits and ornaments in the world. But all her beauty, the splendor of her eye, the delicate crimson of her cheek, the pomp which surrounds her couch, can not conceal the want of health and vigor, the worm which devours her vitals. This, weak luxurious beauty is—South Car'olina.

And after all, she is beautiful. I have inexpressibly enjoyed her peculiar charm, so delightful, so rich, and to me so novel.

I have been fourteen days here, and although the weather for the most part has been rainy, and is so still, yet there have been days when I have wished that all feeble, ailing humanity could remove hither, breathe this air, see this exquisite pomp of heaven and earth, which must invigorate them like a balsam of life, and enjoy life anew. I can understand how the mariners who first approached these shores, and felt these gentle breezes, this atmosphere, believed that they were drinking an elixir of life, and hoped to find here the fountain of perpetual youth.

During these delicious days I have made some excursions into the country, round the city, with Mrs. H.* and some kind acquaintance. In all directions, after we had plowed through an extent of deep sand—but they are now beginning every where to form wooden roads, which are very excellent to drive upon—we arrived at a forest. And the forest here is a sort of paradisiacal wilderness, or abounding with many kinds of trees and plants, which I never before heard of or saw. Nothing is studied or trimmed, but every thing grows in wild, luxuriant disorder: myrtles and fir-trees, magnolias and cypresses, elms and oaks, and a great many foreign trees, the names of which I do not know. The most magnificent and the most abundant of all trees here is the live-oak, an evergreen, an immense tree, from the branches of which depending masses of moss, often three or four yards in length, hung down in heavy draperies. These pendent gray masses upon the heavy branches produce the most unimaginably picturesque effect; and when these trees have been planted with any regularity, they form the most magnificent natural Gothic churches, with arcades, and lofty, vaulted aisles. Beneath these long-branched patriarchs of the forest flourish a number of lesser trees, shrubs, plants, and climbing vegetation, especially the wild vine, which fill the wood with perfume, and make a beautiful show in the hedges, and up aloft in the trees, whence they fling down their wild blossoming branches. Thus with the wild yellow jasmine, which was here and there yet in flower; thus with the white

*Mrs. H. was Harriott Pinckney Rutledge Holbrook (1802–1862), daughter of Frederick and Harriott (Horry) Rutledge of Hampton Plantation, and granddaughter of John Rutledge. Her husband, John Edwards Holbrook (1794–1871), was a professor of anatomy, eminent zoologist, and a founder of the Medical College. They lived at 101 Tradd Street (Furman, "Founders of the Medical College," 36).

Cherokee rose, which also grows wild, and in the greatest abundance; thus with many other showy, creeping plants, which on all sides twine around the boles of the trees, and many of which are said to be poisonous. (And many poisonous things, both of vegetable and animal life, are said to be in these wildernesses.) The magnolia is one of the most glorious of their trees, a tall, green-leaved laurel, the white blossoms of which are said to be the most beautiful flowers of the South; but it does, however, not begin to flower till the end of May.

The city itself is now in full bloom, for the city is like a great assemblage of villas standing in their gardens, which are now brilliant with roses of every kind. The fragrance of the orange blossoms fills the air, and the mocking-bird, the nightingale of North America (called by the Indians *cenconttatolly*) or the hundred-tongued, from its ability to imitate every kind of sound), sings in cages in the open windows, or outside them. I have not yet heard it sing when free in the woods. The nectarine and the fig-tree have already set their fruit. I observed this in Mrs. W.H.'s garden,* where also I saw the Carolina humming-bird flutter, like a little spirit, among the scarlet honeysuckle flowers, sipping their honey as it flew. That is something particular, and very beautiful, and I am fortunate in being here.

I have received many kind visits and invitations. I have, of late in particular, acquired a sort of mercurial sensitiveness to the various temperaments and natures which approach me, and the barometer of my feelings rises or falls accordingly. Thus, as I liked Mrs. W.H. from the first moment, did I like—but in another way—Mrs. Holbrook, the wife of the Professor of Natural History, from the first moment when I saw and heard her. I became animated, and, as it were, awakened, by the fresh, intelligent life which spoke in that lovely, animated woman. There is nothing commonplace, nothing conventional in her. Every thing is clear, peculiar, living, and, above all, good. I felt it like a draught of the very elixir of life—the very fountain of youth. The next day I dined with Mrs. H., at her beautiful, elegant residence, the sea-breezes coming in refreshingly through the curtains of the windows. Her mother, Mrs. R.,[†] a beautiful old lady, with splendid eyes; her sister, Miss Lucas R;[‡] three ideally lovely and charming young girls, her nieces; and three very agreeable gentlemen, composed the party. Mr. Holbrook

---

* Mrs. W.H. was Anne Howland (1805–1860), wife of William Howland (1800–1881), a King Street dry goods merchant. They lived at 21 Lynch Street (now 95 Ashley). The Howlands had seven children, all born in Charleston: Justina (1828), Augustus (1830), Mary Ann (1832), Benjamin (1834), Sarah (1838), William (1841), and Laura (1842).

[†]Mrs. R. was Harriott Horry Rutledge (1770–1858), Mrs. Holbrook's mother.

[‡]Eliza Lucas Rutledge (1810–1893) was Mrs. Holbrook's sister.

is, together with Agassiz, the Swiss,* now on a natural history expedition to the great fens of Florida, called the Everglades.

After an excellent dinner we drove to the Battery, the fashionable promenade of the city, and which consists of a bald inclosure along the beach, where people walk round and round in a circle, so that they see again and again all those they know, and all those they do not know, who are promenading there, a thing that I should have nothing to do with beyond at most once a year, not even to breathe the very best sea-air. Neither did this sort of promenade seem particularly to Mrs. Holbrook's taste; but the people of the New World, in general, are fond of being in company, are fond of a crowd.

After an excellent tea, Mrs. Holbrook drove me home. And that was one day of fashionable life at Charleston; and it was very good. But better still was another day spent in the country, alone with her at her country seat, Belmont, some miles out of town.

She came about noon and fetched me in a little carriage. We were alone, we two, the whole day; we wandered in myrtle-groves—we botanized—we read; Mrs. H. made me acquainted with the English poet, Keats; and, above all, we talked; and the day passed like a golden dream, or like the most beautiful reality. You know how easily I get wearied with talk, how painful to me is the effort which it requires. But now I talked for a whole day with the same person, and I was not conscious either of effort or of fatigue. It was delicious and amusing, amusing, amusing. The air itself was a delicious enjoyment. Mrs. Holbrook was like a perpetually fresh-welling fountain, and every subject which she touched

---

*Dr. Louis Agassiz (1807–1873), Swiss professor and geologist, professor at Harvard from 1846, lectured to large crowds of admirers along the eastern seaboard. Agassiz was in Charleston four times between 1847 and 1853, as a speaker, as adjunct professor at the Medical College, and as chair of comparative anatomy in 1852 and 1853. He established a lab at Sullivan's Island where he studied the flora and fauna of the Atlantic Ocean. Agassiz also performed experiments on blacks in the state. Although he claimed to have abolitionist beliefs, he was one of a group of leading academic physicians who advocated the theory that blacks were biologically inferior to whites. In 1975, disturbing slave daguerreotypes were discovered at Harvard's Peabody Museum from his 1850 experiments in Columbia "to analyze the differences between European whites and African blacks." A number of daguerreotypes were taken on the plantations of Wade Hampton II and other prominent Columbia families. They were the subject of an exhibition at the Amon Carter Museum in 1992. In 2012, the daguerreotypes were the subject of a dispute when Harvard refused to allow their reproduction for an exhibit in Grindelwald, Switzerland, on Agassiz and his racism (Wallis, "Black Bodies, White Science," 39–61; Mary Carmichael, "Louis Agassiz Exhibit Divides Harvard, Swiss Group," *Boston Globe*, June 27, 2012).

upon became interesting, either from her remarks upon it or from the views which her conversation unfolded. Thus we flew together over the whole world, not always agreeing, but always maintaining the best understanding; and that day, in the fragrant myrtle-groves of Belmont, on the banks of the Ashley River,* is one of my most beautiful days in the New World, and one which I shall never forget. Now I became acquainted, for the first time, with the amber-tree, and several other trees and plants, whose names and properties Mrs. H. mentioned to me. Natural science has extended her glance over the life of the world, without diverting it from the religious and heavenly life. For her the earth is a poem, which in its various forms testifies of its Poet and its Creator; but the highest evidence of Him she derives, not from the natural life, but from a still, lofty figure, which once advanced from the shadows of life before her glance, and made life for her light and great, connecting time and eternity. Mrs. H. is a Platonic thinker, who can see (which is rare in this world) system in all things, and dissimilar radii having all relationship to one common centre. I spoke freely to her of what I considered the great want in the female education of this country—and of all countries. Women acquire many kinds of knowledge, but there is no systematizing of it. A deal of Latin, a deal of mathematics, much knowledge of the physical sciences, &c.; but there is no philosophical centralization of this, no application of the life in this to life itself, and no opportunity afforded, after leaving school, of applying all this scientific knowledge to a living purpose. Hence it falls away out of the soul, like flowers that have no root, or as leaves plucked from the branches of the tree of knowledge when the young disciple goes from school into life; or, if they do remember what they have learned, it is but merely remembered work, and does not enter as sap and vegetative power into the life itself. That which is wanting in school-learning, in the great as in the small, is a little Platonic philosophy.

On other subjects we did not fully agree; my imagination could not always accompany the flights of my friend. But the charm in Mrs. H. is that she has genius, and she says new and startling things, in particular as regard the life and correspondence of nature and of the spirit.

When the sun sank in the waters of the river this beautiful day came to an end, and we returned to the city. But I must go again to Belmont, and spend a few days there with its good genius—so it is said; but I know not whether I shall have the time.

---

*Belmont Plantation was on the Cooper River, not the Ashley. Four miles from Charleston on The Neck, it was originally the country seat of Mrs. Holbrook's ancestors, Charles and Eliza Pinckney.

Mrs. H. belongs to the aristocratic world of Charleston; and to one of its noblest families—the Rutledges—but is universally acknowledged as one of "the most intellectual and charming women," and is spoken of as "above fashion;" and how could such a spirit be trammeled by fashion?

She has, however, one twist, but that is universal here, and it belongs to the Slave States.

South Carolina is generally called the Palmetto State. I expected to have seen every where this half-tropical species of tree. I was quite annoyed not to see, either in or out of Charleston, any palmettoes. They have been, in a Vandal-like manner, cut down for piles and for ship-building, because this timber is impenetrable to water. At length, however, a few days ago, I saw this States-tree of Carolina (for the state bears a palmetto-tree on its banner) on Sullivan's Island, a large sand-bank in the sea, outside Charleston, where the citizens have country houses for the enjoyment of sea-air and sea-bathing; and there in various gardens we may yet see clumps of palmettoes. Imagine to yourself a straight round stem, slightly knotted at the joints, from the top of which large, green, waving fans, with finger-like divisions, branch forth on all sides upon long stalks, and you have an image of the palmetto, the representative of the palm. I was invited by Mr. and Mrs. Gilman* to a picnic on Sullivan's Island. Picnics are here the current name for excursions into the country, where they go to eat, and to enjoy themselves in a merry company. These parties are very much liked, especially by the young people; and many a tender, serious union looks back for its commencement to a merry picnic. That at which I was now present was a large party, nor was there any lack of young people, nor yet of young enamored pairs; but the day was cool, and I felt it to be rather laborious than agreeable, which is often the case with me on so-called parties of pleasure. But I really did enjoy a drive with Mrs. Gilman on the beach, along the firm, fine sands, while the waves came rolling in, thundering and foaming even to the horses' feet. There was a wild freshness in this scene, while the air was of the mildest and most delicious character. How romantic is "nature," and how rich in picturesque contrasts! Both Mr. and Mrs. Gilman are of the poetical temperament; she has sung the beauty of quiet and pious life; he the subjects connected with his native land. His splendid song, "Fathers, have ye bled in vain!" written from fervent inspiration at a time when the dissolution of the Union was threatened by the bitterness of party strife, has been sung with rapture throughout the United States, and perhaps may have contributed more

*The Gilmans were first mentioned in the Harriet Martineau account. Caroline Gilman was a close friend of both Mrs. H. and Mrs. W.H. She and Harriet Martineau had arranged Bremer's stay in Charleston.

to arouse the public spirit of fellow-citizenship than any governmental measure which is said to have saved "the Union."*

Mr. Gilman is a highly-esteemed and beloved minister of Charleston, a handsome elderly man, whose inward earnestness and nobility are faithfully reflected in his exterior. Last evening I was at a wedding, that is to say, I was invited to witness the marriage ceremony in the church. It was between a Catholic and a member of the English Episcopalian Church; and they had agreed to select the minister of the Unitarian congregation of Charleston, Mr. Gilman, to unite them. Only the relatives and friends of the bridal pair were to be present at the ceremony, which took place in the evening by lamp-light. The bride was lovely as a new-blown white rose, small and delicate, dressed in white, and with a very pretty garland and veil. The bridegroom was a tall and thin gentleman; not handsome, but had the look of a good, respectable man, is very rich, and desperately in love with his white rose-bud. Their bridal tour is to be a pleasure trip to Europe. After the marriage ceremony, which was worthily and beautifully performed by Mr. Gilman, the company rose from their seats and congratulated the bridal pair. A fat old negro woman sat, like a horrid spectre, black and silent by the altar. This was the nurse and foster-mother of the bride, and who could not bear the thought of parting with her. This parting, however, is only for the time of their journey, as these black nurses are cared for with great tenderness as long as they live in the white families, and, generally speaking, they deserve it, from their affection and fidelity.

You may believe that there has not failed to be here conversations about slavery. I do not originate them, but when they occur, which they frequently do, I express my sentiments candidly, but as inoffensively as may be. One thing, however, which astonishes and annoys me here, and which I did not expect to find, is, that I scarcely ever meet with a man, or woman either, who can openly and honestly look the thing in the face. They wind and turn about in all sorts of ways, and make use of every argument, sometimes the most opposite, to convince me that the slaves are the happiest people in the world, and do not wish to be placed in any other condition, or in any other relationship to their masters than that in which they now find themselves. This in many cases, and under certain circumstances, is true; and it occurs more frequently than the people of the Northern States have any idea of. But there is such an abundance of unfortunate cases, and always must be in this system, as to render it detestable.

*Samuel Gilman was well known for his song "Fathers, have ye bled in vain," which he wrote for a July 4 celebration in 1832, when talk of secession was very much in the air.

I have had a few conversations on the subject, something in the following style:

Southerner. "Report says, Miss Bremer, that you belong to the Abolitionist party?"

Myself. "Yes, certainly I do; but so, doubtlessly, do we both; you as well as I."

Southerner is silent.

Myself. "I am certain that you, as well as I, wish freedom and happiness to the human race."

Southerner. "Y—y—ye—e—e—e—s! but—but—"

And now come many buts, which are to prove the difficulty and the impossibility of the liberation of the negro race. That there is difficulty, I am willing to concede, but not impossibility. This, however, is clear, that there requires a preparation for freedom, and that this has been long neglected. There is here, in Charleston, a noble man who thinks as I do on the matter, and who labors in this, the only true direction and preparation for this freedom, namely, the negroes' initiation into Christianity. Formerly, their instruction was shamefully neglected, or rather opposed; the laws of the state forbidding that slaves should be taught to read and write, and long opposing their instruction, even in Christianity. But better times have come, and seem to be coming. People frequently, in their own houses, teach their slaves to read; and missionaries, generally Methodists, go about the plantations preaching the Gospel.

But the one-sidedness and the obstinate blindness of the educated class in this city really astonish and vex me. And women, women, in whose moral sense of right, and in whose inborn feeling for the true and the good, I have so much faith and hope—women grieve me by being so short-sighted on this subject, and by being still more irritable and violent than the men. And yet it is women who ought to be most deeply wounded by the immorality and the impurity of the institution! Does it not make a family a non-entity? Does it not separate husband and wife, mother and child? It strikes me daily with a sort of amazement when I see the little negro children and think, "These children do not belong to their parents; their mother, who brought them into the world with suffering, who nourished them at her breast, who watched over them, she whose flesh and blood they are, has no right over them. They are not hers; they are the property of her possessor, of the person who bought her, and with her all the children she may have, with his money; and who can sell them away whenever he pleases."

The moral feeling, it is said, is becoming more and more opposed to the separation of families and of little children from their mothers by sale; and that it now no longer takes place at the public slave auctions. But one hears in the

Northern, as well as in the Southern States, of circumstances which prove what heart-breaking occurrences take place in consequence of their separation, which the effects of the system render unavoidable, and which the best slaveholders can not always prevent.

The house-slaves here seem, in general, to be very well treated; and I have been in houses where their rooms, and all that appertains to them (for every servant, male or female, has their own excellent room), are much better than those which are provided for the free servants of our country. The relationship between the servant and the employer seems also, for the most part, to be good and heart-felt; the older servants, especially, seem to stand in that affectionate relationship to the family which characterizes a patriarchal condition, and which it is so beautiful to witness in our good families between servant and employer; at the same time, with this great difference, that with us the relationship is the free-will attachment of one rational being to another. Here, also, may often occur this free-will attachment, but it is then a conquest over slavery and that slavish relationship, and I fancy that here nobody knows exactly how it is. True it is, in the mean time, that the negro race has a strong instinct of devotion and veneration, and this may be seen by the people's eyes, which have a peculiar, kind, faithful, and affectionate expression, which I like, and which reminds me of that beautiful expression in the eye of the dog: true is it, also, that they have a natural tendency to subordination to the white race, and to obey their higher intelligence; and white mothers and black nurses prove continually the exclusive love of the latter for the child of the white. No better foster-mothers, no better nurses, can any one have for their children than the black woman; and, in general, no better sick nurses than the blacks, either male or female. They are naturally good-tempered and attached; and if the white "Massa" and "Missis," as the negroes call their owners, are kind on their part, the relationship between them and "Daddy" and "Mammy," as the black servants are called, especially if they are somewhat in years, is really good and tender. But neither are circumstances of quite the opposite kind wanting. The tribunals of Carolina, and the better class of the community of Carolina, have yet fresh in their memory deeds of cruelty done to house-slaves which rival the worst abominations of the old heathen times. Some of the very blackest of these deeds have been done by—women; by women in the higher class of society in Charleston! Just lately, also, has a rich planter been condemned to two years' imprisonment in the House of Correction for his barbarous treatment of a slave. And then it must be borne in mind that the public tribunal does not take cognizance of any other cruelties to slaves than those which are too horrible and too public to be passed over! When I bring forward these universally-known circumstances in my arguments with the patrons and patronesses of slavery, they reply,

"Even in your country, and in all countries, are masters and mistresses sometimes austere to their servants." To which I reply, "But then they can leave them!" And to this they have nothing to say, but look displeased.

Ah! the curse of slavery, as the common phrase is, has not merely fallen upon the black, but perhaps, at this moment, still more upon the white, because it has warped his sense of truth, and has degraded his moral nature.

The position and the treatment of the blacks, however, really improve from year to year. The whites, nevertheless, do not seem to advance in enlightenment. But I will see and hear more before I condemn them. Perhaps the lover of darkness has established himself principally in Charleston. "Charleston is an owl's nest" said a witty Carolina lady to me one day.

I must now tell you something about the home in which I am, and in which I find myself so well off, and so happy, that I would not wish for a better. The house, with its noble garden, stands alone in one of the most rural streets of the city, Lynch Street, and has on one side a free view of the country and the river, so that it enjoys the most delicious air—the freshest breezes. Lovely sprays of white roses, and of the scarlet honeysuckle, fling themselves over the piazza, and form the most exquisite veranda. Here I often walk, especially in the early morning and in the evening, inhaling the delicious air, and looking abroad over the country. My room, my pretty airy room, is in the upper story. The principal apartments, which are on the first story, open upon the piazza, where people assemble or walk about in the evening, when there is generally company.

You are a little acquainted with Mrs. W.H. already, but no one can rightly know her or value her until they have seen her in daily life, within her own home. She is there more like a Swedish lady than any woman I have met with in this country,* for she has that quiet, attentive, affectionate, motherly demeanor; always finding something to do, and not being above doing it with her own hands. (In the Slave States people commonly consider coarse work as somewhat derogatory, and leave it to be done by slaves.) Thus I see her quietly busied from morning till evening; now with the children, now with meals, when she assists her servants to arrange the table; or when meals are over and removed, and all is in order which needs looking after (for the negroes are naturally careless), she will be busy cutting out and making clothes for them, or in dressing and smartening up the little negroes of the house; then she is in the garden, planting flowers or tying

*Anne Holland's father, Esaias Monefeldt, was from Denmark. Her mother, Marie Hedevig Schottmann, was from Copenhagen. At some point the family settled in Georgia, where Esaias was a planter. After his death, his widow and children lived in Sweden, then immigrated to Charleston around 1830.

up one that has fallen down, training and bringing into order the wild shoots of trailing plants; or she is receiving guests, sending off messengers, &c., and all this with that calm comprehension, with that dignity which, at the same time, is so full of kindness, and which is so beautiful in the mistress of a family, which makes her bear the whole house, and be its stay as well as its ornament. In the evening, in particular; but I will give you a circumstantial history of my day.

Early in the morning comes Lettis, the black-brown servant, and brings me a cup of coffee. An hour after-ward, little Willie knocks at my door and takes me down to breakfast, leaning on my little cavalier's shoulder—sometimes I am conducted both by him and Laura—to the lowest story, where is the eating-room. There, when the family is assembled, good Mrs. Howland dispenses tea and coffee, and many good things, for here, as in the North, the breakfasts are only too abundant. One of the principal dishes here is rice (the principal product of Carolina), boiled in water in such a manner as to swell the grains considerably, yet still they are soft, and eat very pulpy. I always eat from this dish of rice at breakfast, because I know it to be very wholesome. People generally eat it with fresh butter, and many mix with it also a soft-boiled egg. For the rest, they have boiled meat and fish; sweet potatoes, hominy, maize-bread, eggs, milk cooled with ice, all which are really a superabundance of good things. During the whole meal-time, one of the black boys or girls stands with a besom of peacocks' feathers to drive away the flies.

After breakfast all go out on the piazza for a little while, the children leap about and chase one another through the garden, and it is a delight to see the graceful Sarah, now thirteen, leap about, brilliant with the freshness of youth and joy, and light as a young roe, with her plaits of hair and her ribbons flying in the wind. She is a most charming creature. The elder sister, Justina, is also a pretty girl, with something excellent, grave, and demure in her demeanor and manner. Willie has beautiful eyes and brown curls, and Laura is a little rose-bud. Two little black negro girls, Georgia and Attila, the children of Lettis, jump and leap about in the house and on the steps, as quick and dexterous as one might fancy black elves.

After breakfast I go into my own room, and remain there quite undisturbed the whole forenoon. At twelve o'clock Mrs. W.H. sends me up a second breakfast, bread and butter, a glass of iced milk, oranges, and bananas. I am not likely to suffer from hunger. At three o'clock they dine, and there may be a guest or two to dinner. In the afternoon my good hostess takes me out somewhere, which is in every way agreeable to me.

The evening is, nevertheless, the flower of the day in this family (ah, in how many families is the evening the heaviest part of the day!). Then the lamps are lighted in the beautiful drawing-rooms, and all are summoned to tea. Then is Mrs. W.H. kind, and fat, and good, seated on the sofa, with the great tea-table before her loaded with good things; then small tea-tables are placed about (I always have my own little table to myself near the sofa), and the lively little negro boy, Sam (Mrs. W.H.'s great favorite), carries round the refreshments. Then come in, almost always, three or four young lads, sons of neighboring friends of the family, and a couple of young girls also, and the young people dance gayly and gracefully to the piano, in all simplicity and good faith. The children of the house are amiable with one another; they are very fond of one another, and dance together as we used to do in the evenings at home. But they are happier than we were. I generally play an hour for them, either waltzes or quadrilles. Strangers, in the mean time, call and take their leave.

Later, people go out on the piazza, where they walk about, or sit and talk; but I prefer rather quietly to enjoy the fragrant night air, and to glance through the open doors into the room where the handsome children are skipping about in the joy of youth, Sarah always ideally lovely and graceful, and—without knowing it.

Mr. M., the brother of Mrs. W.H.,* and the gentleman who came to fetch me the first morning, is a guest here every evening; he is a man of great conversational powers, and tells a story remarkably well.

April 13th. We had last evening a great storm of thunder and lightning, such as I have never seen in Europe, although I remember one June night last year, in Denmark, at Soro, when the whole atmosphere was as it were in bright flame. But here the flashes of lightning were like glowing streams of lava, and the thunder-claps instantly succeeded them. For the first time in my life I felt a little frightened at a thunder-storm. And yet I enjoyed the wild scene.

Charleston, April 26th. My sweet child, am I in my good, excellent home with Mrs. W.H. I was yesterday present at the funeral procession of the statesman and senator of Carolina, Calhoun, whose body passed through Charleston. The procession was said to consist of above three thousand persons; and it seemed, indeed, to be interminable. The hearse was magnificent, and so lofty from a large catafalque that it seemed to threaten all gates made by human hands.[†]

---

*William Stockton Monefeldt, Anne Howland's bachelor brother, was a successful dentist with a practice on King Street.

[†]John C. Calhoun suffered from tuberculosis. While Congress was involved in the long debate over the admission of California to the Union and other issues relative to slavery, Calhoun was too ill to make a speech. His last speech on the Senate floor, on March 4, 1850, was read by Senator James Mason of Virginia. Calhoun died in Washington on March 31, 1850. His body was sent to Charleston by train, accompanied "by a committee from the U.S. Senate and House of Representatives, the sergeant-at-Arms of the Senate, a committee of

Many regiments paraded in splendid uniforms, and a great number of banners with symbolic figures and inscriptions were borne aloft; it was very splendid, and all went on well. All parties seem to have united with real devotion and admiration to celebrate the memory of the deceased, and his death is deplored in the Southern States as the greatest misfortune. He has sat many years in Congress as the most powerful advocate of slavery, not merely as a necessary evil, but as a good, both for the slave and the slave owner, and has been a great champion for the rights of the Southern States. Calhoun, Clay, and Webster have long been celebrated as a triumvirate of great statesmen, the greatest in all the land. Calhoun was the great man of the Southern States, Clay of the Western and Middle States, Webster of the States of New England, although there is great opposition in the New England States against Webster, particularly among the anti-slavery party. Each of these, although old, has been a mighty champion; at the same time admired and feared, loved and hated. There yet remain two. The third fell on the scene of combat, fighting in death, and, as it seemed, even against it.

His portrait and bust, of which I have seen many, give me the impression of a burning volcano. The hair stands on end, the deep-set eyes flash, deep furrows plow that keen, thin countenance. It is impossible from this exterior, which seems to have been ravaged by sickness and passion, to form any idea of the fascinating man in society, the excellent head of a family, with manners as pure as those of a woman, affectionate to all his relatives, a good master, almost adored by his servants and slaves—in a word, the amiable human being, which even his enemies acknowledge him to have been.

Political ambition and party spirit seem to have been his demons, and to have hastened his death. Clay, in his speech on Calhoun in the Senate, makes some gently warning allusions to this.* His fight for slavery was "a political bravado,"

---

citizens from Wilmington, N.C., a committee of 25 from South Carolina, and a subcommittee of arrangements." On arrival, he was placed on a funeral car "drawn by six horses, caparisoned in mourning trappings which trailed the ground, and was escorted, to the sound of muffled drums, to the Citadel Square," where he was formally surrendered by the Senate committee to the governor of South Carolina and the mayor of Charleston. The funeral cortege proceeded from King Street to Hasell to Meeting, around the Battery, and up East Bay to Broad and City Hall, where he was placed in a "magnificent catafalque" to lay in state "under a guard of honor, composed of 200 citizens." The next day, the bells resumed at dawn, and the body was moved to St. Philip's for his funeral and burial in the churchyard (*City of Charleston Yearbook*, 524–25).

*Henry Clay (1777–1852) gave an obituary address for his friend in the Senate on April 2, 1850 (Butler, *Obituary Addresses Delivered on the Occasion of the Death of the Hon. John C. Calhoun* [see Henry Clay]).

said a clever lady, who was not one of the anti-slavery party. Pity that so good a man should live—and have died for so wretched a thing!

In South Carolina, the idolatry with which he was regarded was carried to the extreme, and it has been said, in joke, that "when Calhoun took snuff the whole of Carolina sneezed." Even now people talk and write about him as if he had been a divine person.

During the procession a whole crowd of negroes leaped about the streets, looking quite entertained, as they are by any pomp. Some one told me that he heard the negroes say, "Calhoun was indeed a wicked man, for he wished that we might remain slaves."

On the evening of this day we had strangers at home, and games, dancing, and music, all merry and gay. After this, we walked in the piazza, in the warm moonlight air, till midnight. On the country side was heard the song of the negroes as they rowed their boats up the river on their return from the city, whither they had taken their small wares—eggs, fowls, and vegetables—for sale, as they do two or three times a week.

"William Makepeace Thackeray," by Francis Holl, after Samuel Laurence
stipple engraving. Copyright National Portrait Gallery, London.

William Makepeace Thackeray (1853 and 1855)

"The Fast Lady of Charleston"

William Makepeace Thackeray (1811–1863) was one of the most popular novelists in the world when he left Britain to make a lecture tour of major American cities from October, 1852, to April, 1853. Famous for *Vanity Fair* and *Pendennis*, his newest novel, *Henry Esmond*, was published to coincide with the tour. Thackeray makes clear in his letters that he embarked on the American lecture circuit for the large sums of money to be made, which he needed to support his wife—incurably insane and in custodial care in England—and his two young daughters, Anny and Minny.

Soon after he arrived in New York City, the author was introduced to George Baxter (1801–1885), a New York businessman who lived near the Clarendon Hotel, where the author was staying. Baxter persuaded the author to accompany him home to meet his family, who had been reading *Henry Esmond.* There Thackeray met Baxter's wife, Anna Smith Strong Baxter (1798–1885), and the Baxter children, Sally, Lucy, Wyllys, and George. He fell in love with the children but was particularly taken with Sally, a popular belle that season in New York. He described her as "eighteen and beautifully brilliant." He wrote his mother: "I have been actually in love for three days with a pretty wild girl of 19. (And was never more delighted in my life than by discovering I could have this malady again.)" Over the duration of six lectures he gave in New York, Thackeray visited the Baxter home many times and attended balls with Sally. He watched "as she whirled by in a Strauss waltz or a polka" or "as she sat on a sofa surrounded by admirers." When he continued on his tour, Americans crowded lecture halls in Boston, Philadelphia, Baltimore, Washington, Richmond, Charleston, and Savannah to

Taken from *Thackeray's Letters to an American Family*, ed. Lucy W. Baxter (Boston: Merrymount Press), 1904; and *The Letters of William Makepeace Thackeray*, ed. Gordon N. Ray (Boston: Harvard University Press), 1946, 1852–56, vol. 3.

hear his lectures on "The English Humorists of the Eighteenth Century." He was entertained with "receptions and dinners, concerts and balls, oysters and champagne every night." Between lectures, he returned again and again to the Baxter home, and from the road he corresponded with Mrs. Baxter, Sally, and Lucy. From Richmond he wrote, "They say at Charleston I shall be in the midst of roses & green pease and Spring."

On March 8, 1853, Thackeray arrived in Charleston with his private secretary, Eyre Crowe (1824–1910), on a steamer from Wilmington. They lodged at the Charleston Hotel and the author began a course of three lectures at Hibernian Hall. Tickets, which for the course cost a dollar and a single lecture fifty cents, were highly sought by Charlestonians. After Thackeray's first lecture, the *Charleston Daily Courier* noted that it was delivered "before the largest audience we have ever seen assembled in Hibernian Hall." Further: "Mr. T's delivery is that of a well educated and practiced reader; clear, distinct and never palling by monotony, yet never seeking elocutionary graces. He was listened to throughout with the greatest attention." His next night's lecture, "Congreve and Addison," was delivered "to an even larger audience than before." On the March 10 he lectured on "Steele and the Humorous Writers of Queen Anne's Reign."

On a hectic round of Charleston parties, Thackeray met Susan Petigru King, the "ungovernable" daughter of lawyer James L. Petigru, and a leading figure in society circles. King was known for her gaiety and "queenly presence." A witty and gay conversationalist, she was considered sarcastic and a notorious flirt. She would soon publish her first novel to much local disfavor. On meeting her, Thackeray said, "Mrs. King, I am disappointed in you; I heard you were the fastest woman in America, and I detest fast women." Mrs. King replied, "And I am agreeably surprised in you, Mr. Thackeray; for I heard you were no gentleman."

In October of 1855, Thackeray returned to America on a second lecture tour. He delivered a second course of lectures on the Hanoverian kings, entitled "King Edward's Ancestors, the Four Georges." This tour coincided with the publication of another new novel, *The Newcomes,* in which Thackeray characterized Sally Baxter as Ethel Newcome. When the author arrived in Boston, he was met there by the Baxters with the news that Sally was marrying Frank Hampton from South Carolina. Thackeray, it is said, took it hard. He did not attend the wedding in December. However, when this lecture tour took him to Charleston a second time, he socialized with Lucy and Sally Baxter Hampton, there for Race Week, and met Sally's new husband. In fact, at a social function, Thackeray and Frank Hampton discovered a shared antipathy for another guest, "the fast lady of Charleston," Susan King.

By this time, King had published *Busy Moments of an Idle Woman* (1853), a satire on Charleston society, and *Lily: A Novel* (1855). Lucy Baxter accompanied Thackeray to a Charleston dinner party, and she wrote:

> At a certain dinner party where I went alone with him, my sister not being well, a lady was present who from their first meeting antagonized Mr. Thackeray. She was clever and rather brilliant, but had written some rather trashy novels, whose reputation had certainly not extended beyond her native city. On this and other occasions she seemed determined to attract Mr. Thackeray's attention, to his great annoyance. At last when something was said about the tribulations of authors, the lady leaned across the table, saying in a loud voice, "You and I, Mr. Thackeray, being in the same boat, can understand, can we not?" A dead silence fell, a thunder-cloud descended upon the face of Mr. Thackeray, and the pleasure of the entertainment was at an end. This annoyance on the part of the lady was the culmination of numerous attacks, and struck just the wrong chord.

The meeting of Thackeray and Susan Petigru King remains a Charleston legend that has been recounted in various renditions down the generations.

The following selection comprises Thackeray's letters from (or about) Charleston over two lecture tours, written to his young daughters, Anny and Minny; to Mrs. Baxter and Lucy Baxter; to his friends Jane Perry Elliot and Kate Perry; to Charlestonian Mitchell King; and from the second tour, to Eyre Crowe, who did not accompany him on his second lecture tour.

SOURCES

Crowe, Eyre. *With Thackeray in America.* New York: C. Scribner's, 1893.

Hampton, Ann Fripp, ed. *A Divided Heart: Letters of Sally Baxter Hampton 1853–1862.* Spartanburg, SC: Reprint Co., 1980.

Mayo, Lida. "Thackeray in Love." *American Heritage Magazine* 13, no. 3 (April 1962): 49–53, 104–10.

Meriwether, James B. *South Carolina Women Writers.* Spartanburg, SC: Reprint Co., 1979.

Ray, Gordon N., ed. *The Letters and Private Papers of William Makepeace Thackeray.* 4 Vols. London: Oxford University Press, 1945–46.

"The Secession Movement.—Entrance Hall To An Hotel at
Charleston, South Carolina," by Eyre Crowe. Engraving. Courtesy of
The Civil War in America from the *Illustrated London News:* A Joint
Project by Sandra J. Still, Emily E. Katt, Collection Management,
and the Beck Center of Emory University.

"The Fast Lady of Charleston"

First Tour: November 1852–April 1853

1853
To Lucy Baxter—*
March 11, Charleston
Upon my word and conscience Miss Lucy I don't know what is going to happen
to me tomorrow; whether I shall go South or take the steamboat and rush upon
New York. But this I know I am getting very brown-house-sick[†] and homesick

---

*Lucy Wainwright Baxter (1836–1922) in 1904 published *Thackeray's Letters to an American
Family*, from which this letter was taken.
[†]The Baxter's brownstone at 286 Second Avenue in New York City was referred to as the
"Brown House."

too—and as for lecture-sick. o Steward! bring me a basin! I loathe and abominate the sight of the confounded old MSS* and persist wherever I go in telling every body that I am a humbug.

Yesterday night the "fast" lady of C—— gave me a supper.[†] How she did bore me! She told me I was the man of all the world she wished to see, though she knew she wouldn't like me—nor I her—on which I didn't contradict her—and when she told me she was disappointed in me—I told her quite simply I didn't care a fig whether she was pleased with me or not—and that is the feeling your humble servant has regarding most people. But I like them as I like, to like me; and you know 3 young ladies and a middle-aged one whom I wish to keep as my friends and about whose good opinion I'm not indifferent at all. If one goes through the world uneasy to know what Jack and Tom are thinking of you, or, as a young lady says, if having got the admiration of Charly & Willy you are still unhappy until you have secured Dick & Harrys—what an insupportable effort & humbug Life would be! Now I shouldn't be surprised, if every body should begin by liking Miss Lucy Baxter a great deal—and I hope and suspect I shall see you move through that pleasant little buzzing and flattering crowd, quite serene and undisturbed by their compliments, until TOMKINS makes his appearance for whom and for whom alone you'll have any flutter or disquiet.

I dont think there is much in this letter—is there? Nor have I much to say—except to tell of a black ball I have been at, and I have just finished talking about that and negroes in general to one Miss Minny Thackeray,[‡] whose turn for a letter it was—so I cant repeat the black talk over again—it would be like the lecture you see. But they interest me very much especially the little pickaninnies with their queer faces and ways which are just exactly half way between the absurd and the pretty, and so create in my mind a strange feeling between pleasure & pity.

*Thackeray was weary of repeating his scripted lectures on the chief English authors of Queen Anne's reign, "The English Humorists of the Eighteenth Century," which he had delivered in England since 1851 and repeated many times on his lecture tour in America. His lectures were later published in *The English Humourists: The Four Georges* (1867).

[†]Susan Petigru King (1824–1875) attended Mme. Talvande's in Charleston and at fourteen was sent to boarding school in Philadelphia. She returned home and married Henry C. King (1819–1862), a lawyer in her father's firm. Her first book, *Busy Moments of the Idle Woman*, was praised in regional papers but did not bring the author great renown. She afterward published *Lily* and *Sylvia's World: Crimes Which the Law Does Not Reach* (1859). "Gerald Gray's Wife," first serialized in *Southern Field and Fireside*, was published in novel form in 1864. In her books, King challenged the local patriarchy's practices regarding wives and plantation mistresses, which did not make her popular in Charleston (Meriwether, *South Carolina Women Writers*, 101–5).

[‡]Harriet Marian "Minny" Thackeray (1840–1875), the author's youngest daughter.

SELLING SWEET POTATOES IN CHARLESTON,

"Selling Sweet Potatoes in Charleston," by Eyre Crowe. Courtesy of
The Civil War in America from the *Illustrated London News:* A Joint
Project by Sandra J. Still, Emily E. Katt, Collection Management,
and the Beck Center of Emory University.

Yesterday where I dined* I felt my elbow pinched by a very little hand, and looking
down saw such a little elfin bit of a brat with such a queer smile and grimace holding me up a silver basket with bread—And the day before at dinner there was one
little negro-boy with a great peacock's feather fan whisking the flies away, whilst
another niggerkin yet smaller was deputed to do nothing but watch the process of
the dinner, which he did standing back against the sideboard and making endless
faces at the child with the fan. The goodness of the masters to these children is
very pleasant to witness. I wish some of our countrymen could see it. I wish we
knew many things about America at home; where there will be one person before
very long please God who will be able to say that people here are not all cruel, & that
there are some gentlemen and ladies, o wonder of wonders! as good as our own!†

*Thackeray recorded in his diary on March 10 he dined with G. A. Hopley. George Au-
gustus Hopley (1802-1859), a wealthy merchant and Belgian consul, lived on Legare Street
at the Sword Gate House. He installed the gates in 1850. (Hagy, *Directories for the City of
Charleston, South Carolina: For the Years 1849, 1852, and 1855,* 74; Ray, ed., *Letters and Private
Papers of William Makepeace Thackeray,* 3, 665; see Belgian consuls in Charleston, 1834–1882,
Louis Manigault Papers, Rare Book & Manuscript Library, Duke University)

†Thackeray was said to have disapproved of slavery and had a continual interest in it throughout his writing career. His letters reveal him to be favorable to slavery and insensitive in his

Good bye dear Lucy and all round your bed & elders and youngers—believe me always sincerely your friend
W.M.T.

To Harriet Thackeray
11 Mar. 1853
My dearest Fininkin. Isn't it your turn now to have a letter? Here is a page with a picture already done on it of a young lady who sells pea-nuts and whom Eyre* brought home the other day when she was so good as to sit for her portrait—

"A Peanut Seller," by Eyre Crowe. Thackeray included it in his letter to Harriet. From Eyre Crowe, *With Thackeray in America* (New York: C. Scribner's Sons, 1897). Courtesy of Thomas Cooper Library, University of South Carolina, Columbia.

———

comments about blacks. When he left the South, he wrote, "I was not so horrified as perhaps I ought to be with slavery, which in the towns is not by any means a horrifying institution. The negroes in the good families are the happiest, laziest, comfortablest race of menials. They are kept luxuriously in working time and cared for most benevolently in old age—one white does the work of four of them, and one negro can't. It is the worst economy, slavery, that can be, the clumsiest and the most costly domestic and agricultural machine that ever was devised. *Uncle Tom's Cabin* and the tirades of the Abolitionists may not destroy it, but common sense infallibly will before long" (Ray, ed., *Letters and Private Papers*, 145–46, 254).

*Eyre Crowe (1824–1910), Thackeray's private secretary on the 1852–53 lecture tour, was the author's cousin. Thackeray called him "the worst secretary and the best creature." Crowe studied art in Paris, Rome, and at the Royal Academy Schools in London, and exhibited at the Royal Academy from 1846 to 1908. In America with Thackeray, he first encountered the reality of slavery, which inspired him to sketch blacks in Richmond and Charleston slave markets. His work ultimately helped to illustrate the growing crisis of the Civil War, and gained him a great deal of lasting renown. Crowe later published an account of the lecture tour, *With Thackeray in America* (1893).

What interests me in this place is the negro-children I think. I am never tired of watching their little queer half pretty half funny faces—It's a great error to suppose they are unhappy, they are the merriest race ever seen—they are tended by their masters with uncommon care—They have the best of food, of doctors when they are ill, of comfortable provision in old age. Slaves they are and that's wrong: but admitting that sad fact, they are the best cared for poor that the world knows of. Eyre & I went to a black ball the other night. It was such queer melancholy fun! The men danced capitally, they are house-servants in the town mostly, as grave & polite as if they had been noblemen. But the women were preternaturally hideous all of them and dressed in such white frocks with tiaras & feathers and white satin shoes (a few) and black scraggy shoulders and arms showing so queer in the white dresses. Not one of them was to compare with the pretty peanut girl with her slim figure & sweet voice. We came from Richmond in bitter frost & snow, & found ourselves here in heat thunder-showers & summer. I get hundreds of visits and scores of invitations to dinners & suppers as usual; and of course more and more wearied of the stale old lectures every day—though everybody seems to like them. I think the pleasantest thing I have had here has been a kiss from a little girl, who was a little a very little like you. Whenever I see 2 young sisters I'm fond of them, and think of *my* 2 women; who either are younger and *will* be their age, or older and *have* been their age. I wish you could have seen the little nigger who sang a song for me last night in the street! a little imp of two feet high who sang the song of the "Figlia del Regimento"* to nigger words of his own! It was quite surprizing to hear the sweetness of the child's voice.

Yesterday at dinner I felt my elbow scratched and looking down saw a little little negro with a bread basket offering to me. His master says the child hits him sometimes in the back to make him attend. At most of the tables there are a couple of these pretty little imps with great peacock-fans brushing the flies away—that is the first part of household duty wch. they learn. The ladies of a family universally wash their own teacups after breakfast—Each slave only does one set of duties—the washerwoman for instance does nothing but wash, & has a little black girl to help her, the cook has a kitchen maid, and so on: besides its being wrong: slavery is 6 times as dear as free labour. People having 12 servants to do what two will do in England. So you have snow at Paris. I wonder whether I am going myself back into snow, or southward into the summer? I don't know

---

*An Italian opera based on "*La fille du regiment*," a Donizetti opera about an orphan girl adopted by a regiment of Napoleon's army, was first performed in Paris in 1840.

a bit what my movements tomorrow will be but there's one thing I know that wherever I am I love and bless my dearest children God bless them & GP and Granny* says
Your Papa.

To sell and shell peanuts is Margaret's occupation. She makes few dollars a day often at this trade—not for herself but for her mistress. Margaret is free. She "dono" how old she is thinks about "6." She earns 5 dollars a month wages. She goes to "Bethels Chapel Methodists."[†] She wears a silk frock Sundays "donoo" what colour frock sortagrey earrings and a bonnet—a blue bonnet and blue ribbons inside. She can't write but she can read a little—not so as to amuse herself—only read. She has heard of England: not much only that it is a fine place. She made her own jacket. She can sing: but she has never been to the play. She laughs, "Coloured people ain't allowed to go," Margaret says. She has no sweetheart never had one Margaret says.
PaPa

To Mrs. Baxter—[‡]
Charleston, 12 March, 1853
My Dear Mrs. Baxter. My fate for the next fortnight at least, seems pretty well decided since I wrote to Miss Lucy yesterday; and it is ordained that I go tomorrow to Savannah, stay a week there and return afterwards to this place to give the rest of my sermons. And from this I shall go to Richmond most probably and say out my say there: if their enthusiasm lasts 4 weeks, I am sure of a great welcome at the pretty little cheery place—such a welcome as is better than dollars,—much pleasanter than the dreary acquiescence of the audiences here. But you will go on writing to Charleston, won't you, please. So Mr. Crowe & I sit up in my room, and draw pictures of niggers & saunter about & get through the day as we can—of course there are dinners & suppers in plenty. Plague take 'em! I wish they did not come so thick.

---

*"GP" was Thackeray's step-father, Maj. Henry Carmichael-Smyth, and "Granny" was Thackeray's mother, Anne Thackeray Carmichael-Smyth. The author's daughters were living with the Carmichael-Smyths in Paris (Ray, ed., *Letters and Private Papers*, 3, 655).

[†]Old Bethel Methodist Church stood at the corner of Calhoun and Pitt streets before 1852, when a new church was built to serve a white congregation. Old Bethel was moved further down Calhoun, where the congregation was made up of free blacks and slaves. In 1880, the building was moved across the street to its present location at 222 Calhoun. It still serves a black congregation, which includes descendants of the 1880 congregation.

[‡]From Thackeray's *Letters to an American Family*.

"The Principal Church in Charleston, South Carolina," by Eyre Crowe. Engraving. Courtesy of The Civil War in America from the Illustrated London News: A Joint Project by Sandra J. Still, Emily E. Katt, Collection Management, and the Beck Center of Emory University.

THE PRINCIPAL CHURCH IN CHARLESTON, SOUTH CAROLINA.—SEE PAGE 147.

Last night a bigwig of the place, Mr. King,* gave a supper in my honor. He promised a small party: he had 40 gentlemen: and of course as many handshakes and introductions took place. Professor Agassiz, (a delightful *bonhommious* person as frank and unpretending as he is learned and illustrious in his own branch) told me Mr. King *dared* not ask a small party: for all who weren't asked of the society here would be offended at the omission.

*Mitchell King (1783–1862) or Judge King, was the father-in-law of Susan Petigru King. A Scotsman, he was a retired circuit judge in his seventies at the time of Thackeray's visit. He had a distinguished career but gained great wealth by marrying two heiresses, Susanna Campbell (1791–1828) and her younger sister, Margaret Campbell (1800–1857). King lived in the Radcliffe-King Mansion at Meeting and George streets, where he entertained in grand style and devoted himself to a fine private library.

Enter the Committee of the Lectures with $665 for your humble servant. That's very well for three lectures isn't it? And outside 3 gentlemen are waiting to take me for a walk into the country. So I shake Mr. and Mrs. Baxter & Mr. Strong* by the hand, and give my paternal benediction to the young ladies & their brothers and put on my hat and sally forth.

Second Tour: October 1855 to April 1856

Thackeray sailed for America on a second lecture tour on October 10, 1855. His second series of lectures was not as well received as the first. He was again scheduled to lecture in Charleston and Savannah. In February of 1856, he arrived in Charleston, where he gave a course of four lectures and doubled the price of admission from his prior tour. He wrote: "I went to Charleston and stayed a fortnight having a pretty merry time."

1856
To Anne[†] and Harriett Thackeray
Feb. 2–7 1856
Your Pa has arrived in the South young ladies which he was very much pleased to git your dkitafle letter of the 8 January. Yesdy was the first lecture here and after leaving behind me the most dismal snows and ices, here I sit at an open winder, have taken off my warm clothes, am pretty well thank you, & shant see the North again until there is some bearable weather. What a weary journey we had from Richmond to this place! We were 48 hours on the road to come not more than 400 miles—we broke down and stopped 8 hours at a roadside hotel we got a little sleep between times we didn't reach Charleston till Tuesday afternoon. We had a conwulsion of nature which occasioned the propriety of calomel we were pooty well on Thursday quite right on Friday with the help of some good Champagne, your very humble servant on Friday when we lectured to a distinguished horditory, and taking our ease and paying our visits on Saturday when we bought a sketch-book and made one sketch and now we come home to dinner—and who do you think is here? Can your beating heart tell you? Sally the mum-mum-married and her jolly husband who is a grand seigneur in these

---

*Oliver Smith Strong (1806–1874), Mrs. Baxter's brother.

[†]Anne Isabella "Anny" Thackeray Ritchie (1837–1919), the author's oldest daughter. He predicted early in her life, "She is going to be a man of genius." She grew up to become a best-selling writer of novels, essays, short stories, and personal memoirs.

parts*—and last night poor Lucy arrived from New York[†]—after a stormy passage leaving winter and ice-blocked ports behind her—and having been ill weeks and week & months past with chill & fever—What has a 'appened to Sally? I declare to goodness she looks 30, & is scarcely handsome. Suppose Anny were to marry would she look 30 six weeks after marriage and lose her beauty, my gentle cheeyild?—How fond you would be of the little blackies—they are the dearest imps—I have been watching them all day, about pumps, crawling in gutters, playing in sunshine—I think I shall buy one and bring it home—and happy they unquestionably are—but, but—I remember telling you of a pretty little child scratching my elbow and holding up a plate to me at dinner when I was here before, and now—now my friend has tired of Charleston and his beautiful luxurious house gardens and establishment, and has sold his home and his wines—and I don't like to ask about the ebony child whom he tickled and used and brought up in luxury, and who I fear may be sold too—Whilst I have been writing this I have been out to pay a visit to my last love—a sweet blond with blue eyes she crows upon my floor and she is 7 months old—and I think Granny & I and you have all got the love of children famously developed.—Enter boy with card & note—Papa reads: Mrs. Barnwell Rhett[‡] requests pleasure" &c—what wonderful names—Bungo is written a little way down the street and in Tradd St. I just saw "Mr. Chevis Jervey"[§] on neat silver plate.

Feb 6. Since I began this is ever so many days off. The communications between here & New York have been interrupted by the snow: and I have the

*On December 12, 1855, Sally Baxter had married Frank Hampton (1829–1863), whom she met when visiting Columbia with her father in 1854. He was the youngest son of Col. Wade Hampton (1791–1858) and Ann Fitzsimons from Charleston. His grandfather was Gen. Wade Hampton, first mentioned in the Stuart account. Frank was described as "a tall handsome man with a fine physique," a "true Southern gentleman, and a great favorite with the ladies." Frank and Sally set up housekeeping at Woodlands Plantation near Columbia and had four children. Sally was increasingly ill in the 1850s and was diagnosed with tuberculosis in 1859. She died at Millwood Plantation in 1862 at the age of twenty-nine. Nine months after Sally's death, Frank, a lieutenant-colonel in the Civil War, died at the Battle of Brandy Station (Wallace, *History of South Carolina*, 3; Ray, ed., *Letters and Private Papers*, 3, 484; Nunn, "Halsted's Carolina Connection," 5–9).

[†]Lucy Baxter joined Sally and Frank Hampton for Race Week. Sally had written Lucy: "You must brisk up for Charleston when we are going to have a topping time—Bring your prettiest ball dresses—you won't need much else—" (Hampton, *Divided Heart*, 28, 31).

[‡]Katherine Herbert Dent Rhett (1821–1882), the second wife of Sen. Robert Barnwell Rhett (1800–1876).

[§]J. C. Jervey, a Custom House inspector, lived at 104 Tradd Street (Hagy, *Directories for the City of Charleston, South Carolina: For the Years 1849, 1852, and 1855*, 141).

satisfaction of knowing that Granny's glum imagination about 10 days hence will be inventing score of reason why I didn't write. It is a pretty good time. Not very profitable and not much to do but pleasant people and agreeable talk over old wine. Poor Charles* awfully bored: he is too shy to make acquaintances and has nothing to do from morning till night. How pleasant it would be to make a trip from Havannah to the West Indies, wouldn't it? But that I am so greedy of money. I might do that—and see, O, what a comfort! Some English people again. A kind letter from my old host Mr. Low of Savannah[†] makes me welcome to his house again, and I go next week, and on the 19 if present plans hold good to Havannah whence to N. Orleans is an easy 3 days run. Last night Mrs. F. Hampton and Miss Baxter went to a ball both looking very bright and pretty—Hampton is a fine young fellow—good looking burly honest and a leterairy cove[‡]—Last year when the Cholera was on his plantation he would not leave it but staid and nursed his poor black people by whom he is adored. His sisters are slaves to the slaves too up at all hours of the night to go see the sick working day & night for these thriftless folk making the best of a bad bargain by the practice of a hindered virtues,[§] O how I should like to set up an Atelier an draw these niggahs! They are endlessly funny. To day is Race day, lecture day.

Feb. 6. Since this young ladies nothing has happened but one lecture, and now there is a great refreshing shower of rain falling—which washes away my blue devils and makes me feel all the more cheery. All the people who are (gone) to the races must be finely flooded: and the dread rain grew as much almost as the dread snow.

I have been this morning to see a crazy portrait painter with a beard like Brotherton[¶]—and not much more skill in his business—I wish I could have praised and did wherever I could get a feeble chance, but of course the praise was not enough, and I left the poor fellow balked of what his soul longed for. What rubbish his pictures were! Yet he talked well enough, and his beard was

---

*Charles Pearman was Thackeray's butler, valet, and sometimes "liveried manservant" from 1853 to 1858, described by the novelist as "not only a manservant but a friend." Pearman served as secretary on the author's second American lecture tour.

[†]Andrew Low (1813–1886), a Scottish merchant and cotton factor with firms in Savannah and Liverpool. On both his lecture tours in the U.S., Thackeray was a guest at Low's Savannah mansion at 329 Abercorn Street.

[‡]Cove being British slang for a "fellow, bloke, or chap."

[§]Frank Hampton's four sisters, Harriet, Catherine, Ann, and Carolina, never married. After the early deaths of Frank and Sally, the sisters would raise their four children.

[¶]This was Charles Fraser (1782–1860), the leading miniaturist in Charleston, who Thackeray compares to his own acquaintance Joseph Brotherton (1783–1857), a crucial figure of Victorian society in England.

beautiful—And to improve my mind yesterday I read Sir S. Romilly's life and letters*—and I went to bed at 9 o'clock and slept till 7 this morning and I think this is all that has happened to me—The mail has taken from Sunday to Thursday to come from New York—as it has to go to Boston—I must shut him up to day and forward him with the balessing to my old and young folks to whom I want to get back so much that I don't know how I shall get the 3 months through. Never mind—they will pass and I shall grumble and one happy day O sich a happy day shall see Liverpool Dock! So God bless all says Papa.

I see it is Feb. 7. Charleston.

To Mrs. Elliot and Kate Perry†
Charleston
6–7 February 1856
The cold has penetrated even here. I fancy one feels it more even than in the North, though there's no snow but the houses are not armed against the cold as in NY & Boston *J'ai froid et je m'ennuie* are not these pleasant incentives to letter-writing? I have been here a week of which two first days were spent in bed. The people are very kind pleasant and hospitable. The newspapers praise the lectures. I know one person who is very sick of them. Can you guess his name? But he will go on spouting them DV for 3 or 4 months to come. He will it is to be hoped earn as much money by them as will pay for his house: and leave 5000 here. Then he will be worth 10,000—very well for one who was worth 000 four years ago—and if he dies there will be bread and cheese at least for Miss Anny-minny. What shall I tell you—Mrs. Frank Hampton Miss S—lly B—xt—r as was is here with her husband and her pretty sister whom I like best now—and I have a new love—living on the same floor with me such a pretty little blue eyed blonde! She is seven months old the only person who moves this glum old heart in the least. *Bon Dieu, comme je m'ennuie*! It is Race day the great day at Charleston— the whole town is on the course three miles off—only what do I care for seeing races? Charles ennuies himself more than his master and with more cause He has nothing to do: not a single companion—I said to him tother day—What do you do in the evening Charles—I read the paper Sir and I lay on my bed and—here his eyes filled with tears—but he remains very good & faithful and is a great comfort to his employer. I want to amuse *mes bonnes soeurs* and only draw a great blue devil? Sh! that is the colour of the day.—We are yet without anything but

---

Memoirs of the Life of Sir Samuel Romilly, published in 1840. Sir Romilly (1757–1818) was an English legal reformer.

†Mrs. Thomas F. (Jane Perry) Elliot and her sister, Kate Perry, were two of Thackeray's intimate English friends.

telegraphic news—the roads between this and New York are blocked—the trains always late—the ice in mountains along the roads.

Feb 6. The child of grief paused here in his complaints yesterday—nor has anything happened since to enliven his mood. It is dreffly stupid that is the fact: and will be for the next 3 months until that welcome Spring sun shines which shall see me on board the returning steamer. With a well constituted mind—a man desirous for information &c. you see this would be different—but I ain't desirous of information. I am frivolous and futile a long course of idleness (which novelwriting is) has wasted my intellect—an impaired digestion or it may be an unhappy passion in early life has made me indifferent to all things in this world—I say? Am I to go on grumbling all day to day too? When I say nothing interests me I fib—the negroes here do considerably. I wish I had a sketch book and a hundred of them drawn—I am not dissolved in pity for them. They seem happy enough here as in Richmond. Two gentlemen beg me to go away to their plantations & see for myself. Colonel Hampton S.S.B's (Sally Baxter's) new father in law—who has a great rank in these parts—is quite like a fine old English gentleman with a pleasant rosy face and white hair & bland simple manners—He is treated as they would treat—whom shall we say? Sir Thomas Acland at Exeter.* He calls for a bottle of Champagne of which he only drinks a glass—we have much better dinners when we dine at his table—than the common table d'hote—The town is alive with balls. Lucy & Sally went the other night and looked uncommonly bright & pretty—but I didn't go—What care I to see Lucy and Sally dancing? My place is by the side of older women—o Lord I wish I were in it!

And this letter is so dreadfully foolish that I scruple about sending it—but you'll be glad of a line ever so dull wont you to say I am always J.J.K's.

To Judge King
9 February, 1856
My dear Sir: I hope you will pardon me for having stolen a volume out of your library which I return with thanks and contrition. I went in to look at Mrs. King's beautiful supper table as I came from the ball the other night, and could not withstand the temptation of a volume of *Old Plays.*† Thank you for your hospitality and believe me always yours
W.M.T.

---

*Sir Thomas Dyke Acland (1787–1871), landed tenth-generation baronet, one of nine Acland males who sat in English Parliament over three centuries. The Acland family properties included acreage that extended into twenty-four parishes.

†*A Select Collection of Old Plays*, edited by English dramatist Robert Dodsley (1703–1764) and published in twelve volumes.

To Eyre Crowe
16 February 1856
My dear Eyre. Thank you for your letter and the welcome news from the old house at home. How I wish I were back in it! I am bored to extinction by this present journey. I make more money than by the last performances: but I hate the business worse and worse hate the parties, eschew the balls, dont like to speak to anybody and make myself so disagreeable that I am sure they will never bear me for a third visit. We are going to Low's comfortable quarters in Savannah next week; and the week after to Havannah perhaps—though if I heard that the infernal winter had broken up in New York I think I should run back thither & cut N. Orleans & the Mississippi. Mrs. Hampton, Miss Sally Baxter that was, is here with her sister & husband. He is a fine fellow—like an Englishman big broad honest handsome gentlemanlike quite unlike the N. York whippersnappers. His wife is very much improved by her marriage and our mutual flame extinguished most satisfactorily. There is one painter here with a fine beard and *mon dieu que sa peinture est affreuse*!

I get famous letters from the girls & they are about my only comfort. Lord! I have already potted $10,000.00 and if health lasts ought to get near as much more before I come home. Pulling in little hauls of dollars along the way—& Charles is great taking the checks—and I think I have nothing to tell you but Lord when June comes shant I be glad to be back again! Goodbye my dear Eyre always yours
WMT

Savannah, 17 Feb. 1856*
My Dear Mrs. Baxter: How well your girls (our girls they almost seem to me) looked at Charleston! Sally in her blue dress and lace—the $10,000 worth wch. I gave her and the $10,000.00 wch. her father gave her—looked as handsome as a fairy Princess going to the ball. I liked her husband more thoroughly every day I saw him. I thought her Papa-in-law a fine courteous old gentleman—and his daughter-in-law happy, improved, bearing her new name and station with a great deal of good sense and cheerful graciousness; and as for Lucy, I must tell you that there was a very strong Lucy party in Charleston, and that all of us young fellows agreed in admiring her looks (which I fear is the first thing we young rogues think of) and her sweet natural manners which win everybody.

F.H.[†] & I got on by feeling and expressing a fellow-loathing for a certain person[‡] whose name I daresay you can guess. And yet vulgar as that Individual is

*From *Thackeray's Letters to an American Family.*
[†]Frank Hampton.
[‡]Susan King.

I rather like h— bless me I was going to mention the individual's sex!—and am glad that Sarah should be kind to the party in question. I write only petty rubbish—I have nothing to say. The wearisome lecturing business goes on, the little heaps of dollars roll in gently, and every week makes the girls about $500 richer; and almost every week brings me in a delightful letter from them. At Baltimore I did not know whether I was going to strike for the West or not and had very nearly done so because Jno Crerar* was so pressing. At Richmond I had a pleasant little time a very pleasant little time—Went to the Virginia University in the snow then to Charleston then to, let me see, to Augusta then on here to my friend Low's house delightful for its comfort and quiet and decorated with a pretty little wife and baby since last I was here.† And I have a passport for Havannah in my desk and should have gone thither on Tuesday had not money-grabbing chances offered at Macon Columbus probably Montgomery; then Mobile and New Orleans. Then the Mississippi and St. Louis and Cincinnati and who knows what other places on my way to New York?—whereabouts please God I shall see Second Avenue again. I see and observe no more and like the life no better than I did; but hold out my hat for the dollars perseveringly, and am determined to go on resolutely singing my dreary old song. Suppose I am stupid and bored, what then? A few months boredom may well be borne for the sake of 2 such good girls as mine. At every place I find kind and pleasant people and am a little melancholy when the time comes to leave them. So let us trudge on till the Summer comes, and the bag is pretty full. It was a comfort to see Lucy smiling and being happy & getting well. A letter at New Orleans I think would find me—or send one to J. G. King's, who will forward to me that is when I and they know who is to be my correspondent in that city. Good bye; my very best regards to all. You know that I am affectionately yours
W.M.T.

---

*John Crear (1827–1889), a member of the lecture committee of the New York Mercantile Library Association, instrumental in bringing Thackeray on his U.S. lecture tours. He later endowed the John Crear Library at the University of Chicago.

†Low's wife and son died before Thackeray's first visit to Savannah in 1853. By his return tour in 1856, he had married Mary Cowper Stiles, daughter of the U.S. minister to Austria, William Henry Stiles. The couple had a new baby in addition to Low's two daughters by his first wife.

"William Ferguson of Kinmundy," by Norman MacBeth (ca. 1870–1885).
Oil on canvas. Courtesy of Aberdeenshire Council, Aberdeenshire
Museums Service, Aberdeenshire, Scotland.

WILLIAM FERGUSON (1855)

"Such a One's Geese Are All Swans"

William Ferguson (1823–1904) was raised on his family estates known as Kinmundy in Aberdeenshire, Scotland, which he would inherit in 1862. He was educated at Marischal College, and trained in business from 1840 to 1852. By 1854, he was a partner in Robert Benson Co., London merchant bankers (today Kleinwort, Benson). From 1849, he contributed to science journals and was a fellow of the Linnean Society, the Royal Society of Edinburgh, and the Geologist Society.

Ferguson traveled to America at least partly on business. He sailed from Liverpool in February of 1855 and visited key northern cities before he left Philadelphia for Charleston, traveling by steamer and rail. His company did business with Gourdin Matthiessen & Co., Factors, a large import-export firm in Charleston with immense connections to European cotton markets. Ferguson arrived with two traveling companions who were not identified. They were entertained by Henry Gourdin and his brother Robert Gourdin, owners of the factorage and members of the extended Gourdin family. The Gourdin brothers were bachelors, often compared to Dickens's Cheeryble brothers in *Nicholas Nickleby*. From their mansion on South Battery, they dispensed so much hospitality it was said that "any guest to Charleston was a guest of the Gourdins." They provided Ferguson and his companions excursions over a large portion of the region, from town to innumerable plantations. Ferguson kept a diary of his travels in America, first published in 1856 as *America by River and Rail*.

Ferguson was later a partner in Messrs. Cropper & Ferguson & Co. in Liverpool. After he inherited the Kinmundy estate, he was in business for himself. In 1867, he was appointed director of the Great North of Scotland Railroad. He published *The Great North of Scotland Railroad* (1881), *Twelve Sketches of Antiquities & Scenery on the Line of the Great North of Scotland Railroad* (1883), and a

Taken from *America by River and Rail; or, Notes by the Way on the New World and its People* (London: J. Nisbet and Co.), 1856.

WILLIAM FERGUSON

number of books on religion. In 1895, he was awarded an LLD from the University of Aberdeen.

SOURCES

Ferguson, Martin Luther, and James Ferguson. *The Ferguson Family in Scotland and America.* Candaigua, NY: The Times Presses, 1905.
Ferguson, William. Papers. Sir Duncan Rice Library, Aberdeen University, Aberdeen, Scotland.
Mosley, Charles, ed. *Burke's Peerage, Baronetage & Knightage.* 107th edition. Wilmington, DE: Burke's Peerage Ltd., 2003.

"Such a One's Geese Are All Swans"

Charleston
Saturday, March 24.—Arrived this morning at four o'clock, and went to the Charleston hotel.* They put us into a room with three beds, which we submitted to for the time, on condition that they should give us other rooms. Americans seem, in travelling, to prefer clubbing together as much as possible, in one bedroom, and even in one bed; and our wish, always to have separate rooms and single beds, appeared quite inexplicable to them. After breakfast, finding that they had no other rooms, we transferred ourselves to the Mills-house,† the announcement of which was followed by the immediate discovery that there were spare rooms, but they were found too late to retain us.

Our hotel is situated in one of the chief streets (Meeting Street), which runs up and down, nearly in the centre, between the rivers, and terminates at the bay. From the end of this street, turning left, a terrace leads to the harbor. There are some fine houses on this terrace, looking out on the bay, and over to the shore of

---

*The Charleston Hotel, where Thackeray stayed earlier, was a fine Greek Revival-style hostelry on Meeting Street. First built in 1814 and destroyed by fire in 1838, the hotel re-opened in 1839. It was four stories with a giant Corinthian colonnade that extended the length of a block of Meeting Street. In 1839, it advertised "142 parlors and chambers, a large Dining saloon" "Ladies Dining Room with a suite of private parlors," "Bar Room, Reading Rooms and Offices," and a ballroom (advertisement in the [Greenville, SC] *Southern Patriot*, Oct. 21, 1847).The building was demolished in 1960.
†The Mills House, opened by Otis Mills in 1853, advertised 125 rooms with the "luxury" of "piped in" steam heat and running water, both rare commodities. It was located on the site of the present Mills House Hotel at 135 Meeting Street.

St John's Island.* These shores are low, being but little elevated above the surface of the water. At one point there is a little swelling hill, and it is crowned with a clump of Scotch firs, the picturesquely rugged masses of which redeem the landscape from an insipid uniformity.

Our first walk was in this direction. We passed down Meeting Street, and along the battery, as the terrace I have alluded to is called, to the harbor. Here, on a wharf covered with cotton bales, we found the establishment of my companion's father's friends; and so hearty was the welcome they gave us, that we soon found they were our friends too. Their sample-room is the head-quarters of the trade in Sea Islands cotton.

It was not long ere I got involved with one of them in a deeply-interesting conversation upon the subject of slavery. My friend is so far a strong pro-slavery man, that he believes it will be abolished, but not now, and he does not think it should be meddled with. I said we had met with a friend of his in Boston, and delivered a message he had sent by me about a bet. "Ah," said my friend, "D. is a fine fellow, but he holds extreme views. The constitution of the United States neither prohibits nor provides for the extension of slavery. D. and the Northerners hold that because it is silent about the extension of slavery, it must be construed as prohibiting it. We, on the other hand, maintain that it may and must be construed as permitting it. To us it is a vital question, as unless we can hold our own in this respect, the free States will soon be a majority and swamp us. Therefore we must have slave States increased."

I said that I, as an Englishman, objected to slavery entirely, but that I did not approve of the way followed by the abolitionists in the North to procure its abolition.

"Look for yourself," was the reply; "pay no attention to what any one tells you; and just see if the slaves, as such, are not happier and better treated than many of the working classes in England."

"We have everywhere been told that this is the case," I said, "and I quite expect to find it is so; but that does not alter the fact of *property in the men,* which cannot be brought against us."

To this he replied, that it was a most difficult question to deal with, and that the abolitionists made no allowance for the difficulties which there are in the way of immediate emancipation.

In entering the slave States, we have much to unlearn as well as much to learn. There are many preconceived notions and prejudices to get rid of, as well as information to obtain. Coming from the Northern States, where contact with a black

*Ferguson apparently mistakes "St. John's" for James Island.

man is avoided, where they are not allowed to enter the same conveyance with the whites, and where they have to suffer many other degradations, it surprises us to find no such distinctions here, but, on the contrary, to have to notice the familiarity which exists between the whites and their slaves. They entrust their children to them. They allow them to join in conversation, and take many other liberties. As an instance of this familiarity, my friends told me the following incident:—An Englishman was staying with them on one occasion; and the night of his arrival, they had sat together talking till one o'clock or later. On retiring for bed, they told him they would breakfast and go to business as usual, but that he had better rest in the morning, and that Charles, their "boy" (that is, black servant), would have breakfast for him at any hour he chose. When they met again at dinner, the hosts asked the visitor when he had breakfasted? "Well," was the reply, "I think it was about twelve." "Oh, no," chimed in Charles, who, standing behind his master's chair, heard the conversation, "Mr H. is mistaken; it was half-past one when he came down to breakfast." Unused to such familiarity in servants, Mr H. was a little nettled at it."Why, G.," said he, "what an insolent fellow that servant of yours is!" "Don't you quarrel with him too soon," was the quiet reply, "and you will find Charles will take excellent care of you."*

Coming up with one of our friends, he pointed out to us, at the foot of Broad Street, a building now used as the Post-office, which was a Colonial building, that is, a British government-office before the revolution. In one of the basement rooms of it, Haynes, executed by Lord Roden, was confined.† A little way from this, a large palmetto tree was growing in the street, surrounded by an iron railing. We gazed with interest on this first specimen of vegetation of a sub-tropical type we had seen. I believe it had some revolutionary association connected with it also. These palmettos grow in large quantities on the Florida coast, and they are very valuable for constructing jetties and other works within tide-water, as the endogenous stem has the property of resisting the action of sea-water.

At the corner of Broad Street and Meeting Street is another Colonial building, now the City-hall of Charleston. In the entrance-hall is a fine statue of Calhoun,

*G. was one of the Gourdin brothers, Henry (1803–1879) or Robert Newman Gourdin (1812–1894), who lived together in a mansion that stood on the east corner of Meeting and South Battery. Henry was senior partner, and Robert a co-partner in Gourdin Matthiessen & Co. on Adger's Wharf. Born on Buck Hall Plantation near Pineville into an old family of French Huguenots, the brothers were model citizens, active in civic affairs, and well-loved. For more on the Gourdins and their slave, Charles, see Philip N. Racine, *Gentlemen Merchants: A Charleston Family's Odyssey, 1828–1870* (Knoxville: University of Tennessee Press, 2008).

†This was Hayne not "Haynes," and Lord Rawdon not "Roden." Isaac Hayne was confined there after his arrest by the British in the Revolution.

said to be very like him. It is by Power, the author.* In the mayor's room and council-chamber were pointed out to us portraits of Washington, of General Jackson, General Taylor, &c. In the mayor's room is a portrait of Gadsden, who was the first to raise the standard of rebellion (they call it independence) in Carolina. It was pointed out to Thackeray, when he was here, and he was overheard muttering to himself as he looked at it in retiring, "So you are the scoundrel who began it, are you?"†

Sabbath, March 25.—The family of our friends, as they told me, came over from France on the Revocation of the Edict of Nantes, along with many other Huguenots; and to the French Protestant church, founded then, I this forenoon accompanied one of them, while my companions went with a nephew to St Michael's Episcopal church. At the French Protestant church they are without a regular minister at present. The service—a translation of that used by the old Huguenots in France—is short, simple, and evangelical, and was in striking contrast to the sermon. The text was Romans VIII. 10, 11, and the preacher's "argument," as he called it, to prove that a resurrection was practicable, notwithstanding the constant change in the substance of our bodies, and their ultimate dissolution. He had two theories for securing "personal identity," his favorite one being that there might exist a "germ of life," "infinitesimally attenuated," which was "persistent" through all changes, and formed the basis of the new body, &c. Dreadful rubbish! As G. remarked, "How foolish to waste time in a useless argument on a point with which we have utterly nothing to do, and can know nothing beyond the fact as revealed!"

Having an hour to spare before dinner, we strolled out Meeting Street, north, the longest diameter of the city, till we reached the fields. We saw woods beyond, but had not time to go so far. Hanging over a garden wall was an orange-tree, with a large yellow orange upon it, reminding us we were in warmer latitudes than our wont. Indeed, although the people here call it cold, we have had to adopt a lighter garb than we found necessary in the north.

*Hiram Powers (1805–1883) was a sculptor, not an author. Awarded the last antebellum commission for monumental sculpture, he executed a marble statue of John C. Calhoun dressed as a Roman senator. At the end of the Civil War, the statue was sent to Columbia for safe-keeping, where it was destroyed in a fire during Sherman's March in 1865. Powers is now considered the most famous American sculptor of the mid-nineteenth century in the neoclassical style. Among his patrons were the Preston and Hampton families of Columbia.

†Three of these portraits still hang in Charleston City Hall: George Washington by artist John Trumbull, Andrew Jackson by John Vanderlyn, and Zachary Taylor by James Henry Beard. The Christopher Gadsden portrait by Rembrandt Peale, still part of the City Hall Collection, hangs in the Old Exchange.

We became acquainted, this afternoon, with a third brother of our friends, the owner of cotton and rice plantations up the Cooper river;* and we went all together to have tea with them previous to going in the evening to hear Dr Thornewell, president of South Carolina College,[†] preach to the graduates of Charleston College.

In Meeting Street, we met a negro funeral. Four negroes and negresses walked first. Then came the hearse; then a long procession of darkies, men and women, about three hundred, walking two and two, most of the women dressed in white. Mr G., with whom I was walking, told us that a great funeral was the ambition of the negro. He said, he supposed there was not one of those we might meet who would not be willing to die to-morrow, if he could be assured of a grand funeral.

We went upon the Battery, a walk along the bay. There is a grass-plot between the street and the water, and the look-out is towards the sea. There are walks and benches, but to-night it was too cold to lounge much. The sun set amid a purple glory, not in the sea, but behind the land. On this battery, in summer, from half-past six till dark, you may see almost every one of any notability in Charleston. It is the universal resort. G.'s house looks out on this esplanade, and beyond it on the bay. In his garden we saw several shrubs and flowers which were new to us; and, among other plants belonging to the climate, an old friend, the common primrose,—here, however, a carefully tended exotic.

Dr Thornewell, whom we went to hear to-night, president of the South Carolina College at Columbia, is considered one of the most powerful and talented men in the State. The place of meeting was the Circular church, belonging to the Presbyterians.[‡] It is a large beautiful house, quite a circle in form, painted white inside, and so light and clean as to be a great contrast to the generality of our English churches. The gallery here, as in all churches in the Southern States, is reserved for the colored people, and was filled. One of our friends pointed to it with much satisfaction, as a proof that their "domestic institution" recognized and provided for the religious wants of the slaves. I was much struck with their appearance. Old and young, men and women, were there, of every shade of color;

---

*Peter Gourdin (1814–1893), younger brother of the Gourdin brothers, was a cotton and rice planter who owned Cotebas; however, he also planted Mepkin, Dean Hall, and the Hut, among others.

[†]James Henley Thornwell (1812–1862) had been a schoolmate of R. N. Gourdin at South Carolina College. He was now the leading Presbyterian in the South and a proslavery theologian.

[‡]Ferguson refers to a prior church building (ca. 1804) that stood on the site of the present Circular Congregational Church. Designed by architect Robert Mills (1781–1855), the building was destroyed in the fire of 1861.

and all sat and listened with marked attention and decorum, though the tenor of the discourse must have been far above their capacity. Some of the female costumes were very gaudy, and those of both sexes evidenced the characteristic love of showy dress. I was very much amused by one dark exquisite, who sat fanning himself, evidently with great self-complacency, and no small idea of his irresistible attractions.

The text was John XII. 24, "Except a corn of wheat fall into the ground and *die,* it abideth alone: but if it die, it bringeth forth much fruit." The doctrine deduced from this was, that the principle of success is sacrifice. Life out of death. The history of Jesus, the preacher said, was a great example of this. It was through death that he brought life and immortality to light. Having expounded this, and unfolded very clearly the substitutionary expiation of the cross, he went on to say that the principle was illustrated in its lowest form—1st, In the education of the intellect. It was only by hard study, great self-denial, and determined sacrifice of pleasure and ease, that greatness could be attained in intellectual pursuits. 2d, Next to this, the principle was illustrated in the attainment of morality. It was possible to attain a high degree of morality without a particle of religion, but not without the sacrifice of all those desires which are natural to the depraved condition of man. But, 3d, Its highest development is in religion. To open the way for return to God's favor, the sacrifice of Jesus was necessary. To attain to a life of holiness, a constant sacrifice is necessary. He closed by pressing upon those to whom his discourse was specially addressed, now on their outset in life, to ponder much this principle, and to be prepared to sacrifice everything to duty. He said the maxim, "Self-preservation is the first law of nature," is not only fallacy, but wickedness. In a sense, it is true that we should take all right means to preserve the life which God has given; but if the maxim means, as too often thought to do, that danger and duty are to be shunned—that we may live on the earth as beasts do—then it is of the father of lies. Life is secondary to duty, not duty to life. The true hero takes his life in his hand, and goes forward in the path of duty God has called him to. If he loses his life, it is but God reclaiming his own. It was theirs to set out prepared to suffer, and even to die. "For except a corn of wheat *die,* it abideth alone; but if it die, it bringeth forth much fruit."

Charleston
Monday, March 26.—We had a long stroll through the town to-day. The chief docks or jetties for shipping are on the East bay or Cooper river, but not many ships come here. Above them are floats for timber, saw-mills, &c. Crossing the town from the one river to the other, we passed in front of the arsenal or military school, and immediately beyond, the orphan hospital.

We walked on till we came near the West or Ashley river. Here, even more than on East river, there are a great many timber-floats, and mills of various kinds, interspersed with some good houses. As we were looking at a large aloe through the garden-rails of one of these houses, an ancient negro came up and asked, in a quiet tone, "If massas would not like to step in and see the garden?"* We said we should be glad to do so, which seemed to delight the old man much. The garden contained a most magnificent red japonica,—a tree we afterwards found to be one of the floral wonders of Charleston. It is probably twenty feet high, and covered with flower-bearing branches almost to the ground. The first flush of full blossoming was gone, but still it was a noble mass of crimson and green. This garden, a large and fine one, suffered, along with nearly every other garden in Charleston, from a severe storm last November, from the effects of which it has not yet recovered. In a yard beside it, was a small collection of water-birds and other animals.

Our black friend was most respectful. The quiet way in which he spoke, and his extreme politeness and kindness, made me feel a lively interest in him. The house and grounds, he informed me, belonged to the owner of some large rice-mills near by. To-day, he was gone to his plantation in the country; but Sambo said it was quite the same—he was pleased that he should shew anybody the garden, even when he was at home. "Come back and see me—be sure—come back soon," was the earnest parting request of our dark cicerone. Three other ne-groes were in the garden, whom gardener Sambo contemptuously characterized as "them black fellows," he himself the while being as black as coal, with short curly white beard and moustache.

We next threaded our way through timber-floats and saw-mills to one Mr Lu-cas's rice-mills on the river-side.†

Unfortunately, it was not working, but we were able to examine and compre-hend the machinery. The rice is first passed through an ordinary mill of two hori-zontal stones; this breaks the husk. It is then passed down into iron mortars in which heavy iron pestles are worked. A revolving drum with short arms, catching a knob on the wooden shaft of the pestle, lifts it, and it falls by its own weight.

*This was the Jonathan Lucas House (ca. 1803–1809), now at 286 Calhoun Street.
†Three generations of the Lucas family constructed mills throughout the lowcountry. The Lucas Mill enterprises stood nearby their home mentioned earlier. Jonathan Lucas III (1800–1853) inherited the Lucas enterprises in 1832. In 1840, he built West Point Rice Mill on the Ashley River. It was the largest rice mill in the state. When Lucas died of pneumonia in 1853, the mill was purchased from his estate by his son, Thomas Lucas Bennett (1827–1858), who died soon after Ferguson's visit.

When the rice is sufficiently pounded in this way to remove the hard shell, it is raised again to an upper floor by a kind of chain-pump or elevator. It is then cleaned by a brushing-apparatus, and returned by another shaft to be packed. A barrel is placed on a revolving table on the floor, and the rice runs into it. A hammer is so arranged and worked by machinery as to strike this barrel every two or three seconds, and at the same time the table on which it is placed is turned half-round with a jerk. By this contrivance, the rice is equally filled in and shaken down. We wished much to see the process of preparing the rice, and the article itself in its different stages; but the man in charge could not tell us when there would be any in to grind.

In answer to inquiries about the Sea-Islands cotton, we were told that the average crop for the last two years was about 35,000 bags, an average reduced by the short crop of last year. Some years, it amounts to 40,000 and even 45,000 bags. It is a long-stapled cotton, and is produced upon the rich alluvial islands which lie along the coast south of Charleston. It varies in price from 8 cents to 80 cents, or 4d. to 3s. 4d. per lb. We were shewn the finest sample of the present season, valued at 70 cents per lb. This would cost, laid down in Liverpool, 3s. 2d. per lb., the ordinary average cost of American cotton being 6d. per lb. Messrs Houldsworth, of Manchester, spun for the Exhibition eleven hundred yards of thread from one pound of Sea-Islands cotton.* The usual production of one pound of this cotton is from six hundred to eight hundred yards. It is used for laces, and to mix with silks, and other fine work.

In the course of conversation at dinner to-day, we were told that there are oaks here which it takes six or even nine people to clasp in their outstretched arms— oaks larger, they maintain, than any in England. These are not in the forest, however, where they grow tall and slender, but in open ground. The complaint of the Earl of Carlisle, in his published lectures, of the want of large trees,[†] they therefore hold to be based on the absence of information.

---

*Henry Houldsworth & Sons, mill owners and cotton spinners in Manchester, England. For a description of the experiments shown at the London Exhibition in 1851 with Sea Island cotton, see Wells, *The Annual of Scientific Discovery*, 35.

†George William Frederick Howard, the seventh Earl of Carlisle (1802–1864), better known as Lord Morpeth, visited Charleston in 1850, when he made the comment about trees. A British politician associated with social reform and abolition, he was a popular figure who gave travel lectures and published his opinions on literary taste and culture. See Carlisle, William Frederick Howard, Seventh Earl, *Two Lectures: On the Poetry of Pope, and His Own Travel in America; Delivered to the Leeds Mechanic's Institute & Literary Society, December 5th and 6th, 1850* (Leeds, 1850).

Tuesday, March 27.—Another long walk this morning before breakfast along East bay. We visited a large rice-mill in that direction* in hopes to see it working, but were disappointed again in this.

In the forenoon, a friend came to take me to the college. On our way thither, we met a procession of the students going to the South Carolina Institute Hall,[†] to a public recitation which is called "Commencement," although it is, in fact, the breaking-up of the session. At this, the more distinguished graduates of the year declaim in public. The programme of the procession, as it appeared in the newspaper this morning, looked very imposing, but the reality was a very miserable affair.

The chief object of interest at the college is the natural history collection. We hoped to find Professor Holmes, the curator,[‡] there, but did not, so we looked very cursorily through the museum by ourselves. There is the nucleus of a very fine collection, wanting arranging sadly. It is peculiarly rich in the palæontology of the neighbourhood, the fossiliferous deposits of which are chiefly tertiary. The black bear (*ursus Americanus*) is still met with in Carolina. The beaver (*castor fiber*), the elk (*cervus strongyloceros*), and the bison (*bos Americanus*), formerly existed in the State, but are now extinct. Fifty species of mammifers are still found. Among birds, one of the most prominent is the turkey-buzzard (*cathartes*), of which there are two species. Two hundred and seventy-one species of birds have been enumerated as occurring in South Carolina; along with ninety reptiles, one hundred and forty fishes, sixty-nine crustacians, seven cirripedes, thirteen annelides, one hundred and ninety molluscs, twelve echinoderms, two acalephs, and seven polyps. The lists of all after the birds, however, are not at all complete.

A room in the college is set apart for a debating society. It is fitted up for the purpose, being comfortably curtained and carpeted, while the members are provided with chairs and desks, and the president, vice-president, and secretaries have seats on a raised daïs, in front of the society. It is, in fact, a miniature hall of assembly. I like a little "pomp and circumstance" in the conduct of these societies, and think that there is a good influence, of a refining and polishing nature, in the comfort and tidiness of the room, upon those who frequent it.

As we returned, we slipped into the hall, where "Commencement" was coming to a close, and heard some of the recitations, which were very creditable. We

*Bennett Mill on East Bay Street first operated as a saw mill in the 1830s. Thomas Bennett, Jr. (1781–1865) expanded the building as a rice mill beginning in 1845.He was the father-in-law of Jonathan Lucas, III.

[†]Institute Hall stood in the vicinity of 134 Meeting Street, next to the Circular Congregational Church. It was destroyed in the fire of 1861.

[‡]Francis S. Holmes (1815–1882), planter and naturalist, was curator of the collection.

went out afterwards to drive. We had one of the peculiar buggies, or light-trotting waggons. This was the first time I had been in one. They are extremely light, and, from being hung low between two pairs of very high wheels, closely set together, it is rather a feat to get into them. Your knowing driver gives them a twist, which puts one wheel on the off-side nearly under the body of the vehicle, and widens the space between the two on the ascending side, and this facilitates the getting shipped. Once fairly in, and off, they go rattling over the stones at a great rate, but shake you pretty well. Magnolia cemetery,* a few miles out on the Columbia road, was our first point; and, on the way thither, we became acquainted with a "plank-road." These are formed of sawed deals, laid even and close. When in good order they are pretty smooth, but, we are told, break up both horses and carriages in half the time a common road will, from there being no "yield" in them. When they are out of repair, as they almost always are (that is, when every here and there a plank has got loose, or rotted out altogether), travelling on them is the reverse of pleasant. Although naturally level, some variety has been artificially given to the grounds of Magnolia cemetery. They lie upon the bank of Cooper river, and are very extensive. We saw scattered through them some large "live" or evergreen oaks—very fine trees. When they have space to grow freely, these oaks, though not equal to our forest oaks, are picturesque objects.

We then drove on, partly through the pine-woods, to a wild point, called "Old Magazine."[†] The forest comes quite down to the river, and here, in the war a station was erected to establish a check upon the British attacking Charleston from the river. There are only some ruins of brick buildings to be seen now. They are overgrown with brushwood, which makes them a little picturesque. The charm of the place, however (for there was a charm about it), lay in its solitude.

---

*Magnolia Cemetery, founded in 1849 on the banks of the Cooper River, was a regular feature on the antebellum tour circuit.

[†]Originally the site of what was known as the Old Powder-Horn, "Old Magazine" refers to a state-owned arsenal designed by Robert Mills, located on Laurel Island (then five acres of high ground) in the Cooper River off Charleston Neck, south of Magnolia Cemetery. Initially nine circular powder magazines (said to resemble a "collection of assorted pill bottles") with barracks and a gateway, they were built beginning around 1823. Two of the magazines were demolished during the late nineteenth century in the building of a right-of-way by the Seaboard Air Line Railroad. The remaining buildings were in ruins when they were studied and photographed by the Federal Historic American Buildings Survey in the 1930s. They were completely dismantled in the 1960s (Dr. Nic Butler, Charleston County Library, email to author, September 23, 2009; "Powder Magazines 1822–1915," Historic American Buildings Survey, Prints and Photographs Collection, Library of Congress; Historic American Building Survey documentation, Preservation Society, Charleston).

Behind, the pine forest; in front, a reedy swamp, with the open water of a reach of the river beyond, backed again by the low wood-crowned shore of Sullivan's Island. The mouldering walls added a feeling of desolation to that of solitude, and a tragic interest was not wanting, as a wretched clergyman had not long before selected the place as a spot fitting to take self-imposed leave of life. We were, however, more disposed for the enjoyment of the native features of the scene than its exotic associations. The air was delightfully balmy; the smell of the pine-trees was delicious; we were exhilarated by the rapid ride. It was our first visit to the woods, and it was worth enjoying.

Then a rattling ride back to town—a long conversation with a banker about the railways of the Southern States, which, in the estimation of the Carolinians, are far safer than those in the North—a sumptuous dinner, with orange-leaves in the finger-glasses, imparting a pleasing fragrance to the water—generous wines— cheerful conversation—music—Carolinian beauties to look at and talk to—and so the day drew to a close.

Up the Cooper River

Thursday, March 29.—Just returned from a most interesting and delightful visit to plantations on Cooper river. Our friend Mr G. arranged our trip for us on Tuesday evening, and yesterday morning we started by the steamer *Massasoit*, at nine o'clock.

The Cooper river is a broad winding creek running northwards into the interior, and at a distance sufficiently far up to be beyond the influence of the salt-water; it is bordered by rice plantations. On some of these, cotton is also grown. The windings of the river nearly double the direct distance. It flows through swamps, into which the elevated ground or bluffs project like capes into the sea. Opposite Mr G.'s plantation, Cotebas, the river is forty feet deep.

We reached the landing of Cotebas about twelve, and Mr G. got out there, while we went on under charge of Mr L. of Mepkin,* to visit his plantation, which is considered as possessing the finest scenery in the neighbourhood. We reached Mepkin, forty-two miles above Charleston, about two o'clock.

Each plantation has a little pier or jetty—"landing" is the local term. It was the first day of the Easter holidays, and the boat was crowded with families going

*Mepkin was the seat of Henry Laurens from 1762 until his death in 1792, when the estate passed to his descendants. Peter Gourdin now had some stake in a portion of the property. Ferguson likely encountered John Ball Laurens (1824–1865), the fourth Laurens generation to own the plantation. In 1855, John Ball signed over the title to the South Carolina Society; however, a Laurens descendant lived on the property until 1916. It is now a Trappist monastery.

up to spend April at their plantations. We stopped at every landing, and put ashore whites, blacks, beds, pots, pans, carriages, horses, &c., &c.

The peculiarity of the distribution of their time here prevents the planters from attempting to have their places in the country surrounded with fine pleasure-grounds. They can only reside on the plantations in winter, when everything is bare. In summer, by the 1st of May, swamp-fever drives them away, and they cannot return with impunity till the first black frost sets in. Frost is called black when it produces ice, and a single night of this effectually destroys the fever.

Many of the planters' houses are extremely picturesque. The finest of all is said to be Mepkin. It is the highest bluff on the river, and it is varied with oak-wooded dells and water. We landed at one of the wooden jetties, on a shelf of rock not much above the level of the water. Beyond this, the bluff rises in a cliff of chalk marl sixteen or seventeen feet vertically. It then slopes gently up till it is probably sixty or seventy feet above the water, receding in table-land. This bank is wooded chiefly with large well-grown live-oaks and other evergreen trees. A little dell, through which a streamlet finds its way to the river, runs from the landing back into the bluff, widening and ascending till it shades off into the table-land. On its left stands the house, fronted by a lawn of some extent, sloping gently towards the dell, the water in which, collected into a little lake, can just be seen from the windows. Some very magnificent oaks grow on the lawn—huge fellows, which it takes six men to span with outstretched arms. They are "live oaks," so called because the leaves continue upon the trees, and remain green all winter. They are falling now to give place to fresh ones. The trunks are not lofty, fifteen or twenty feet, at which height they branch. The limbs spread out and the branches bend down, forming a tree of great beauty of outline.

On landing, Mr L. led the way to the stable, and singing out for "January," told him to saddle four horses. While these were getting ready, we explored the corn-house, and saw the Indian-corn as it is stowed for keeping.

The driver, Tom, an ancient negro, was with us. "Tom," said his master, "this," pointing to Y., "is my brother." "Ah, massa, him berry like you." "You did not know I had a brother, did you, Tom?" "No, massa, him berry good broder!" "And, Tom, these," pointing to us, "are my cousins." "All your family, massa?" "Yes, Tom." "All berry like you, massa. What a many family you hab, massa!" I need hardly remark that four persons more unlike could hardly have been brought together.

We then got on horseback, and rode round the plantation for about an hour. It had been very cold on the river, but in the woods it was most pleasant. The sun was shining out, the air was fresh and balmy, and full of the fragrance of the yellow jessamine. Everything was new and interesting. All conspired to make the hour one of great pleasure. We cantered along a fine open avenue, and then turning abruptly off by a bridle-path through the wood, came to a large cleared field, in which some negroes were at work, preparing it for corn. The soil is sandy, and so friable that it is easily worked. The instrument used is a hoe. It is large, perhaps about eight inches square, and has a long handle. With this the soil is raked up into ridges, and the corn is planted on the ridges. It is the custom to keep on planting corn, year after year, in the same field; and it shews how rich the soil is, that it continues to produce good crops for years in succession. Usually before winter, when the ridges are covered with weeds, the earth is hoed down into the furrows, and the weeds are thus covered up and rot. In spring the ridges are made up again with the hoe. Three or four seeds are planted together, and when the plants are a certain height, they are thinned out to one. They are then hoed, to destroy the weeds and earth-up the plant. After this the growth of the corn itself is sufficiently strong to keep down the weeds. The fences on these plantations are almost all of the kind called zigzag.

Through a field behind the house, through another pine-wood, where many a prickly creeper, hanging from the trees, and across the pathway, menaced danger to the face and hands, unless all the more carefully avoided, we reached the brow of the bluff. We had been rising gradually as we rode along, and now we halted our horses amid fine old pines which crest the cliff, and overhang the river. It is the picturesque site of the plantation graveyard. A small brick enclosure contains the tombs of the whites, with marble memorial-stones. Outside, among the pines, lie the blacks,—a wooden cross, or a board with a diamond-shaped head, marking their resting-place. It was a chapter on the separation of the races. It reaches hither, but no further. Beyond this, all are equal. I shall not soon forget that spot. The rustling of our horses' feet among the dried leaves and pine-cones—the tall rough stems of the pines, with their foliage overhead, throwing down a dim sepulchral light on that out-of-the-way place of graves—the steep wood-covered bank, abruptly descending on three sides, and the dark deep water below,—it was all in keeping, while the bright yellow jessamine which festooned many of the trees might have been taken as an emblem of the life even in death.

In another direction we rode down by a steep path to the edge of the swamp, preparing for rice. All along the sides of the river, at a distance from the sea, sufficient to get quit of the salt water, the swamp lands are very valuable for raising rice. The river is embanked, and the surface of the land is under the level of the water in the river at high-tide. The fields are divided by embankments, furnished with sluices, and water is thus put on the fields when the tide is up, and allowed to run off at will when the tide has receded. This year no rice has been planted yet, although the usual planting-day is the 20th of March. The season has been so dry, that there is not current enough in the river to carry out the salt water, and consequently the lands cannot be irrigated except where there are reserves of fresh water, independent of the river. As few have these, there are fears entertained that unless there comes wet weather soon, the rice crop will be a failure. A part of Mr L.'s embankment had given way, and to facilitate the transportation, in punts, of the material required to repair it, he had flooded one of his fields to the depth of about two feet.

We thus saw how the fields usually look when under irrigation. It was like a large lake. We rode along between the bluff and it. There are sluices or water-gates at short intervals in the river embankment, and in the dividing banks; with these, large ditches, cut all across the rice fields, communicate, and smaller trenches again lead into these larger ones. The whole fields are thus under command. The water can be put on to a given portion and to a given depth, and let off again when the recession of the tide makes a downward current in the river.

So far as I could gather, after the seed is sown, water is put on for a few days. It is then run off till the plant springs. When the plant is well up, water is again put on, and allowed to remain for thirty days or so. The plants grow vigorously to keep above the water, which is gradually deepened, till they are a sufficient height. It is then gradually lowered, to allow the plants time to strengthen as uncovered. If run off all at once, the plants would not have strength to stand up, and would be scorched; but by running it off by degrees, they become strong, and gain a foliage which so covers the ground as to shield it from the sun. As the rice ripens, the water is drained off altogether.

These fields are entirely wrought by negroes. Whites do not go into them at all when wet. The soil is a rich vegetable mould, so deep that a ramrod can be thrust into it easily its whole length, and so rich as to be seemingly quite inexhaustible.

Our ride led us past a considerable escarpment of the bluff, and the marl I observed is fossiliferous. The previous owner of this plantation left orders that his body should be burned.* The spot where the incremation took place is just opposite the house, on the other side of the little dell. As we rested there on horseback, for the spot was pretty, as well as the view from it, and we had stopped to enjoy it, the gang of negroes we had seen at work in the fields passed us on their way home. They had finished their work for the day. They are, after all, the feature in

---

*In 1760, Henry Laurens's infant daughter, Martha was declared dead of smallpox. She was placed on a windowsill while the household prepared for her funeral, when she suddenly revived. As a result, Henry Laurens left specific instructions for his body to be burned at Mepkin at his death. He was the first known person to be cremated in the United States (Wallace, *Life of Henry Laurens*, 457–58; Gillespie, *Life and Times of Martha Laurens Ramsay*, 22).

the scene which most interests me. It is pleasing to know that many masters take pains to have their negroes instructed and well cared for.

Already the short March day is drawing to a close, and it is a long way to Cotebas, so we must bid Mr L. good-bye; but not till we had enjoyed his hospitality at luncheon, and still further experienced his kindness.

His carriage conveyed us two miles to a ferry at Strawberry, for Mepkin is on the opposite side of the river from Cotebas. All the way we had the "forest primeval" on one side, and cleared fields on the other. There is an old chapel at Strawberry,* beautifully situated among the trees on the bluff. It is built in the form of a cross, with low walls and high-pitched roofs, and is quite a fine thing to see amidst the prevailing wooden houses of the country.

As we passed down to the ferry, our black charioteer "hollered," which produced two sable ferrymen, one of them a very old man, who came tottering down to the "batteau" in a long white greatcoat. There was a "smart lot" of water in the coble, but they managed to row us over, for which they asked sixpence, or twelve and a-half cents, and they showed their teeth most beautifully when they received half a dollar, or four times as much.

Colonel Carson, of Dean hall, had sent his "carry-all," at Mr G.'s request, to convey us to Cotebas.

It was waiting for us when we landed. Deanhall,[†] which we were now crossing, is one of the finest plantations, in the economic point of view, on the river. Colonel Carson plants about 700 acres of rice, and owns about 280 negroes. It was he that said to Lord Carlisle that he did not approve of negroes going to church, because it spoilt them for work. Lord Carlisle mentioned this in his lectures on America, afterwards published; and the Carolinians find fault with it as an unfair expression of their opinions, and think Lord Carlisle should have added, that his informant is an avowed disbeliever in all religion, and will not allow his own children to go to church, putting them in this respect on a par with his negroes.[‡]

---

*Strawberry Chapel (ca. 1725) remains the only building left of Childsbury, a town built on a bluff on the Cooper River by Englishman James Childs beginning about 1707.

[†]Dean Hall, the plantation of Col. William Augustus Carson (1800–1856), a planter who owned the factorage Carson & Snowden. The original house burned but Carson rebuilt in 1827. He was the estranged husband of Caroline Petigru Carson (1820–1892), elder daughter of James Petigru and sister to the "fast lady of Charleston," Susan Petigru King. The site of Dean Hall is now Cypress Gardens.

[‡]The Earl of Carlisle wrote in *Travels in America*: "I went with a remarkably agreeable party to spend a day at the rice plantation of one of their chief proprietors; he had the credit of being an excellent manager, and his negroes, young and old, seemed well taken care of and

A considerable portion of the six miles we had to traverse, lay through pine-woods by a long road, straight for miles together. These roads require little making. The country is level, and almost all that is necessary is to remove the trees. The soil is sandy and dry, and does not hold wet. The dried pine leaves are put on the road, and they make a compact and solid roadway, and yet so soft that the horses are driven upon it without shoes.

An hour from Mepkin, brought us to Cotebas, which we reached just as it was getting dark, and where a hearty welcome awaited us. Our host has been building a new house on a new site, and is forming a lawn in front, and flower-gardens.* On one side, he has a little way off the Cooper river, and from the end windows of his dining-room he looks out on the Medway or Back river, with two very pretty houses, "Parnassus,"† and "Medway Cottage,"‡ on the opposite bank. My bed-room window also looked out upon this view, which is a very pleasing one. It has more of the home-look of English scenery than is usually met with.

We spent a pleasant evening around a huge log-fire till ten o'clock, when we separated for bed. The butler was absent from ill health, and his place is supplied by another negro, "Smart," and a little fellow, "Jim." An Englishman who was here lately took a great fancy to Jim, and Mr G. gave him permission to go to England, but Jim asked about the water, and was afraid to cross. If he could have got back to "mammy" in five or six weeks he would have gone.

As we were sitting after dinner (I was lying at full length on a most luxurious sofa) a tap came to the door, and in walked an old negro about seventy, named John. John is one of the old family negroes, and always comes in to ask after them all, when any one comes from the city to Cotebas. So John came in, making a tremendous bow, and pulling his wool, to ask for massa, and if "he had brought any baccy from the city." But, alas! no tobacco had been brought, as Mr G. had

---

looked after; [but] he repelled the idea—not of educating them—that is highly penal but the law of the State, but of letting them have religious instruction" (*The Traveller's Library* 25: 35).

*Around 1845, an earlier plantation house was designed and assembled by slaves in the yard of the Gourdin brother's house on South Battery. It was carried up the river and situated on a neck of the land at Cotebas (Neuffer, *Names in South Carolina* 12: 26; Irving, *A Day on the Cooper River*, 77–78).

†Parnassus stood on a bluff above the Back River. From 1842 to 1867, it was owned by the family of Dr. Charles Tennent. The property later became part of Medway. It is now part of the Naval Weapons Station in Goose Creek.

‡Medway, north of Parnassus, remains the oldest house in the region. Built in 1682 by a Belgian nobleman, it was owned by Peter Gaillard Stoney (1809–1884) at the time of Ferguson's visit. For more on Medway, see Virginia Christian Beach, *Medway* (Charleston, S.C.: Wyrick & Co., 1999).

come out with us sooner than he intended. However, he gave John some cigars, and told him he was going back soon, when he would bring him some "baccy." John and another negro had built the house, and proud John was of it. "Fine house—good timber—not bad piece—John not let them put bad piece in—no, no!" The old man was hale and hearty. They don't seem to like to hear about dying, or any allusion to it. "How old are you, John?" "Plenty old, massa," was the reply; "I hope dat you will live to be as old!" "And how long will I need to live to be as old?" "Maybe sixty year," said John; "and I hope you will live more," he added, "even till a hundred." "What! John, do you want to live as long as that?" "Oh yes, massa, me don't want to go yet!" John was told we were "cousins," which seemed to interest him. I suppose this means friends. He was a fine old fellow; a capital specimen of the old domestic negro, identifying himself with his master and his family, and treated quite as a member of it.

I was awaked at six this (Thursday) morning, by Smart coming in to build me a fire. I have not sufficiently described the dining-room fire of last night. Our ride from Mepkin was a very cold one; we therefore appreciated the magnificent fire of logs that was blazing in the ample hearth when we arrived. This was the first wood-fire I had seen, and truly they are glorious things. Two brass "dogs," familiar from drawings of old English fire-places, sustain the blazing fagots. Yesterday, those of Cotebas supported hickory-logs four feet long and a foot thick. One at a time forms the great staple of the fire. Two or three smaller ones laid in alongside, and a lump or two of pine with the resin in it, thrown in below, made the finest fire that could be wished.

Such a fire, though on a smaller scale, did Smart build for me this morning. The pine-sticks are so full of resin that they light very easily. Smart only required to hold one of them for half a minute to a common candle-flame, to light it thoroughly. I watched the flame curling upwards with cheerful blaze and crackling noise till I fell asleep again. Once more I was awaked, an hour after, by Smart coming to open the Venetians, and fill the bath. Augh! How cold the water was! It was a black frost. Presently Jim came to say breakfast was ready, so I hurried down. "Jim, what did you do to the water to make it so cold?" "Didn't do nothin', massa." "Are you sure, Jim?"

"Yes, massa. De water just as it come from de well!" Jim taking it all quite seriously.

Presently our host came in, and we had breakfast—and such a breakfast! First, there were herrings and wings of turkeys, toast, and tea and coffee, and hominy and butter put up in the shucks of the Indian corn; then there were eggs, and muffins, and hoe-cakes—cakes made of Indian corn baked with milk, put out quite thin, and fired on oak boards—very fine, as were the muffins. The sharp frosty air and good sound sleep had given us all appetites for breakfast, and we did ample justice to the good things provided.

Then out over the plantation—first to the corn-house to select some heads of Indian corn to carry to England, then to the cotton-house. There are three stages which the cotton passes through before it leaves the plantation—first, the condition in which it comes from the field, with the seed on; second, noted, a sort of sorting or selection; third, ginned, separated from the seed by a gin, and fit to be put into bags and sent to market.

There were lots of small sables about. To one tiny urchin, three or four years old, perhaps hardly that, Mr G. put the question, "How do you find yourself this morning, Sammy?" "Tho, tho, massa," was the reply. One of our party went into one of the negro houses,—an invasion of their peculiar territory which frightened the young ones sadly. He wanted to know if there were any opossums about, but "piccaninny hab no possum, massa."

In a field which had been caught by the frost, and consequently so much spoiled as not to be worth picking, we found the plants with the cotton remaining in the pods. I picked up a small gourd, and filled it with the peculiar-looking seed-vessels of the sweet gum. This is the opossum's favourite tree. It climbs it to lick the gum which exudes from the bark. Hence the allusion in the negro melody, "Possum up a gum-tree." The "possums" are timid creatures, and run away; the "coons" (raccoon) are bolder and show fight, and it takes a good dog to kill a raccoon. We made a pleasant round through some of the woods and fields. As we returned to the house, we passed an old negress walking leisurely up and down in a field, beating very gently two sticks together. "What are you doing, Mammy?" "Minding corn, massa." "What is that for?" "Keep birds away, massa." "Are these oats?" "Rye." "What do you do with rye?" "For cow, massa." "And do you give the cow the oats too?" "No, massa; oats too good for cow. Oats for horse, massa." This old lady, and many of the old negresses, smoked short clay-pipes. "Baccy" is their sole luxury.

It was two hours till boat-time, so Mr G. led us again into the forest, to point out some trees worth seeing—magnificent magnolias, fifty or sixty feet and more high, and some hickory-trees. When the long-leafed pine, which is the one that is used for timber, and which yields turpentine, is cut down, a growth of another species, called the old-field pine, or loblolly pine, springs up. This has a long leaf too, but a short depressed cone. It was delightful in the forest. There was no road, merely a track, barely marked, and we had to push our way through brushwood, and wild brier, and jessamine vines, which make a pretty tangled and difficult maze to get through.

There is a proverb in use here, when it is meant to institute a sarcastic comparison. Such and such a thing is a "hurlberry above our persimmon." The persimmon is a large pulpy, luscious fruit, while the "hurlberry," or whortleberry, is like ours (blaeberry, *vaccinium*), and the proverb is therefore severe. The proper form of the adage is, "Your whortleberry is above our persimmon," but the usual use of it is as I have written it down. The proverb is analogous to our own—"Such a one's geese are all swans."

Smart and another negro, by the aid of a horse and waggon, had conveyed our two hand-bags the couple of fields' breadth from the house to the river, and were now stationed at the landing with a towel tied to a stick, and hoisted as a signal for the steamer to stop. We sat on a log in the sun, on the edge of the pine-wood, and had nearly an hour's chat before the *Massasoit* hove in sight. At last, about one o'clock, she came to the landing, and we embarked, Mr. G. going with us as far as the next plantation. The very fat little captain of the *Massasoit* shook hands with us all fraternally as we got on board, and was quite jolly and affable, as captains are *not* always.

We were introduced to nearly everybody on board on the way down; among others, to the proprietor of the rice-mills we visited the other day, and to the British consul.* The passage down was speedy and agreeable, and we got back to Charleston about four o'clock.

There was a review, and we went out to see it. We encountered some of the volunteer and artillery companies, but the whole affair was stopped for half an hour by some stupidity in loading a cannon,—not stopping the vent, or something of that sort. It went off, and blew off a fellow's hand. There was a great cannonading down at the battery, the point of attack being a bathing-boat near by. The thing was supposed to be fine, but we soon tired of it.

By ten o'clock all was still. We walked down to the guard-house to hear the tattoo, which is very well beaten. To-night, it was "Rory O'More."†

These two days' experiences have not taught me to love slavery, though I am impressed more than ever with the practical difficulty of the subject.

Sea-islands
Friday, March 30.—To-day we have been, all three, to see another plantation, one of the Sea-Islands ones, namely, Bellevue, on St John's Island, belonging to Mr L.‡

*Robert Bunch, British consul at Charleston from 1853 to 1863.

†"Rory O'More" was a song made popular in the 1830s and 1840s by British actress and opera singer Madame (Lucia Elizabeth) Vestris (1797–1856). It was based on a novel about an historical Irish rebel of the same name.

‡Mr. L. was Winborn Lawton (1782–1861) of James Island, not "St. Johns Island." Bellevue was a plantation and mill establishment originally built by Thomas Bennett, Sr. (1754–1814). A dam and causeway were constructed to provide water power for the mill, which included a rice mill, saw mill, and cotton gin. Winborn Lawton, now owner of the plantation, was

Having expressed our wish to cross the bay to the island, one of our friends at once took steps to put us over. He went with us to the wharf, and introduced us to a son of Mr L.'s, who lent us a canoe-boat and sent a negro with us, telling us to call upon his father. So we got into the boat, the others pulling, and Adam and I in the stern-sheets. On reaching the opposite shore, in front of Mr L.'s house, we found that, the tide being out, the water was so shallow we could not bring the boat near the beach. There was nothing for it but to take off our shoes and socks and wade ashore. Adam would have carried us, but the mud was so soft this was impossible. As it was, we sank every step to mid-calf in the mud, while the water was above our knees. It was a most disagreeable sensation to feel the feet sinking in the mire, the mud oozing through between one's toes, and then to pull the foot out again. However, we reached the firm ground, with no worse result than very dirty feet, and trousers a little wet.

A little negro fellow came down to see what we wanted. "Did Massa L. send you?" "Yes." "Massa L. send you, and no tell you walk in mud?" He seemed to think we had been slightly sold. We sent Adam up to the house with our cards and his son's message to Mr L., as well as to borrow towels, while we made our way after little Sambo through the yard to the well and trough. The bucket and swing soon brought us up some fresh water, and Adam appearing with the towels, we speedily regained our usual appearance.

Mr L. was not in, so we started off through the fields at a venture. Crossing one, we came to a small swamp, with a dyke and zig-zag paling, which combination makes a pretty good fence. As we passed through the next field, we saw going towards the house, in a different direction, an old gentleman led by a negro boy; and having been told Mr L. was blind, we made no doubt this was him, so went up and introduced ourselves. We were right in supposing he was the owner, and a welcome characteristic of Southern hospitality awaited us. He immediately said he would be happy to shew us everything, but first he despatched Peter to the house, to tell Mam Betsy that three English gentlemen would dine with him, and

---

blinded when he removed his bandages too soon after a cataract operation. His son, Winborn Wallace Lawton (1837–1906) would manage the plantation at his death. The Lawton properties—Bennett, Dill Bluff, and Cuthbert—were acquired over time and consolidated into Lawton Bluff Plantation. A grandson, St. John Alison Lawton (1869–1947) developed crops and was a dairy farmer on the property, operator of Battery Dairy (Charleston County, South Carolina, wills and miscellaneous probate records, 1671–1868: St. Philips Parish Wills, Book 12, March 1814, 388; *News and Courier*, St. J. Alison Lawton obituary, February 15, 1947; *James Island and Johns Island Historical Survey*, National Register, nationalregister.sc .gov/SurveyReports/HC10002.pdf [accessed July 15, 2013]).

furthermore to tell Cain to put in the horses, and send the carriage to meet us beyond the wood. Then taking my arm in lieu of the sable messenger's who had been sent off, he turned and led us towards the wood. With the floral productions of this wood he had made himself well acquainted before his blindness came on, for he could tell us where to look for several plants, and then by the touch he could tell us their names.

He indicated a spot where we should find the mandrake of the Bible. He had been told it was so by two botanists from Charleston. We found the plant. It is the May-apple (*podophyllum*). It has a simple stem which bifurcates. Each division bears a circular five or six partite leaf. The flower is white, and is supported on a short footstalk in the centre of the bifurcation. It is in flower now. In June or July the fruit ripens. It is then about the size, shape, and colour of a common hen's egg, and is eatable. We did not find them in flower at first, and the driver, an intensely black negro, coming up, Mr L. sent him to find them, describing them as "the things which the Biblefolks told the story about the old fellows long ago going out to pick and eat when they were too lazy to work," &c.; somewhat of his speech being on the principle of "All this for your instruction tends, / If you could take it so."

We had passed through the wood, and were now in a lane which led along its outward side, with cleared fields beyond. A prettier lane I have seldom seen. There were casino-bushes on each side, festooned with jessamine, China-apple, and several other varieties of creeper,—and mixed with bay, dogwood, sassafras, &c., many of them just bursting into flower.

Mr L.'s son came up with us here, and presently the carriage overtook us. So we all got in, and were driven about half-way down the island, then across, and so up the other side to the house. We passed a school-house and two churches,— one a Presbyterian, and the other an Episcopalian. There are from thirty to forty families resident on the island, which is a triangle of about nine miles to the side. There are some pretty views of forest scenery, with others in which the city of Charleston comes in as a background.

The most interesting plant we saw was the cactus. It grew pretty abundantly upon a sandy dyke by the road. It bore the cochineal insect, and by bruising one of these we expressed the scarlet dye. The plants were in fruit, which is eatable. It is a fleshy fruit, of rather a sickly taste. The species bears groups of minute barbed prickles.

The dwarf palmetto grows abundantly on [James] Island. It is called the Spanish bayonet, or bayonet palmetto. It bears in "the fall," or autumn, a largish bell-shaped white and purple flower, in bunches. The tiny seedling cotton-plants were beginning to peep through the ground. The sugar-cane, too, was just sprouting. The whole cane is laid horizontally on the ground, and covered with earth. It shoots at the joints, each shoot forming a new cane. It is raised for home use and sale in the green state.

In the cotton-houses we were shewn the common and McCarthy's gins.* The gin is a machine for separating the cotton from the seed. The common one is a simple instrument, formed of two rollers made to revolve opposite ways. The cotton is passed between them, and torn from the seed. It is wrought by the foot, and a good workman can gin 25 ft. of cotton per day with it. The M'Carthy gin passes the cotton through something like a long pair of scissors, which takes off the cotton from the seed. It is driven by horse-power, and one of them can clean 450 ft. in a day.

At three we sat down to dinner, which was sumptuous, for it consisted of roast sucking-pig, bacon and eggs, oyster-paties (the oysters occur abundantly on the beach), &c., and we were waited upon by Mam Betsy, a "yaller" woman, the housekeeper, Peter and Cain, two young negroes, and Eliza and another, two small black girls, one of them kept waving a huge fan of peacocks'-tail feathers, to brush away the flies.

Our new friend is a most intelligent man, a thorough planter and slave owner. To our question, whether they punished their slaves, the reply, "Not often," sufficiently indicated that they do sometimes. He spoke constantly of them as one would do at home of his horses; still, in speaking to them his manner was quiet and kind. He shewed us the lash or cow-skin. He had a new one, which he had bought lately on a special occasion. He had been rearing some wild-turkeys, and just as they were fit to eat they were stolen, and he had provided himself with the new cow-skin to chastise the thief. Whether they were his own negroes, and whether the guilty confessed, or whether he went over them all, he did not tell us. Eliza, who brought the cow-skin, looked very like as if she feared she was going to get it, which made me think that the poor thing was not unaccustomed to it.

Mr L. says that he feels that slavery is slipping away from them. He regrets it, but he cannot deny that it is so. Emancipation, he admits, is gaining ground in public opinion, and will, he fears, become universal. He seems to think that it is helped by over indulgence. The slaves in Carolina are allowed to go about from plantation to plantation when their work is done, and they meet, he says, and talk, and he thinks they are becoming independent and insolent, and, he added, he would not be surprised if it ended in revolt. In Cuba, he says, they act much

---

*Fones McCarthy's gin, invented in Alabama in 1840 and patented as the "Smooth Cylinder Cotton-Gin," was the most important roller gin invention of the century. The gin's popularity fluctuated, but by 1850 it had found a niche in the small but profitable Sea Island cotton market.

more wisely. No slave is allowed to cross the border of the plantation without a white man being with him. And everything, he says, is regulated by law, while here there is none. All this shewed a feeling intensely unfavourable to the slave.

Even in that island, where there are only about thirty plantations, he says there is immense variety in the mode of the treatment of the slaves. Some masters think it good policy to treat, and feed, and clothe them well; while others think such conduct does not attach them any more to you, and only serves to make them lazy and indolent. So they half-starve them; and the consequence is, that the negroes on such plantations steal from those around. He told us that, *by law*, each negro is entitled to four pounds of beef or bacon a-week, but that this is universally set aside, and many never get any meat at all. His policy with negroes is, "*plenty* to eat, and a *little* cow-skin." He feeds them well, and does not overwork them. The usual period of labour is eight hours a-day. Sometimes, as in picking seasons, it is more, and at other times it is less. My own observation led me to the opinion that the work was light.

As we approached the house, we passed the "quarters," or negro-huts. "Ah," said Mr L., "there's a niger nursery here. Do you see the ugly-looking, odd-like little black rascals?" He evidently regarded them much as I would do a litter of pigs. Their parents were at work in the fields, and they were left in charge of an old negress. The sight and the idea almost sickened me.

The tide was up when we left, and we embarked at their pier. Adam, our negro boatman, is a slave belonging to a lady, who lets him out. He is hired by his present employer, his mistress receiving the chief part of his wages. He must work, work, work, for what barely keeps him alive. How can it be expected that hearty service can be obtained in this way. Adam is a likely man—can boat, hoe, work in the field, load cotton, work on the wharf, "anyting, massa, can do anyting, oh yes, massa." He has a wife and children, who are, I suppose, slaves too. My heart bled at the tone of his reply to our question, "Are you free?" "No, massa, me no free!" It was all he said, and we studiously avoided a word which would raise a longing for what we had no means of helping him to attain. On my mentioning our friend's name, "Ah," said Adam, "dat fine man. Me like to belong to him most as well as any man."

We went to a store in Charleston, to which Mr L. had directed us, to buy "cow-skins." They cost ten cents, or fivepence each. On asking where they were made, the reply was, "In the North!" Significant this! Is the North quite consistent on the subject of slavery? I think very much the reverse. These lashes are made of a stripe of cow-skin twisted, and can be used with terrible effect.

We heard of one planter who, for punishment, makes use of the system of solitary confinement. The cells are not so high as to permit the negro to stand upright. There is a bed in them *shaped like a coffin*. With the negro characteristic of superstitious sensibility, this is a refinement of torture. They implore "anything but dat, massa!" The fear of it is said to be so very effectual, that it is never required to be put in requisition.

In the course of the evening, we strolled down to the wharves to see the pressing and roping of the cotton-bales. It is a very rapid operation. There is a steam press, on the principle of the Bramah, I suppose. The bales, as they come from the plantations, are placed on one side. One is then put in this press, which in a second or two reduces it to less than half its former size. Two men speedily sow up the canvas and cord it, and the press relaxing, it is rolled out on the opposite side, and carted away, while a fresh bale succeeds it in the press without the loss of a second. The time occupied to put in a bale, press it, rope it, and put it out, is not more than a minute to a minute and a quarter.

Saturday, March 31.—It has rained so to-day that we could not go out. This has continued from twelve till now (ten o'clock at night), and there is no apparent symptom of intermission. The heaviness of the fall has been surprising to us. There has been thunder and lightning too, so that we have had a specimen of a juxta-tropical storm. It has prevented us paying some farewell visits to-day, which we hoped to have accomplished, as we leave on Monday.

A Coloured Church and School.
Sabbath, April 1.—I looked out last night about twelve, before going to bed. The rain had entirely ceased. The moon was shining out with only a few fleecy clouds in the sky, and the roofs and pavements were already dry,—rapid are the changes of weather in this climate. To-day the thermometer has been at 66°. With the rain yesterday and the sunshine to-day, vegetation has made a marked progress in thirty-six hours. The air has been most delicious.

I went to the Scotch Presbyterian church in Meeting Street this morning, and heard Mr. Forrest.* In the afternoon I went to Calvary, a church chiefly devoted to the colored population. The clergyman is Mr. Trappeir.† He has been connected with this colored church for more than five years.

*Rev. John Forrest, DD (d. 1879), minister to First Scots Presbyterian Church from 1832 until his death.
†At the Fifty-eighth Convention of the Diocese in 1847, a resolution was introduced to provide slaves with religious instruction. The same year, Calvary Episcopal was organized for black Episcopalians as a distinct congregation. Rev. Paul Trapier (1806–1872), a white Episcopal clergyman, was rector. Construction of the church building at Beaufain and Wilson streets was completed in 1849, with special seats set aside for whites. Unlike other local churches, blacks and whites were seated on the same floor (Smith, "Slavery and Theology," 506; Trapier, *Incidents in My Life*.)

Some pews round the pulpit are on an elevated platform, and separated from the rest of the church by a division and passage. This portion is for such whites as attend. The remaining part of the church is appropriated to the colored folks. Mr. Trappeir would prefer wanting the whites altogether, but he must have them as assistant teachers.

The attendance was small at first, but increased till the church was pretty full. Probably about two hundred of all ages were present. It was intensely interesting to me to watch the variety of faces, and to observe the attention which many of them paid to the service.

The usual afternoon service of the Episcopal Church was read, followed by a sermon from Matthew xxvi. 58—"Peter followed him afar off unto the high priest's palace, and went in, and sat with the servants, to see the end." The singing was conducted by a negro of the darkest dye. It was remarkably sweet. Mr. Trappeir read each two lines of the hymns, so that all might join, all not being able to read. "Gloria Patria" and the other psalms were chanted.

As soon as the benediction was pronounced, Sabbath-school began. There were fifteen classes of boys and girls, all colored, taught (with I think three exceptions) by ladies, whites of course. The attendance of scholars was about 130. Mr. Trappeir began by giving out the hymn, "There is a happy land!" which the children sang most sweetly. The talent of the colored race for music is remarkable. Teaching then went on in the different classes. Few or none could read; it was therefore vivâ voce. Prayers, catechism, &c., are taught and explained. There was one class of grown young men, and one of married women, distinguished by the peculiarly-tied kerchief they wear upon their heads.

Owing to a lack of teachers, my friend was impressed to take a class, and I stood beside him. The little dark fellows (there were more shades than one in the class) repeated after their teacher "a prayer for a young child," which was explained and made the basis of questions. This over, I had an opportunity of examining them, which I did with great pleasure. I found them familiar with the story of creation and of the fall. They know that we are sinful and out of God's favor and they could tell of Jesus, God's Son, our Savior. I was much interested with their answers, and they seemed to be deeply interested also. We were, however, brought to a stop by the bell ringing. After a short hymn, Mr. Trappeir proceeded to examine the whole school upon his sermon, and upon the lesson for the day, concluding the service with a prayer, during which all knelt.

I was truly delighted to find so much is doing for the slaves. I am informed that there are Sabbath-schools for the colored youth connected with nearly all the churches. In the class of nine which we had, there was a Tony, a Pompey, a Henry, a Joe, a Philander; the second name given by them being those of their masters and mistresses. Thus, "Henry belonging to Colonel So-and-So," and "Joe belonging to Mrs. Such-an-One." Such a mode of taking a Sabbath-class roll sounded very strangely to me. Mr. Bancroft, the historian, was present at the sermon,[*] but did not wait to see the school. He seems about sixty, and is tall and thin, with gray hair.

I was introduced to Mr. Trappeir, and we had much talk about slavery. All say that much more is being done now to teach the slave than used to be; and all admitted, too, that the separation of families was the crying evil of the system, and unavoidable; although there was an inclination to palliate it, by pointing to the early separation that takes place in the families of the working-classes in England. It is true; but the one is forced and the other voluntary and that makes all the difference.

Walked on the battery with Louis Young[†] in the moon-light. It was lovely! The tide was full. The waters of the bay rippled up against the stones with a pleasing gurgle. The shores of the opposite island of St John's were seen dimly in the distance; the clump of tall pines standing out a darker shade in the haze. The whole bay was light, silver-like, with ships spotting it, their watch-lights trembling like stars, and reflected below in the water. The sky was perfectly cloudless, intensely blue. The moon full and sharply defined—no haze tip there. The air full of fragrance. The houses along the bay with their piazzas, so strange, so tropical-looking. All still and calm. Is it reality? or I am dreaming, and in fancy conjuring up the shadow of some half-forgotten story? It is real. I have seen it. And I love to remember it as the farewell scene of Charleston.

[*]George Bancroft (1800–1891) from New York, former statesman and minster to England, was a historian, and author of the ten-volume *History of the United States, From the Discovery of the American Continent*, published in series over four decades, beginning in 1834.

[†]Louis Gourdin Young (1833–1922), a nephew of the Gourdin brothers, worked for his uncles in their firm, Gourdin Matthiessen & Co. He was the youngest son of their sister, Anna Rebecca Gourdin Young (1805–1881) and Thomas J. Young (1803–1852). Since the death of her husband, Mrs. Young and her sons had lived with the Gourdin brothers.

The Battery—Charleston.

"View on the Battery, Charleston, South Carolina," by James Wells Champ-
ney. From Edward King, *The Great South . . . . Profusely Illustrated by J. Wells
Champney* (1875; rpt. New York: B. Franklin, [1969]), vol. 2. Courtesy of
Thomas Cooper Library, University of South Carolina, Columbia.

JOHN MILTON MACKIE (1859)

"The Last Hour of Repose"

John Milton Mackie (1813–1894), born in Wareham County, Massachusetts, attended Phillips Academy and Andover before he graduated in 1832 from Brown University in Rhode Island, first in his class. He afterward studied at Andover Theological Seminary, worked three years as a tutor at Brown, and attended a German university before he returned to the United States to pursue writing. Mackie lived in New York City. He later moved to Great Barrington, Massachusetts, where he may have practiced law briefly before he purchased an estate, Pine Cliff, and devoted himself to literary pursuits, agriculture, and the importing and breeding of Jersey cattle. He was one of the founders of the American Jersey Cattle Club, and its president from 1876 to 1879. His wife, Estelle Ives Mackie (1831–1901), was a cousin of Julia S. Bryant, the wife of author William Cullen Bryant.

Besides contributing to the *North American, American Whig, Putnam's Magazine, North American Review, The Dial* and *Christian Review,* Mackie published a number of books, including *Life of Godfrey William yon Leibnitz* (1845); and "Life of Samuel Gorton" in Sparks's "The Library of American Biography" (2nd series, 1848); *Cosas de Espana, or Going to Madrid via Barcelona* (1848); *Life of Schamyl, the Circassian Chief* (1856); *Life of Tai-Ping-Wang, Chief of the Chinese Insurrection* (1857); and *From Cape Cod to Dixie and the Tropics* (1864).

The publication of *From Cape Cod to Dixie and the Tropics,* an account of his travels just prior to the Civil War, was halted "as letters very properly yielded to arms," and the book was not published until 1864. He wrote in the preface: "When the public mind is turning to books for momentary relief from the long drawn story of battles and campaigns, it may not be ill-timed to give to the press an account of a pleasure journey, made, in part, through the Southern States; and a portion of which may serve as a memento of the happy days—not soon to return, I fear—when there existed between the inhabitants of the Northern and Southern sections of the country a free interchange of services and hospitalities."

Taken from *From Cape Cod to Dixie and the Tropics* (New York: G. P. Putnam, 1864).

Indeed, Mackie's depiction of the Charleston aristocracy continuing on at the apex of society only two years before the start of war, seems to describe the calm before the storm, that "last hour of repose."

In 2006, Mackie's Whig analysis of George Washington's presidency, which had first appeared in *The American Whig Review* in 1849, was republished in book form. *The Administration of George Washington* was published by scholar Frank E. Grizzard Jr., then senior associate editor for the Papers of George Washington, an editorial project at the University of Virginia.

SOURCES

Bryan, Clark W. *The Book of Berkshire*. Great Barrington, MA: Clark W. Bryan & Co, 1887.

Cook, George Willis. *An Historical and Biographical Introduction to Accompany the Dial as Reprinted in Numbers for the Rowfant Club*. Vol. 2. Cleveland: Rowfant Club, 1902.

Wilson, James Grant, John Fiske, and Stanley L. Klos, eds. "Mackie, John Milton." *Appleton's Cyclopedia of American Biography*. New York: D. Appleton and Co., 1887–89 and 1999.

"The Last Hour of Repose"

Charleston

The rail from Richmond to Charleston took me through a country exhibiting fewer marks of civilization than I had anticipated. To the very end of the journey, my surprise was repeatedly excited at passing through forests beyond forests, interspersed only by more or less extensive clearings. Even in these, many of the corn and cotton fields were pretty well filled with stumps and the stems of broken, half-decayed trees, left standing by the axe and the firebrand. The two Carolinas I found as rough as Ohio; while Illinois with its cultivated prairies, might almost pass for an old country in comparison with them. Nearly the whole stretch of these Southern pine woods is as level, too, as any prairie; and many districts, in consequence of recent heavy rains, were little better than a succession of dismal swamps. Even the noble pines themselves, tall, slender, and tapering as were their stems, and sometimes beautifully spreading their tops, like the stone pines of Italy, yet being disfigured by the axe for the sake of their sap, which is manufactured into turpentine, present such conspicuous scars as to make the otherwise fair woods look ghastly enough to be the haunts of ghosts.

Indeed, the poor whites who mostly inhabit these openings in the forests are scarcely less haggard than sprites. They would be equally pale, also, but that they are so yellow. Theirs is the genuine fever-and-ague complexion, more or less modified in this rainy season by the color of the mud wherein they live, and move, and have their being. Fortunately, their hovels are made of logs instead of clay; otherwise these, too, would gradually be dissolved in water. The dress of these natives of the woods was, certainly, when I saw it, in a great many instances fast coming to nought. At best, it was coarse and neglected; while the general aspect of life was low and almost brutish.

At the end of two days of travelling, it was truly a relief to emerge from these pine-grown regions, and see, on approaching the suburbs of Charleston, a greater variety of forest trees. The oaks now preponderated, their boughs hung with gray moss and their trunks often draped with climbing evergreens. In low places, the maples were hanging out their crimson buds and fringes. At the same time, the sun, breaking through the heavy clouds which had for several days obscured the heavens, poured a flood of golden light over the tender foliage, over the city, and the bay; and, genially warming the air, gave promise that I was here to meet the spring thus far advanced on its way northward from the equator and the shores of the Caribbean.

FIRST of all I went to the races. For I had begun to hear the February races in Charleston talked of as far north as Washington, and had been told much of the fine horses, much of the beautiful women, who, in grande toilette, grace these festive occasions. Unfortunately, the twelfth of February brought with it gentle showers of rain; but, heavy as was the course, I had rarely seen in the States better running. The horses were ridden by slips of black boys, whom, at first sight, I thought scarcely equal to the task, but who, in the end, proved themselves to be born Jehus. Like the steeds, they must have been bred specially for the race course. I forget, at this moment, what the time made was; but the horses were so well matched as to come in almost neck and neck.

As to the ladies, they were not to be cheated out of their holiday by the rain. They were there in full feather; in ermine and point lace; in light brocades and cashmeres of India. They were there in the latest nouveautes; gay with flowers and graceful with fringes, as well as the perfect little loves of two dowagers sported their diamonds and jewels more appropriate for the ballroom. Nearly all, as it seemed to me, were rather over-dressed for the occasion; though, as it is the fashion of the Charlestonians to put on new bonnets for the February races, as the Philadelphians do at Easter, perhaps the temptation to make too much of the toilet at this time might well be irresistible. Still, bright colors do not harmonize with dark skies; the reason why they are always so becoming in the *tierras calientes* of Spain and Italy being because the air there is full of resplendent light, and so many of nature's tints are high-toned. But at the Charleston race course, nothing was gorgeous save the silks and ribbons; for, while heavens of lead overhung an earth scarcely yet green, even the cheeks of the fair were pale, and their eyes lacked the lustre of the south of Europe. They were, however, sufficiently pretty and highbred.

The lords of this part of creation, likewise, were tall and fine-looking; though it struck me that their easy morning costumes, if adapted to the occasion, were not quite in harmony with the elaborate toilets of the sex. Certain it is, that the tip-top beaux were generally dressed in overcoats, sacks, raglans, sticks, and umbrellas. I could but think, also, that many of them carried a trifle too much weight in the watch chain, and, in some instances, selected their waistcoats of a crimson slightly too emphatic for the black of their pantaloons. But, on the whole, the crowd of clubmen were well attired; and I did not see among them a single specimen of the black-satin vest gentry.

For the rest, considering that ladies came to the race in full dress, I was a little surprised at seeing that the floor of the saloon wherein they were assembled was, in places, wet with tobacco juice, and sprinkled with nutshells. Lads, whose bringing up in the best families of the town should have taught them better, threw the shells on the floor as unceremoniously as if they had been in a beer garden, or a cockpit. Even a lady arrayed in ermine, and deep frills of Chantilly lace, who was holding a court, at the moment, consisting of four gentlemen, all in waxed mustaches, suffered two out of the four to stand in her presence munching peanuts.

It may be added, that, with few exceptions, the elegantly arrayed ladies present on this occasion to witness the running, and receive the admiration of the handsome members of the Jockey Club, were unmarried; and that the presence of a somewhat larger number of matrons would have imparted a little more dignity to the festivity, without detracting too much from its grace.

To return to town. My first impressions of Charleston were extremely agreeable. It was a pleasant thing to find an American city containing so many memorials of the times colonial, and not wearing the appearance of having been all built yesterday. The atmosphere, charged with an unusual dampness in consequence of the low position of the town on coast and river bank, helps materially to deepen the marks of years; soon discoloring the paint upon the houses and facilitating the progress of the green moss, which here is ever creeping over the northern side of roofs and walls. The whole town looks picturesquely dingy, and the greater number of buildings have assumed something of the appearance of European antiquity. The heavy brick walls and the high gateways are such as one sees in London or Paris. Many front doors and piazzas had been wrought after the graceful models brought from England in the old colonial period. The verandas, story above story, and generally looking toward the south, or the sea, form another pleasant feature in the prevailing style of building. Nor less attractive are the gardens and courtyards invariably attached to the best houses, where, in winter, the hedges are green with pitosporum and the dwarf orange; and where blow the first fragrant violets and daffodils of spring. Here, in February, I beheld with delight the open rose, and camellias so numerous as to redden the ground they fell upon; also, the wild orange bursting with white buds, and the peach tree in full blossom, as well as the humble strawberry at its foot. Stopping at one of these lofty gateways, and looking through the quaint, old-fashioned gratings, I could not help repeating lines of Goethe: "Ein sanftcr Wind vom blauen Hiinmel weht / Die Myrte still und hoch der Lorber steht."*

These charming gardens, in connection with the piazzas resting on ornamental pillars, make the whole town graceful. One sits, in the morning, in these open chambers, inhaling the refreshing air from the sea, its perfume mingled with that of the flowers below; and, at midday, closing the Venetian shutters to exclude the sun, he rests in grateful shade. Here, too, throughout the longer portion of the year, may be spread, at evening, the tea table; while the heavens still glow with the purple and amber of the sunset. And here lingers the family until the bells from the tower of St. Michael's, sweetly ringing their silver chimes through the calm, starry air, announce, at last, the hour of repose.

Many invalids from the North, delighted with these Southern balconies and these melodious evening bells, with this soft air and genial sunshine, with the lovely promenade of the ever grass-green Battery, and with the pleasing prospect of the bay, never the same with its coming and going ships, are tempted to linger here the winter through, nor go farther southward in their search for health or pleasure. But the climate of Charleston, if soft—soft, even, as that of Rome—is damp, and exceedingly variable. The consumptive invalid, therefore, should never daily long with these sea breezes, nor stay to pluck these flowers. He should proceed onward as far as St. Augustine, or inland to the dry, sandy hill country.

In winter, many of the wealthy South Carolinian planters come to Charleston to enjoy the gay season of February; and a few spend several months here for the sake of the greater advantages in educating their children. But all come to town with less parade than did the grand seigneurs of the generation preceding. For a quarter of a century, the number of coaches and four has been gradually diminishing. Fewer outriders herald the planter's advance. The family carriage has grown a little rickety, and the worse for wear; though the horses are still well blooded, and Sambo holds the reins with cheeks as full, and shoulders as widely spreading.

*A gentle wind blows from the blue sky / The myrtle still and high the laurel stands.

Comparatively few are the masters who nowadays pass through the country with a retinue of from fifteen to twenty servants; who, at a wedding, or other festive occasion, open wide their doors to all comers, entertaining troops of friends, two score—and more, with for every one a couch, as well as for every one a month's welcome. Fiddling, indeed, has not died out; and Pompey still draws his bow, and beats his banjo with as much ardor as in the days of yore. At the merry-makings, there is dancing every night in the parlor, as well as plenty of giggling and roaring in the kitchen. Five-and-twenty varieties of corn cake may be served at breakfast; the pot of hominy, like the widow's cruse, is inexhaustible; the bacon makes the table groan; though certainly the number of pipes of wine annually laid down is getting every year less; nor do I believe there can be many nabobs left, who, in purchasing their supplies in town at the beginning of the season, do not fail to include a hogshead of castor oil for their little negroes.

The February balls in Charleston are scarcely less known to fame than the races. The most select and fashionable are those of the Saint Cecilia, and they have been given here from times running back past the memory of all the dancers now living. Only the gentry and the more favored strangers are admitted. They go at ten o'clock, and stay until three. The attendance, however, is principally confined to the younger portion of the fashionable community, who, before setting off for the dance, see the mammas and papas comfortably to bed. I observed that even the young married ladies attracted but little attention from the beaux; and, in fact, I was repeatedly told, that whenever a bride was led to the altar, she, afterward, went in society, as a matter of course, to the wall. Even the bride, who comes from other parts of the country to find in this hospitable city a home, runs imminent risk of receiving but few marks of courtesy from any gentleman not married. She may be beautiful, accomplished, and elegantly dressed; but the beaux will look at her, if they deign to look at her at all, with blank, mute admiration. This, in a city so famed as Charleston is for gallantry of manners, struck me as a little singular. I saw many fair young ladies among the dancers, and the prevailing style of toilet was characterized by simplicity as well as elegance. Some waltzing, also, I noticed, as graceful as that which may be seen in the countries where the waltz is at home. Of flowers, however, whether as an ornament for the person, or the apartments, there were quite too few; and it seemed as though the profusion with which nature, in the more genial seasons of the year, furnishes these decorations, had led to the neglect of their cultivation by artificial means in winter.

From the presence of two races, the streets of Charleston have a pepper-and-salt aspect. The blacks are almost as numerous as the whites, but are generally of smaller stature. I saw very few slaves, either male or female, who were of large size; still fewer who were good-looking. As an exception, however, in the matter of size, I noticed one portly dame striding down the street in broad-brimmed hat, and staff, who appropriated to her own use nearly the whole of the sidewalk, and swaggered with an importance which plainly marked her as having authority in the kitchen of one of the proudest families of Charleston. On Sunday, the negroes I saw airing themselves on their way to church appeared to good advantage, being respectful in manners, and, for the most part, becomingly plain in dress. The aged dames were in turbans containing only a few modest stripes, though worn pretty high. The younger damsels showed, of course, more love for dressing like white folks. One dainty miss, with large, liquid eyes, and the deep red breaking through her colored cheek, like the vermilion streaming through dark clouds that lie athwart the sunset, made herself gay in a French cashmere; another displayed her jaunty modesty in Canton crape; while the principal colored belle of the promenade held up her rich black silk to exhibit an elaborately embroidered petticoat. The other sex were decently clad, and scarcely in a single instance that came under my observation, grotesquely. They showed, occasionally, a little red in their cravats—sometimes a little buff. But not even on the coach box did Pompey go much beyond a brass buckle in his hat, and purple plush in his waistcoat. On the whole, therefore, the colored palmetto gentry seemed to me to have learned demureness from their betters; though there was, perhaps, as much grinning and giggling as was decent on a Sunday.

But the next day being a half holiday, in consequence of the Governor's review, I was surprised at seeing crowds of nurses in bandanna turbans, and sable urchins in caps so gay as to need nothing but belles to set them all ringing. The sunny afternoon air was quite filled with the kites of these small black boys. Their loud, tumultuous laughter mingled pleasantly with the music of drum, and fife, and bagpipe; while, by nightfall, the circles of all eyes had grown visibly larger from gazing at the plumes and glitter of the militiamen. With special pleasure I remember the sight, on that afternoon, of a pair of brats about the size of Murillo's beggar boys,* and as much like them as blacks can be like Spaniards. They occupied the same position, also, against a sunny wall, and were in the same need of having their heads combed; the one being happily intent on smoking a broken clay pipe, and the other gazing at vacancy with a degree of tranquil animal satisfaction which distended his half-shining, half-unwashed skin well-nigh to cracking.

It was but a sorry entertainment to visit the slave market; yet, one fine morning, attracted by the auctioneer's flag, I dropped in. There was but one small lot on the block, evidently a badly damaged lot of merchandise; and I did not

*Bartolomé Esteban Murillo (1618–1682), an artist whose genre paintings feature the street urchins of seventeenth-century Seville.

hear a single bid for them. One old woman, however, by trade a cook, was put up for sale separately. She was, at the time, half seas over, and might very likely have been thus exposed by her master for the sake of frightening her into better behavior. But, if such had been the purpose, the failure of the experiment was complete; for, when she saw that not a single bid was made for such a sinner, she exclaimed, with a prodigiously broad leer of satisfaction, "Nobody want dis ole nigger? Well, I goes back to massa."

For piety and church-going the negroes are as remarkable as the Charlestonians themselves. They like to sing psalms and to deliver to each other the solemn word of exhortation. Their labor in prayer resembles the wrestling of Jacob with the angel; though, in this exercise, they sometimes get themselves on the hip. Their masters and mistresses, however, I am sorry to say, are in the habit of making the observation, that a negro's Sunday faith has but a loose connection with his week-day conduct. Moved, myself, one Sunday evening, to sit under colored preaching, I accepted the invitation of a friend to visit one of the conventicles attended exclusively by negroes. On entering the large and commodious building, we were politely shown up the broad aisle to a seat directly in front of the pulpit, it being the chief seat in the synagogue, and one expressly reserved for white folks. Thereupon the wink was tipped to the sable sexton, who was made to understand that, inasmuch as I was a distinguished gentleman from New York city, the performers in Divine service would be expected to do their best. At length, after a tolerably long pause of preparation, a venerable negro was called up by the clergyman to open the service with prayer. This he did with not a little solemnity, not forgetting, at the close of the exercise, to intercede expressly in behalf of the "gemman present from York." The prayer ended, a devout old negro, called Pete, immediately struck up the hymn beginning, "I'm bound for de kingdom." But old Pete had, apparently, forgotten, in his zeal, the presence of the eminent gentleman from New York, and had to be snubbed by the sexton.

"Stop dat, you nigger!" quickly exclaimed the official, looking, at the same time, sharply at the singer's face, and then, after a pause, pointing upward, he called out, authoritatively: "Choir, sing 'Vital spark.'"

The singing was not bad; the tone of voice being pure, and the chief deficiency consisting in the lack of expression. All the other exercises, likewise, were done decently and in order.

From the negro, whether under the sounding board of the conventicle, or the hammer of the auctioneer, to Powers, the sculptor, may seem a pretty long stride; but the statue of Mr. Calhoun, by this great American bust maker, stands in the old State House, at but a short distance from either the meeting house, or the slave market. With a disposition to speak well of native art, I cannot, however, attribute to this statue of the distinguished Carolinian any high degree of merit beyond that of possessing a good head. Unfortunately, the marble, too, has the fault of being the least bit smutty at the tip of the nose, and suggests the homely idea of snuff-taking. The body is encumbered by the drapery, which, though wrought with very great pains, seems to be heavy with the water of the wet garments after which it must have been modelled. The three folds on the left shoulder are particularly stiff and monotonous. The figure, represented as stepping forward, is impeded, in so doing, by two supports, one on either side.—The left arm is elevated awkwardly, to hold a scroll bearing an inscription, which, at a little distance, looks as though it were done in red chalk, and produces rather a burlesque effect than otherwise. But the weakest points in the statue are the hands and arms which look still weaker when contrasted with the remarkable strength and boldness of the head. It was a pity, indeed, to impair the effect of so excellent a bust by adding a body to it.

Before leaving Charleston, I did not fail to take à look at its environs. On a bright, sunny afternoon, the soft southwest wind gently blowing, I was driven out by a friend to his farm, situated a few miles out of town. The rather quiet landscape was made attractive by numerous liveoaks, with sturdy, broadly spreading branches, by tall, dark-leafed magnolias, and by the graceful wild oranges, all being evergreens. Some of these trees were draped with grapevines climbing to their summits; and the hedges were green with the Cherokee rose, and the yellow jessamine. In a stroll through the gardens of a farmhouse, I gathered a nosegay of fragrant violets, snowdrops, jonquils, and Christmas berries, which, brought home, filled my apartment for hours with a sweet, summer perfume.

But the most pleasing feature of the scenery which came within my observation, on this excursion, was an avenue, or, rather, a couple of avenues, of live oaks of unusual size and beauty. The trees being fully grown, the crooked branches stretched themselves high in the air, numerous as the masts in the crowded seaport, and strong enough to supply the joints and knees of the proudest ships of war. They stretched high overhead, and apparently halfway to heaven, until gradually lost in the tapering twigs, and evergreen leaves, and gracefully pendent mosses. The stems had the strength of the columns of some great temple in Thebes or Palmyra. And yet, I was told that these monarchs of the plain had scarcely yet attained their threescore years and ten. When the old men of Charleston were in their cradles, these oaks were tiny acorns, such as I trod under foot as I walked thoughtfully in the vast, checkered shade of these green avenues. So vigorous and rapid is the growth of vegetable forms in this clime of the sun.

On returning from the country, I drove through the Mount Auburn of Charleston, called, from the beautiful trees interspersed through it, the Magnolia Cemetery. But, entertaining always a decided disposition to keep out of places of this sort as long as may be, I was scarcely in the mood to do justice to this promenade among the graves. As it was, the situation seemed to me little better than a collection of low sandhills, the monotony of which was varied, after the manner of the Chinese, by a few pools of standing water. The principal monuments, as is generally the case in cemeteries, had a look of more or less vain ostentation about them; their proportions being rarely good, and the carving being almost always tawdry. The simplest forms, and lines of ornament, certainly, sympathize best with heartfelt grief; and we generally raise the monument to ourselves, rather than to the dead, whenever we overdo it. Some new tombs in the Egyptian style were pointed out to me as particularly "nice;" one of them having a glass door which allowed all curious persons to look in, and see the coffins. But, thinking the sight could not possibly prove entertaining, I drove out of the grounds at as fast a walk as the regulations of the place would admit of.

Returning to town, we passed along the Battery, the principal promenade of the Charlestonians, and a truly beautiful one. Two rivers flow past it into the bay, which here spreads out to view a pleasant expanse of waters. Almost entirely landlocked, the Palmetto Islands bound it on the south; to the eastward project into the water the two salient points of Forts Sumter and Moultrie; while in the west, when I first saw it, lay diffused over all the beautiful tints of the sunset. And, night after night, as I returned to the Battery at that hour, the sky was ever aglow with the same hues of purple and salmon color, of saffron, rose, and green. On the first evening, too, the full moon, rising above the eastern horizon, scattered innumerable sparkling points of light in a line across the dancing waves, laying a necklace of diamonds on the bosom of the bay. A little later in the year, all the fashion of Charleston will be met, at the hour of twilight, promenading on this smoothly laid sea wall. Nightly the cool breeze from the water fans them, and refreshes their languid spirits, when May-day introduces the season of hot weather. And hence has grown up the proverb, that the Charlestonians live but during two months of the year—in February, for the sake of the races, and in May, for that of the promenade upon the Battery.

WITH pleasant regrets I took my leave of Charleston, and, passing the long Palmetto Islands, saluted once more the open, broad Atlantic. As the sun came up higher, its rays, agreeably tempered by a slight haze in the air, made for us a summer sea in February. And such the sea remained the livelong day; a soft southwest breeze just raising a ripple over the azure expanse, and the bosom of the ocean only so much heaving as when it is most at rest. It was but mere pastime for the white sea-gulls to follow us on lazily flapping wings; often resting poised in the air, now dipping, for a moment, in the ship's white wake of foam, and then alighting gracefully upon their watery nests, to be rocked asleep by the gently rolling waves, as from the branches of trees the birds' nests hang swinging in the summer winds.

HARPER'S WEEKLY
A JOURNAL OF CIVILIZATION

Vol. V.—No. 227.]   NEW YORK, SATURDAY, MAY 4, 1861.   [SINGLE COPIES SIX CENTS. / $2 50 PER YEAR IN ADVANCE.

Entered according to Act of Congress, in the Year 1861, by Harper & Brothers, in the Clerk's office of the District Court for the Southern District of New York.

THE HOUSETOPS IN CHARLESTON DURING THE BOMBARDMENT OF SUMTER.

"The Housetops in Charleston During the Bombardment of Sumter."
Harper's Weekly 5, no. 227 (May 4, 1861), title page. Courtesy of Irvin
Department of Rare Books and Special Collections, Thomas Cooper
Library, University of South Carolina, Columbia.

Anna C. Brackett (1861)

"Charleston, South Carolina 1861"

Anna Callender Brackett (1836–1911) was the daughter of a Boston dry goods merchant. She attended Boston schools and Abbott's Academy at Andover before she graduated in 1856 from the State Normal School (now Farmington State College) at Framingham, Massachusetts. She taught in Farmington schools, then served as assistant principal in Massachusetts schools. In 1860, she was recruited to Charleston as teacher and vice-principal at Girls' High and Normal School. Charlestonians, who traditionally sent their children north to be educated, had been long advocating for southern education for their youth. From the 1850s, Christopher Memminger had been promoting a public education system with southerners as teachers, and with the further hope of "bringing together the children of rich and poor" in the same classroom. Toward the end of the decade, northern educators trained in the latest pedagogical methods were recruited to Charleston to train southern teachers to take over future classrooms. In 1859, Girls' High and Normal School (later renamed Memminger School) opened in a handsome building at the corner of Beaufain and St. Philip streets as a training school for (white) southern women.

On Christmas Eve, 1860, state leaders signed the "Declaration of the Immediate Causes Which Induce and Justify the Secession of South Carolina from the Federal Union," soon followed by ten states. Charleston became a closed city. The northern teachers and administrators recruited to town remained at their posts until the firing on Fort Sumter in 1861, then most departed for the North, leaving their pupils in native hands: newly educated graduates of Girls' High and Normal School. Anna Brackett stayed longer. Finally forced to flee herself, she was the last northerner to leave town before the blockade was established. She later wrote a stunning article for *Harper's*, testament to the last days of antebellum Charleston.

In St. Louis in 1863, at the age of twenty-five, Brackett was the first woman in the United States to be appointed principal of a secondary school. She became

Taken from *Harper's New Monthly* 88, no. 528 (May 1894): 941–51.

an educational theorist and ardent feminist, who wrote and lectured on women's rights to equal education and employment opportunities. She published innumerable books and wrote for magazines and newspapers. In 1870 she and her lifelong domestic partner, Ida Mitchell Eliot, opened a prominent private girls' school at 9 West Fifty-first Street in New York City, which operated for decades. They adopted two daughters in the 1870s

SOURCES

James, Edward T., ed. *Notable American Women, 1607-1950: A Biographical Dictionary.* Vol.1. Cambridge: Harvard University Press, 1971.

Jennings, Laylon Wayne. "Education for Community: C. G. Memminger and the Origination of Common Schools in Antebellum Charleston." *South Carolina Historical Magazine* 83, no. 2 (April 1982): 99–115.

Obituary. "Miss Anna C. Brackett Dead." *New York Times.* March 19, 1911.

Turnbull, L. Minerva. "The Southern Educational Revolt." *William and Mary Quarterly Historical Magazine,* 2nd ser., vol. 14, no. 1 (January 1934): 60–76.

"CHARLESTON, SOUTH CAROLINA 1861"

PERHAPS there are no two States which stand more as representatives of their two sections than Massachusetts and South Carolina. In the history of the country they have never been silent, and they have spoken with no uncertain sound. Though they have often been bitterly opposed, yet in their sturdy and uncompromising allegiance to what each has believed to be the right way of acting they have found certain sympathy with each other, and a certain large measure of mutual respect. Each has felt that in the other she had a foeman worthy of her steel when in opposition and when in conjunction a friend not to be misunderstood or distrusted. In the same way it might be said that their two largest cities are worthy antagonists, and now heartily respected friends. Boston is Massachusetts boiled down, and Charleston may be spoken of as a very strong decoction of South Carolina. Both think what they must, and say what they think. The people of both have a very strong attachment for and a hearty pride in their city, and an injury to it, an insult aimed at it, or even a humorous remark bearing on any of its peculiarities, is sure to call to their feet a host of indignant defenders.

More than all others, these are the feminine cities of the Union, being all through and everywhere just what they are anywhere, and, like women, arousing a chivalric love. Both have a glorious past and a living present, such as in kind and intensity of personal life can scarce be easily found elsewhere—at any rate in the

East, or in the original thirteen colonies. There is among their merchants a fine sense of honor, which holds itself high for the sake of the city as well as from personal motives, and in social life an aristocracy not based upon wealth. Both have a line of noble names, the very possession of which is a presumption of breeding and refinement. Both are the holders of the kind of firmness that begins with "o," and are ready to maintain their opinion with any and all arms. Both have strongly marked peculiarities in their English, and hold to these as firmly as to any other characteristic. They are noble and consistent members of the great family of cities, standing proudly side by side in spite of their well-marked differences, and acting as constant foils to the beauty of each other. While seeming to be opposed, they understand each other, and hold alike to the old motto concerning the obligations resting on real nobility.

In the old times it was especially Boston that hated slavery, and it was Charleston, above all other cities, that hated antislavery. It has always been the boast of Boston that her public schools were absolutely perfect, and one would hardly have expected that any resemblance could be found to them, or to the spirit which runs through them, in the public schools of Charleston, differing as did the two cities for so long in the very principles of their existence. But there is a story about the public schools of Charleston before the war which is worth telling, and worthy of the noble city, and which shall not go untold so long as I, who was a part of it, do not forget the duty of recognizing noble deeds.

It was easy in Boston to carry on the schools. They were a part of the tradition of the city, and it took no great amount of courage to support and defend them. They were filled by the children of rich and poor alike, and it was the boast of the city that the child of the mechanic sat side by side with the children of the richest and noblest families. To be a teacher had always been to be respected, if not honored, and there was no thought of accepting charity in the children who enjoyed their advantages. This was generally the case in the Northern States. But in the South it was different. The public schools were supposed to be only for those who could not afford to pay for education, and consequently they had many of the characteristics of charity schools. The teaching in them was poor and far behind the times, and none of the families of breeding ever thought of sending their children to them. These were educated in small private schools, or at home under tutors and governesses, or were sent North. But about the year 1857 some of the best men in Charleston became dissatisfied with this state of things, and determined to see if it could not be bettered. They studied the ways of other cities, and the outcome of the movement was the building, of three large school-houses after the New York plans, having each one accommodations for primary and grammar departments, and of one noble house of different idea, to be called the

Girls' High and Normal School. They meant to have good schools, and they were determined to have good teachers, and in time to have them educated in their own city. The men who initiated the movement and who gave it their personal attention, and not merely the weight of their names, were the men who should begin such enterprises. They were a power in the community, and commanded universal respect and confidence. They made up their minds that as to schools they must learn of the North, and they faced the necessity of the situation with a noble courage. Their ultimate purpose was to supply their city with good schools, taught by native teachers, and they hesitated at no sacrifice of their life—long prejudices to attain their end. They must have large and convenient houses. They built them, sparing no expense and no trouble to make them as good as any. They needed teachers in line with the best theories and familiar with the most tested practice of the profession. They took them from the principals of New York and Providence grammar-schools. They demanded the best, and they offered those men and women salaries sufficient to draw them from their positions in those two cities, and to make the question of their acceptance of the offers only a matter of time. They made these schools free to all the children of the city, and bought the books which were to be used. They furnished the rooms with every-thing that could make them attractive and healthful. They sought in the city for the best teachers, men and women, that they could find, and made them assistants to the Northern principals, to learn of and to be trained in their ways; and when all this had been done they put their own children, not only boys, but girls, into these public free schools, side by side with any who might choose to come. Never was there a nobler instance of entire singleness of purpose and of the sacrifice of preconceived opinions to conviction. It seems worth while to give the names of the Commissioners for the year 1860 as a testimony. Some of the names will be easily recognized as familiar: C. G. Memminger, chairman;* William C. Bee; W. J. Bennett; G. P. Bryan; George Buist; W. G. De Saussure; C. M. Furman; William Jervey; Hon. A. G. Magrath; Hon. W. A. Pringle; F. Richards; John Russell; E. Montague Grimke, secretary.[†]

*Christopher G. Memminger (1803–1888), state legislator and partner in the law firm Memminger & Jervey. He would later serve as Confederate Secretary of the Treasury.

[†]William C. Bee (d. 1881), rice factor, owner of Wm. C. Bee, Factor and Commissions; Washington Jefferson Bennett (1808–1874) had succeeded his father, Thomas Bennett, Jr. in operating the family mills; "G.P. Bryan" was likely George Seabrook Bryan (1809–1905), lawyer and federal judge; George Lamb Buist (1838–1907) was admitted to the bar in 1860; Wilmot G. De Saussure (1822–1886), a lawyer who served in the state legislature; Charles Manning Furman (1797–1872), president of the Bank of South Carolina, the son of Rev. Richard Furman (1755–1825), Baptist leader for whom Furman University was named;

Of the building for the Girls' High and Normal School something more should be said. Situated in St. Philip Street, a square, three-story building with a crowning dome, it attracted the eye of whoever passed that way. Below there were ward-robes, and a large room for the use of the girls at recesses in stormy weather. The second story was filled by a hall and class-rooms leading therefrom, while above was a still larger hall, to which the increased size of the school drove the daily sessions in the second year of its life. The glory of the place, however, was the garden in the midst of which it was set, and which, surrounded by a high stone wall, gave perfect freedom and seclusion to the pupils. This garden was overflowing with all sorts of roses and flowering plants, was laid out with gravelled walks, and well cared for by the Irish janitor, who had a little house on the premises.

Dan was very proud of the garden and his care of it, though he used often to assure us that, for real beauty, now, there was no place like Ireland, adding, "And sure if ye were there now, I could show yez a spot where this blessed minute ye could stand knee-deep in clover." In the second story, and fronting this garden, was a piazza two stories in height, with lofty pillars reaching to the roof—a pleasanter spot than which, during the heats of the early summer, I have never found.

For this school, in which was the hope of the entire system, the teachers were all selected from the Northern States—the most convincing proof, if anything further were needed, of the noble courage and fearlessness of purpose which characterized every act of the Board of Commissioners. The principal was a teacher of long experience in the public schools of Boston, a native of New Hampshire;* two of the assistants were Massachusetts born and bred, and one came from Pennsylvania. To show how conservative and wise were the board, it may be stated that of the seventy-seven teachers in all the public schools, only nine were of Northern birth and home. But in the Normal School, where the future teachers were to be trained, they were all Northern, that the very best and most modern work might be done there. Of those three women, coming thus into a new home and a strange city, I was one, and am therefore telling what I know and saw.

William Jervey (1810–1870), law partner in Memminger & Jervey; Andrew Gordon Magrath (1813–1893), U.S. judge for South Carolina from 1856; William Alston Pringle (1803–1884), attorney and recorder of the city from 1858; Frederick Richards (1817–1875), partner in Edgerton, Richards & Co., Drapers & Tailors; John Russell (1812–1871), proprietor of Russell's Bookstore on King Street; and Edward Montague Grimke (1832–1895), secretary of Girls' High and Normal School.

*Frederick Adolphus Sawyer (1822–1891), a graduate of Harvard, taught in Massachusetts, Maine, and New Hampshire until 1859, when he became principal of the school. He fled north during the war but afterward, he returned and was active in Reconstruction.

It was a fresh experience, the voyage thither in one of the beautiful steamers which then ran between Charleston and the Northern cities—the Massachusetts and the South Carolina. But stranger to our Northern eyes was Charleston itself, with the cross on old St. Michael's rising high above it as the steamer came in view of the garden-loving city. The harbor is bad, like those of all the sand-line cities; and the steamers, though drawing at the utmost only sixteen feet, were often obliged to lie outside waiting for high water, and had always to time their departures by the almanac. But, once within the bars and on shore, there were no bars in the welcome of the people. Not only by our personal friends, but by all connected with the schools, were we made to feel at home. The exquisite breeding of the city asserted itself, and at once took us, though from an alien land and a different civilization, into its charmed circle. The commissioners who had invited us there spared no pains to make our stay pleasant, making us welcome to their homes as well as to those of all the best people in the city. Courtesies of all kinds were offered to us. How beautiful and strange it all was—the rides about the country, where, while our Northern homes were still shivering in frost and snow, the Cherokee rose spread its white petals along the dusty roads, and we picked the yellow jasmine where the gray moss hung from the live-oaks! Camellias blossomed unafraid in the open air, and our desks at school were beautiful with them and magnolia blooms, or weighted with daintily arranged baskets of the purple or the large lemon figs which our girls had picked as they came to school from before their doors. The memory even now lies in my mind, sweet and still, persistent as the odor of orange blossoms from the Charleston trees. The orange-tree is not safe in that latitude; a sudden frost might stifle its life; but they were sometimes planted, and were of course found in conservatories or raised in parlors.

It was with a curious interest that we studied the buildings and customs of the town, so different in every way from those of our Northern homes. The long, airy houses with their three stories of piazzas, the negro quarters in the yards, often much larger and more imposing than the dwelling of the master and mistress, swarming with happy and careless life, as the many servants passed to and fro between house and quarters; and the little darkies of all ages were free to play and tumble to their hearts' content, unless, indeed, a sweet-voiced call came from the rear of the piazza, "George Washington and Columbus, come notice Miss Elvira" followed by the rush of perhaps half a dozen small darkies of varying ages, all eager to play with and care for the heiress of the house and of them. And the loving and reverent care which they did take of the little Elvira was beautiful to see! Then the long stretch of the yard, with its pump in the middle, where a buxom serving-maid was filling her pails of water, which came into the house afterwards, one poised on her stately head, while she carried two in her hands; the queer wooden shutters, and the bewildering arrangement of the numbers of the houses on the street, where it was said that every citizen, if he moved, carried his number with him as a part of his personal property; the inevitable negro everywhere, waiting on and serving us at every turn; the beautiful gardens, whose high gates opened mysteriously and swiftly by invisible hands at the appeal of the loud-echoing bell. While one negro led us up the path, another opened the front door, a third escorted us to the drawing-room, while a fourth announced our arrival to the gracious mistress, and a fifth chubby little girl or boy appeared before we were fairly seated with a tray of cooling drink! And the procession of servants from the kitchen when dinner was in course of serving, one servant for each dish, so that everything was smoking hot, though it had come some distance in the open air! The queer and fascinating dialect of the negroes, and the altogether fascinating accent of the Charlestonians, the flare and live sighlike breath of the pitch-pine knots in the fireplace in the evening or the early morning, when the servant who came to make our fire entertained us all the time of her stay by her remarks, and never quitted the room—which she did half a dozen times during the process—leaving us in doubt as to what her errand might be, but announcing encouragingly each time, as she opened the door and disappeared, "Now I'm going for the matches," "Now I'm going for to fetch the dust-pan," etc. All was new, and full of interest and suggestion.

The regulations under which it was considered necessary to keep the colored population were to us new and interesting. The law at that time forbade their being taught to read. A colored woman could not wear a veil in the street, nor were two negroes allowed to walk arm in arm except at funerals. A curious and suggestive thing happened, therefore. Every negro funeral was largely attended, and the corpse was sure to be followed to the grave by an imposing line of mourners, all walking arm in arm. One very marked figure in the city was the old man at the ladies' entrance of the Charleston Hotel. I think I have never seen a man who had more the appearance of being somebody's grandfather than this kindly old Marcus. One day he had disappeared, and there was no one at the door. After long and futile search for him, a messenger brought word that he wanted the loan of money in order to return, and the mystery was finally solved by the discovery that he could not come not because he had bought either oxen or land or married a wife, but for the simple reason that, having become more than specially interested in his one only pastime of gambling the night before, he had, in a fit of noble rage at his persistent ill luck, rashly hazarded his clothes—and lost the game. A contribution from his friends at the hotel soon restored him, clothed and in his right mind, which was a very positive one. There was a tradition current that one evening, as a party of lately arrived Northerners were having a pleasant

conversation in the parlor somewhat late, they were surprised by the appearance
of Marcus, who gravely informed them that he had come to sweep the parlors,
and that "our folks in dis house always goes to bed by half past ten, sah !" The
intimation was humbly heeded. Of course no one could resist the law of the hotel
when the decisions were handed down from such a height.

Old St. Michael's Church was well worth a visit, with its tiled aisles and square
pews. In its steeple, 193 feet in height, were the chimes which marked the quarters
of the hour, and here too were rung, morning and evening, the bells which regulated the negroes in their perambulations. In winter the evening bells ring from
quarter of six to six, and for a quarter of an hour before nine. This last was called
the "last bell-ringing," and after it had ceased to sound any unfortunate negro
found in the streets, unless he could show a pass from his master, was summarily
deposited in the guard-house for the remainder of the night. During the ringing
of the last bell two men regularly performed on the fife and drum on the corner
opposite where the guard-house was situated, and the negroes who came out to
listen to the music dispersed in quick time as the last tap was given the drum, and
the last stroke of the bell lingered in the air. The watchman in the tower called the
hour, and all relapsed into silence again. I give a literal copy of one of these passes:

"CHARLESTON, March 12, 1855.
Paris has permission to pass from my residence in Beaufain St., near Rutledge,
to the corner of Vanderhorst's wharf and East Berry [sic], and from thence
back again to my residence, before drum-beat in the morning, for one month.
JAS. B. CAMPBELL.
T. L. Hutchinson, Mayor."

One of the most interesting places was the church of Rev. J. L. Girardeau,
a very large building, capable of seating perhaps fourteen hundred persons.* In
the morning the lower floor was occupied by the white congregation, and the
negroes, as in the other churches, sat in the galleries, but in the afternoon the
negroes filled the body of the house, the whites being seated only at the sides and

---

*Rev. John Lafayette Girardeau (1825–1898) had become famous for his dynamic preaching
to an integrated congregation. In 1850, a meeting house was built on Anson Street for the exclusive use of slaves. During 1858 and 1859, the church experienced a revival. They moved to
a new church building at Meeting and Calhoun streets, which the black membership named
"Zion." From 1859 through 1861, Girardeau preached to over fifteen hundred weekly. From
thirty-six black members, church membership expanded to over six hundred by the time
of the Civil War (Powers, *Black Charlestonians*, 15, 209; PCA Historical Center, Archives
and Manuscript Repository for the Continuing Presbyterian Church, www.pcahistory.org/
periodicals/spr/bios/girardeau.html [accessed August 1, 2013]).

in the galleries. To one not accustomed to the sight, the church then presented a striking appearance, and we had an opportunity of seeing all shades and varieties of color, in both complexion and dress. The old and staid negro women generally wore bright handkerchiefs twisted around the head, sometimes with the addition, though not the amendment, of a bonnet perched upon the top thereof, crown uppermost; but the younger and gayer portion of the community wore bonnets of all styles, from the most fashionable to the most obsolete. The only music was by the negroes, and it was really worth hearing. As of course they could not read, the hymn was retailed, two lines at a time, by the minister, who usually began the singing, and it welled out refreshingly strong and true. Before the services commenced the audience sometimes struck up a voluntary, greeting the ear as we entered in the form of some grand old tune sung by the assembled throng. The courtesy which surrendered the main part of the church to the negroes for half the time was only one out of many customs in the city which testified to the general kind feeling existing between master and slave, where true nobility asserted itself in relation to inferiors as well as to equals. In the homes of Charleston the Negroes were treated like a sort of children of the household, and this because of a real affection.

The strength of family feeling on the part of the negroes was often queerly put, as thus: "Law sakes! Balaam Preston Hamilton Smith," a venerable old Negro was heard to exclaim to a young man who was understood to be thinking of marrying, "don't say you'd go fur to 'liberate fur to take up wid any middlin' set. If you want a wife, you'd better marry into de Middleton family. De Middletons is a mighty good family. Hm! De Roses is 'spectable too; but jes look at me! I married into de Middleton family!"

The closeness of the relation was amusingly illustrated by an incident which occurred in school when we insisted that certain words should be pronounced according to authority, and not in the way in which the girls had been accustomed to sound them. "But," they said, "you know we grow up with the negroes, they take care of us, and we hear them talk all the time. Of course we can't help catching some of their ways of talking. It sounds all right to us." They were told that if they could find in any dictionary the least authority for the pronunciation dear to them, there would be no objection to it; that we were only trying to give them the best, and that it was not for any notion of ours that we insisted. "But," they said, quickly and sadly, "the dictionaries are all Northern dictionaries!" and so the matter came to an end. For it was by no means nothing but flowers and fruit from their gardens that these Southern maidens were in the habit of bringing to us, their Northern teachers; they brought to our aid every morning the sweetest docility, the greatest eagerness to learn, and the most perfect breeding. Even in the days after the *Star of the West* had been fired on, and the whole city was full of devotion to the Palmetto State and of denunciations of the North and of the people there; when for a Northern woman it was sometimes difficult to be calm; when we could neither listen to the prayers offered from the pulpits nor read the newspapers; when threatening anonymous letters came to our hand, and we grew tired with the constant strain and uncertainty—even then, and perhaps even more than before, to cross the threshold of that school-room was to pass at-once into an atmosphere of peace and unfailing courtesy. Those girls came from homes that were full of bitter feeling and opposition to the North, but there was never an ungentle look or word from them to their Northern teachers. The school-room was an asylum, a safe and sure place for us; and what this meant of good-breeding and loyalty is comprehensible perhaps only to those who have spent their lives in contact with young and warm-hearted girls. There is nothing but sweet and dear memories of those girls, light-hearted and happy then, but with heavy clouds of war and trouble hanging over them—war and trouble which in more than one instance broke up happy homes, and struck down at their sides the brothers and the friends whom they so loved. I have before me now a card on which the girls of the first class wrote their names together for me, and to look it over is to recall much of sadness, though much of devotion, faithfulness, and high courage. The planning of this work is exquisitely neat, as was all the work that they did. Here are the names of two sisters, who afterwards became teachers in our places when we came away. Underneath, a name that recalls all gentleness and grace; next it, that of a girl whose parents had been born in New England, and who showed it in every fibre. Then comes Sallie, tall and slender, full of dash and fire, and the indescribable charm of the Southern girl, with her haughty, "Who'd stoop to quarrel?" so often said when some difference arose in the class; then Lizzie, with her beautiful dark eyes and her no less beautiful disposition, whose after-life was so full of sadness and sorrow; then the carefully written signature of the girl who took up the teacher's life, drawing her inspiration from what we brought her in those long-past days, and who has become a tower of strength to a new generation in her chosen profession; and then Celia, who, leaving her gracious and luxurious home, gave up her life to caring for the poor and suffering, and died at her post, mourned by the whole city. Sweet and strong they pass before me in memory, the girls of that first class, with the happy days in which we lived together in the close relation of teacher and taught. They had never before been in a large school, and its life and regulations were new and striking to them. They grew mentally like plants given a new sun and soil, and the work to the educator was beyond measure delightful, yielding a rich harvest.

We had visitors, men and women, to all of whom our work was of the greatest interest, and to whom it was a comparative novelty to be allowed to visit a school, and to see the work going on. I was greatly puzzled at first by the saying, which I heard often, that they had come to "see the system," as if we had some patent method of conveying information and of training, which had to be applied in some well-defined manner. I have since learned that this idea is not peculiar to the South.

Not different from the cordiality with which we were welcomed to the city homes was the thoughtful kindness which provided for our Christmas holidays. To see the rice plantation, with its long avenue of live-oaks, and the noble mansion standing on the wide lawn; to go over the store-house, where were kept goods of all kinds ready to be distributed to the field hands, the piles of dress goods and provisions, and all presided over by the gracious mistress of the house; to watch the men laborers, tall and brawny, splendid animals, with their fully developed muscles, and their rows of perfect white teeth, and the not-so-fortunate negro women who also toiled in the rice-fields, bent and knotted with the labor; to see the great supper provided for them on Christmas eve, and to listen to their rejoicing and songs—all this was a great pleasure and a great lesson.

But it all was to pass away. The Democratic Convention in April, 1860, to which we devoted all our spare time, was a highly interesting and significant event.* Political meetings grew more common and more enthusiastic. Then followed the election of President Lincoln, and the immediate resignation of the Federal judge, one of our commissioners, the Hon. A. G. Magrath, and of the district attorney.† The streets bloomed with palmetto flags, and with a great variety of mottoes, and the air grew more and more charged with electrical feeling. The banks all suspended November 30, 1860.

---

*The Democratic Convention was held at Institute Hall in Charleston on April 23 to May 3, 1860, but was torn apart by sectionalism within the Democratic Party as delegates were split over the issue of slavery. Failure to nominate a candidate required the convention to be in Baltimore in June.

†On November 7, 1860, Andrew Gordon Magrath (1813-1893), U.S. judge for South Carolina and one of the strongest advocates of secession, was presiding over a session of the grand jury in a Charleston courtroom when telegrams arrived confirming the election of Lincoln the day before. Robert Gourdin, another leading advocate of secession, was serving as foreman in the same court. Gourdin declined to continue with any proceedings of the federal government. Magrath's response was to "divest himself of his judicial robes and resign his office," thereby becoming the first paid federal official to do so. These resignations were immediately followed by those of James Conner (1829–1883), U.S. district attorney, and the court clerk.

The convention met December 16th, and the act of secession was passed on
the 20th, between one and two o'clock.* The firing of guns and the ringing of
bells announced the fact to the eager populace, and we began to live in a scene of
the wildest excitement—a double- distilled Fourth of July. Business was at once
suspended, and stores were closed. The chimes of old St. Michael's rang merrily
at intervals all the afternoon. Fire companies of both colors paraded the streets,
noisily jingling their bells, and one continually met members of the Vigilant
Rifles, the Zouaves, the Washington Light-Infantry, or some other of the many
companies, hurrying in a state of great excitement to their headquarters. Boys
in the street shouted, "Hurrah! Out of the Union!" with all the strength of their
lungs; and the negroes, who, on hearing any unusual noise always made their
appearance at all the gates, stood in groups at every passage-way. The young men
devoted themselves to drinking the health of the State, and exhibited indubitable
evidence of having done so as they walked or drove furiously along. On Meeting
and King streets in several places the sidewalks were covered with the remains of
Indian crackers and the whole air was redolent of gun-powder.

The excitement by no means came to an end as the day wore to its close, with
a rosy sunset over the rippling waters of the Ashley, and when the twilight had
died away an illumination of the principal business streets by means of blazing
tar-barrels produced a strong and bodeful light. Meeting Street, from above the
Charleston Hotel to below Institute or "Secession" Hall, was ablaze with burning
tar, which overflowed so that sometimes the whole width of the street was aflame.
Ladies as well as gentlemen crowded Secession Hall at an early hour. About half
the floor was reserved for members of the convention and the Legislature, the remainder being filled with an excited crowd of men. The meeting was opened with
a prayer, short but comprehensive, acknowledging the possibility of suffering and
privation, but asking, after that was passed, that their sails might whiten every sea,
and their agriculture and commerce be greatly prospered. The ordinance of secession was then handed to the president,† and by him read from a large parchment
with the seal of the State hanging therefrom. At its close tumultuous applause

*The Democratic Convention reopened in Columbia on December 16, 1860. However, an
alleged outbreak of smallpox caused delegates to flee to Charleston and reconvene on Broad
Street at St. Andrew's Hall, where the Ordinance of Secession passed on December 20. Delegates, with a celebratory throng of representatives and citizens, then paraded down Broad
Street to Institute Hall, where the ordinance was signed later that same day. On December
26, 1860, U.S. Major Robert Anderson secretly moved his small command at Fort Moultrie
to Fort Sumter, hoping to better control Charleston Harbor.
†David Flavel Jamison (1810–1864), lawyer, planter, jurist, was president of the Secession
Convention.

shook the building, and the delegates, called in the order of their districts, were summoned to affix their names. The table upon which the signing was done was that upon which the ratification of the Federal Constitution had been signed. The whole evening there was a constant discharge of fireworks, crackers, and fire-arms in the street below, so that during the prayer it was at times impossible to hear what was being said. Bands of music passed at intervals, and the crowd outside shouted and cheered without intermission.

At last the signing was over, and the president, taking up the parchment amid profound silence, said, "The ordinance of secession has been signed and ratified, and I proclaim the State of South Carolina to be an independent commonwealth." This was the signal for an outburst of enthusiasm such as is not often witnessed. Every one rose to his feet, and all broke forth into tumultuous and ever-renewed cheering. Handkerchiefs waved, hats were swung round and wildly tossed into the air, or they were elevated on canes, swords, or muskets, and spun round and round. The act of secession was then read to the crowd on the outside of the building, who greeted it with their shouts. The two palmetto-trees which stood on either side of the platform were despoiled of their leaves by the audience as mementos of the occasion, and the meeting slowly dispersed.

It was in the assembly-room of the old school-house, early on the morning of January 9, 1861, as I sat at the desk bending over my books preparing for the day's work, that I heard the report of the first gun which was fired at the *Star of the West,* * and lifted my head to listen, with a great fear at my heart, and an effort to persuade myself that the sounds were only the effect of my excited imagination as they came again and again. On the morning of April 12th I was twenty miles away, in one of the beautiful homes where we had been so often welcome guests, and on coming down to breakfast found anxious faces and much excitement among the servants, who reported that they had heard firing all the night in the direction of Charleston.† We ate breakfast almost in silence, our only thought being whether we could get to the city that day; and after the meal was over stood

---

*Gov. Francis W. Pickens (1805–1869) had ordered Maj. Peter Fayssoux Stevens (1830–1910), superintendent of the Citadel, with a detachment of Citadel cadets to man a battery on Morris Island. They had orders to fire on any merchant vessel flying the U.S. flag that attempted to enter Charleston Harbor. When President Buchanan sent a civilian steamship, the *Star of the West*, to reinforce Maj. Anderson and his garrison on Fort Sumter, cadets fired on the supply ship. Subsequently, the mission was aborted and the ship fled the harbor for New York.

†President Lincoln, newly in office, had notified Gov. Pickens that he was sending reinforcements to Fort Sumter. This resulted in an ultimatum by the Confederacy that Maj. Anderson evacuate and surrender the fort. Anderson refused, and on April 12, 1861, at 4:30 a.m., Confederates fired on Fort Sumter from artillery batteries surrounding the harbor.

on the broad piazza waiting till the big strong farm wagon could be arranged to take us to the railroad station. At last it appeared.

The driver went to the kitchen for a last word, and detailed one of the house-servants who stood looking on to stand in front of the horses till he should return. The latter, attracted by the play of two children, turned away to watch them; some sudden noise startled the horses, and away they went, big wagon and all, in a mad run round and round over the great field, in and out among out-houses, sheds, and trees, while we stood helplessly looking on, and heard the sound of the guns. It seemed a long time before they made for the opposite sides of a tree, which they saw stood directly in their way, and smashing the pole of the wagon on its trunk, were brought to a standstill. There was the wagon hopelessly ruined, so far as any journey in it for that day was concerned, dripping as to its back end with broken eggs; there was the terrified negro, tears streaming down his face, and crying out, "Oh, I only looked away from dose horses one minute, and now I have done more harm dan I can pay for all my life long!" And again and again we heard the sound of the far-off guns. The brother of one of our company was on duty at one of the forts; the families of all of them were there whence came the ominous sound.

But there was absolutely nothing to do on that isolated plantation but to sit still or pace up and down while the servants hunted for some other vehicle in sufficient order to be trusted to carry all of us over the roads, floating with the spring rains. They worked at an old carry-all, which they found stored away in a shed, till they thought it safe to trust, and it was some time after dinner before we finally set off for the railroad station miles away. When we reached there in safety, in spite of the ominous groans and creaks of the crazy old carriage in which we sat crowded, the air was full of rumors, but we could hear nothing definite. At last came the train, delayed, and with troops on board, whose number was augmented at several stations where we stopped, to be still farther delayed, and when we were finally landed in a shed on the side of the river opposite Charleston, we found it swarming with citizen soldiery. We crossed the river, and said hasty good-byes. I rushed to my boarding-place, flung down my packages, and hastening through the streets, filled with an excited crowd, reported myself to the principal of the school as being in the city, to be greeted as soon as seen by the exclamation, "By Jove! I knew you'd get here somehow."

The night came and passed, and the sun rose cloudless and bright on one of the April days which are like the June days of New England, but the wind had shifted, and we heard no reports. It was believed that the firing had ceased—why, no one could tell—but at the Battery the smoke still showed that it had not, even though there it was almost impossible to hear the sound.

Let us go thither. Many of the stores have their doors open, but no shutters are unclosed, and only necessary business is transacted. We go down Meeting Street, past Institute or Secession Hall, and remember the scene of the 20th of last December there. Saddled horses stand waiting at the door, and remind us that General Beauregard's office is within.* As we turn down Water Street towards the East Battery the crowd becomes visible, lining the sidewalk. Making our way between the carriages which fill the street, we mount the steps leading to the walk, and taking up our position at the least crowded part, turn our attention to the harbor. The reports come deadened to the ear though one can easily tell whence the shot come by the smoke.

The crowd increases, and is composed of all materials. Women of all ages and ranks of life look eagerly out with spy-glasses and opera-glasses. Children talk and laugh and walk back and forth in the small moving-space as if they were at a public show. Now and then a man in military dress goes hastily past. Grave men talk in groups. Young men smoke and calculate probabilities and compare conflicting reports, and still the guns send forth their deadly missiles, and the light clouds suddenly appearing and hanging over the fort till dispersed by the wind tell of the shells which explode before they reach their destination.

"There goes Stevens again! He gives it to 'em strong!" and a puff of white smoke rises from the iron-clad battery.

"Look! Did you see the bricks fly then from the end of the fort? She struck that time!"

"What is that smoke over Sumter? Isn't it smoke?" and all glasses and eyes are turned in that direction and watch eagerly. It increases in volume and rolls off seaward. What can it be? Is he going to blow up the fort? Is he heating shot? What is it? Still the batteries keep up their continual fire, and Anderson's guns, amidst a cloud of smoke, return with two or three discharges. Suddenly a white cloud rises from Sumter, and a loud report tells of the explosion of some magazine—"Probably a magazine on the roof for some of his barbette guns"—and the firing goes on.

"Look out! Moultrie speaks again!" and another puff of smoke points out the position of that fort, followed by one from the floating battery of the others. We listen and watch.

"I don't believe Anderson is in the fort. He must have gone off in the night and left only a few men. It was a very dark night."

---

*Brigadier Gen. Pierre Toutant Beauregard (1818–1893), the first general officer of the newly formed Confederate States of America, was sent to Charleston in March as commander-in-charge of Confederate forces. He had been a student in Maj. Robert Anderson's artillery class at West Point, and now they stood directly on opposing sides of the conflict.

"See the vessels off there? No, not there; farther along to the right of Sumter. That small one is the *Harriet Lane*."*

"Yes, I can see them plain with the naked eye. Ain't they going to do anything? The large one has hauled off."

"No; they are still."

"Look! Can you see those little boats? Three little boats a hundred yards apart. They are certainly coming."

"Yes," said a woman, an opera-glass at her eyes, "the papers this morning said they were to re-enforce with small boats, which were to keep at a great distance from each other." Another, incredulous, says they are nothing but waves, and you can see plenty anywhere like them. "Doubleday is killed," remarks another. "They saw him from Moultrie, lying on top of the ramparts."†

This is set at naught by a small boy, who says, "Look, do you see that mosquito just on the corner of that flag in Sumter?" and a dignified silence follows.

Now the smoke rises over Sumter again, black smoke and curls away, but no other signs of life. We watch, and as we watch it grows blacker and thicker. The fort must be on fire!

"Yes! Can't you see the flame? There at the south angle! You can see it through this glass. Look now!"

The smoke hides all one side of the fort, and the leaping flames leave no room for doubt. They spread till it seems as if the whole fort must be a sheet of flame within and the firing goes on as if nothing had happened, but no signs of life at Fort Sumter. Why doesn't the fleet do something? How can men with blood in their veins idly watch the scene and not lend a helping hand when they have the power? They must be armed vessels! Is Anderson still in the fort? No signal comes from there, and the firing continues, and the shells explode around and within, and the dense black smoke rolls away, and the flames leap round the flag-staff.

"Now you'll see that old flag go down," cries a boy with a spy-glass.

"*That old flag!*"

I listen and watch in mournful silence, and hear the beating of my heart as the flames rise higher and higher. What does it mean? Anderson can't be in the fort! He must be on board the fleet, or they could not stand idly by.

---

*The *Harriet Lane*, a revenue cutter transferred to the U.S. Navy, was sent to relieve the garrison at Fort Sumter. In a standoff, the *Harriet Lane* fired on the steamer *Nashville*, attempting to enter Charleston Harbor without displaying a U.S. flag.

†Captain Abner Doubleday (1819–1893), who had been transferred in 1858 to Fort Moultrie, was now stationed on Ft. Sumter where he was second-in-command to Maj. Robert Anderson. He was not shot or killed. Rumors flew as he was particularly hated by Charlestonians.

"He has probably left slow matches to some of his guns. He means to burn up the fort—to blow it up!"

"Captain Foster intimated that it was undermined," says another.*

Still the flag-staff stands, though the flames are red around it.

"It would be a bad omen if the flag should stand all this fire," says a gentleman at my side as he hands me his glass. I level it and look.

A vessel has dropped anchor just between, and the flag of the Confederate States, fluttering from the fore, completely conceals the staff at Sumter. I move impatiently to the right to get rid of it, and see with throbbing heart the flag still safe, and watch with sickening anxiety.

Another explosion, which scatters the smoke for a while.

"He is blowing up the barracks to prevent the fire from spreading," says one. Can it be that he is still there?

Still the flag waves as of old. The flames die down, and the smoke somewhat clears away, and the shells explode as before, and Major Stevens fires continually.

"It is West Point against West Point to-day," says one.

"Stevens was not at West Point."

"No, but Beauregard was a pupil of Anderson's there."

The tide has turned and is going out, and now the vessels cannot come in.

What does it mean? Still the people pass and repass; the crowd thins a little; they jest idly and remark on the passers, and conversation goes on. Friends meet and greet each other with playful words. Judge Magrath stands in a careless attitude, a red camellia in his button-hole, at the window of one of the houses overlooking the scene. Beauregard passes, observant. Carriages drive by. People begin to leave.

"The flag is down!" A shot has struck the staff and carried it away. "Look! The flag is down!" and an excited crowd rush again through the streets leading to the Battery, and a shout fills the air.

The flag of the United States has been shot down in the harbor of Charleston, South Carolina.

"It is up again on a lower staff! " "Yes!" 'No!" "It is a white flag!"

A white flag waves from the walls of Fort Sumter, and the colors which have been repeatedly lowered to-day as a signal of distress in vain have fallen at last.

The firing ceases, and Anderson surrenders unconditionally, with the fort a blazing furnace.

---

*Captain John Gray Foster (1823–1874) of the U.S. Corps of Engineers was in charge of the forts around Charleston. He was on duty at Fort Sumter when the shelling began. At the evacuation of Fort Moultrie, Foster had spiked the guns, burned the carriages, and blown up the flagstaff.

The school went on, and everything of added gravity, and a sense of sorrow over teachers and taught; if it had been possible, an increased docility and loving gentleness on the one hand, a greater tender watchfulness and earnestness on the other. The shadow grew heavier and the parting nearer as the months went on, full of stir, till the day in early June when I left my class to meet the chairman of the special commissioners for our school in the dome-room, not to stand there again. Mr. Bennett had brought me my salary, then due; he paid me as usual in gold, and he said: "We are very sorry that you feel you must go. We want you to say that when this trouble is over you will come back to us," and he reached out his hand for a leave-taking with the old-time courtesy of which we had so much since we had made our home in Charleston. I said: "Mr. Bennett, I am so sorry to go! But I cannot promise to come back. I am afraid that neither you nor I nor any one knows how long this trouble is going to last, and I cannot say anything about coming back."

And so I had to turn away from my girls, and travel to Massachusetts by way of Georgia, Tennessee, Kentucky, Indiana, Ohio, Pennsylvania, and New York. I have the notes of that journey still, kept in pencil as we went, full of excitement and wonder. As the war went on, the schools had to stop; all the beautiful fabric so wisely and so nobly planned was destroyed, and the labor seemed to have been in vain. The shells went ploughing their way through the roof into the old class-rooms, so full of sweet and gracious memories and fell in the flower planted garden where we had walked with the eager girls. Trouble and anguish fell upon the dear old city. And when her people fled to Columbia, fire and destruction met them there, such realities as we at the North never knew, even with all that came to us. That was the time when a young woman remarked to my friend one evening, "Well, whatever happens, I am sure that we shall not be utterly ruined, for my father has put our goods in seven different places in the city, so that we shall be sure to have something," and said "Good-night." In the lurid glare of the next morning, before daybreak, the same girl knocked at the same door with the piteous appeal: "Have you got a dress you can lend me to wear? I have not one thing left." That was what war meant to those people. We thought it was hard!

But the work on those schools was not lost, for one by one they who had been our girls took up the task with the spirit we had helped to inspire in them, and one of them has made not only on her city, but on the wide Southern country from which her girls come to her wise guidance, an abiding mark. After the war was over, and the time of mismanagement and misuse, the seed that had been sown in earnest faith, unswerving purpose, and singleness of spirit brought forth a hundredfold.

And the two cities, so alike in so many ways, so different from all the other cities of the land, even through the bitter war learned to know each other better, and to recognize more fully their common character. As is the case often with two human sisters, they repelled each other simply because they were at heart and in all that constitutes true nobility so much alike. But as two sisters, taught better to understand each other by the experience of life, find their former repulsion changed into attraction, and finally into a complete unity that no outside influence can in the least affect, so is it with Boston and Charleston. When fire and earthquake fought for the possession of their beauty and their old and sacred places, they reached out tender hands to each other; for in the new dispensation the Lord was in both fire and earthquake. The great and strong wind bears now only peace and good-will for message on its Northern and Southern way, and if ever henceforth there be heed of defending "that old flag," no two States will stand closer shoulder to shoulder than Massachusetts and South Carolina.

Bibliography

MANUSCRIPT COLLECTIONS

Boston

Harvard University Archives.
Massachusetts Historical Society.
Quincy Family Papers. Josiah Quincy Jr. Journal.
Josiah Quincy (1772–1862). Papers.

Washington, DC

Library of Congress, Manuscript Division. Samuel Finley Breese papers, 1793–1944.
Library of Congress, Manuscript Division. Margaret Hunter Hall Papers, 1827–28.

Preservation Society, Charleston, SC

Historic American Building Survey Documentation.

Sir Duncan Rice Library, Aberdeen University

William Ferguson Papers. 1857 Journal.

University of North Carolina Libraries, Southern Historical Collection, Chapel Hill

William Colcock Papers.

William L. Clements Library, University of Michigan, Ann Arbor

Joseph Woory Typescript.

REPRINTED SOURCES

Baxter, Lucy, ed. *Thackeray's Letters to an American Family.* Boston: Merrymount Press, 1904.
Benwell, John. *An Englishman's Travels in America: His Observations of Life and Manners in the Free and Slave States.* London: Binns and Goodwin, 1853.
Brackett, Anna C. "Charleston, South Carolina 1861." *Harper's New Monthly* 88 (1894): 941–51.
Bremer, Fredrika. *The Homes of the New World; Impressions of America.* New York: Harper Bros., 1853.

Davis, John. *Travels of Four Years and a Half in the United States of America; during 1798, 1799, 1800, 1801, and 1802.* London, 1803.

Ferguson, William. *America by River and Rail; or, Notes by the Way on the New World and Its People.* London: J. Nisbet and Co., 1856.

Lambert, John. *Travels through Lower Canada and the United States of America in the Years 1806, 1807, and 1808.* London: C. Cradock & W. Joy, 1814.

Lawson, John. *A New Voyage to Carolina; Containing the Exact Description and Natural History of That Country: Together with the Present State thereof. And A Journal Of a Thousand Miles, Travel'd thro' several Nations of Indians. Giving a particular Account of their Customs, Manners, &c.* London, 1709.

Mackie, John Milton. *From Cape Cod to Dixie and the Tropics.* New York: G. P. Putnam, 1864.

Martineau, Harriet. *Retrospect of Western Travel.* London: Saunders and Otley, 1838.

Schoepf, Johann David. *Travels in the Confederation.* Trans. and ed. Alfred J. Morrison. New York: Burt Franklin, 1911.

Stuart, James, Esq. *Three Years in North America.* Edinburgh: Printed for R. Cadell, 1833.

PRINTED PRIMARY SOURCES

Bates, Susan Baldwin, and Harriott Cheves Leland, eds. *Proprietary Records of South Carolina.* Charleston: History Press, 2006.

Bernhard, Duke of Saxe-Weimar-Eisenach. *Travels by His Highness Duke Bernhard of Saxe-Weimar-Eisenach through North America in the Years 1825 and 1826.* Trans. C. J. William Jeronimus. Lanham, MD: University Press of America, 2001.

Bridges, Anne Baker Leland, and Roy Williams III. *St. James Santee, Plantation Parish: History and Records, 1685–1925.* Spartanburg, SC: Reprint Co., 1996.

Brunhouse, Robert L. "David Ramsay, 1749–1815: Selections from His Writings." *Transactions of the American Philosophical Society,* new ser., vol. 55, no. 4 (1965): 1–250.

Butler, C. M. *Obituary addresses delivered on the occasion of the death of the Hon. John C. Calhoun: A senator of South Carolina, in the Senate of the United States, April 1, 1850, with the funeral sermon of C. M. Butler, chaplain of the Senate, preached in the Senate, April 2, 1850.* Washington, DC: Printed by J. T. Tower, 1850.

Carson, James Petigru. *Life, Letters and Speeches of James Louis Petigru: The Union Man of South Carolina.* Washington, DC: Lowdermilk & Co., 1920.

Childs, Arney. *Rice Planter and Sportsman: The Recollections of J. Motte Alston, 1821–1909.* Columbia: University of South Carolina Press, 1953.

City of Charleston Yearbook. Charleston: News & Courier Books Press, 1883.

Clough, B. A. *A Memoir of Aunt Jemima Clough by Her Niece, Blanche Athena Clough, Vice-Principal of Newnham College, Cambridge.* London: Edward Arnold, 1897.

Cody, Cheryl Ann Cody. "There Was No 'Absalom' on the Ball Plantations." *American Historical Review* 92, no. 3 (June 1987): 563–96.

Easterby, J. H. "South Carolina Through New England Eyes: Almira Coffin's Visit to the Lowcountry in 1851." *South Carolina Historical and Genealogical Magazine* 45, no. 3 (July 1944): 127–36.

Fisher, Eliza Middleton, Mary Hering Middleton, and Eliza Cope Harrison. *Best Companions: Letters of Eliza Middleton Fisher and Her Mother, Mary Hering Middleton, from Charleston, Philadelphia, and Newport, 1839–1846.* Columbia: University of South Carolina Press, 2001.

Fraser, Charles. *Reminiscences of Charleston.* Charleston: John Russell, 1854.

Hagy, James W. *Charleston, S.C. City Directories for the Years 1816, 1819, 1822, 1825, and 1829.* Baltimore: Clearfield Co., 1996.

———. *Directories for the City of Charleston, South Carolina: For the Years 1849, 1852, and 1855.* Baltimore: Clearfield Co., 1998.

———. *People and Professions of Charleston, South Carolina, 1782–1802.* Baltimore: Genealogical Publishing Co., 1992.

Hale, James W. *Authentic Account of the Loss of Steam Packet Home, from New York Bound to Charleston.* New York: J. F. Trow, 1837.

Hall, Basil. *Travels in North America, in the Years 1827 and 1828.* Vol. 3. Edinburgh, 1829.

Jefferson, Thomas. *Notes on the State of Virginia.* Paris, 1785.

Martineau, Harriet. *Autobiography.* Boston: James R. Osgood Co., 1877.

Morison, Samuel Eliot. *Life and Letters of Harrison Gray Otis, Federalist.* Boston: Houghton Mifflin, 1913.

Quincy, Josiah, and Eliza Susan Morton Quincy. *Memoir of the Life of Josiah Quincy, Jr., 1744–1775.* Boston: Little, Brown, 1875.

Ramsay, David. *History of South Carolina: From Its Settlement to the Year 1808.* Vol. 2. Newberry, SC: W. J. Duffie, 1858.

Sandford, Robert, "A Relation of a Voyage on the Coast of Carolina, 1666." In *Narratives of Early Carolina, 1650–1708,* ed. Alexander S. Salley Jr. New York: C. Scribner's, 1911.

Schackleford, William F. *Directory and Strangers' Guide for the City of Charleston: Also, for Charleston Neck, Between Boundary-Street and the Lines; to which is Added, an Almanac for the Year of Our Lord 1825; with Other Useful and Important Information.* Charleston: A. E. Miller, 1824.

Stedman, John Gabriel. *Narrative of a Five Years Expedition against the Revolted Negroes of Surinam: In Guiana on the Wild Coasts of South America from the Year 1772, to 1777.* Ed. Richard Price and Sally Price. 1796. Rpt. Baltimore: Johns Hopkins University Press, 1988.

Taylor, Robert J., ed. *The Adams Papers, Papers of John Adams, vol. 2, December 1773– April 1775.* Cambridge: Harvard University Press, 1977.

Texas Legislature. *Obituary Addresses on the Occasion of the Death of James Hamilton, of South Carolina.* Delivered in the Supreme Court, Senate and House of Representatives of the State of Texas. Austin: John Marshall & Co., 1857.

Trapier, Paul. *Incidents in My Life: The Autobiography of Paul Trapier.* Charleston: Dalcho Historical Society, 1954.

Virgil. *Æneid.* Trans. John Dryden. New York: P. F. Collier & Son, 1909.

Zubly, John Joachim. *The Journal of the Reverend John Joachim Zubly, March 5, 1770 through June 22, 1781.* Savannah: Georgia Historical Society, 1989.

SECONDARY SOURCES

Avery, Kevin J. *John Vanderlyn's Panorama of the Palace and Gardens of Versailles.* New York: Metropolitan Museum of Art, 1988.

Ball, Edward Ball. *Slaves in the Family.* New York: Farrar, Straus and Giroux, 1998.

Bellot, H. Hale. "Presidential Address: The Leighs in South Carolina." *Transactions of the Royal Historical Society,* 5th ser., vol. 6 (1956): 161–88.

Brown, Ralph H. "Jefferson's Notes on Virginia." *Geographical Review* 33, no. 3 (July 1943): 467–73.

Brown, Richard Maxwell. *South Carolina Regulators.* Cambridge, MA: Harvard University Press, 1963.

Calhoun, Joanne. *Circular Church: Three Centuries of Charleston.* Charleston: History Press, 2008.

Chase, George B., "The Lowndes Family of South Carolina." *New England Historical and Genealogical Register* 30 (April 1876): 141–64.

Chevalley, Sylvie. "The Death of Alexander Placide." *South Carolina Historical Magazine* 58 (April 1957): 63–66.

Cobau, Judith. "The Precarious Life of Thomas Pike, a Colonial Dancing Master in Philadelphia and Charleston." *Dance Chronicle* 17, no. 3 (1994): 229–62.

Côté, Richard. *Theodosia Burr Alston: Portrait of a Prodigy.* Mt. Pleasant, SC: Corinthian Books, 2002.

Curtis, Julia, "John Joseph Stephen Leger Sollee and the Charleston Theatre." *Educational Theatre Journal* 21, no. 3 (October 1969): 285–98.

Dale, Elizabeth. "Getting Away with Murder." *American Historical Review* 111, no. 1 (2006): 95–103.

Davidson, Chalmers Gaston. *The Last Foray: The South Carolina Planters of 1860.* Columbia: University of South Carolina Press, 1971.

Davis, Richard B. and Milledge B. Seigler. "Peter Freneau, Carolina Republican." *Journal of Southern History* 13, no. 3 (August 1947): 395–405.

Dethloff, Henry C. "The Colonial Rice Trade." *Agricultural History* 56, no. 1 (1982): 231–43.

Earland, Ada. *John Opie and His Circle*. London: Hutchinson & Co., 1911.

Easterby, J. H. *A History of the College of Charleston*. New York: Scribner, 1935.

Egbert, Donald Drew. "Two Portraits by Thomas Sully." *Record of the Art Museum, Princeton University* 19, no. 1 (1960): 11–16.

Friedman, Winifred H. "Some Commercial Aspects of the Shakespeare Gallery." *Journal of the Warburg and Courtauld Institutes* 36 (1973): 396–40.

Furman, Annabelle W. "Founders of the Medical College of the State of South Carolina, 1. John Edward Holbrook (1794–1871)." *Bulletin of the Medical Library Association* 31, no. 1 (January 1943): 35–39.

Gillespie, Joanna Bowen. *Life and Times of Martha Laurens Ramsay*. Columbia: University of South Carolina Press, 2001.

Glickman, Sylvia, and Martha Furman Schleifer, eds. *Composers: Music through the Ages*. Vol. 4: *Composers Born Between 1700 and 1799—Vocal Music*. New York: G. K. Hall / Gale Group, 1998.

Groves, Joseph A. *The Alstons and the Allstons*. Atlanta: Franklin Co., 1901.

Harrell, Carolyn L. *Kith and Kin: A Portrait of a Southern Family 1630–1934*. Macon, GA: Mercer University Press, 1984.

Hatfield, Mark O., with the Senate Historical Office. *Vice Presidents of the United States, 1789–1993*. Washington, DC: U.S. Govt. Printing Office, 1997.

Heyward, Dubose. "Charleston: Where Mellow Past and Present Meet." *National Geographic* 75, no. 3 (March 1939): 273–312.

Heyward, James B. "The Heyward Family of South Carolina." *South Carolina Historical Magazine* 59, no. 3 (1958): 143–58.

Highfill, Philip, Kalman A. Burmin, and Edward A. Langhans. *Biographical Dictionary of Actors, Actresses, Musicians, Dancers, Managers & Other Stage Personnel in London 1660–1800*. Vol. 14. Carbondale: Southern Illinois University Press, 1991.

Hoole, Stanley. *The Antebellum Charleston Theatre*. Tuscaloosa: University of Alabama Press, 1946.

Irving, John. *A Day on the Cooper River*. Columbia, SC: R. L. Bryan Co., 1969.

Johnson, Michael P., and James L. Roark. *Black Masters: A Free Family of Color in the Old South*. New York: Norton, 1984.

———. *No Chariot Let Down: Charleston's Free People of Color on the Eve of the Civil War*. Chapel Hill: University of North Carolina Press, 1984.

King, William L. *The Newspaper Press of Charleston, SC*. Charleston: Edward Perry, 1872.

Kovacik, Charles F., and Lawrence S. Rowland. "Images of Port Royal, South Carolina." *Annals of the Association of American Geographers* 63, no. 3 (September 1973): 331–40.

Krumpelmann, John T. "Duke Bernard of Saxe-Weimar: An Emissary of Goethe to the American South." *South Central Bulletin* 30, no. 4 (Winter 1970): 201–3.

Lawton, Edward P. *A Saga of the South*. Fort Meyers, FL: Island Press, 1965.

Leiding, Harriette Kershaw. *Historic Houses of South Carolina*. Philadelphia: J. P. Lippincott, 1921.

Linder, Suzanne Cameron. *Historical Atlas of the Plantations of the Ace Basin*. Columbia: South Carolina Department of Archives and History, 1995.

Lindsay, Maurice. *Burn's Encyclopedia*. London: Hutchinson, 1959.

Lounsbury, Carl. *From Statehouse to Courthouse*. Columbia: University of South Carolina Press, 2001.

Mabee, Carleton. *American Leonardo: A Life of Samuel F. B. Morse*. New York: A. A. Knopf, 1943.

Marsh, John L. "John Vanderlyn, Charleston and Panorama." *Journal of American Culture* 3, no. 3 (Fall 1980): 217–429.

McCandless, Peter. "Mesmerism and Phrenology in Antebellum Charleston: Enough of the Marvellous." *Journal of Southern History* 8, no. 2 (May 1992): 199–230.

McCrady, Edward. *South Carolina under the Proprietary Government 1670–1719*. New York: Macmillan, 1897.

McInnis, Maurie D. *The Politics of Taste in Antebellum Charleston*. Chapel Hill: University of North Carolina Press, 2005.

Mills, W. Jay. *Historic Houses of New Jersey*. Philadelphia: J. B. Lippincott Co., 1902.

Moore, Alex, Lawrence Rowland, and George Rogers Jr. *History of Beaufort County, SC*. Vol. 1. Columbia: University of South Carolina Press, 1996.

Nelson, Charles Alexander, and Lucy Morris Carhart. *Genealogy of the Morris Family: Descendants of Thomas Morris of Connecticut*. New York: A. S. Barnes Co., 1911.

Neuffer, Claude Henry, ed. *Names in South Carolina*. Volumes 1 through 30, 1954–1965. Columbia, SC: The State Printing Company, 1976.

Norton, Charles Eliot, "The First American Classical Archaeologist." *American Journal of Archeology* 1 (1885): 3–9.

Nunn, D. B. "Halsted's Carolina Connection: The Story of Caroline Hampton." *Pharos*. Alpha Omega Honor Medical Society, 53 no. 4 (Fall 1990): 5–9.

O'Neall, John Belton. *Biological Sketches of the Bench and Bar*. Charleston: H. G. Courtenay, 1859.

Orvin, Maxwell Clayton. *Historic Berkeley County*. Charleston: Comprint, 1973.

Patrick, J. Max. *Savannah's Pioneer Theater from its Origins to 1810*. Athens: University of Georgia Press, 1953.

Pearson, Edward A. *Designs Against Charleston: The Trial Record of the Denmark Vesey Slave Conspiracy of 1822*. Chapel Hill: University of North Carolina Press, 1999.

Perry, Grace Fox. *Moving Finger of Jasper.* Jasper County, SC: Confederate Centennial Commission, 1962.

Powers, Bernard E., Jr. *Black Charlestonians: A Social History, 1822–1885.* Fayetteville: University of Arkansas Press, 1994.

Rogers, George. *Charleston in the Age of the Pinckneys.* Columbia: University of South Carolina Press, 1980.

———. *Evolution of a Federalist: William Loughton Smith of Charleston (1758–1812).* Columbia: University of South Carolina Press, 1962.

Rutledge, Anna Wells. "Artists in the Life of Charleston from Colony and State from Restoration to Reconstruction." *Transactions of the American Philosophical Society* 39, no. 2 (1949).

———. "The Second St. Philips, 1710–1835." *Journal of Architectural Historians* 18, no. 3 (October 1959): 112–14.

Salley, Alexander S., Jr., ed. *Warrants for Land in South Carolina 1672–1911.* Columbia, SC: State Co., 1910.

Scarborough, William Kauffman. *Masters of the Big House.* Baton Rouge: Louisiana State University Press, 2003.

Smith, Timothy L. "Slavery and Theology: The Emergence of Black Christian Consciousness in Nineteenth-Century America." *American Church History* 41, no. 4 (December 1972): 497–512.

Sonneck, Oscar George Theodore. *Early Concert Life in America.* Leipzig: Breitkopf & Härtel, 1907.

Schantz, Mark S. "'A Very Serious Business': Managerial Relationships on the Ball Plantations, 1800–1835." *South Carolina Historical Magazine* 88, no. 1 (January 1987): 1–22.

Simons, Harriett P., and Albert Simons. "The William Burrows House of Charleston." *South Carolina Historical and Genealogical Magazine* 70 (1969): 155–76.

Staiti, Paul. "Samuel F. B. Morse's Search for a Personal Style: The Anxiety of Influence." *Winterthur Portfolio* 16, no. 4 (Winter 1981): 275.

Taylor, Emily Heyward Drayton. "The Draytons of South Carolina and Philadelphia." *Publications of the Genealogical Society of Pennsylvania* 8, no. 1 (March 1921): 1–25.

Taylor, Rosser H. *Antebellum South Carolina: A Social and Cultural History.* Chapel Hill: University of North Carolina Press, 1942.

Tharp, Louise Hall. "Professor of World's Wonders." *American Heritage* 12:2 (February, 1961.)

The Traveller's Library. Vol. 25. London: Longman, Brown, Green & Longman, 1856.

Van Ruymbeke, Bertrand. *From New Babylon to Eden: The Huguenots and Their Migration to Colonial South Carolina.* Columbia: University of South Carolina Press, 2006.

Wallace, David Duncan. *History of South Carolina.* New York: American Historical Society, 1934.

———. *Life of Henry Laurens.* New York: G. P. Putnam's Sons, 1915.

Wallis, Brian. "Black Bodies, White Science: Louis Agassiz's Slave Daguerreotypes." *American Art* (Summer 1995): 39–61.

Waring, Joseph I. "Lionel Chalmers and Williams Cullen's Treatment of Fevers." *Journal of the History of Medicine and Allied Sciences* 3 (October 1953): 445–47.

Wells, David Ames. *The Annual of Scientific Discovery or, Yearbook of Facts in Science and Art.* Boston: Gould and Lincoln, 1863.

Willis, Eola. *The Charleston Stage in the XVIII Century.* New York: B. Blom, 1968.

INDEX

Thackeray, William Makepeace, 282n1, 185; *ill.* 262; letters of, 266–279; life and works of, 263–65
Thomas Pike's New Assembly Room (concert hall), 25, 42n2
Thornwell, James Henley, 286
Tidyman, Philip, 172, 176, 180, 192, 196–97
Tidyman, Susannah Somers, 176n1
Titian, *see* Vecellio, Tiziano
Tobacco Inspection, 68n1
Tom (Laurens slave), 293
Tradd Street, 82n1, 249n1, 274
traders, 13, 19n2, 106, 107, 108, 112–13, 215
Trapier, Paul (Rev.), 305–7
Trapier, Paul (Trapier's Mill), 146
Travels in North America in the Years 1827 and 1828, 172
Trumbull, John, 165, 285n2
Tryon, Thomas, 35n1
Tuscarora Indians (North Carolina), 10
Twelve Sketches of Antiquities & Scenery on the Line of the Great North of Scotland Railroad, 281

Unionstreet, *See* State Street.
Unitarian Church, 206, 254
Upstate, S.C., 110

Van Bibber, Jacob, 69n3
Vanderhorst, Arnoldus, 52
Vanderhorst Street, 101n1
Vanderhorst's wharf, 328
Vanderlyn, John, 128n3, 135–36, 153, 154, 165, 285n2
Vanity Fair, 263
Vassall, Henry, 29
Vaughan, Charles R., 178
Vauxhall Gardens, 93, 101, 103, 111

Vecellio, Tiziano (Titian), 125, 140, 144n1
Vendue Range, 228
Vesey, Denmark, conspiracy (1822), 201–2, 212n3
Vigilant Rifles, 332
Virgil (Publius Vergilius Marjo), 63n1

Waccamaw River, 37, 86, 125, 128n3, 130, 136n2
Wagner, Dr. John, 157
Walker, Mr. and Mrs. Charles, 131, 132
Wallace, Mr. (stage driver), 179–80, 182
Walter Kennedy: An Interesting American Tale (1805), 58
Wambaw Creek, 19n2
Wanderings of William, 58
Warley, Maj. (Felix), 78
Washington, D.C., 142–43, 178, 205–6, 211, 214–15, 241, 259n2, 263, 311
Washington, George, 69n3, 224, 310; portrait of, 165n1, 285
Washington Light Infantry, 112n2, 332
Washington Race Course, 108–109
Water Street, 335
Waterhorn, 19n2
Waterton, Charles, 239
Webster, Daniel, 213, 214, 247, 260
Webster, Noah, 61
Wesleyan Connection, 230
West, Benjamin, 125, 128n3, 135, 136n1, 144n1
West Indies, 11, 44, 45, 47, 48, 51
West Point Rice Mill, 288–89
Wheatley, Phillis, 80–81
Whipple, Abraham, 41
White, John Blake, 97
White Hall Plantation, 185n1
Wilds, Samuel, 200–201
William Burrows House, 193n1